Arabella Boxer's
Book of
Elegant Cooking
and Entertaining

Arabella Boxer's Book of Elegant Cooking and Entertaining

The Planning, Preparation,
and Presentation
of 350 Delicious Dishes

Arabella Boxer

x

Times
BOOKS

Publisher's Note

Where dishes are referred to with capital letters
(e.g., Potato Purée, Horseradish Sauce), recipes are given in full
elsewhere in the book. See index for page numbers.

Published by TIMES BOOKS,
The New York Times Book Co., Inc.
130 Fifth Avenue, New York, N.Y. 10011

Copyright © 1983 by The Sunday Times
First published in Great Britain in 1983 by
George Weidenfeld and Nicolson Limited

ISBN: 0-8129-1125-3

Printed and bound in Italy
84 85 86 87 88 5 4 3 2 1

CONTENTS

INTRODUCTION

Like most daily habits, our cooking can be cultivated and improved immeasurably, without making vast efforts. I have spent the past year working on this book with these aims in mind. Into it I have poured all my enthusiasms and prejudices: my love for food, and for cooking, in all its traditional forms, and my growing irritation with phony and unrealistic trends. I would like to put in a particular plea for cooking more fresh vegetables, fish, and farm-raised chickens – not just for special occasions but as a general rule, until it becomes second nature.

I suspect that many of us have become too pretentious about our food. Every meal doesn't have to be a culinary experience; such expectations soon escalate, and the pleasure of eating simple dishes is lost. Some of the dishes I remember with most pleasure have been the simplest imaginable, but served with style, and the necessary confidence. A green salad made from the first pickings of different sorts of lettuce fresh from the garden, served as a first course; the first of the new spring vegetables, poached and served warm, with a garlic mayonnaise; whole avocados, each perfectly ripe, laid in a huge bowl for each guest to prepare himself, with a jug of vinaigrette. The French, who rarely make mistakes in such matters, have not undergone the same confusion about their food as we have; they continue to serve simple family dishes at home, and enjoy the fantasies of *haute cuisine* occasionally, in the restaurant of their choice.

We must not be fooled by food writers into thinking that such things are "not good enough for dinner parties," as someone remarked about the recipes in my first book. A mere change in scale, with appropriate serving dishes, is often all that is needed to give a sense of occasion. I remember Cecil Beaton describing Dorelia John's carrying an immense bowl of green peas to the table during a lunch party in Augustus John's kitchen. Although no cook himself, Beaton was perceptive enough to recognize this as a symbol of generous hospitality, since the task of shelling peas on such a scale represented some herculean labor, devoid of pretension.

For me, the bowl of green peas could serve equally well as a symbol of "real food." This, rather than "good food," is now my aim. By "real food" I mean fresh ingredients, cooked, for the most part, in classic ways – nothing ersatz or contrived, no clever mixtures of convenience foods. I should like to reinstate the classic arts of poaching and braising, both out of fashion and largely forgotten. These involve many good examples of genuine dishes, based on tradition, yet open to individual variation, as the French term *á la mode de chez nous* indicates.

I see little point in striving for perfection. When I produced a perfectly made apple tart for dinner some time ago, it aroused no comment, and I realized that my guests assumed that it had been bought. So for this book I decided to substitute a rectangular tart, and to show it still in its baking pan. This is how I would serve it another time, obviously home-made, and still warm from the oven.

The first part of this book is devoted to choosing, buying, and storing fresh produce. This is vital information, for raw ingredients lie at the root of our cooking and must be treated with respect. Ideally, buying should be done with a combination of daring and common sense. Sticking rigidly to a shopping list compiled before leaving home may be safe, but it is unadventurous, for it does not allow for the unexpected. Yet impulse buying demands flair and sound instincts, or, like unsuccessful clothes buying, it can leave one with an ill-assorted array of things, none of which complements the other. Learn to think in general terms and make your shopping list general rather than precise.

The main body of the book is devoted to the actual cooking. Unlike most authors, I have chosen to concentrate on the techniques rather than the ingredients. Instead of a chapter on fish, for instance, you will find one on poaching, steaming, boiling, and pressure cooking. First comes an explanation of the method, with background information and tips, and a guide to the best equipment that is available. Then come the recipes. In each case, I have chosen one typical recipe which is given in detail, called the Master Recipe. This is followed by a series of other recipes – the Family of Recipes – which explore the various foods that may be cooked by the same method. Thus, in one chapter, you see how to poach chickens and fish, boil beef and ham, cook root and leaf vegetables, steam fish, poach eggs, and make compôtes of fruit. The more complicated techniques are illustrated with step-by-step drawings, invaluable for such tricky processes as making your own pasta. Also included are the best accompaniments: a velouté sauce of watercress to go with a poached chicken, or a vanilla-flavored cream to serve with a compôte of apricots. All the recipes are thoroughly indexed at the end of the book; you will find them listed under their chief ingredient as well as under their full title.

Lastly comes entertaining. In order to demonstrate my belief that the heart of entertaining lies in the personality of the hosts, rather than in the actual recipes, I asked eight different cooks to suggest and cook dishes for specific occasions. Their styles and attitudes are diverse, and there is much to be learned from these masters in the art of hospitality.

Fashions change, not only in the choice of foods and in the manner of their presentation but also in the style of entertaining itself. Gone are the formal meals of pre-1940; gone are the bring-your-own bottle parties of the 1950s and 1960s; and on the way out are the extremes of the Nouvelle Cuisine of the late 1970s. In this decade, I sense a feeling for moderation; nothing too elaborate is required, either in the number of dishes or in their presentation.

In the end all that we can bring to our entertaining is the essence of our own personality. This is reflected in the atmosphere, both in the surroundings and in the manner of the meal, be it carefully planned long in advance and executed or spontaneous and casual.

In my own home, I care more about creating an ambience in which my friends feel relaxed and at ease, than about stunning them with elaborate dishes. It takes time and effort to build up a pleasant atmosphere, yet once it has been established, it is easy to maintain. Comfortable chairs, restful lighting, pretty china and glass, music, and good smells – all make their contribution and give a sense of place. As Brillat-Savarin said: "The invitation of a guest implies responsibility for his whole contentment while he is under our roof."

– Arabella Boxer 7

FISH

The fashion for health is good for fish, as the oils in fish are polyunsaturated, which helps to avoid heart disease. Fish is also an excellent source of protein, vitamins and minerals. Best of all, fish is delicious, and gives the cook one of the most adventurous and rewarding areas of cooking.

The first thing is to find a good fish market. In most big cities the best fishstore is usually independent, though some pioneering supermarkets are beginning to take an interest by selling fresh-chilled fish in some stores. The sign of a good fishstore is there in the fish on display, in the flow of regular customers, and in sales so brisk the slab will be almost empty by mid-afternoon.

A good fish market will order almost any fish for you, and will behead, split, gut, scale and fillet fish according to type and the way you plan to cook it. Take home heads and bones of white fish for stock. There is no mistaking really fresh fish. The skin gleams, gills are red, eyes are bright. The flesh is plump and elastic, firm enough to leave no dimple mark when pressed with a fingertip. If fish smells aggressively fishy, looks flabby and depressed, with cloudy, sunken eyes, it is stale.

Fish frozen at sea, or immediately on landing, may be a good deal fresher than the "fresh" fish in some shops. If transportation and distribution are poor, "fresh" fish can be stale by the time it reaches the retailer.

Eat fish fast once you have bought it. Shellfish and oily fish should always be eaten on the day of purchase. White fish can be kept overnight, smoked fish for a couple of days. Refrigerate all fish as soon as possible: put it on a plate, sprinkle it with salt if it's a fresh sea fish, and cover loosely with plastic wrap or foil.

Oily Fish

Oily fish contain 5–15% oil, distributed throughout the flesh. Because they are naturally rich, they are well suited to grilling. The more oily the fish, the more welcome are garnishes such as tart gooseberry sauce, a squeeze of lemon, the clean green taste of fresh herbs, the smoky anise touch of fennel. Oily fish are natural candidates for pickling, and emerge succulently from smoking.

Mostly oily fish are small enough to be sold whole and are therefore quite easy to identify. The tiniest are **whitebait**, silvery shoals of the inch-long small fry of sprats and herring. They are at their best from February to early summer. Because whitebait are so small, they are eaten head, tail, gut and all: dust with flour and deep-fry so they rustle crisply on to the plate. **Sprats** are about 3 inches long, less delicate in flavor and much cheaper than whitebait. Gut them before you fry them.

Sprightly fresh **sardines** are not easy to find, but look for them. Canned sardines can be a great delicacy; the most highly prized are grilled, then matured for a year in olive oil before canning. Sardines grow up into **pilchards**, not sold except canned, which improves their flat taste a little.

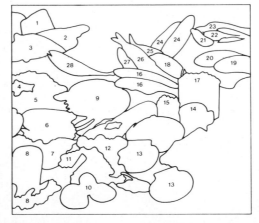

1 Skate 2 Dover Sole 3 Plaice 4 Squid 5 Octopus
6 Crab 7 Crayfish (freshwater) 8 Shrimp
9 Langoustines 10 Clams 11 Oysters 12 Whelks
13 Scallops 14 Cockles 15 Winkles 16 Kippers
17 Mussels 18 Cod's roe 19 Carp 20 Haddock
21 Whitebait 22 Sardines 23 Red mullet 24 Mackerel
25 Herring 26 Finnan haddock 27 Bloater
28 Sea trout

Herrings used to be cheap and plentiful and in prerefrigeration days the surplus gave rise to major salting, smoking and pickling industries. Now they are sadly over-fished and more costly and scarce. **Mackerel** has also become more expensive, but is still plentiful. Both mackerel and herring make exquisite dishes when dramatically fresh, but become stale exceedingly quickly.

Red mullet, nicknamed the woodcock of the sea because it can be cooked without gutting, is a beautiful rosy-armoured little fish. Wonderful to eat fresh from the Mediterranean, they are often an expensive disappointment. **Gray mullet**, which are unrelated, are larger and less esteemed, but better value.

Tuna, **bonito** and **swordfish** are great ocean fish. On the rare occasions you see them on sale they will probably have been frozen and will usually be cut into steaks. Marinate them well before cooking for although technically oily fish, the flesh is so dense and meaty it dries out easily.

Salmon is known as the king of fish, and fresh river salmon from Washington State in May, June and July, the peak season, is said to be unsurpassed. Many would agree, however, that **salmon trout (sea trout)** 9 makes finer eating for it combines the best of both salmon and trout. The less extravagant price and smaller size of sea trout makes it more practical than salmon for most households. Farmed salmon is now available all year round and makes very good eating.

Varieties of **trout** can be found fairly readily from coast to coast. **Rainbow trout**, often frozen, tastes better.

White Fish

White fish may not always have truly white flesh: they are called white fish if they contain less than 2% oil, and this oil is usually concentrated in the liver (thus cod liver oil). Because the flesh is very lean, white fish appreciates moist cooking.

Flat varieties: Most flat fish dwell on the seabed and their topside skin is heavily pigmented to camouflage them. Small varieties are usually sold whole for cooking on the bone, although if large enough they can be filleted.

Dover sole is an aristocrat. Regrettably inordinately expensive, its flesh is firm and its flavor superb. **Lemon sole**, the best substitute and considerably cheaper, will benefit from a garnish of mushrooms and herbs or a delicate wine sauce. **Witch** has a high proportion of bone to flesh and, like **megrim**, is not very interesting. **Flounder** is plentiful, popular and cheap. **Dab** has better flavor and texture.

John Dory, not strictly a flat fish but decidedly flattened, is easily identified by the black mark behind the head. Small landings make it expensive, but it is fine in flavor and texture.

Five of the larger varieties of white fish are only available in small quantities, and best in autumn and winter. **Turbot** is very expensive and very princely, but it is beginning to be farmed with good-tasting results and with luck prices may come down before long. **Halibut** is slightly less costly, and **brill** more reasonably priced. All are most often sold as steaks, cutlets and fillets. Whole fish cooked on the bone are even more of a treat: ask for **chicken turbot** or **chicken halibut** (chicken being the name given to the youngsters).

Skate and **monkfish** are no beauty competition winners and fishsellers tactfully refrain from displaying them whole, offering only the choice edible parts. Very choice they are too: skate wings are classically served *au beurre noire*, while the tail end of monkfish has such good flavor and dense, lobster-like flesh it makes superb kebabs, casseroles and salads.

Round varieties Although it is fashionable to be dismissive of **cod**, I find it very versatile and useful. Its succulent firm flakes are extremely pleasing in salads, and in hot dishes when carefully cooked. **Haddock** is finer – but a lot of it goes for smoking. **Pollack**, **ling** and **whiting** are best treated as what I call "background" fish. They make, for example, good fishcakes, while the modest whiting makes a surprisingly good basis for quenelles. **Red fish** is another acceptable cod substitute. **Hake** and **dogfish** (**huss** or **rock salmon**) make excellent soups.

Sea bass, **grouper** and **sea bream** are fairly expensive, and not widely sold, but wonderfully welcome for they enable us to cook Mediterranean dishes. Sea bass is an excellent, family-size fish which can be poached or stuffed and baked whole. The fillets and steaks are best poached or fried like the same cuts of grouper. Sea bream is smaller, has coarser juicy flesh, and is best in autumn.

Two freshwater species are **carp** and **pike**. Carp is *the* fish of Jewish cuisine. Pike is the fish for quenelles – if you have the patience to deal with its vicious and fiddly little bones.

Smoked Fish

Some varieties of smoked fish need no cooking and are generally served cold. Prime Scotch or Irish **smoked salmon** is magnificent; Canadian imports simply cannot compare. Other smaller smoked fish are also very good, and have more everyday prices. **Smoked trout** is delicate of flavor. **Smoked mackerel** is richer and cheaper, and fast becoming a best seller. **Smoked sprats** are a bit fiddly but very reasonably priced and **smoked eel** is in a class of its own, beautifully rich and filling.

With the exception of smoked salmon, all the above fish should be bought whole, and skinned and filleted as close to eating as is practicable. Check that skins are not jaded and that the flesh is plump and juicy.

The next group of smoked fish need to be cooked. Like the first group they should be bought whole, as fish smoked on the bone tastes far sweeter.

The **kipper** is generally regarded as king of this group. The best come from the Isle of Man, where the raw herring is split, gutted, brined and smoked by traditional slow methods which leave the fish fragrant in flavor and a pale tawny color. They are much more expensive than the artificially dyed kipper generally on sale, but are very much better to eat. **Bloaters** are a Yarmouth speciality. They are herrings, too, but this time smoked whole with their guts for a "gamier" flavor. Split and gut before cooking.

For me, **smoked haddock** is the most versatile and excellent smoked fish but regrettably, like kippers, often dyed. Deep saffron yellow specimens lack the fine character of the real thing, which is the color of honey and split before curing. **Arbroath smokies** are young haddock, beheaded and gutted but not split, and are always sold in pairs. **Kipper fillets, smoked haddock fillets** and **golden fish fillets** (which may be any white fish) often do not have flavor and, again, are dyed.

Salted or smoked **fish roes** (the eggs of female fish) can be very grand or modest. **Caviar** is salted sturgeon roes, glisteningly expensive, clinging together in blackcurrant clusters. Overpriced, and in my view overrated. **Red "caviar"** is dog salmon roe, translucently red, saltier and considerably cheaper, as is beady, blackdyed **lump-fish roe**. Look also for **gray mullet roe**, the ingredient for authentic taramasalata.

I would swap any of these salted fish roes for smoked fish items: **smoked cod's roe** is excellent, inexpensive and extremely useful, my "Best Buy." Check it is firm and moist, its skin not split or torn. **Smoked oysters** and **smoked mussels**, available in cans, make wonderful savories.

Shellfish

Fishy little morsels of boiled **winkles** can be winkled out of their shells with a pin. The bigger **whelks** and **cockles** are easier to get at. All are sold boiled, and are at their best in summer.

Mussels have fine blue-black beauties of shells, and are only sold in winter. Exquisite eaten raw, like oysters (if you are certain of their purity), cooked mussels make superb soups, sauces, rice dishes and salads. **Clams** are more expensive. They vary in size depending on variety, and I think of them as halfway between mussels and oysters in taste.

Knobbly rock-shelled **oysters**, opened with a dagger-like oyster knife, are an acquired taste for some.

Scallops are perhaps the sweetest tasting and most delicate of all shellfish. The discs of tender white flesh and curling coral roes need to be cooked gently – fierce or prolonged heat toughens and ruins them, as does freezing. Buy them only when they are really fresh and plump.

Octopus and **squid**, like mussels, are often cheap, though a bit time-consuming to prepare. The tinier the squid, the more tender and good they are. Octopuses need pounding to tenderize them before stuffing and baking, or gentle casseroling.

Size is no guide to the quality of **shrimp** but all small shrimp are sold already boiled. Next best are shrimp freshly-boiled then frozen in the shell. Cold water varieties have better flavor than warm water varieties. If you buy them already defrosted, they will spoil quickly. Pre-boiled, already-shelled frozen shrimp have least flavor. If you can't find any other sort, defrost them in the refrigerator, sprinkled with lemon, salt and pepper in a covered bowl. Drain off liquid next day. Like all cooked shrimp, these are only suitable for cold dishes or for heating very gently. If cooked again they become rubbery. Buy fresh shrimp whenever possible.

Crayfish are miniature freshwater lobster, rarely found in stores, except in Louisiana. **Lobster** itself is in peak season May–October. The price is crippling but the taste magnificent when in peak condition. Lobster and **crawfish (langoustine)**, its almost clawless cousin, are a waste of money when frozen: fresh **crab**, relatively cheap and plentiful in May and June, is a better choice. Buy crab live, as fresh as possible. They should feel heavy for their size but are best when not too big.

MEAT

Meat is the most difficult food to buy well, because its good qualities, or lack of them, are not easily discernible to the eye. The way meat looks is, of course, important and provides valuable pointers, but it is not the whole story. A lot depends on the age and breed of the animal, how it was reared, at what temperature and, most important of all, for how long it was hung after being slaughtered.

It is obviously impractical for shoppers to become a walking encyclopedia of Master Butchery. The answer is to employ an expert – a good butcher. Look for a shop that is scrupulously clean. Do not be impressed by the quantity of meat on display, for it is quality that counts. The meat should be properly hung, freshly butchered, appetizing and clean scented. Bones should be neatly sawn, not jagged, rolled roasts should be carefully tied – not pierced with skewers which allows moisture to escape. The quality of the ground meat on sale is a good guide, and another excellent sign is good sausages made on the premises.

A good butcher will salt his own beef, and prepare meat to order: he will bone out awkward joints, and make up a crown roast given good notice.

If you do not see what you want on display, ask. Much of a butcher's stock is kept off-stage, stored as a carcass in his chill-room. Hanging, or ageing, is vital to the flavor and tenderness of meat, particularly beef and game. However, as the enzymes break down the tough muscle tissues, moisture evaporates and, with it, weight, and consequently, money. Too many butchers shortsightedly cut corners on this count – selling beef that was only slaughtered a few days before, but a butcher who cares about the eating quality of his meat will hang beef for about 10 days and lamb for about 5 days.

Choosing meat Because butchering is done in different ways in different regions, the names of cuts, their shapes, and the way bones are dealt with, can vary considerably, but the principles of butchery and meat cookery are the same because the animals are built the same.

It is helpful to think of the human anatomy – tough and bony in the extremities, plump and tender in the rump. Thus the front half of animals contains the muscles that do the most work, and neck, foreleg, ribcage and belly areas are bony and sinewy. The meat on them is every bit as nutritious as other parts, and often well flavored, but it is tough and these cuts need gentle, moist cooking. The rear half (loin, rump and top part of the hindleg) leads a less strenuous life compared to the laboring front end, and here the muscles are large, fleshy and tender, with less connective tissue; they can therefore be cooked more quickly, using fiercer dry heat – roasted, grilled or fried. For intermediate cuts like chuck steak or brisket, which are neither very tender nor very tough, it is best to use halfway-house cooking methods such as pot-roasting and braising.

Storing meat All meat should be lightly covered, not wrapped in a tight parcel, and refrigerated until you are ready to cook it. Pork, poultry and small pieces of meat (eg escalopes) will keep for 2–3 days; joints and large cuts of beef and lamb, for 4–5 days.

Beef

Beef is the meat of cattle, and is mainly steer and heifer meat. Beef from retired cows goes to make manufactured meat products such as burgers, sausages and pies.

The flesh should be firm and the fat creamy. If the meat is corally red it is fresh; when properly hung, beef is a darker red, slightly drier looking and will taste much better. The prime lean cuts should be delicately marbled with fat to keep them moist and succulent during cooking.

Fillet, **medallion**, **tournedos** and **Chateaubriand** steaks all come from the fillet, the tenderest part of all. Better flavored steaks, including **T-bone**, come from the **sirloin** (which also makes a superb roast) and from the **rump**. I also use rump for steak tartare, beef olives and special steak and kidney puddings. **Rib**, which lies next to the sirloin, gives **entrecote** steaks and the huge and impressive **forerib** produces spectacular roasts.

The rib cage yields **thick** and **thin ribs**. Bonier and less tender, these are secondary cuts and better pot-roasted than open roasted. Other secondary cuts include **rump** (leanish meat from the buttocks) and **brisket** (coarser, fattier meat from the fleshy part of the belly). All are good for pot-roasting and braising, while brisket and rump are favourites for salt beef. **Blade** and **chuck**, from the shoulder area, and **flank** from the thigh are mainly used for braising and casseroling. **Shin** and **leg**, and the neck pieces such as **clod**, are sinewy, tough, and are well flavored. They are good for stews and pies if slowly and gently cooked in liquid from cold (rather than browned in fat).

Veal

Veal is the meat of calves. There are two types: **milk-fed veal** which comes from very young calves, and **grass-fed veal**, which comes from calves about 4 months old. Milk-fed veal is very pale in color, grass-fed is slightly more rosy.

Because veal is such young meat it contains little fat and is very tender and delicate in flavor. It therefore needs careful protection against drying out in cooking and welcomes flavorsome garnishes such as anchovies, lemon, and Marsala.

Large joints such as **leg** and **loin** need to be well larded for roasting, and are better if mostly braised or pot-roasted. **Chops** should be gently fried rather than grilled or broiled, generously anointed with butter, bacon fat or olive oil; when sautéed they are usually given a protective egg and breadcrumb coating. Cubed veal makes delicate blanquettes and mixes well with other meats for pie fillings. The bony **foreleg** or **knuckle**, sawn into thick slices, makes osso buco.

Lamb and Mutton

Lambing is timed to coincide with the growth of new grass. Lamb fed on hilly pastures is sweeter-tasting but a little less tender than fat lowland lamb. Very young milk-fed lamb, meltingly tender and pale pink, is a great delicacy, wildly expensive and not easy to buy.

Young lamb should be firm and pinkish, the bones should be small with a blue tinge and the fat creamy white and crisp. The more mature the lamb the redder its flesh and the more richly colored its fat – but it should not look waxy.

Leg of lamb (or **gigot** as it is called in France) is the prime roast; **shoulder** is sweeter but fattier, and more trouble to carve. The juiciest **chops** come from the chump, which lies between the leg and loin. Loin chops come, of course, from the loin, and so does the handsome roast, cut in one piece from both sides of the loin, called **saddle**. **Cutlets** are individual ribs taken from the **best end of neck**; whole best end of neck is called a **rack**. Two racks can be curved, fat side in, to make a **crown roast**, or stood face to face, fat side out, to make a **guard of honor**. Best end of neck can also be boned, rolled and cut into thick slices to make choice little **noisettes**.

Middle neck, which lies under the shoulder, and **scrag**, which is neck proper, are progressively bonier and fattier. Trimmed of surplus fat (and boned if appropriate) the meat is good for pies, pasties and stews. **Breast** is the cheapest and least meaty cut, but if it is taken from good lamb and is cooked with care it can be very good.

Pork

Pork comes from young pigs and is the most versatile of all meats. Although the traditional family pig was fed on scraps, the pig is, in fact, a gourmet rather than a glutton, and will search out such delicacies as truffles and windfall apples. Traditionally, the more the pig was allowed to decide its own menu, the better the pork tasted. Pork is available all year round, but often cheapest in summer, partly because the demand for rich meats drops in summer, and partly because some people still will not eat pork unless there is an "R" in the month, which was a wise precaution in pre-refrigeration days, but totally unnecessary now.

Good pork has smooth lean meat, the color of pale pink silk, and firm white fat. Bones should be pinkish-blue and rind should be thin and supple. Unlike beef and lamb, pork is sold newly-killed and thoroughly chilled, and for safety it must be cooked right through, never served rare.

"Every part of the pig can be eaten except his squeak" is the traditional view: even the intestine is used for sausage casing. Only the gall bladder is not eaten. **Tenderloin** or **fillet** is the most tender and lean cut. It can be roasted, or sliced and beaten out thinly to make an excellent substitute for veal escalopes. **Loin** and **leg** make splendid roasts. **Blade** (shoulder) is also good, very rich but not as handsome. **Hand and spring** (the foreleg) is even more awkwardly shaped, but delicious if boned and rolled for roasting or braising.

The meatiest **chops** come from the chump, but loin chops are excellent. **Meaty upper spare ribs** can also be sliced and treated as chops. **Spare ribs** are the bony ends of the rib cage with little meat on them. **Belly** is sold in joints on the bone, or cut into slices, and it is sold salted or fresh. The richest and fattiest of cuts, it is particularly good cooked with cabbage or mealy textured foods such as chestnuts and potatoes, and is valuable for pâtés. Strips of hard **fatback** from the loin can sometimes be bought separately, for larding and barding lean meats and game, and for enriching pâtés.

Bacon

Bacon comes from slightly older pigs, especially bred to be longer and leaner. Mild and other cures involve briefer brining, while sweet cures use syrup and other flavorings in the brine. After curing, the meat may be smoked for greater flavor. Unsmoked bacon may be called "green" or "pale."

Ham comes from the hind leg of a pig, but it is cured as a separate joint (not as part of a whole side of bacon) and is left to mature after curing.

Variety Meats

This is where true delicacies can be found at bargain prices, because in general supplies exceed demand.

All variety meats are highly perishable and must be very fresh. They should glisten with health and smell clean and sweet.

Pale colored **liver** usually has the best flavor. Calves' liver is exquisite and lambs' fine if neatly sliced and lightly sautéed. Pigs' liver is not sufficiently delicate for such treatment, but can be casseroled or used in meat loaves and pâtés. Chicken livers are the best of all bargains. They are essential for giving a rich note to pâtés, and marvelous for savories on toast and in rice dishes, as are the livers of game birds.

Buy **kidneys** wrapped in their own suet jackets if possible. Calves' and lambs' kidneys are a succulent treat roasted in their jackets. They are also delicious cored and grilled or sautéed. Milk-soaked pigs' kidney makes economical braises and casseroles.

Hearts have little flavor, calves' being particularly insipid, while ox heart is far too tough. Lambs' hearts, delicately stuffed, wrapped in bacon and braised, have a certain charm, not least the fact that the dish is called "Love in Disguise."

Sweetbreads (the pancreas) are regarded as a greater delicacy than **brains**, but both have a creamy lightness of flavor and texture. Both need to be carefully rinsed, blanched in simmering acidulated water, and skinned before final cooking – all fiddly but worth the effort. Calves' are best, lambs' very good and cheaper.

Tripe is the lining of an ox or cow's stomach. Too much neglected, except as a regional speciality, the best of several types is honeycomb.

Whole pig's **head** is first rate for brawn-making. Carve them across so that everyone gets a section of fat, lean and tongue. Ox cheek has excellent flavor and is a cheap basis for slow cooked casseroles and the like.

Try as I do, I really cannot get worked up about even the finest **tongue** (ox tongue), even less about calves' and lambs' tongue, although I love the traditional accompanying sauces: Salsa Verde, mustard, Marsala and Cumberland. The best tongue is salted and lightly smoked.

Calves' **feet** produce the most velvety rich jellies, stocks and gravies. Pigs' **trotters** are easier to come by and make a good substitute, as well as being eaten as meat in their own right. Chicken **gizzards and necks** are also invaluable for the stockpot and can be bought cheaply in frozen blocks from some supermarkets. **Oxtail** is richly flavored meat with a high proportion of bone. Sliced, it makes an excellent, warming and inexpensive dish. For best results, always trim off surplus fat before cooking and skim surface fat from the stewpan before serving.

Poultry

If you have a good butcher, you need not settle for fresh-chilled birds but may buy freshly dressed farm birds – which are the best, and especially good for roasting. Take home everything the butcher will give you; all the bits and pieces are valuable for stock-making.

I do not recommend frozen poultry under any circumstances. Supermarkets and chainstores come into their own, however, in providing chill-fresh chicken and turkey portions of plump meat and consistent clean flavor. I find chicken breasts and thighs particularly useful, while escalopes of turkey breast, carefully cooked, make a very passable pauper's "veal."

Poussins, very young chickens, are so tiny you have to allow 1 per person. They are pretty, but too young to taste of chicken and almost impossible to find. Cornish game hens are a better bet and can be split to share with a friend. **Spring chickens** (it is always "spring" where these battery birds are raised) weigh up to 5 lb., while **roasters**, the family size bird, range from 3–6 lb. and are 8–10 weeks old. A spring chicken is sometimes called a **broiler**, but at a few weeks old it has nothing to do with a **boiler**, a hen of such advanced years it must be gently simmered for hours. The young chickens sold can be of either sex. The older chicken normally on sale is the meat of the hen, considered finer than that of the cockerel, which only graces the table in its castrated form. These **capons** reach 8 lb., twice the size of more *macho* cockerels, and have a fine fat flavor for the grander occasion.

Turkeys are usually too big for everyday consumption and cold turkey remains nagging you in the larder for days. The minimum weight is usually about 10 lb.

Guinea fowl are slightly smaller than chickens but much more expensive. They have fine black and white speckled feathers like a Liberty print – plucked on the wings to avoid confusion with plebeian chicken. The flesh can be dry unless the breast is generously stuffed with butter, or well coated with bacon; the flavor is deliciously gamey: the Victorians thought of guinea fowl as out-of-season pheasant.

Geese are so testily mannered they have eluded standardization. Goose is at its best when 6–9 months old and weighing about 10 lb. Like duck, it exudes copious quantities of beautifully flavored fat when roasted. Red cabbage is the classic accompaniment, a good foil for the rich meat.

Duck is a truly delicious food. Domestic duck is readily found, and is usually fleshy-breasted: wild duck can be stringy and taste muddy in comparison. But there is always far less meat to any duck than mets the eye. A 4 lb. duck is ample for 3, but for 4 the carver may panic.

Game

Game is richly flavored and provides such a splendid change from routine meats it is worth seeking out. A butcher who is a game dealer (Laws regulate the season for game and the retailing of it) sells game ready prepared for cooking, and will tell you whether it it young enough to roast. Smooth legs, pliable feet and beaks which open easily are signs of youth. If you receive game as a present, you must prepare it yourself. The object of hanging freshly-killed game is to develop its flavor by giving it the chance (literally) to go beyond being a "stiff," so the muscles relax and become less tough. Hang game, undrawn, in a cool dry place – by the feet if an animal, by the neck if a game bird. It is hung when it looks extremely relaxed: this happens quite quickly if the weather is warm, if cold it takes longer. If you cannot face skinning or plucking game, and drawing it yourself (which is easier than you may think) the butcher will usually do it for a small charge.

All game tends to be lean and dry. If it is young enough to roast, keep it moist and succulent by buttering it generously. Marinate older game before casseroling, braising or pot-roasting.

The cock **pheasant** is the handsome fellow with peacock trails of tail feathers. The hen may be plain, but makes juicier eating. This is my favorite game bird and not atrociously expensive. The **partridge** is much smaller than pheasant and more expensive. One pheasant will feed 3 people, but it is best to allow 1 partridge for each person when roasting. Buy partridge young (avoid the red legged variety) and not hung for too long as this diminishes the subtlety of flavor.

Grouse is considered by many to be the finest-tasting game bird there is. This may have something to do with the fact that it is available earliest (Aug. 12–Dec. 10), but is mainly because the grouse is a gourmet of the best berries and herbs. Allow 1 grouse per person. **Capercaillie** are jumbo grouse, as big as geese, which feed on pine trees and therefore can taste a little like bath salts.

Because they are both farmed and shot as game, **quail** are available all year round from specialty shops as well as game dealers. Quail are tiny and form a delectable centerpiece to a main course, no more. **Snipe** and **woodcock** again are tiny – and very hard to come by. **Pigeons** as big as Bantam hens, which grow fat on farmer's corn and all the tenderest shoots in the garden, have nothing to do with their seedy city cousins. They have no season, are often available and reasonably priced. I find them delicious: they are much better fresh than frozen, and better braised than roasted. Cook them breast downwards to keep the flesh moist.

Venison is rich, sweet gamey meat if well hung. Like beef, some cuts are suitable for roasting, others for gentler cooking, but always marinate venison, and protect it against drying out during cooking.

Despite its humble status, good fresh **rabbit** can make first-class eating. It is cheap, contains less cholesterol than other meats, and is very versatile. Wild rabbit is gamier and less tender than plump farmed rabbit, which is mildly flavored. Both are available all year round. **Hare** is in season September–March. The meat is not the pinky-gold of rabbit, more the color of a good claret, and the taste is appropriately much richer. Often jugged or casseroled in red wine, hare also makes excellent pâté, and the saddle is a fine roast.

DAIRY PRODUCTS

Every year the chilled food cabinets devoted to dairy foods take up more and more supermarket space. Traditional farmhouse products like buttermilk are returning to the shelves, alongside relative newcomers like yogurt. Today there are hundreds of domestic and imported cheeses on sale in city shops, and the list of dairy products continues to proliferate. So much choice can seem bewildering. But milk, cream, butter, cheese and eggs have long been staple foods, wholesome and enriching ingredients in many dishes, and it is well worth learning how to buy and store the best and most appropriate items for your needs.

Eggs

The **hen's egg** is delicious and versatile in cooking, and an extremely good source of nourishment. It is not true that brown eggs are better than white: the difference is simply in the breed of hen. Nor does the color of the yolk reveal anything about its food value, or its freshness: it only reflects the hen's diet. Free-range birds feeding on corn and grass usually produce deeper colored yolks, but if carotene is included in a battery hen's food it has the same effect of enriching the color.

Eggs can only be labelled "free range" if a lot of the hen's diet comes from open pasture. It may not be applied to battery farm eggs. Any other terms, such as "farm eggs," mean battery farm eggs. There is no nutritional difference between free range eggs and battery ones, but the taste of a free range egg will vary a little according to the food the hen finds.

What matters far more than whether an egg is free range or battery is its freshness. When you break a fresh egg it looks fresh: it sits up properly on the saucer and has a plump dome of yolk, surrounded by a translucent gelatinous white, with an outer layer of thinner white. The staler the egg, the flatter the yolk and the more the two layers of white mingle and spread in a rather watery way.

The freshest eggs come direct from an egg producer who sells fresh stocks at his farm gate, from his own delivery round, or his own market stall. A few stores, especially those who buy direct from such a producer/packet, may have very fresh eggs. The next freshest eggs come from large supermarkets supplied direct and frequently from an egg packing station. These will be about nine days old on arrival in the supermarket, but may have to wait for existing stocks to clear before they are put on sale. Less fresh still are eggs from small stores who buy from a wholesaler. These are about 12 days old on reaching the stores and, again, may not go straight on sale.

The rule is to buy eggs as directly as possible, and buy little and often, especially when you are serving eggs in their own right, when freshness really counts. For most other cooking purposes, less fresh eggs will do quite well.

Storing eggs The yolk rises as the egg ages. Store eggs pointed end downwards so the yolk rises towards the air pocket in the rounded end, or it will drift to the pointed end and may stick to the shell. Store in a cool larder, or in the refrigerator; or in the kitchen if they are used up fast. Bring them to room temperature before using so they won't crack in boiling, or curdle in cake mixtures. Chilled egg whites are hard to whisk and chilled yolks will not emulsify reliably.

Once the shell is broken, the egg must be kept in the refrigerator. Store yolks and white separately, and use within 3 days. The smaller and more airtight the container the better; an egg cup covered with plastic wrap works well. To prevent hardening of yolks, cover with a thin layer of water, then plastic wrap.

Remember, loose eggs can be tainted through their shells from adjacent foods. By the same token, they can be flavored with herbs placed with them in a paper bag.

Duck, goose, turkey, guinea fowl and **quail eggs** are all richer than hen's eggs. Duck, goose and turkey eggs are, frankly, best used in custards, mousses and savoury omelettes. Gull, guinea fowl and quail eggs, being small, make pretty starters. Quail's eggs are sold fresh and take 3 minutes to boil; allow 5 minutes for a guinea fowl egg. Serve them with brown bread and butter, cayenne pepper and celery salt. Duck and quail eggs are farmed now, and available fresh in specialty shops and supermarkets. Quail eggs are also available in bottles, less good but just as pretty. Goose, guinea fowl and turkey eggs are hard to find.

Milk, Cream and Yogurt

The quality of **milk** is standardized by law in degrees of richness which range from **skim**, which has virtually all the fat removed – and with it vitamins A and D – to whole milk which contains a minimum of 4% fat and is particularly good for making milk puddings. **Raw milk** has the freshest, milkiest taste, but is sold only in a few rural areas. Virtually all of our milk is heat-treated before sale to kill off harmful bacteria, usually by pasteurization. **Pasteurized milk**, the nation's staple milk, contains an average 3.25% fat content. Most pasteurized milk is also **homogenized**, which distributes the cream evenly through the milk. **Sterilized milk** is also 15 available: useful in emergencies, but does not taste like fresh milk.

Cream: most cream is pasteurized. The minimum butterfat content is fixed by law: half-and-half contains $10\frac{1}{2}\%$ to 18% butterfat, **light cream**, **table cream** or **coffee cream** contains 18% to 30%. **Whipping cream** comes in two varieties: **light whipping cream** which contains 30% to 36% butterfat and **heavy whipping cream** which contains 36% to 40% butterfat. Avoid ultra-pasteurized whipping cream. **Clotted** cream contains over 50% butterfat.

Only whipping cream can be whipped successfully. Light cream and half-and-half have too low a fat content. Heavy cream is better than light in cooking (light cream, for no apparent reason, sometimes tastes floury when heated). To avoid curdling, either scald the cream before adding it to a hot dish, or stir a little hot liquid into the cream before carefully blending it into a hot dish. Once cream has been added, do not let the mixture boil.

Heavy cream will whip more smoothly and to a greater volume if 1 tbsp. of milk is added to every $\frac{1}{2}$ cup cream. Alternatively, 1 tbsp. yogurt can be added to make it less rich tasting, more like crème fraîche. A whisked egg white or a little sour cream or yogurt can be folded into whipped cream to lighten its texture and taste, but the consistency then makes it unsuitable for piping.

Crème fraîche is fresh cream left to ferment long enough to develop lactic acid, which thickens it without souring it and gives it a fresh, clean taste. It can be bought in a few specialty shops.

Sour cream is made from light cream, with the addition of bacterial culture. Smooth and rich, with a hint of acidity, it makes a refreshing change from the blandness of thick fresh cream.

Buttermilk is thicker and slightly sourer today than the old variety made from unpasteurized milk. Traditionally used for making biscuits and soda bread, it is good for cool summer soups, sauces and drinks.

Yogurt: commercial varieties are often made with skim milk, to give fewer calories, but richer milk gives a better taste. Some yogurts proudly proclaim they are "live" but in fact all yogurts are live except those specifically labelled pasteurized. Pasteurized and frozen yogurt cannot be used as a starter to make your own yogurt. Drinking yogurts, plain and flavored, are beginning to become more popular and more widely available.

Usually eaten on its own, or used in cold dishes and marinades, yogurt is also excellent in many hot dishes. However it does tend to separate out at high temperatures:

the risk can be minimized by stabilizing yogurt before cooking, either by mixing a little cornflour into it or by draining off some of the whey – put the yogurt in a muslin-lined sieve and leave it to drain for a few hours.

Storing milk, cream and yogurt All milk products deteriorate swiftly if left on a sunny doorstep or in a hot car. Refrigerate them as soon as possible, and keep well covered or they will pick up flavors from other foods. An unopened bottle of pasteurized milk will keep 4–5 days; raw milk 2–3 days. Fresh and sour creams, yogurt and buttermilk should be used within a week of the sell-by date and you must use them quickly once opened.

Butter
The butter you buy may be salted or unsalted. Unsalted butter is known as sweet butter, made from sweet cream. Which combination you prefer is a matter of taste and it is worth trying different types, simply spread on bread, to see which you really like.

Unsalted butter is essential for delicate sauces such as Hollandaise. It is also better than salted butter for cake-making, and for frying, since it contains fewer deposits to blacken and burn. Better still, for frying, is clarified butter (see recipe below).

Storing butter The flavor and texture of butter is spoiled by exposure to air, light and heat. Pats of butter stored naked in the refrigerator invite tainting and drying out. It needs to be brought gently to room

1 Yogurt 2 Cottage cheese 3 Mozzarella
4 Parmesan 5 Brie 6 Camembert 7 Pont l'Evêque
8 Double Gloucester 9 Dolcelatte 10 Cheddar
11 Emmental 12 Stilton 13 Salted butter 14 Unsalted butter 15 Cream cheese 16, 17, 18 Milk
19 Unpasteurized milk 20 Skim milk 21 Goose egg
22 Duck egg 23 Turkey egg 24 Hen's egg 25 Guinea fowl egg 26 Gull's egg 27 Quail's egg 28 Crème fraîche 29 Caboc 30 Clotted cream 31 Heavy cream
32 Light cream 33 Buttermilk 34 Milk

temperature for spreading and creaming, but should not be left around longer than necessary.

Unsalted butter will keep in the refrigerator for 2 weeks, salted for 3 weeks. But paradoxically unsalted butter can be deep frozen longer than salted butter, 6 months instead of 3.

MAKING CLARIFIED BUTTER

Heat the butter in a saucepan over gentle heat until it is frothing but not colored. Let it cool a few minutes, then strain it slowly through a damp, muslin-lined sieve to remove the froth and milky sediment, into a screw-top jar. Refrigerate as soon as cold.

Clarified butter keeps for weeks, so it is worth making a good quantity; it is used for frying and making *beurre noire*, and as an airtight seal for potted meats and fish pastes.

Cheese
Shops which stock a wide selection of cheeses, in peak condition, are few and far between, but worth seeking out. But even the best shops sometimes sell cheese a little underripe, overripe or otherwise slightly imperfect if they have miscalculated which cheeses will sell best. So it is best to set out intending to buy "cheese of some sort," but make your final choice in the shop.

It is wiser to buy a big piece of one or two cheeses than a large selection of bits. The larger pieces look more handsome on the table, and the high proportion of cut edges on small pieces encourages fast deterioration.

In the days when cheeses were all made from unpasteurized milk, cheeses had seasons. For example, the glut of rich milk from summer pastures, yielding a cheese with a maturing time of 6 months, would make winter the peak eating season: hence the custom of Stilton for Christmas. A few cheeses are still made with raw milk. For example you can, if you have stamina, find **Fermier Brie** and **Fermier Camembert**. Since raw milk Camembert takes a month to mature, its eating season is from early summer to autumn. Raw milk Brie takes a little longer to mature, so the season begins later and lasts to early winter. American law requires cheese sold to be made from pasteurized milk. However, occasionally raw milk cheeses are found.

The bulk of cheeses today are made from treated milks, and are "in season" all year round. The main groups of cheeses have different ripening times, so let us take them in turn, from those requiring no ripening time – fresh cheeses – to those needing the longest: hard matured cheeses.

Fresh cheeses These are soft, with a high moisture content, and include **cottage**, **curd** and **cream** cheeses, **Crowdie**, **Fromage Blanc**, **Quark**, **Petit Suisse**, **Mozzarella**, **Ricotta** and **Caboc**.

Their richness varies enormously. Those made with cream are labelled so. Cheeses labelled "full fat soft cheese" sound enormously fattening, but it only means the cheese is made with full strength milk, not skimmed. Cheeses made with skimmed milk are labelled "medium fat soft cheese," "low fat soft cheese" or "skimmed milk cheese" as progressively lower fat milks are used.

Fresh cheeses should look and smell very fresh, and should be eaten up quickly. Avoid any which look at all tired or yellowing, or whose packaging is damaged.

Soft matured cheese These include **Bries** and **Camemberts**; they are creamy and buttery in texture and taste, and mostly have white rinds with a soft bloom to them.

Buy a good-sized wedge cut, in the shop, from a whole cheese if you can. Look for plumpness and resilience, with no sign of sinking in the center. A chalky layer signifies immaturity and such cheeses are hard to ripen once cut. A faint scent of ammonia indicates the cheese is past its best. If the cheese is very runny and smells strongly of ammonia it will be unpleasant to eat and could be dangerous.

Firm matured cheeses These are firmer in texture, with shinier rinds colored pale straw to orangy-brown. Some notable ones are **Pont L'Evêque**, **Reblochon**, **Port du Salut** and **St Paulin** (the main difference between the last two is that St Paulin is cheaper). All should be creamily firm, evenly colored, and show no signs of drying out. If so, they are relatively easy to keep well at home.

Hard matured cheese These cheeses are pressed during their making, some only lightly and briefly, others are left to mature under firm pressure for months. **Cheddar** and most other British cheeses are hard cheeses, as are **Emmental**, **Jarisberg**, **Gruyère** and **Parmesan**. All have a relatively low moisture content and a dense texture. Since they keep well, they are usually in good condition. Avoid any which seem to be sweating greasily, have deep cracks, or any signs of mold.

It is best to buy a good wedge of properly aged **Farmhouse Cheddar** cut from a whole cylinder. The plastic covered bricks on sale share the name Cheddar, but not much else. Cheddar, Gruyère and Parmesan are the cook's principal cheeses; **Lancashire** and **Leicester** are particularly good for toasting. All five melt well, but too fierce or sudden a heat can cause curdling and make the cheese stringy, so add cheese at the end of making a sauce, without then letting it boil; grill toppings gently.

Grated Parmesan sold in jars or boxes tastes nothing like true Parmesan, which is identified by the words 'Parmigiano-Reggiano' pinpricked all over the rind. Buy a wedge and grate it as you need it. It is the most heavily pressed of all cheeses, and keeps the longest.

Blue cheeses Blue varieties of cheese such as **Stilton**, **Lymeswold**, **Roquefort**, **Gorgonzola**, **Dolcelatte** (a mild version of Gorgonzola) and **Cambazola** (a new German cheese sometimes called **Blue Brie**), regardless of whether they are soft or firm, should have blue veins which contrast sharply and cleanly with the body of the cheese. Avoid blue-veined cheese with dark brown blotches in the body color, or where the veins do not spread evenly.

Storing cheese Cheese needs protection from loss of moisture and extreme heat or cold. Wrap it tightly (plastic wrap or foil is best), taking care not to trap air in the package. Store in a cool place (50–55°F) like a cellar, old-fashioned larder or the vegetable compartment of the refrigerator (the least cold part). Bring cheese back to room temperature an hour before serving, but keep it wrapped until the last moment. Re-wrap and return it to cool storage as soon as possible, and change wrappings every few days.

Cream cheeses and all matured cheeses can be frozen quite successfully. Freezing arrests the development of cheese, so freeze only when the cheese is at the perfect stage for eating and freeze in small enough portions to eat at one sitting – once defrosted it is best eaten up quickly.

VEGETABLES

Under-rated and over-cooked for too many years, vegetables are at last beginning to be treated with kindness and respect. What has probably done most to inspire our greater appreciation of vegetables is the splendidly wide variety now available in stores and supermarkets.

Very roughly speaking, vegetables can be divided into the tender and the hardy. Both types are best to eat young and freshly-picked, but freshness is of paramount importance when choosing tender types.

By tender vegetables I mean those that will only flourish in the mild summer months – butterhead lettuce, spinach and allied delicate leafy greens; snow peas, runner and other beans; eggplant, zucchini, and similar fruit-like vegetables. Once picked they are cut off from the copious supplies of moisture they need, and become exceedingly vulnerable. Having few reserves on which to draw and sustain themselves, leafy varieties wilt fast, fruit-like vegetables turn limp and soggy and peas and beans convert their sweet sugary sap to blotting paper starch in a desperate attempt to survive.

Vegetables hardy enough to withstand less favorable growing conditions are more resilient when picked, having been bred as survivors. Brassicas (the cabbage family), with their relatively coarse leaves packed into tight heads, are tough enough to combat cold, wind and rain in the field. Bulbs, roots and tubers shelter underground as they grow, while stem vegetables such as celery and leeks have protective walls of earth built up around them. All these are literally more solid, and have built-in reservoirs on which to feed after cropping, so they survive a bit longer.

We can't complain about the delays between cropping vegetables and getting them into the shops as it is usually a fairly rapid process from field to store. What is of great concern is the stage at which they are harvested.

Almost all vegetables are only good to eat if picked young, and some (peas and beans especially) need to be very young indeed. Small is beautiful and youth is vital. But on the principle of the greater the weight of the crop the bigger the income, it obviously makes financial sense for growers to delay picking crops until they grow large. They will not change their habits until a sufficient number of customers refuse to buy the "big baddies" and demand young produce, and are willing to pay higher prices. Large, elderly vegetables – megaton bomb-sized zucchini, leeks as stout as marble pillars – are coarse and fibrous, their flavor faded or crude, and however cheap they are almost worthless. A good young vegetable is worth the extra.

Inspect all vegetables closely before buying and avoid any which look miserably turned in on themselves. If a vegetable is unhappy or tired, its good eating qualities are lost and no amount of cossetting by the cook will revive it.

The shade of green to look for in vegetables depends so much on variety that it is best simply to say that all green vegetables should look vibrant and lively in color.

Where to buy vegetables The basic guidelines for vegetable shopping are quite straightforward: trust any source which offers fresh, high quality produce, with a fast turnover.

I buy most of my vegetables from a supermarket which meets all these requirements but I prefer to buy produce at the farm gate when I can. This is because I feel strongly in favor of such things as whole leeks, "dirty" celery, carrots complete with their plumy foliage, and cauliflowers whose curds nestle creamily under protective, unstripped leaves. Vegetables sold with their leaves intact and earth still clinging to their roots are more cumbersome, but retain their moisture and freshness far better. Trimming a vegetable always reduces its life expectancy and if the vegetable is fragile, trimming can prove a death-blow. For example, the right time to snap juicy stalks and leaves from radishes is when you eat them, not a moment before.

Storing vegetables Ideally, vegetables should be eaten just after picking, but this is clearly out of the question for many cooks, as is daily shopping. If you only shop once or twice a week, it makes sense to eat on the day of purchase those vegetables to which freshness matters most, and save for subsequent days those which suffer least from delay.

The less cold parts of the refrigerator (the vegetable compartment and shelves furthest from the freezing compartment), or a north-facing larder, are the best places to store vegetables. Take care not to squash or pack them too tightly. Vegetables which have been blanched as they grow (eg. Belgian endive and leeks) must be protected from light and so must bulbs, roots and tubers.

Many vegetables can be preserved as chutneys, pickles and relishes – a delicious way to enjoy the garden surplus out of season. Most vegetables can also be frozen, and will generally keep for several months.

Roots and Tubers

All roots and tubers should feel smooth and very firm, never flabby and should be free from cuts made during lifting, and other blemishes. New potatoes and radishes must be exceedingly fresh. The rest store well in cool, dark conditions.

Swedes and **turnips** are root members of the brassica family. I never bother with swedes, but really baby turnips can taste delicate. Even better is **kohlrabi**, a swollen stem brassica with crisp, pale green flesh. Buy all of them small: if larger than tennis balls this group tends to be coarse.

Celeriac and **Jerusalem artichokes** look unprepossessing but the intense nutty-sweet celery flavor of celeriac and the subtle, smoky taste of artichokes are excellent. Both make lovely soups and purées. Peel and cook in acidulated water or milk (don't let artichokes become mushy); roast in bacon fat; grate for salads. Fresh baby **beets** sold in bunches with foliage attached are a treat. Check for skin damage, and trim and peel after cooking. Beet leaves are very nutritious; cook them like greens.

Early summer **carrots** are delicately flavored, maincrop carrots are richer and sweeter. When sugar was expensive, carrots were used for sweet dishes, as were **parsnips**.

Salsify and **scorzonera** are subtly-flavored, thin tapering roots available from early autumn until spring. Scorzonera is slightly more flavorsome, but peeling the thick black skin after cooking is tiresome. **Mooli** (**winter radish** or **daikon**) looks like a giant white carrot. It is more expensive, coarser, less pretty and less tasty than our own pink **radishes**.

The home-grown new **potato** season is May–August. Waxy new potatoes are essential for salads and the best potatoes for gratins and other sliced potato dishes. Maincrop potatoes, harvested in September and able to be kept in store till May, are more floury – good for mashing, baking and roasting.

Sweet potatoes and **yams** are unrelated though the names are sometimes used interchangeably. True yams have bark-like brown skins and are moister and sweeter than purply-red skinned sweet potatoes, which have floury, chestnutty flesh. Both can be boiled and buttered, or glazed.

Bulbs and Stems

Onions are one of the most valuable flavorings in cooking – tight round onions for pungency, and the flatter-shaped Spanish varieties for sweeter, milder flavor. Always look for dry-necked onions and refuse any that are sprouting. Button or pickling onions can usually be substituted for **shallots** which are expensive and difficult to find. **Scallions** taste good cooked as well as raw.

Leeks have a more subtle taste: a beautiful vegetable when young, tender and slim, carefully washed and gently cooked. Beware of fat elderly leeks: the coarse greenery may signal a wooden core in the white part. **Celery**, like leeks, used to be earthed to blanch as it grew, but most varieties are now self-blanching. Blanched (white) celery tastes more delicate than the self-blanching (pale green) sort. The generous furl of leaves on whole, untrimmed celery looks and tastes especially good. A juicy crisp head of long white stems has a more delicate flavor than green varieties.

Looking like a squat bulbous version of celery, **fennel** has a smoky aniseed flavor. Like celery, it is excellent both raw and cooked and is superb with fish. Scrape lightly to remove any bulbous strings and save the fronds for salads or stuffing.

Asparagus is lovely but often expensive and loses its flavor quickly after picking, so it is best to wait until a variety is in season in May and June.

Brassicas

Always check the base of a brassica. If it looks nicotine-stained it is stale; if slimy it is rotten.

Red cabbages should have a bloom to them and make wonderfully rich braised dishes. **White cabbage** is traditional for coleslaw but **Chinese cabbage** is infinitely preferable – juicy crisp with a less aggressive brassica flavor. Water is anathema to Chinese cabbage and to **green cabbage** – the school dinner image of the latter is due to death by drowning. Steaming, stir-frying, stuffing and braising are kinder. Check all cabbages for firm-heartedness.

Brussels sprouts are a delight when tiny, tight and delicately steamed, a disaster when blowsy, yellowing or boiled to death. Still sometimes called **collards** (heartless cabbages), **spring greens** have little to recommend them, but young **kale** is very good if lightly steamed; when old it is too mineral.

Technically, all flower-headed brassicas are cauliflowers, but shops and cooks use the name **cauliflower** only for the large, white-headed varieties. Green or purple headed varieties, which are smaller and more delicate in flavor, are generally called **broccoli**. But the best broccoli are those bought as budded shoots in asparagus-type spears – either substantial, tender and green (which are called **calabrese**) or thinner and purple (called **purple sprouting broccoli**). The curds or florets of all flower-headed brassicas should be firm, tight and wide-awake looking, never feeble or cringing. Cook with care, standing the vegetables in a pan so the stalk cooks in gently bubbling water while the tender florets soften in steam.

Leaves

Spinach and **sorrel** should be vibrant green and squeaky fresh. Sorrel has such a direct acid taste it is used in tiny quantities – a small handful makes a delicious addition to a large bundle of spinach. Tender summer spinach is exquisite both cooked and raw.

Some vegetables are grown for the juicy stalks and central ribs of their leaves, which are steamed and served with butter sauces. The leafy parts are cooked separately, like spinach. Of these, **Swiss chard**, **seakale beet** and **spinach beet** are delicate and good. **Red chard** is particularly pretty but hard to find and you will probably have to grow your own. Real **seakale**, a seashore plant, and **cardoons**, which have a faint, globe artichoke flavor, both have enormous ribs and scant leaf area.

Salad Greens

Lettuce can only be used fresh. Soft leaved varieties, like Butterhead, flop completely very quickly; Webbs Wonder, with crispish, crinkly leaves, stands up a bit better. The crispest, like Iceberg (as tight and round as a cabbage heart, but inclined to be low on taste) and Cos, with its elongated leaves, survive best. There are also loose-headed varieties, called "butterflies" in the trade, such as Salad Bowl which has pretty, ribbony leaves.

Endive is a curly winter lettuce which has beautiful frizzy leaves and a fresh taste – don't eat the outer dark green leaves, they are disagreeably bitter. **Escarole** is a broader-leafed type. **Lambs lettuce** (or **corn salad**) is nutty tasting and another good vegetable for winter salads.

Purslane is an old fashioned salad vegetable chewy in texture, slightly sour and worth experimenting with. **Rocket**, which has quite the greenest-tasting leaves, is also good and can be found in some Greek and Italian shops. **Rape and cress** is the only vegetable that comes complete with its own garden to keep it fresh. **Watercress**, with its beautifully crisp slightly peppery tasting leaves is perhaps the most versatile salad vegetable.

The succulent great buds of delicate white crispness called **Belgian endive** are blanched as they grow and must be kept in the dark. Look for plumpness with no sign of bruising. Leaf tips should be yellow – they turn green and bitter if exposed to light. **Radicchio** (sometimes called **red** 21

Grading and cleaning scallions.

chicory) look like gigantic Brussels sprouts with the pigment of red cabbage. A popular alternative to chicory, they are more peppery, more definitely savory.

Peas and Beans
Peas and **beans** contain sugary sap which begins to convert to starch when the pod reaches maturity, so youth is vital. Pods should be a sappy healthy green. Snap to check crispness and lack of stringiness. Never buy pods bulging with contents like a snake fed on cricket balls. **Mangetouts (sugar peas)**, eaten pod and all, have the beauty of fresh young peas but with a luxurious bite.

Broad beans can be eaten pod and all when they are real juveniles, but I have never seen them on sale so babyish and tender. And the fibrous giants that fill the shops in the name of **runner beans** have given this vegetable a bad reputation – unfairly, because when young and tender they are truly delicious. **Green beans (French beans)** are superb when pencil slim, youthful, tender and fresh.

Pale crunchy **beansprouts** are sprouting seeds of mung or soy beans. Good in salads and much used in Chinese cuisine, absolute freshness is essential, so it is best (and fun) to grow them at home in a jam jar.

Dried peas and beans are enjoying a revival because they make cheap, filling and warming winter dishes. Favorite varieties are whole gray-green **lentils**, delicate green **flageolets**, knobbly and nutty **chickpeas**, small white **haricot beans** and red **kidney beans**. All, except lentils, need soaking before cooking, and red kidney beans must be fast-boiled for at least 15 minutes to destroy a poisoning agent.

Fruit and Flower Vegetables
Glossy, plump and firm good looks are important qualities in fruit-like vegetables. Avoid any that show the slightest sign of wrinkles, bruising or soft patches.

The **tomatoes** generally found in stores out of season are characterless: uniform in size, cottonwoolly in texture and lacking real flavor. Slightly green tomatoes are the least disappointing.

Large, fist-sized **green peppers (capsicums)** are mild, crisp and clean tasting. Yellow and red colors are riper and taste more tomatoey. White and black varieties are also available now: the taste is much the same, only the color is a novelty. Tiny Aladdin's slipper-shaped **chili peppers** are for those who like it hot.

Regal purple **egg plant** has many fine qualities once its bitter juices are removed by salting, or by squeezing after grilling or baking. It is impossible to cook Mediterranean or Middle Eastern dishes without its generous smoky meatiness.

Avocados are now available all year round. They may be pear-shaped or round, rough or smooth skinned, green or almost black (the knobbly, purply-brown skinned Hass variety is said to be best of all). Avocados are easy to ripen at home and must be gently yielding all over to eat well. Squashy avocados, sold off cheaply, are a good buy for soups and sauces.

Zucchini, the tinier the better, are exquisite. The **chayote** (or **chocho** or **christophene**) is a pear-shaped **squash**, the taste of which might be described as like an uninteresting zucchini, and, Cinderella apart, the **pumpkin** is not a very magical or interesting vegetable.

Hooray, for once, for plastic packaging which enables you to inspect the increasingly found English **cucumber** closely, and helps to keep it fresh. Leave the peel on for flavor and color when eating raw, but remove it for cooking because it tastes bitter when heated. Smaller ridged **gherkins** are best for pickling.

Corn cobs should be densely packed, sappy looking and a pale creamy yellow; if deep golden they are over-mature and will taste very starchy. Do not add salt when cooking: it toughens the cob. The scaly leaves of **artichokes** should be pearly green and plump with no sign of browning or bruising. Check stalk end for freshness, and leaf tips for splits. Cooked too far ahead of eating, all artichokes taste stale. **Okra (ladies' fingers, bindi)** are small fluted green darts, delicate, pretty and popular in Southern as well as Asian and West Indian cooking. They should be freshly green and snap crisply. Snip off the stalks carefully before cooking, without cutting the pod.

Fungi
Open or flat cultivated **mushrooms** have more flavor than younger cups or buttons, but their taste still falls far short of fresh field mushrooms. **Horse mushroom**, **ceps**, **puff balls** and **shaggy caps** can also be picked in the wild but distinguishing the edible from the poisonous is so risky for the amateur picker that many, like me, consider it wiser to buy rich tasting dried mushrooms instead.

FRUIT

Fresh fruit, being rich in fiber and vitamins, is good for you, and needs only to be served simply and prettily – a gift to the cook.

In the days when local fruit in season was all one could buy, there were times of plenty and times of nothing. But the arrival of cold storage systems has greatly extended the eating seasons of fruit and brought a variety of imports from abroad. Now the choice at all times is so wide it can seem bewildering.

Where to buy fresh fruit Open air markets are enticing but it is unrealistic to expect a fair deal from every barrow. Some stallholders do sell good quality fresh fruits at low prices – they are worth seeking out if you intend to become a regular customer.

If you are unsure, it is wiser to buy from a specialty fruiterer. He or she will advise you which fruit is now in peak condition, and will pass on tips about how to bring on the fruit you want to eat tomorrow.

In a supermarket there is usually no specialist help or advice to turn to but, if it is part of a large and efficient chain, the produce should be very fresh and of high quality, the range may be much wider than a small shop can manage and prices are sometimes exceedingly low.

Choose a supermarket which sells fruit loose so you can really see, select and weigh out what you want. I avoid pre-packed fruit because it is hard to check the quality, and more expensive than loose fruit.

One of the most agreeable ways to buy fruit is from a Pick-Your-Own orchard or soft fruit farm. This is more time-consuming, of course, but there is no surer way of obtaining truly fresh produce.

If you want fruit grown without the aid of modern chemicals, you will have to seek out a natural food store and be prepared to pay a premium price.

Choosing fruit In general it makes sense to buy fruit only when it is perfectly ripe and fresh, buying little and often, and eating it without delay. There are, however, exceptions. The fruit used in jam-making should be slightly under-ripe, because then it contains more acid and pectin than very ripe fruit, and good acid and pectin levels are essential if jam is to set properly.

Buying overripe fruit may also make housekeeping sense at times. For example, cheap, blackened and soft bananas will make a perfectly good mousse, and cheap windfall apples will make as good a purée as perfect ones providing, of course, that all the bruised and overripe parts are conscientiously cut out before cooking.

Sometimes, search as one may, it is impossible to find fruit in tip-top condition and a tactical approach is necessary to make the best of what is available. Using citrus juice as an "improver" is a useful Italian trick. Sprinkle overripe strawberries with a little fresh orange and lemon juice (two parts orange to one part lemon) and a sifting of sugar half an hour or so before serving and it will sharpen their overblown flavor admirably. Paradoxically, this is equally effective in rounding out the thin flavor of underripe strawberries, and other soft berry fruit, peaches and melons that fall short of perfection can be made more choice in the same way.

But what is choice fruit? Irrespective of type, fruit that is fresh and ripe, looks plump and vibrant, glowing with good health. Colors should be bright, skins taut, scent deliciously evident but not overpowering. If fruit looks in need of a good night's sleep it is past its prime – the longer it has been separated from the sap-giving branch, the duller and more sad looking it becomes.

Storing fruit Ideally, fresh ripe fruit should not be stored at all, but, if you have to, this is the way to do it.

Ripe fruits should be stored in a cold place to inhibit over-ripening – and the more delicate the fruit the more mollycoddling it needs. Berries must be refrigerated if not eaten on the day of purchase. Spread them in a shallow dish to prevent them being bruised and crushed, with an airtight covering, and they will keep 1–2 days.

If space permits, most other ripe fruits are also best refrigerated. The next best place to store them is in a north-facing larder, with a normal temperature of 45–50°F. This is cool enough to keep fruit such as apples for several weeks.

A kitchen store cupboard, if not properly ventilated, will have a temperature of about 62°F. This is fine for storing fruits that are fairly protected from their surroundings, such as pomegranates, which have hard casings, and citrus fruits, which are literally more thick-skinned than most other fruits. But hard and stone fruits will ripen and go over the top very quickly under such conditions and delicate fruits could go moldy overnight.

Fresh Berries

Each berry should be distinct and sparkle with color. Don't buy if the fruit is beginning to slur and sink into the punnet, or if the base of the punnet is stained. Cranberries have relatively tough skins. For all others, buy fresh and ripe and eat right away.

Strawberries from home and abroad are available May–August, small supplies later. Taste before buying: some strawberries are grown for high yield and good looks at the cost of flavor. **Alpine**, or **wood strawberries** are tiny and wonderfully fragrant. Not grown commercially, but well worth growing at home.

Raspberries are perhaps the choicest soft summer fruit, available late June–early August. They are beginning to be supplemented in quantity by **loganberries**, an American cross, grown here and sold in July–August. Loganberries are larger and darker than raspberries, less intensely flavored but seedless.

Cultivated blackberries, hard to find in stores, are larger and less seedy than **wild blackberries** gathered in the autumn. Cultivated blackberries have a fairly bland flavor compared to wild blackberries in a good year, but are superior if the weather has been bad.

Black currants, **red currants** and **white currants** are found wild in July–August. Black currants are pungent and aromatic, with a high vitamin C content. Red and white currants (white currants are simply albino versions of red currants) are less popular because of their seeds.

Cultivated **blueberries** look rather like very large, plump black currants with a beautiful blue bloom to their skins. A longstanding favorite, they are available in the spring. Delicious raw, in ice creams, pies, pancakes and waffles.

Cranberries are available in late autumn and winter, need a lot of sugar to be used in desserts, slightly less when making sauces to accompany turkey and game.

Gooseberries are rather out of fashion today. Early cooking varieties, hard as hailstones and bright green, are excellent if you add scented elderflower blossom or sweet geranium leaves to the cooking pot. Dessert varieties are larger, softer, sweeter globes of amber or red. Their season starts later and continues through August.

Hard Fruits

Apples and **pears** should be complete with stalks, and free of bruising and other damage. Skins should be smooth and firm and there should be no overall softening or middle-aged wrinkles.

Dessert apples are excellent raw and better than cookers when neat slices are desirable, for instance in open tarts. Good varieties include Red and Yellow Delicious, Granny Smith, the three most popular apples worldwide. Good all-purpose apples include Jonathan, McIntoch, Rome Beauty, Macoun, Winesap, Baldwin, Gravenstein, and Grimes Golden. Autumn is apple season, but modern storage techniques and varied growing seasons make them available year round.

Of pears, Comice, Anjou and Boscs are excellent for dessert and cooking. Pears are unpredictable ripeners and once ripe can go over exceedingly quickly. Buy them underripe, put in a warm place, check once or twice a day and eat each one as soon as it ripens.

Quinces are strongly scented and impart a blossomy flavor to cooked apple dishes. Also good for jellies and jams, they are only patchily available, in late autumn.

Stone Fruits

Many **plums** (available July–October) are acidic and only fit for cooking, but many, on their way back after years of neglect, are delicious raw. Dusky purple **damsons**, the smallest and most tart of plums, are available in September–October. All plums should be plump and smooth with a shy bloom to their skins, resilient not oversoft. Check for bird and insect damage.

Cherries are available from the end of May onwards through the summer. All varieties should look shiny and bouncy, free of pecks and pitting, with fresh looking stalks intact. Montmorency, derived from the morello strain is the main cooking variety. Some dessert varieties are soft fleshed, others firm, and there is a confusing array of colors – so it is always wise to taste before buying.

Peaches, primarily from Southern states, ripen in the summer. Check for soft spots and bruising. Peaches should yield to slight pressure when cradled in the hand, and have downy fresh skins. If tennis ball hard, or tinged with green when bought, the fruit will possibly never ripen properly. Ask for a freestone variety of peach if you want to serve them peeled and sliced. In clingstone varieties the flesh digs deep into the stone cracks. White-fleshed varieties of peach, regrettably rare in the stores, are better than the yellow-fleshed ones. **Nectarines** are close relatives, with a smoother, plum-like skin and fine flavor.

Apricots, like peaches, are hard to ripen once picked. Colors vary from pale to tawny depending on variety rather than ripeness, although deeper colored fruits are usually sweeter. Feel them (they should be neither hard nor very soft), smell them, and taste one. If in doubt, cook them by poaching in syrup.

Citrus Fruits

Citrus skins should glow, be filled with headily scented zest and hug the fruit tightly. If they are lacklustre or feel spongy, the fruit may be dry. The heavier the fruit feels for its size the juicier it will be.

Sweet **oranges** are available all year round. The majority are termed Navels, including the fleshy, reliable Jaffas. Valencias and Blood Oranges have smoother, thinner skins. Sevilles and other bitter varieties on sale briefly in January–February are intended only for marmalade and cooking. **Kumquats** look like miniature oranges and are eaten peel and all, sometimes candied.

The **tangerine** family with its loose-fitting skin comes into season in winter. Tangerines (sometimes called mandarins), **clementines** and **satsumas** have a more floral taste and scent than oranges; muscats and temple oranges are crosses between tangerines and oranges and taste like it. All, including a stream of new hybrids with pretty names, are worth trying.

Grapefruit are available primarily in two colors: white-fleshed and pink-fleshed. Keep an eye out for the more rare Texas ruby grapefruit. The skin of pink grapefruit is sometimes patchily colored, but the flesh is beautifully sweet. **Ugli** fruit are aptly named, with bumpy, heavily-mottled skins. A cross between a grapefruit and a tangerine, the flesh is delicately flavored and scented.

Lemons are not a fruit to eat, as such, but the juice and zest are invaluable in the kitchen. Giant lemons are no better than small ones, but smooth skinned lemons are usually juicier than those with knobbly skins. Basically **limes** are lemons in tropical kit (the lemon will not grow in the tropics where the lime thrives and vice versa). Limes should be pale or dark green; if yellowish the juice may have lost some of its enviable tang.

Vine and Other Fruits

Impeccable looking **grapes** are available year round at a price. For the sweetest "white" grapes look for a honeyed shade of green. Seedless varieties are usually labelled as such.

A good ripe **melon** feels heavy for its size, firm, not rock hard overall, and softer at one end. It should also smell fragrant and sound a little hollow when gently tapped. Musk types have "hair net" skins. Canteloupe types, such as Charentais and Ogen, are the most aromatic. Galia tastes like a cross between Ogen and Honeydew.

As for **watermelons**, Sugarbaby is less tasteless than most.

Bananas are easy to ripen at home, eat them when all the skin has turned from green to yellow and is beginning to spot with brown. Never refrigerate bananas – the flesh will turn black. **Plantains** are a cooking banana, but starchier and less sweet. Best treated as a vegetable, they can be used while still underripe.

The need to harvest **pineapples** underripe for the long shipment to market often leaves them bereft of much of their sweetness and goodness and with too much acidity. It is only worth buying a pineapple if it is fully, or almost ripe. Look for a heady scent, uniform coloring, a soft but not damaged stalk end, a fresh pinecone of leaves, and no signs of bruising.

Brilliant pink forced **rhubarb** brings a breath of spring early in the year. The outdoor summer crop is coarser in texture and flavor. Avoid limp, sad rhubarb, and very large and aggressively green stems. Big is not beautiful to eat.

Newcomers

The **Chinese gooseberry**, now better known as **kiwifruit**, surely owes its huge success to its decorative qualities – jade green flesh speckled with tiny black seeds in a rose window pattern. The taste, though pleasant, is pallid, but the fruit makes a very pretty ingredient in all kinds of salad.

The **pomegranate** is beautiful. Its rosy-flushed hard shell encases hundreds of pulp-covered seeds, which burst their aromatic, refreshing juices as you bite them: If you find the seeds tiresome, squeeze the flesh in cheesecloth to extract the juices.

Fresh **dates** are an improvement on dried dates, and fresh **figs** wonderfully different from dried figs. Fresh "white" figs (which are green) are exquisite, while "black" ones (which are winey-purple) have a more aromatic taste. Buy as ripe as possible, but not stickily over-ripe.

The Israeli development of a seedless, easy ripening variety of **persimmon** called **sharonfruit** has rescued what would otherwise be an oddity – persimmon is a blowsy tomato-like fruit packed with seeds and uneatably astringent until almost rotten. Sharonfruit is ready to eat when plump and firm and a pale orangey color, and is agreeable in salads.

The most exciting thing about **passion fruit** is, perhaps, its name. When the purply-brown, hard papery skin is wrinkled and dimpled, the fruit is ripe. The seed-packed yellowy pulp, eaten like pomegranates, is sweet but dull.

Amongst the best new fruits are **lychees** and **rambutans** from China and South-East Asia. Inside their thin shield-like shells (rambutans are also covered with spines) the flesh looks like a giant translucent grape. Even better is the **mangosteen**, unrelated but not dissimilar. Inside its purple-brown skin, the pearly white flesh is divided into five neat segments. All three fruits are juicy, with an intriguing balance of sweetness and acidity, and available December–February.

Mangoes, **guavas** and **papayas** (also called **pawpaws**) are all scented fruits which people either love or hate. Yellow-skinned, pink-fleshed guavas have a very pervasive fragrance and are very sweet, even cloying. Best made into jelly or jam, they will also give a fruit salad some mystery.

The orange-pink flesh of a perfectly ripe papaya is a little like musky sweet melon (papaya is known as tree melon in some places). It can be ripened like an avocado, in a warm room: check for softness at the calyx end.

Some people liken mangoes to slippery, overscented soap. Others, like myself, rate the mango as the most beautiful of all fruits. The skin color varies according to the variety, but totally green mangoes are underripe and heavily blackened fruit are overripe, while any whiff of turpentine signals underripeness. When it is ready to eat, a mango is lusciously scented and feels just soft all over.

HERBS

Herbs have suffered twice over in recent years. First they went out of fashion almost completely, so that the only reference to them in many cookbooks was the vague instruction, "Add a pinch of herbs." Then they lost out again when they reappeared in the kitchen not as the fresh green plants they really are, but as rows of cute bottles and packets, filled with dried herbs – the least successful way of using them.

Buying fresh herbs: if you possibly can, buy fresh herbs for your cooking, on the day you need them. They will keep for several days in the refrigerator if you wrap the stems in damp paper towels and put them in an airtight container or in a plastic bag, blown up like a balloon and fastened around the neck with a rubber band or twist tie.

Buying dried herbs: if you have to buy dried herbs, try to find a reliable source with a quick turnover and look for the smallest packet you can find. There is no point in buying huge quantities of dried herbs when only a pinch or two is required in each recipe. And when you use dried herbs, remember that weight for weight their flavor will be more concentrated than fresh ones.

Growing herbs: try to find a corner where you can grow your own herbs. A balcony or even a window sill offers room enough for a few pots and the plants thrive on being cut again and again. Don't worry if your pot does not face the sun: many herbs prefer damp soil and some shade. Some herbs are annual and only flourish in the summer, but fortunately these seem most suited to the food we eat in summer. Those that you need for winter casseroles and soups are mostly perenial, shrubby herbs.

Freezing herbs: if you want to preserve herbs, they can be frozen very successfully in small quantities. For soups, stocks and casseroles, freeze the chopped herbs in icecube trays with a little water; store the cubes in a labelled bag and use as few or as many as you need. This is the best method of preserving the annual herbs that only flourish in the summer months.

Drying herbs: the shrubby herbs can be dried for winter months. Pick them on a dry summer morning when all the dew has evaporated: they are at their best before the plants flower. Do not wash them, or put them into a plastic bag, as this will encourage mold. Spread them on a piece of cloth stretched tight over a wooden frame, in a single layer. Put them in a shady place to dry, turning them from time to time to expose every side to the air. When they are completely dry, rub the leaves from the stems and crumble them into small pieces. Store in airtight jars in a cool, dark cupboard. If you must keep them in the kitchen, make sure it is not too hot and that you use dark glass jars.

Preserving herbs in oil and vinegar: herb-flavored oils and vinegars are perfect partners for your winter salads. After gathering your herbs in the usual way they can be put into bottles of wine or cider vinegar and left in the sun for a couple of weeks. Shake the bottles every day, then pour off the vinegar into labelled bottles, discarding the herb. If the flavor is not quite strong enough, repeat the process with fresh herbs until the required strength is achieved.

Fresh herbs can be preserved very successfully in oil for use in winter. Pick the herbs as for drying, chop them finely and pack into jars covering them with light olive or sunflower oil. Add more herbs to the jars as they become available, always making sure there is more oil than herbs in the jar. Keep covered in the refrigerator, or a cold dark larder, for use in winter. A spoonful of the mixture can be put into salad dressings, soups and casseroles, or used for coating vegetables after they have been cooked.

Herb teas, or tisanes, are becoming increasingly popular because they are soothing and refreshing, aromatic and delicate. They are made much like ordinary tea; the proportion of herb to water is generally 1oz. fresh herb ($\frac{1}{2}$oz. dried) to 1 pint of boiling water. Leave it covered for up to 15 minutes before pouring. The tea may be served either hot or cold, and if sweetening is required, use a teaspoon of honey.

Sweet Basil *Ocimum basilicum*
Bush Basil *Ocimum minimum*
These are favorite summer herbs. Their flavor is at its best in any tomato dish, but basil is also a wonderful addition to green salads, or those made with rice and pasta. Basil is good, too, with omelettes or scrambled egg dishes and mushrooms.

Basil can be dried, though the leaves are a little too thick to dry quickly. The best method is to freeze it on its own or in ice cubes. Basil can also be preserved in olive oil to use in sauces and with pasta dishes and is an essential flavoring of the classic Italian preserve, *pesto*.

Bay *Laurus nobilis*
This handsome tree supplies fresh leaves all year round. Often used to flavor soups, casseroles and fish, bay leaves are essential in the making of stock and milk-based sauces, and are well worth trying in custards and milk puddings. A bay leaf is one of the essential ingredients in a *bouquet garni*, and is a welcome addition to marinades and kebabs. When making a terrine or pâté place one or two bay leaves on top, and let their flavor permeate the finished dish.

Chervil *Anthriscus cerefolium*
This ferny-leaved herb with its delicate anise taste is good in all egg dishes, with cream sauces or cream cheese, in soups or with summer vegetables. It can also be used in potato salad or with mashed potatoes. It is one of the herbs used in "*fines herbes*." Its flavor is fugitive and will not stand prolonged cooking, so use it as a garnish, or as a last minute addition.

Dried chervil is not very good so freezing or making chervil vinegar are the best methods of preserving it.

Chives *Allium schoenoprasum*
Chives are the most delicate in flavor of the onion family and one of the earliest green herbs to arrive in spring. Snip them with scissors to make a garnish for summer dishes, with eggs, cream cheese and for soups – Vichysoisse is traditionally flavored with chives. Like chervil, their taste will not stand prolonged cooking; add them to your dishes at the last minute.

Fresh chives can be available all year round if kept in pots on the kitchen window sill during the winter. Outdoors they can be encouraged to sprout early by covering with cloches.

Coriander *Coriandrum sativum*
This pungent herb is much used in cooking in the Middle East, India, Mexico and China and can often be found in shops catering for people from these countries. For some people the taste of the green leaves is too strong, but if you like it at all, it may become quite addictive. The ground seeds are generally better liked for their aromatic flavor, especially in curries.

In Mexico, where it is known as cilantro, the green leaves are used in the preparation of eggs. Guacamole (made with mashed avocado), green and red tomato sauce and mixed with rice and vegetables. In the Middle East coriander is combined with chick peas, used in salads, and added to soups and stews.

Gather the seeds when ripe and dry for the winter. The green leaves do not dry well, but they can be frozen.

Dill *Anethum graveolens*
Dill is a tall feathery plant with aromatic leaves and seeds. Dill pickles are made from both stalks and seeds while the leaves alone are best chopped into salads and as a garnish for summer vegetables. Cucumber salad made with cream, lemon juice and chopped dill is delicious and the Scandinavians use dill to flavor their pickled salmon, *gravad lax*. The seeds can be used to flavor root vegetables and cakes, sauces and to make dill vinegar.

Dill is not altogether satisfactory dried, but it can be frozen.

Fennel *Foeniculum vulgare*
Fennel is a fairly large feathery plant. For cooking, use the fresh young leaves and the thin juicy stalks. It is particularly good with oily fish such as mackerel or red mullet, and also with pork. The larger stalks can be used to flavor fish soups, or put in the bottom of the casserole when cooking a chicken. Dried stalks should be kept to put on the barbecue when grilling fish, and the seeds are sometimes used when baking bread and as a flavoring for cream cheese.

To gather the seeds, cut the whole heads from the plant as they ripen and hang them upside down over a piece of paper. The stalks of fennel are the only bits worth drying. You *can* freeze the leaves, but the seeds are a better source of fennel flavor to see you through the winter.

Lemon Balm *Melissa officinalis*
Fresh balm will add a pleasant lemon flavor to stewed fruit, or to tea if it is popped into the pot when brewing. It is excellent used in summer drinks, iced tea, wine punches and lemonade. The dried leaves are useful in stuffings, and they make a particularly good herb tea.

Pick the leaves for drying before the flowers are open, dry quickly and store in dark airtight jars in a cool place.

Lovage *Levisticum officinale*
This strong plant can reach six foot, and is too large for the average garden, but you may like to sample its pleasant, celery-like taste. The green leaves can be chopped up for soups, stews and salads, and are also used to improve the taste of gravy. The seeds can be collected to add flavor to hearty dishes with meat or cheese.

Pick the leaves to dry for winter. The flower heads should be picked as the seeds begin to turn brown, and hung upside down in a cool place over a sheet of paper, to collect the seeds as they fall.

Pot Marjoram *Origanum onites*
Sweet Marjoram *Origanum marjorana*
Oregano *Origanum vulgare*
Marjoram is an excellent herb to use in the preparation of meat dishes and also has a strong affinity with tomatoes. The Italians make great use of its stronger cousin, **oregano**, in their pizzas. The Greeks use it in marinades for their kebabs.

Dried marjoram keeps well and, if you like the flavor, try growing oregano and preserve it in oil or vinegar. Its flavour will last all winter long and will remind you of hot hillsides and blue skies.

Applemint *Mentha sauveolens*
Spearmint *Mentha spicata*
There are many members of the mint family, and Applemint and Spearmint are among the best. Mint sauce with lamb is a classic combination, but mint jelly, made with apple, is equally good. Veal and lamb chops are very good served with a pat of mint butter and new potatoes and fresh peas benefit from a fresh mint garnish.

In India, a cool sauce to serve with hot flavored curries is made with grated cucumber, yogurt and mint. The leaves can also be made into a soothing tea and iced tea made with mint and lemon is very refreshing on a hot day.

Mint can be dried, but its flavor is stronger if it is frozen, or chopped and put into honey or syrup for use in mint sauce during the winter.

Parsley *Petroselinum crispum*
Parsley is obtainable year-around and should be used often for it is rich in Vitamins A, B and C and contains calcium, iron and other minerals.

Parsley sauce, once so popular, is still good if carefully made and parsley can be added to other sauces and soups. It is an important part of a *bouquet garni*, essential in the preparation of stews and stock, and good when added in handfuls to stuffing. Finely chopped parsley mixed with breadcrumbs and lemon peel can be rubbed on to a leg or shoulder of lamb while it is roasting to make a crunchy surface to the meat, and fish cakes or fish pie made with plenty of parsley are especially delicious.

Preserving parsley is hardly necessary as it is so generally available.

Rosemary *Rosmarinus officinalis*
The presence of a rosemary bush in your garden or on your balcony is essential if you are interested in herbs and will delight you with its delicious scent as you pass.

A few sprigs added to lamb, pork or chicken dishes will fill the kitchen with their aroma. Don't use too much as it can be a rather overpowering flavor, but it combines well with garlic. The stiffer twigs, shorn of their needles, can be used to spear kebabs for the grill. The Italians make a delicious bread flavored with rosemary, and it can also be added to biscuits or dumplings to serve with your main course.

Rosemary can be preserved (in vinegar) but there is no need if you have a plant as it is available all the year round.

Sage *Salvia officinalis*
This rather strongly flavored herb is not popular with everyone but it is a traditional herb to serve with fatty meats – pork, goose and duck. It is often used in stuffing for these, and can also be mixed into apple sauce for a more subtle flavor. Home-made sausages are excellent .seasoned with sage. In Italy many veal and calves' liver dishes are cooked with sage. Sage leaves are also used in the making of Derby sage cheese.

The leaves of sage can be dried for winter use, but as it is an evergreen, fresh leaves are always available if you grow your own plants.

Sweet Cicely *Myrrhis odorata*
A fern-like plant, up to 3 feet high, the leaves have a sweet anise taste and are good in salads or when cooked with fruit. Sweet Cicely is a natural sweetener and can be used instead of some of the sugar when cooking sour fruit. The seeds are also sweet and can be gathered, dried and used during the winter.

Collecting the seeds as they turn brown and ripen is the only way of preserving the flavor: the leaves do not dry well.

Tarragon *Artemisia dracunculus*
Once you have tasted this excellent herb, no summer will be complete without it. It has an aniseed flavor and a certain bite to it that is never forgotten.

In the kitchen its best known use is in the cooking of Tarragon Chicken, but it lends itself equally well to flavoring veal, salads and eggs. It is also very good combined with tomatoes. It is an essential ingredient of the Sauces Tartare, Hollandaise, Béarnaise and Ravigote.

It does not dry well as the essential oil, and therefore much of the flavor, is lost. It can, however, be frozen successfully, and preserved in vinegar.

Thyme *Thymus vulgaris*
There are many varieties of this aromatic bush plant, some with variegated or colored leaves. Thyme can be used fresh or dried as it keeps its flavor well. It is most often used in stuffings, casseroles, soups and marinades. Fresh thyme is a delicious seasoning with fresh spring vegetables. It can be used to flavor bread or dumplings, and it combines well with cheese and olives, and with other herbs.

The leaves of thyme can be dried successfully for use in the winter, but it does not freeze very well.

PICK HERBS ON A DRY SUMMER MORNING

FENNEL

TARRAGON

CHERVIL

MARJORAM

BASIL

CORIANDER

DILL

ROSEMARY

THE COMPLETE COOKING TECHNIQUES

SOUPS

Soups are one of the most rewarding fields for the beginning cook to explore since they are extremely varied and not hard to master. Nor do they take forever to make: many can be made in an hour.

My favorite soups fall into four main categories. There are the thick soups, sustaining enough to make a meal – or the basis of one – in themselves. These include such comforting foods as minestrone, chicken noodle soup, and bean and lentil soups. Then there are the vegetable purées. These make a healthy and inexpensive start to a meal and range from the homely carrot and tomato soup to the elegant Vichyssoise.

Fish soups vary widely in character, from the exotic Mediterranean soups, flavored with saffron and garlic, to the nursery-like simplicity of American fish chowder made with milk and water biscuits. In a category of their own are the consommés. A consommé is the test of a good restaurant for it demands much time, care and expense. Yet it is a delicacy the true gourmet never fails to appreciate. I rarely make one from scratch, except for special occasions like Christmas, but when there is a good beef or game stock in the larder, it is little extra trouble to make it into a consommé.

All soups can be greatly enhanced by the way they are served. Peasant soups like minestrone look best in earthenware, shellfish soups in shallow china bowls, and cold soups in cups.

"Sous la Lampe – Alfred Sisley et sa Femme," by Marie Bracquemond, 1841–1916. By courtesy of Galleries Maurice Sternberg, Chicago.

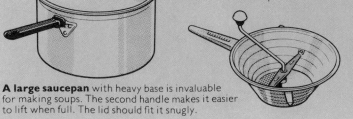

A food mill or *mouli-légumes* with three interchangeable discs gives varying degrees of smoothness. This is good for making vegetable soups, where texture is important.

A large saucepan with heavy base is invaluable for making soups. The second handle makes it easier to lift when full. The lid should fit it snugly.

Stock pot. Also useful for making large quantities of soup. Must not be used for preliminary frying as the base is too thin.

Large ladle for spooning soup into food mill, or for serving.

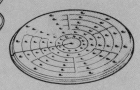

A heat diffuser enables soup to simmer gently, even on old stoves with imperfect heat control.

TIPS ON MAKING PERFECT SOUPS

✳ *Soups must be freshly made, with carefully chosen ingredients. They must never be treated as a repository for leftovers.*

✳ *When soups are made using a number of different ingredients, the flavors need time to blend and grow used to each other. Whenever possible they should be cooked a few hours before serving, and reheated. If this is not possible, leave the finished soup to stand, covered, for 10 minutes before serving.*

✳ *Most flavors are predominantly "warm" or "cool." The warm ones can be emphasized by adding spices, such as coriander or saffron, and cream, while the cool ones are enhanced by yogurt, fresh herbs and fruit juices.*

✳ *Vegetable soups range from the thick bean soup to a smooth Vichyssoise. I don't like smooth hot soups; they seem too much like sauce. The only smooth soups I like are those that are served icy cold. On the whole I think almost all soups need some texture. This can be achieved by serving the soup as it stands, without sieving or blending, or by simply*

mashing some of the contents with a fork. A compromise is to push it through a coarse food mill, or to process half the contents of the soup before mixing it with the other, unsieved half.

✳ *All vegetable soups are made in roughly the same way. The chopped or sliced vegetables are first softened in butter or oil, then simmered in light stock or water until tender. The finished soup may be served as it stands, or puréed to the consistency you desire. It is then reheated and often enriched with cream, butter or oil may be added at this stage. A*

31

Canouras

Batatas

Cebolas

Nabos

Alho Porró

Caixa para o sal

garnish of chopped herbs is added at the very end, since herbs lose their color and freshness if allowed to cook with the soup.

✳Except in the case of certain soups from the Mediterranean countries, the preliminary softening is best done in butter. With certain French, Italian and Spanish soups, however, an authentic flavor is attained by using olive oil. With soups like minestrone, a little fresh olive oil is added at the table.

✳Never use flour as a thickener, except for Crème Sénégale, a cold cream of chicken. A thicker consistency is usually reached by adding potato or other soft vegetables, or simply reducing the liquid content.

✳Use light stock instead of water for the main body of the soup. Stock cubes are perfectly adequate for most soups, since so many flavors are added. Consommés must be made with genuine stock, however, and a few other soups are not worth making except with a really good home-made chicken stock.

MASTER RECIPE

MINESTRONE

Serves 6–8

¼ lb. dried cannellini beans
1 large onion, sliced
2 leeks, white parts only, sliced
4 tbsp. olive oil
2 stalks celery, sliced
2 carrots, sliced
¼ cup fennel, sliced
small zucchini (unpeeled), sliced ½ inch thick
⅓ lb. chard or cabbage, shredded
¼ lb. string beans, cut in 1 inch lengths
½ lb. tomatoes, skinned and chopped
7½ cups chicken stock
salt and black pepper
1 cup elbow macaroni, plain or wholewheat
Garnish:
4 tbsp. chopped parsley
2 tbsp. virgin olive oil
grated Parmesan

Soak the dried beans for 3–4 hours, drain, and throw away the water. Cover with fresh cold water, bring slowly to the boil, and simmer until they are soft; this may take 25–45 minutes, depending on the age of the beans. When they are cooked, turn off the heat and leave them standing in their cooking water.

Cook the onion and leeks in the oil in a casserole for about 8 minutes, without allowing them to change color. Then add the celery, carrots, and fennel, and cook a further 8 minutes. Add the zucchini and the chard, or cabbage, and finally add string beans and tomatoes. Cook for 5 minutes, then add the hot chicken stock, bring to the boil, add salt and black pepper. Simmer, half covered, for 50 minutes.

Add the drained beans and the macaroni, bring back to the boil, and cook for 15 minutes, or until the macaroni is cooked. Turn off the heat and let stand, covered, for 5–10 minutes before serving.

To serve: pour into a tureen, stir in the parsley, pour in 2 tbsp. fresh olive oil, preferably a "green" oil from the first pressing, and have a bowl of grated Parmesan on the table.

Variation: in Tuscany, in the autumn, they make a delicious soup called *ribollita* with yesterday's reheated minestrone. The soup is poured over a mound of freshly cooked cabbage piled on a slice of home-made bread in each soup plate. They use a purplish cabbage called *cavolo nero*. The nearest thing is chard. When making *ribollita*, omit the chard or cabbage, and the macaroni, from the minestrone and make the minestrone a day in advance. Next day, boil some chard or cabbage, drain, and chop coarsely, then pile on slices of bread in individual soup plates. Heat the soup (without its garnish), pour over the vegetable, and serve a small jug of fresh olive oil separately.

Jancis Robinson's Wine Choice:
Soups are notoriously difficult foils for wine. A good minestrone is a food and drink in itself and hardly needs a wine accompaniment, although some may find their hand stretching out for a light Italian red such as a youthful Chianti, Bardolino or even the much-scorned Valpolicella. The toothsome tradition of serving dry sherry or madeira with soups, especially clear ones, deserves to be revived. Fino and Sercial are, respectively, the descriptions to look for in these dry appetizing fortified wines.

Chopping an onion

Halve onion through its root. Lay cut side on board and slice.

Slice again, at right angles to first cuts. Onion is now chopped.

To chop finely, hold knife as shown and swivel the blade.

Crushing garlic

Lay unpeeled clove on board; crush with blow to flat of knife.

Remove skin, which slides off easily, and chop garlic.

Sprinkle with salt, to draw out juices, and crush with knife.

FAMILY OF RECIPES

BORSCHT

Serves 8

1 large onion
2 large beets, uncooked
2 large carrots
2 stalks celery
3 tbsp. beef dripping (or duck, goose or chicken fat, or butter)
2 cloves garlic (optional)
4 large tomatoes, skinned
7½ cups homemade duck, beef, game, or chicken stock
salt and pepper
parsley
1 bay leaf } *tied in a piece of cheesecloth*
2 cloves
1–2 tbsp. lemon juice (optional)
¾ cup sour cream

Cut the onion, beets, carrots and celery into strips like thick matchsticks. Heat the fat in a casserole and stew them for 10 minutes over low heat, stirring now and again. Crush the garlic (if used), chop the tomatoes and add them to the casserole. Continue to cook for another 5 minutes. Pour on the heated stock, adding salt, pepper and the herbs and spices tied in a piece of cheesecloth. Cover and cook gently for 1½ hours. When the time is up, remove the cheesecloth bag, and taste for seasoning. Add lemon juice if bland (this depends on the acidity of the tomatoes), and more salt and pepper if needed.
Serve in a large tureen, if you have one, or in soup bowls, with the sour cream in a separate bowl.

SIMPLE BORSCHT

This is worth making only if you have a pressure cooker.

Serves 6

1¼ lb. raw beets
2 cups homemade chicken stock
1 can (11½ fl. oz.) V8 juice
juice of 1 lemon
½ Spanish onion, thinly sliced
¾ cup sour cream

Start a day in advance. Chop the scrubbed beets in a food processor and put in the pressure cooker with 2 cups cold water. Cook under pressure for 30 minutes.

Borscht with bread and sour cream

Strain, and cool, discarding the beets. Mix with the chicken stock, V8, and lemon juice. Pour into a bowl, add the raw onion, and leave overnight in the refrigerator.
To serve: next day, strain again and serve chilled, in cups, or reheated. Garnish with sour cream, either in a blob or swirled in, or serve it separately in a small bowl.

SOUP OF MIXED ROOT VEGETABLES

Serves 6–8

½ lb. carrots
½ lb. turnips or swedes
½ lb. parsnips or kohlrabi or celeriac
4 tbsp. beef dripping or butter, or goose or duck or chicken fat
6 cups beef stock
salt and black pepper
3 tbsp. chopped parsley

Cut the vegetables in quarters, then in small thick slices. Heat the fat in a sauté pan and sauté the vegetables gently for 5 minutes to soften without letting them brown. While they are cooking, heat the stock in a deep pan. When it is almost boiling, transfer the vegetables from the sauté pan to the stock, using a slotted spoon to strain off all the fat. Simmer for 10 minutes, until the vegetables are tender without being mushy. Push through the coarse mesh of a food mill, or purée very briefly in the food processor – it should not be too smooth. Reheat in a clean pan, adding salt and pepper. Stir in the chopped parsley, and serve.

LEEK AND POTATO SOUP

Serves 6

6 leeks, white parts only, chopped
4 tbsp. butter
1 large potato, peeled and sliced
5 cups chicken stock (homemade)
3 stalks parsley
1 stalk celery
salt and black pepper
⅔ cup double cream

Cook the leeks gently in the butter for 5 minutes, then add the potato. Stir to mix and coat with the butter, then pour in the heated stock, adding the parsley tied inside the celery stalk. Bring to the boil, add salt and pepper to taste, and simmer for 25–30 minutes until the potato is soft. Discard the parsley and celery, and cool slightly.

Purée briefly in a food processor, stopping before it is smooth, or push through a coarse food mill. If using a food processor, add the cream while processing; if using the food mill, add the cream later, while reheating. Reheat in a clean pan, adding more salt and pepper as required.

One of the best vegetable soups, this can be made into a chilled vichyssoise with very little extra trouble.
Variation: to make Vichyssoise, you need really good, homemade chicken stock, plus ⅔ cup heavy cream, and 2–3 chopped chives.

Start a day in advance, if possible, or several hours beforehand at least. Make the soup as above, adding the extra cream while blending. (Ideally it should be puréed in a blender, which gives an even smoother texture than a food processor, but this is not essential. Without either, however, it just isn't possible to make a good vichyssoise – at least without lengthy sieving.) Chill overnight.

Serve in cups which have been chilled for an hour or two. Sprinkle with chives before serving (chives should be snipped with scissors, rather than chopped with a knife).

MIXED VEGETABLE BROTH

This nourishing soup can be made in just half an hour, using a pressure cooker.

Serves 6

2 large leeks, coarsely chopped
2 large carrots, coarsely chopped
2 potatoes, coarsely chopped
⅛ green cabbage, coarsely chopped
4 tbsp. butter
¼ cup green lentils
5 cups beef, game or chicken stock or
* vegetable stock*
salt and black pepper

Melt the butter in a pressure cooker and add the leek, carrots, potatoes and cabbage. Stew them gently for 6–8 minutes, then heat the stock and add, with the lentils. Bring to the boil, adding salt and pepper, cover, and cook for 20 minutes under pressure. (Or cook for 1 hour in a covered saucepan.) When the time is up, reduce the pressure, uncover, and cool for 10 minutes. Put half the soup in a food processor and reduce to a purée, mix with the unsieved soup, reheat, and adjust seasoning. Pour into a tureen to serve.

THICK BEAN SOUP

Serves 6

½ lb. cannellini beans
2 leeks, chopped
2 carrots, chopped
2 stalks celery, chopped
½ lb. tomatoes, skinned and chopped
⅓ cup olive oil
salt and black pepper
⅓ cup chopped parsley

Soak the beans for 3–4 hours, then drain. Put them in a pan and cover generously with fresh, cold, unsalted water, and bring slowly to the boil. Cook gently until they are tender, adding a little salt towards the end of the cooking (salt tends to toughen dried vegetables). This will probably take 25–45 minutes. When they are soft, drain them and reserve the cooking water.

Heat the oil in a casserole and cook the leeks for 3 minutes, then add the carrots, cook for another 3 minutes, then add celery and tomatoes at 3-minute intervals. When all are lightly colored and starting to soften, reheat 4 cups of the strained bean stock and pour on. Bring to the boil and cook gently for about 20 minutes, until the vegetables are soft. Add the drained beans and reheat, adding salt and black pepper.
To serve: pour into a tureen and stir in the chopped parsley.
Quick version: put the soaked beans in a pressure cooker with unsalted water to cover and cook for 15 minutes under pressure. While they are cooking, stew the chopped vegetables in olive oil in a frying pan, as described above. When the beans have finished cooking, reduce pressure and add the vegetables, salt and pepper, and cook for a further 10–12 minutes under pressure. Cool slightly, stir in the chopped parsley, and serve.

LENTIL SOUP

Serves 8

1 medium onion, chopped
1 carrot, chopped
1 leek, chopped
2 stalks celery, chopped
3 tbsp. olive oil
½ lb. brown lentils, washed and picked over
6 cups game, or duck stock or chicken stock
salt and black pepper

Heat the oil in a flameproof casserole, and cook the chopped onion for 3 minutes. Add the carrot, leek, and celery, and cook for another 5 minutes. Then add the drained lentils and stir around for a minute or two before adding the hot stock. Bring to the boil, adjust the heat, and simmer, half-covered, until the lentils are soft, 45–50 minutes. Thin the soup with a little extra stock if necessary, and season to taste with salt and pepper. When this is made with a good game stock, it is very delicious, and if there are any scraps of game left they can be chopped and added to the soup at the end, to just heat through.

GARNISHES FOR SOUP

Croûtons: fry cubes of dry bread in butter and oil till golden, drain and scatter over vegetable soups just before serving.
Bacon dice: fry strips of bacon until crisp, drain well and chop or crumble. Scatter over onion, leek, potato or lentil soup just before serving.
Parmesan: scatter freshly grated Parmesan over minestrone, ribollita or onion soup just before serving.
Noodle strips: when making fresh pasta, reserve any scraps, cut in strips and poach for 1–2 minutes in consommé.
Tiny dumplings: drop into consommé and poach for 5 minutes before serving.

Cleaning leeks

If leeks are to be kept whole, or sliced, slit leek in half from leaf end to center.

Stand leeks, cut side down, in water for 30 minutes and dirt will pass into water.

If leeks are to be chopped, make two cuts at right angles, from leaf end almost to the root.

Ruffle cut ends under cold running water to remove dirt particles. Cut across to chop.

CARROT AND TOMATO SOUP

Serves 6

¾ lb. carrots, thickly sliced
4 tbsp. butter
1½ tsp. ground coriander seeds
1 lb tomatoes, skinned and coarsely
    chopped
4 cups chicken stock
¾ cup heavy cream
salt and black pepper
2 tbsp. chopped coriander leaves or 3–4
    tbsp. chopped parsley

Cook the carrots gently in the butter for 2 minutes, adding the ground coriander and stirring often. Then add the tomatoes, stir to mix, and cook for another 5 minutes. Heat the stock and add to the pan, stirring. Bring to the boil, cover the pan, and simmer for 35 minutes, or until the carrots are soft. Purée briefly in a food processor, or push through a coarse food mill; it should not be too smooth. Return to the pan and reheat, adding the cream, salt and pepper to taste, and the coriander, stirring in well. (It looks like flat parsley, and has a curious taste that some people love and others hate. If you don't like, or can't get coriander, add chopped parsley instead.) Cover and let stand for 5 minutes before serving, to allow the taste of the herb to permeate the soup.

FRESH TOMATO SOUP WITH BASIL

Serves 6

2 lb. ripe tomatoes, skinned and quartered
4 cups homemade chicken stock, free from
    fat
sea salt and black pepper
1½ tsp. sugar
1–2 tbsp. lemon juice
4 tbsp. fresh basil, cut in strips (when
    available)

Heat the stock in a large saucepan to boiling point then drop in the tomatoes. Add salt, pepper, and sugar, bring back to the boil, and simmer gently for 5 minutes. Remove from the heat, push through a medium food mill – a food processor is no use here, since it will not remove the seeds – and return to the clean pan. Reheat, adding lemon juice to taste, and more salt and pepper if needed.

To serve: sprinkle the basil over the top before serving but do not let it cook. This is also good served ice-cold.

CREME SENEGALE

This delicious iced soup must be made with good chicken stock, prepared the day before, strained and chilled overnight in the refrigerator so that all the fat can be removed.

Serves 6

2 tbsp. butter
1½ tsp. light curry powder
2 tbsp. flour
4½–5 cups chicken stock
juice of ½ lemon
¾ cup light cream
salt and black pepper
2 raw chicken breasts, or the cooked white
    meat of 1 chicken

If using chicken breasts, allow 5 cups of chicken stock and steam them over the stock for 20 minutes. Leave to cool, and add water to make 4 cups. Heat the butter in a saucepan, shake in the curry powder and the flour, and cook for 1 minute, stirring. Then pour on the chicken stock, reheated if necessary, and stir until blended. Simmer for 4 minutes, stirring often, then add the lemon juice, cream, and salt and pepper to taste. Cool quickly by standing the pan in a sink of very cold water. Stir the soup frequently to prevent a skin forming. Chill for several hours, as it must be very cold.

To serve: chop the white meat into neat dice, discarding all skin, and divide it between 6 soup cups. Pour the soup over it, and keep chilled, until ready to serve.

Watercress Soup

CHICKEN NOODLE SOUP

This excellent soup can be made with the remains of a roast or poached chicken.

Serves 5–6

5 cups good chicken stock (homemade),
    strained and free from fat
¼ lb. cooked chicken, chopped (optional)
4 small carrots, thickly sliced
4 small leeks, thickly sliced
¼ lb. green beans, cut in 1 inch lengths
4 small zucchini, thickly sliced
4 small tomatoes, skinned and quartered
1 cup noodles
salt and black pepper
3 tbsp. chopped parsley, or chervil when
    available

Bring 4–5 cups very lightly salted water to the boil. Have the vegetables, sliced about ½ inch thick, in separate piles. When the water boils, drop in the carrots and cook for 10 minutes, then add the leeks and beans and cook a further 5 minutes. Add the zucchinis and tomatoes and cook for another 5 minutes.

Heat the stock in a deep pan, and when it is almost boiling transfer the vegetables into it, using a slotted spoon. Drop the noodles into the vegetable water and cook until tender; 5 minutes will probably be enough. Then strain, and add to the soup. Add salt and pepper to taste, and the chopped chicken, if you have any. (If not, you can increase the noodles to 1½ cups.) Remove from the heat, let stand, covered, for 5 minutes to heat through, then stir in the chopped parsley.

Serve in large bowls, with crusty bread and butter. When it includes some chicken meat, this soup makes a meal in itself. If small vegetables are unobtainable, you can buy larger ones and chop them coarsely, but it will not be as pretty.

WATERCRESS SOUP

Serves 6

2 large bunches watercress, trimmed
4 tbsp. butter
1 large potato, peeled and sliced
4 cups chicken stock
salt and black pepper
¾ cup cream, light or heavy

Chop the watercress, sauté gently in the butter for 4 minutes, stirring occasionally, then add the potato and cook another 2 minutes. Heat the stock and pour it on the vegetables, adding salt and pepper. Simmer gently for 25 minutes, or until the potato is soft. Cool for a few moments, then pour into a food processor and purée. Pour back into the clean pan and reheat, adding salt and black pepper as needed.

To serve: pour into a tureen or into individual soup plates, swirling in the cream at the last minute. (I use light cream, but heavy cream gives a richer soup, which you may prefer.)

MEDITERRANEAN FISH SOUP

Serves 6

2 lb. mixed white fish (grey mullet,
   monkfish, conger eel, lemon sole, cod,
   snapper, etc.), filleted, with their bones
1 onion, halved
1 carrot, halved
1 stalk celery, halved
1 bay leaf
salt and black pepper
2 tbsp. olive oil
1 leek, or 4 shallots, sliced
1 clove garlic, crushed or finely chopped
2 tomatoes, skinned and finely chopped
2 sprigs fennel
a 2 inch strip orange peel
$\frac{1}{8}$ tsp. saffron, in powder form
a pinch cayenne
2–3 drops Tabasco
a few slices French bread, dried in the oven
grated Parmesan

Put the fish bones in a pan with the onion, carrot, and celery; cover with 6 cups water, adding the bay leaf, salt and pepper. Bring to the boil slowly, skimming off the scum that forms on the surface, and boil gently, half covered, for 30 minutes. Strain the stock and throw away the bones and vegetables.

In a heavy pan, heat the oil and cook the sliced leek (or shallots) for 3 minutes, add the garlic, cook for 2 minutes, then add the tomatoes and cook for 2 minutes. Bury the fennel and orange peel among the vegetables. Cut the fish fillets in small pieces, about 1–1½ inches, keeping the coarser varieties (monkfish, conger eel, cod, haddock) separate from the softer ones (mullet, snapper, sole). Lay the coarser fish pieces on the vegetables, cover the pan, and steam gently for 3–4 minutes. Then pour in the fish stock and bring to the boil. Boil steadily, quite fast, for 10 minutes, then lower the heat, add the softer fish, and simmer another 5 minutes. Turn off the heat, and add the saffron, a pinch of cayenne, and a few drops Tabasco. Stand, covered, for 5 minutes before serving.

To serve: accompany with the French bread, and a bowl of grated Parmesan.

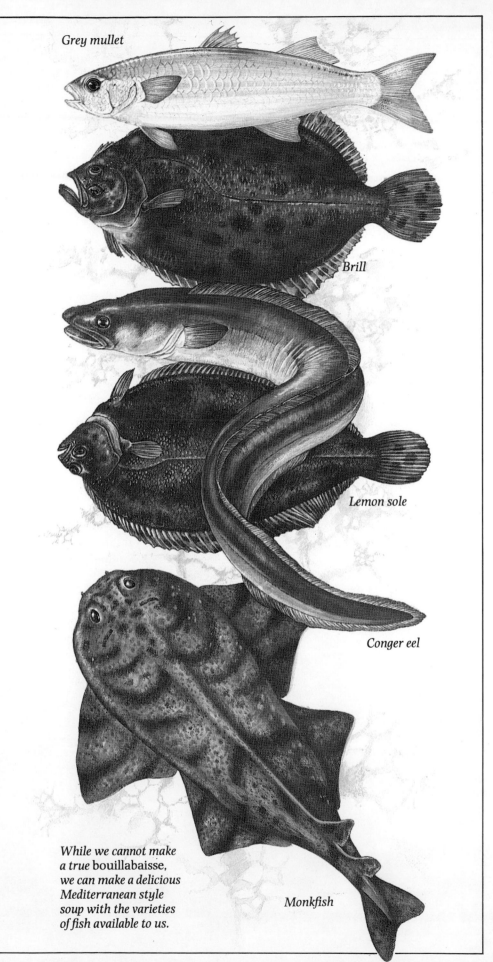

Grey mullet

Brill

Lemon sole

Conger eel

Monkfish

While we cannot make a true bouillabaisse, we can make a delicious Mediterranean style soup with the varieties of fish available to us.

MUSSEL SOUP

Serves 6

2 lb. mussels
4 shallots
2 tbsp. butter
1 tbsp. olive oil
2 leeks
2 stalks celery
a few shreds grated lemon peel
black pepper
⅔ cup dry white wine
⅛–¼ tsp. saffron
1 cup light cream, or ½ cup each heavy and
*   light cream*
1½ tbsp. parsley, finely chopped

Put the mussels in a sink full of cold water and leave for 10 minutes. Then go through them carefully, throwing away any with broken shells, or that are not tightly closed. Use a small strong knife to scrape off any barnacles, and to pull out any beard that protrudes from between the shells. Then brush each one hard with a stiff brush under cold running water. After several changes of water, leave them to soak in fresh cold water while you get on with the soup.

Peel the shallots and cut in quarters. Put them in a food processor and process finely, or chop them very finely by hand. Heat the butter and oil in a sauté pan and cook the chopped shallots gently. Cut the cleaned and trimmed leeks in thick slices then chop them and add to the shallots. Destring the celery with a potato peeler, cut in thick slices, chop, and add to the leeks after a minute or two. Cook all together

gently for 5 minutes with lemon peel. Add 2 cups hot water, a little pepper but no salt at this stage, and simmer, partly covered, for 25 minutes. (This dish can be made in advance to this point.)

Shortly before serving, put the mussels in a deep pot with the wine and an equal amount of water. Bring to the boil, lower the heat, and boil steadily, uncovered, for 3–4 minutes, until the mussels have opened. Any that refuse to open should be discarded. Lift them out with a slotted spoon, put in a warm bowl, cover with a cloth, and keep hot while you finish the soup. Add the saffron to the fish stock; if using saffron in strand form this must be left for 6–8 minutes to infuse, but powdered saffron needs only a moment to release its flavor. Strain the stock (to remove saffron stamens) into a clean pan and pour in the vegetable soup. Reheat, adding the cream. (I prefer this soup made with light cream, but some people prefer the richer version, using heavy and light cream.) Taste for seasoning; you may add salt at this stage, if it needs it, remembering that the mussels are slightly salty, and plenty of pepper. (Purists insist on white pepper for pale dishes, but I don't mind little specks of black pepper and find the flavor more than makes up for any lack of elegance.) If the mussels need reheating, they can be put back into the soup for a minute or two at this stage, without allowing it to boil, but they will not look as good, since their shells will lose their pristine quality if they are submerged in the hashed vegetables. If you do this, keep back a few to lay over the top.

To serve: pour the soup into a tureen, add the mussels and sprinkle with the parsley. If you prefer, the mussels can be served on the half-shell (simply remove the empty half shell from each mussel), or taken completely out of their shells. This makes a more elegant dish for a party, since you needn't use your fingers to eat it. In this case, it may be served in individual cups (or plates), with the mussels divided between them and the soup poured over.

AMERICAN FISH CHOWDER

Serves 6

2 tbsp. butter
¼ lb. unsmoked bacon, or salt pork, cut in
*   strips*
1 large onion, chopped
2 stalks celery, chopped
4 cups hot water, or fish stock (see recipe)
2 large potatoes, chopped
1½ lb. haddock or cod fillet, skinned
1 tbsp. seasoned flour
2 cups milk
salt and black pepper
2 tbsp. chopped parsley
2 Matzos, broken into pieces, or chowder
*   crackers*

If you have the time, ask the fish market for some extra fish bones, or a cod's head, and make fish stock with these, together with the fish skin and some flavoring vegetables, to use instead of hot water for added flavor.

Heat the butter in a flameproof casserole and fry the bacon strips gently, allowing about 15 minutes for them to become crisp and yield all their fat. Then add the onion and fry with the bacon until it softens, about 8 minutes. Add the celery and cook another 2–3 minutes, then add the hot water (or stock), and the potatoes. Cover and simmer for 20 minutes, until the potatoes are almost cooked. While they are cooking, cut the fish into pieces about 1–1½ inches square, and dust with seasoned flour. Add them to the pan and cook for 5 minutes. Scald the milk (bring to boil in a separate pan) and add it to the chowder. Season with salt and pepper.

To serve: if you have a suitable pot (a black cast iron one is ideal), this looks good served straight from the pot; otherwise pour it into a tureen. Sprinkle with chopped parsley and scatter broken Matzos or chowder crackers over the top. Eat in soup plates. This makes a meal, followed by a vegetable dish or a salad and cheese.

BEEF CONSOMME WITH GINGER GARNISH

This is a lengthy soup to make, but it is very delicious for a special occasion, like the start of a Christmas dinner, when there is a lot of rich food to follow. Start a day in advance.

Serves about 10

First day:
beef bones
1 calf's foot
1 piece knuckle of veal
2 tbsp. lard
2½ lb. shin of beef, roughly chopped
1 Spanish onion, unskinned, roughly chopped, plus some extra onion skins
3 leeks, roughly chopped
3 carrots, roughly chopped
3 stalks celery, roughly chopped
¼ raw chicken, or 1½ lb. wing tips, or legs
2 bay leaves
4 stalks parsley
1 tbsp. salt
10 black peppercorns
1 cup dry white wine
Second day:
½ lb. ground beef
2 egg whites with their shells
¼ cup dry sherry
2 small carrots
4 scallions
a piece of fresh ginger, peeled

Melt the lard in a casserole or roasting pan, put in the beef bones, calf's foot and veal knuckle and brown them for 15 minutes, either on top of the stove, or in the oven preheated to 400°F, turning them over once or twice. When the time is up, transfer them to the stock pot, and put the ground beef, onion, leeks, carrots, and celery into the same fat. Brown in a similar fashion for 10–12 minutes, stirring occasionally, then add to the stock pot, too. Add the chicken, herbs, salt and peppercorns, and the wine, then pour in 3½–4 quarts cold water. Bring slowly to the boil, skimming the surface as it nears boiling point. When it boils, add a cup of cold water and bring back to the boil, skimming. Do this twice, then adjust the heat so that it boils gently. Half cover the pot, and cook for 3–4 hours, until reduced to about 2 quarts, skimming every now and then. (The constant skimming will ensure a clear consommé.) Strain, throw away the meat, bones, and vegetables, leave the stock to cool, then chill overnight.

Next day, remove the fat from the surface (keep it to fry potatoes or make vegetable soups) and pour the stock back into the clean stock pot. Add the ground beef, and the egg whites beaten to a froth (but not stiff), together with their crumbled egg shells. Bring to boiling point, beating constantly with a wire whisk, then stop whisking and allow the stock to boil up until it reaches the top of the pan. Remove from the heat and allow it to settle for a moment or two, then replace over the heat and leave to boil gently for 20–30 minutes.

Have a strainer lined with a piece of muslin standing over a deep bowl. When the time is up, boil up the stock and pour, boiling, through the muslin. Leave it to trickle through; if you squeeze the cloth you may force through some of the solids. The egg whites form a crust which absorbs the impurities, and the strained consommé should be crystal clear. If not, put it back in the pot with the egg whites and boil up once more, and strain a second time.

Prepare the garnish: cut the carrots and scallions into the thinnest possible strips, about 1 inch long. Chop the ginger finely, and measure 2 tbsp. Put the carrot and scallion slivers into some of the simmering consommé in a small pan; poach for 1 minute, then drain. Repeat with the chopped ginger, allowing 30 seconds. Remove from the heat and add the carrot and onion. Just before serving, reheat the consommé, adding the sherry. Heat the garnishes separately.

To serve: add the contents of the small pan to the stock pot, and serve in small cups, with a little of the garnish. The reason for keeping the garnish separate is so that it does not overcook and lose its crispness while the soup is being reheated.

Variations: to make Consommé en Gelée, make beef consommé as above, but start 2 days in advance and omit the garnish. After clarifying the stock, leave to cool, then chill overnight in the refrigerator. To serve: chop the jelly roughly with the edge of a thin spatula, pile into small cups and serve with lemon quarters.

For a Simple Consommé, make 1½ quarts good stock using 2 duck or pheasant carcasses, or 1 of either plus 1½ lb. raw chicken pieces, and flavoring vegetables. Make a day in advance and chill overnight. Next day, remove all surplus fat. Heat, adding sea salt, black pepper and a little lemon juice to taste. Garnish with scallions and ginger, as above; or with thin matchstick strips of carrot, turnip and leek, poached in the consommé for exactly 1 minute; or take 2 tbsp. finely chopped ginger and 12 small sprigs watercress. Poach the ginger in the consommé for 30 seconds, then turn off heat and add the watercress.

—MENUS—

Some suggestions for well balanced meals based on the soup recipes

MINESTRONE

STEAMED MEATBALLS
with vegetables and dipping sauce

SLICED PEACHES
with orange and lime juice

MEDITERRANEAN FISH SOUP
with Saffron Bread

COLD BEEF VINAIGRETTE
green salad

CHEESES

CREME SENEGALE

BOILED FRESH BEEF
with Salsa Verde
boiled potatoes, carrots and leeks

APPLE CRUMBLE
with cream

Vegetarian Menu
MIXED VEGETABLE BROTH
with Cabbage Piroshkis

EGG CROQUETTES
with Tomato and Pepper Sauce

GRILLED GRAPEFRUIT

CASSEROLES

A casserole is a relatively simple, inexpensive and adaptable dish, ideally suited to home cooking, which takes its name from the dish in which it is cooked. It uses the less expensive cuts of meat which, with tenderizing agents such as wine or vinegar, and long slow cooking, are transformed into dishes full of flavor.

Ideally they should be cooked in a low oven, where they are surrounded by an even heat, but they can be cooked on top of the stove. This may be more convenient: to save fuel perhaps, or if the oven is needed for something else, or if a big casserole is too heavy to lift in and out of the oven.

A preliminary browning helps to seal in flavor and improves color. The finished result should be meat that is soft and melting, never fibrous, the sauce a rich blend of vegetables, herbs and seasonings carefully balanced, no single flavor being allowed to dominate. A casserole is a wholesome meal for friends or family, needing little accompaniment other than potatoes (boiled, baked or mashed), rice, noodles, or just fresh bread, and a green salad. For a family meal it may be served out of the fish in which it is cooked. For a party it can be made more elegant by transferring it to a serving dish and garnishing with croûtons spread with mustard or rubbed with garlic.

TIPS ON MAKING CASSEROLES

✳The beef casserole (Master Recipe) can be made with cheaper cuts of meat by simply extending the cooking time. All things considered, I find it worth buying the best stewing beef, however, since the shorter cooking time prevents the vegetables overcooking and saves fuel. If using a cheaper cut, allow 4 hours cooking, but only remove the lid for the last hour.

✳Any fat or oil can be used for the preliminary browning. I use a mixture of olive oil and butter, since the oil has a higher boiling temperature and prevents the butter burning, while the butter gives a good flavor.

✳Garlic burns easily, so it should be added to onions only toward the end of their cooking.

✳The addition of flour to thicken the sauce can be done in a number of ways. Simplest is to coat the meat with seasoned flour just before frying: this encourages browning, and the meat only takes up as much as is needed. Beginners may find it helpful to measure the amount of flour, to avoid waste. Only coat the meat just before frying or the flour will be moistened by the meat juices and become soggy. For the same reason it is best to sprinkle the flour on the meat with a flour sifter, rather than dipping the meat in flour.

✳If using an earthenware or porcelain casserole, the preliminary browning must be done in a frying pan, then the food transferred to the casserole to be cooked in the oven. In this case be careful to swill out the hot frying pan with the heated stock and wine, scraping up the residue of flour and meat juices in the bottom of the frying pan, and allow it all to bubble together for 2 or 3 minutes.

✳The proportions of wine to stock are not important: simply adjust according to what you have available. If you don't want to open a bottle of wine, use half as much dry vermouth, or a quarter as much red or white wine vinegar instead. Or keep a boxed wine on tap in the kitchen for cooking with. Stock for casseroles may be made with a stock cube, but use them sparingly, roughly half as strong as the manufacturer's recommendations.

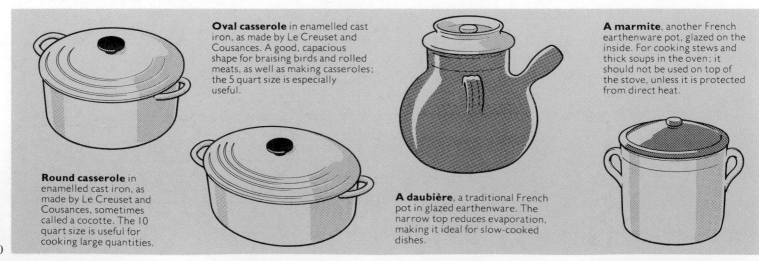

Oval casserole in enamelled cast iron, as made by Le Creuset and Cousances. A good, capacious shape for braising birds and rolled meats, as well as making casseroles; the 5 quart size is especially useful.

Round casserole in enamelled cast iron, as made by Le Creuset and Cousances, sometimes called a cocotte. The 10 quart size is useful for cooking large quantities.

A daubière, a traditional French pot in glazed earthenware. The narrow top reduces evaporation, making it ideal for slow-cooked dishes.

A marmite, another French earthenware pot, glazed on the inside. For cooking stews and thick soups in the oven; it should not be used on top of the stove, unless it is protected from direct heat.

"Le Benedicite," by Jean-Baptiste Chardin, 1699–1779. Musée du Louvre, Paris.

MASTER RECIPE

BEEF CASSEROLE

Serves 6

2½ lb. chuck steak
1 large onion
2 large carrots
1 turnip
1 parsnip
3 stalks celery
2 tbsp. butter
3 tbsp. olive oil
2 cloves garlic, crushed
1½ tbsp. flour
salt and black pepper
2 cups beef stock
¾ cup red wine
1 tbsp. tomato purée
1 orange
1 bay leaf
3 drops Tabasco
2 tbsp. chopped parsley

Preheat the oven to 300°F. Trim the beef, cutting away all the membrane, and cut into neat rectangles about 1½ × 1 inch. Cut the onion in half, then cut across in semicircles. Cut the carrots, turnip, parsnip and celery into matchstick strips.

Heat the butter and 2 tablespoons of the olive oil in a heavy casserole, add the sliced onion, and cook for 2–3 minutes. Then add the other vegetables and cook all together for 5 minutes, adding the garlic halfway through. Lift the vegetables out with a slotted spoon and lay them in a dish, or on the upturned casserole lid, if it is large and steady enough. Mix the flour with a good pinch of salt and a few twists of the peppermill, and shake over the meat in a shallow dish, turning it so that it is lightly coated all over. Add the remaining tablespoon of olive oil to the pan, reheat until it is quite hot, and put in the meat. Fry until lightly browned all over, doing it in 2 or 3 batches so it is not crowded, as it should be in constant contact with the bottom of the pan. Once browned, lift meat out and add to the vegetables, until all is done. Then return meat and vegetables to the pan.

Heat the stock and wine together in a small pan, and pour into the casserole, stirring to mix thoroughly. When all is blended and starting to bubble, stir in the tomato purée, then add a 2 inch strip of orange peel, the juice of the orange, the bay leaf, Tabasco, and more salt and freshly ground pepper.

Cover the casserole and transfer to the oven. Cook for 1 hour, then remove the lid and cook for a second hour, basting 3 or 4 times with the sauce, and turning over the cubes of meat on top so they do not dry out too much. The vegetable strips, on the other hand, may be allowed to caramelize.

This somewhat unorthodox method produces a most excellent dish, since it causes a reduction of the sauce, and a delicious meaty glaze forms over the surface of the dish. If you are unable to baste it, however, it is better to keep it covered throughout. It may be cooked in advance for the first hour, either the day before, or in the morning. Later, bring back to the boiling point on top of the stove, then cook a further hour in the oven, as above.

To serve: this stew must be transferred to a clean dish for serving, since the reduction of the sauce makes the inside of the casserole unsightly. Lift out the meat with a slotted spoon and lay in a shallow earthenware dish. Spoon the vegetable strips over it, and pour the sauce over all. Sprinkle with parsley and serve with baked, boiled, or mashed potatoes, and a green salad.

Jancis Robinson's wine choice:
The comforting mixture of flavors offered by most casseroles provides the perfect foil to some of the best wine value in the world. Full-bodied Rioja, Chianti and Rhône reds have just the right sort of rustic appeal, and should have enough flavor to stand up to the richest of stews. Look out for Riojas in sloping-shouldered Burgundy bottles, Chianti from the big, soft and easy 1979 vintage and, for a special occasion, upgrade from a simple Côtes-du-Rhône to a lovely, spicy Châteauneuf-du-Pape, a casserole in a bottle if ever there was one.

FAMILY OF RECIPES

CARBONADE OF BEEF

This is an adaptation of a Flemish dish, useful because most of the work can be done in advance; the stew can then be simply reheated and thickened at the last moment. It can be made with beer, ale, or stout, according to taste. Brown ale is probably closest to Flemish beer, but I prefer to use a lighter beer.

Serves 6

2½ lb. stew beef
¾ pint beer, ale or stout
1 bay leaf
3 tbsp. butter
1 tbsp. olive oil
2 large onions, chopped
2 large cloves garlic, finely chopped
2 tbsp. tomato paste
2 tbsp. flour
salt and black pepper
Garnish:
3 large slices dry brown bread
3–4 tbsp. Dijon mustard
a few sprigs watercress

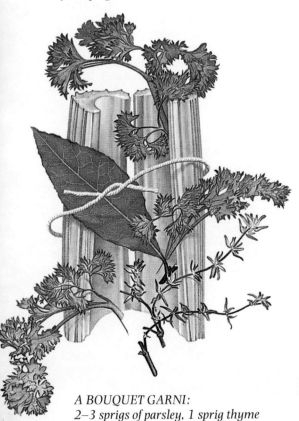

A BOUQUET GARNI:
2–3 sprigs of parsley, 1 sprig thyme
and a bay leaf, tied inside a stick
of celery to hold them all together.

Preheat the oven to 300°F. Cut the meat in neat pieces and put in a flameproof casserole, pouring the beer over it. Add the bay leaf, bring to the boil, cover and cook in the oven. For tender steak like chuck, allow 2 hours, for cheaper cuts like shin, allow 3½–4 hours.

If made in advance up to this point, reheat gently on top of the stove while you proceed.

Half an hour before serving, cut the bread in triangles, 4 to each slice, and dry out in a slow oven until crisp.

Heat the butter and oil in a deep frying pan and cook the onions slowly until light golden, adding the garlic halfway through. Stir in the tomato paste, then the flour, and cook for two minutes, stirring.

Transfer the casserole to the top of the stove, and gradually add the onion mixture, stirring until each addition is amalgamated. Simmer over low heat for 4 minutes, to cook the flour, stirring now and then. If it seems too thick, thin down with a little boiling water or stock, and add salt and pepper to taste.

To serve: tip into a serving dish. Spread the pieces of bread generously with Dijon mustard and lay on top of the stew, with a small bunch of watercress tucked into the center. Serve with boiled potatoes and a lettuce and watercress salad.

OXTAIL STEW

Serves 6

First day:
2 oxtail, cut in 2 inch sections
3 tbsp. flour
salt and black pepper
2 tbsp. olive oil
2 tbsp. butter
2 cloves garlic, finely chopped or crushed
2 tbsp. tomato paste
1 large onion, halved
1 large carrot, halved
1 stalk celery, halved
1 bay leaf
3 stalks parsley
3 cups beef stock
⅔ cup red wine
Second day:
1 leek
2 medium carrots ⎫
2 small turnips ⎬ cut in thick strips
2 stalks celery ⎪
1 parsnip   ⎭
3 tbsp. beef dripping, or fat from the stew
2 tbsp. chopped parsley

Start a day in advance. Preheat the oven to 300°F. Trim excess fat off the oxtail. Season flour with salt and pepper, and

shake over the oxtail pieces, turning them so they are lightly coated. Heat the oil and butter in a casserole and brown the oxtail on all sides, lifting pieces on to a dish as they are done.

Add the minced garlic and tomato paste to the casserole, replace the meat, and add the halved vegetables, bay leaf and parsley. Heat the stock and wine together and pour over the meat; bring to the boil, adding more salt and pepper. Cover the pan and cook for 4 hours in the oven. Take out and leave to cool overnight.

Next day preheat the oven to 350°F. Remove the fat from the surface, reserving it. Lift the meat into a shallow earthenware dish (I use a round Provençal *tian*), and discard the flavoring vegetables and herbs. (If you cannot start a day in advance, simply transfer the meat to its dish after the first stage of cooking, discarding the vegetables and herbs, and cool the sauce quickly by pouring it into a bowl standing in a sink half full of ice-cold water. After 30 minutes you should be able to remove most of the fat before proceeding with the next stage.)

Keep the meat warm while you cook the fresh vegetables. Take 3 tbsp. of the fat from the stew, or a good beef dripping, and heat it in a sauté pan. Put in all the second batch of vegetables which, except for the sliced leeks, you have cut in strips like thick matchsticks (this is best done using the julienne black of a food processor). Sauté them all together gently in the fat for 8 minutes, then add 1 cup of the oxtail stock, bring to the boil, and simmer another 15 minutes.

When the time is up, scatter the vegetable sticks over the surface of the oxtail, pouring over their stock and the remainder of the oxtail stock. Bake in the oven for 1 hour, basting from time to time with juice from the edges of the dish, without disturbing the vegetables. These should acquire a crisp, browned exterior, because they will have slightly caramelized from the evaporation of the meat juices.

To serve: sprinkle with chopped parsley and accompany with a dish of potatoes boiled in their skins, or the hollow pasta, like giant macaroni, called penne, and a green salad.

Lamb Tagine

salt and pepper and shake over the veal. Push onions to one side of the pan, put in the veal, and brown lightly all over. Mix with the onions and scatter the chopped tomatoes over all.

Heat the stock and wine together and pour over, stirring to blend with the flour. Add the bay leaf, parsley and thyme, all tied inside the folded celery stalk. Cover the pan and simmer gently, either on top of the stove or in an oven preheated to 300°F, for 1½–2 hours, turning the pieces of veal over and basting them once or twice. Be careful to keep them upright so the marrow does not fall out. When ready, the meat should be very soft and melting.

Just before serving, make the Gremolada: chop the peeled garlic, lemon rind and parsley very finely together.

To serve: lift the veal into a serving dish and spoon sauce over, discarding the celery and herbs and scatter the *gremolada* over all. Serve with a risotto Milanese, or plain rice, or a Potato Purée, and a green salad.

LAMB TAGINE

Serves 5–6

2½ lb. boned shoulder of lamb
2 tbsp. flour
salt and black pepper
4 tbsp. olive oil
2 medium onions, sliced
2 green peppers, de-seeded and cut in strips
1 head fennel, sliced
¼ tsp. ground ginger
2 cups chicken stock
¼ tsp. saffron (powder, not stamens)
1 strip orange peel, about 2 × ½ inch
¼ lb. dried apricots, chopped
2 tbsp. lemon juice

Cut the meat in neat cubes, discarding all fat. Season the flour with salt and pepper, and shake over the meat, turning so that it is evenly coated. Heat the oil in a casserole, add the meat and fry gently, turning over, until lightly browned. Take it out, put it aside, and put the sliced vegetables into the casserole, cooking them gently for 5 minutes, stirring often. Then replace the meat and add the heated stock, ginger, saffron, orange peel, and more salt and pepper. Bring to the boil, adjust the heat so it merely simmers, cover, and simmer for 1 hour or bake at 300°F. After an hour, add the apricots and cook for a further 15 minutes, then add lemon juice to taste.

Serve with brown rice, kasha or couscous, and a green salad.

OSSO BUCO

Serves 6

6 slices knuckle of veal, about 2 inches thick
⅓ cup olive oil
2 medium onions, chopped
2 tbsp. flour
salt and black pepper
1½ lb. tomatoes, skinned and roughly chopped
1 cup veal or chicken stock
⅔ cup dry white wine

1 bay leaf
3 stalks parsley
1 sprig thyme
1 stalk celery
Gremolada (to garnish):
1 large clove garlic, peeled
rind of 1 lemon
⅓ cup chopped parsley

Choose a casserole broad enough to hold the pieces of veal in one layer. Fry the onions until they start to color. Mix flour,

Chicken Niçoise

IRISH STEW

Serves 4–5

2½ lb. middle neck of lamb
2 lb. potatoes
1 lb. large onions, thinly sliced
salt and black pepper
2 tbsp. chopped parsley

Leave the meat on the bone, trimming off excess fat. Slice half the potatoes thinly, the second half thickly. Put the thinly sliced potatoes in the bottom of a heavy flame-proof casserole, layering them with the onions and the meat, sprinkling each layer with salt and pepper. Use the thicker potatoes in the upper part of the dish. Add 2 cups hot water and bring to the boil, then lower the heat and simmer, covered, 2–2½ hours.

Made this way, half the potatoes should dissolve and thicken the sauce, while the thicker ones should retain their shape.
To serve: sprinkle with parsley, and accompany with boiled carrots.

CHICKEN NICOISE

Serves 4–6

2 broilers, about 3 lb. each, cut in quarters
4 tbsp. olive oil
4 tbsp. butter
2 medium onions, chopped
2 cloves garlic
½ lb. tomatoes, peeled and chopped
salt and black pepper
1 tbsp. flour
¼ cup dry white wine
¼ cup chicken stock
6 oz. small mushrooms
Garnish:
2 slices dry bread, crusts removed
2 tbsp. chopped parsley

Trim the chicken pieces. Heat 2 tbsp. olive oil with 2 tbsp. butter in a casserole, or sauté pan with lid. Fry the chicken pieces in

NAVARIN OF LAMB

This is a delicate dish which can only be made in early summer, using tender vegetables carefully timed so that they are all cooked at the same moment. It is a good example of a casserole that is thickened by the beurre manié method.

Serves 6

2½ lb. boned leg of lamb
2 tbsp. butter
1 cup chicken stock
1 cup white wine
1½ cups V8 or tomato juice
½ lb. small new potatoes, peeled
½ lb. small carrots, scrubbed
½ lb. small turnips, peeled
½ lb. small zucchini, cut in chunks
½ lb. green beans, trimmed and cut in 2–3
  pieces or ¼ lb. shelled broad beans and ¼
  lb. shelled peas
salt and black pepper
⅓ cup chopped parsley
Beurre Manié:
3 tbsp. butter
4 tbsp. flour

Cut the lamb in neat square pieces. Melt the butter in a casserole and fry the meat, stirring, until lightly browned all over. Heat the stock, wine and vegetable juice in a saucepan and pour over the lamb. Stir until it reaches boiling point, then adjust the heat so that it simmers gently; cover,

and simmer for 1 hour. Then add the whole potatoes, carrots and turnips. Bring back to the boil and simmer for 30 minutes, and then add the zucchini and beans (or peas). Cook for another 20 minutes.

While it cooks, make the beurre manié. Mix the butter and flour to a paste, mashing against the sides of a small bowl with the back of a wooden spoon. When the cooking time is up, gradually drop this paste into the stew, stirring until amalgamated into the sauce. Simmer for another 3 minutes to cook the flour, add salt and pepper to taste, and stir in the parsley.
Serve with crusty bread, and a green salad.

Peeling tomatoes

1 Pour boiling water over tomatoes; leave for 1 minute.

Remove tomatoes and hold under cold running water to cool.

Skin will now slide off easily when pierced with a knife.

Cutting up a chicken

1 Pull the leg gently away from body, and cut through skin.

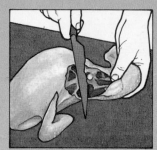

2 Locate the thigh joint, and cut right through.

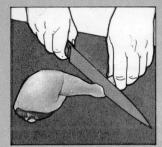

3 Remove third joint of leg, and keep for making stock.

4 Divide leg into two joints, the thighs and the drumstick.

5 Cut the breast away from the breastbone.

6 Remove the breast, together with the wing.

7 Divide in two, taking some of the breast with the wing.

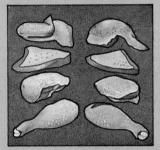

8 You now have 8 joints, plus carcass, neck etc. for stock.

it, turning them over until they are an even light golden brown. Remove them and cook the chopped onions in the remaining oil and butter. Stir them around often, adding 1 crushed clove of garlic after about 4 minutes. After another 2 minutes, add the tomatoes, stir well, and cook gently for another 4 minutes.

Heat the wine and stock together in a small pan; set aside. Shake the flour into the casserole and cook gently for 1 minute, stirring, then pour in the wine and stock. Stir until blended, adding salt and pepper. Replace the chicken, cover the pan, and cook for 50 minutes. (If more convenient, this may be cooked in the oven, preheated to 325°F.) Then take out the breasts and wings and keep warm in the serving dish. Continue to cook the dark meat for another 5 minutes.

Trim the mushrooms, using the whole caps. Fry them in 1 tbsp. butter, stopping as soon as they soften; keep warm. Cut the bread into 8 triangles. Heat the remaining oil and butter in a clean frying pan; when hot, put in the bread and fry until golden on each side. Drain on paper towels and rub each side with a cut clove of garlic.

To serve: when all the chicken is cooked, lay it in a serving dish and pour the sauce over it. Lay the mushrooms over the dish, and the croûtons all around the edge. Scatter chopped parsley over all, and serve with boiled rice or noodles, and a simple green salad.

A VERY SIMPLE CHICKEN CASSEROLE

Serves 4–5

3½ lb. roasting chicken, cut up
2 tbsp. flour
salt and black pepper
3 tbsp. butter
3 tbsp. olive oil
1 lb. onions, coarsely chopped
1 clove garlic, crushed
1 lb. tomatoes (peeled fresh tomatoes cut in eighths, or canned tomatoes with juice, roughly chopped)
¼ lb. small mushrooms, caps only
1–2 tablespoons chopped parsley

Trim the chicken pieces, cutting away excess fat and odd flaps of skin. Lay the pieces in a flat dish and lightly coat with seasoned flour. Heat 1½ tbsp. butter and 3 tbsp. olive oil in a casserole and cook the chicken pieces until they are golden, turning them over to brown evenly. Remove them from the casserole and put in the chopped onions. Cook gently for 4 minutes, then add the garlic and the roughly chopped tomatoes. Add salt and black pepper, replace the chicken pieces, cover the pan, and simmer gently for 1 hour. Just before the time is up, heat the remaining butter in a frying pan and sauté the mushroom caps for a few minutes, just until they soften slightly.

To serve: when the chicken is ready, lift the mushrooms out of their juices with a slotted spoon and lay over the chicken in its casserole (the juice would discolor the dish). Sprinkle chopped parsley over all, and serve with boiled rice or noodles, and a green salad.

Any remains will make an excellent sauce for spaghetti: simply cut any chicken off the bone and chop it, then reheat in the sauce.

Variation: this is a good simple dish, but it can be improved by squeezing the juice out of the fresh tomatoes before chopping, or discarding the canned tomato juice, and substituting ½ cup dry white wine, which will concentrate the flavor.

Removing tomato seeds

Cut in half horizontally and squeeze, extracting juice.

RABBITS, TAME AND WILD. On the left is a domestic rabbit, kept in captivity and fed on pellets. This is the rabbit usually eaten in France, Italy and Greece. It has a mild flavor, not unlike chicken. The wild rabbit (right) feeds on brambles, dandelions etc. and it has a slightly gamey flavor, closer to hare than chicken.

GREEK RABBIT STIFADO

Serves 6

6–8 pieces domestic rabbit (the best parts
  of 2 rabbits)
2 tbsp. flour
salt and black pepper
5 tbsp. butter
6 tbsp. olive oil
1½ lb. pearl onions, peeled
1 clove garlic, crushed
1 tbsp. tomato paste
1 cup dry white wine
1 cup chicken stock
3 sprigs thyme
Garnish:
2 slices dry bread, crusts removed
2 tbsp. chopped parsley

If planning to use the oven, preheat to 325°F. Then peel the onions as this is a fiddly business and takes some time; get someone to help you, if possible. Trim the rabbit pieces, removing any extraneous flaps of skin. Season flour with salt and black pepper, and shake over the rabbit pieces so they are lightly coated all over.

Heat 4 tbsp. butter with 5 tbsp. olive oil in a casserole. When it is hot, put in the rabbit pieces and brown them slowly, turning them over, until they are very pale golden, then remove them. Put the peeled onions into the casserole and cook gently, stirring often, until they are lightly colored,

too. Add the garlic and tomato purée, stir well to mix with the onions, and cook for 2 minutes. Heat the wine and stock together and pour over the onions; stir to blend, then replace the rabbit pieces. Add salt, pepper and thyme, bring back to the boil. Lower the heat, cover the pan, and cook for 1½ hours, either on top of the stove or in the

Greek Rabbit Stifado

oven. (If using wild rabbit, allow 2 hours.)

Just before the time is up, cut the bread into triangles. Heat the remaining butter and oil in a frying pan, and sauté the little pieces of bread until they are golden brown on both sides, then drain on paper towels.
To serve: transfer the rabbit to a serving dish. Lay the onions all around the edges of the dish, garnish with the bread croûtons, and scatter the chopped parsley over all. Serve with boiled potatoes or noodles, and a green salad.

RABBIT WITH MUSTARD AND HERBS

Serves 6

6–8 pieces domestic rabbit (the best parts
  of 2 rabbits)
¼ lb. shallots, chopped
4 tbsp. butter
2 cloves garlic, crushed
2 tbsp. flour
salt and black pepper
3 tbsp. Dijon mustard
2 cups chicken stock
3 sprigs thyme, or ½ tsp. dried thyme
3 sprigs marjoram, or ½ tsp. dried oregano
¼ cup heavy cream
4–5 tbsp. chopped dill, or 3 tbsp. chopped
  parsley

Trim the rabbit pieces, removing any extra flaps of skin. Cook the shallots in the butter in a flameproof casserole until they are pale golden, adding the crushed garlic towards the end. Season the flour with salt and pepper and shake all over the rabbit so it is lightly coated. Push the shallots to the side of the pan and brown the rabbit, turning, until pale golden all over. Add the mustard, then heat the stock and add it to the pan, with more salt and pepper, the thyme and the marjoram. Stir until all is blended smoothly, then cover the pan and cook gently for 1½ hours, stirring now and then. (If using wild rabbit, allow 2 hours.)
To serve: when the rabbit is tender, transfer it to a serving dish. Cool the sauce for a few moments, discarding the herbs, then purée it in a food processor. Return to a clean pan and reheat, adding the cream, more salt and pepper, and the chopped dill (if fresh dill is unavailable, sprinkle a little chopped parsley over the dish). Pour the sauce over the rabbit and serve with boiled potatoes and a green salad.

BUCKWHEAT CASSEROLE

Serves 4

1 cup roasted buckwheat
salt and black pepper
3 tbsp. butter
4 tbsp. sunflower oil
1 medium onion, sliced
2 medium leeks, sliced
2 medium carrots, sliced
3 medium zucchini, sliced
¼ lb. tomatoes, peeled and thickly sliced
1 egg, beaten
1 tbsp. flour
1 cup yogurt
3 tbsp. sesame seeds.

Bring 2 cups lightly salted water to the boil, shake in the buckwheat, and bring back to the boil. Boil hard for 1 minute, then lower the heat and cook as slowly as possible for 12 minutes, by which time all the water should have been absorbed. Do not stir. If there is still some moisture left, simply uncover the pan and cook for a minute or two longer. Put the cooked buckwheat in the bottom of a well-buttered casserole; it should half fill it.

Heat the butter and oil in a sauté pan and cook the onion and leeks until they soften and start to turn golden. While they are cooking, put the carrots in a small pan with very lightly salted water to cover; bring to the boil, and cook for 5 minutes. Then drain the carrots, reserving the water, and add them to the onion and leeks, with a couple of spoonfuls of their cooking water. Cover the pan, and cook gently for 5 minutes. Then add the zucchini, cover, and simmer for another 5 minutes. Finally, add the tomatoes, stir gently, adding salt and black pepper, and cook another 4–5 minutes. (All this can be prepared in advance, and left until the evening.)

When ready to cook, pour the vegetables and their juices over the buckwheat. Mix the flour into the beaten egg, beating until smooth with a small wire whisk or fork, then stir it into the yogurt and beat again. Add salt and pepper to taste, and pour it over the vegetables, smoothing with the back of a spoon.

Heat a dry frying pan and toast the sesame seeds for 2–3 minutes, watching them carefully to see they don't burn, and turning them with a spatula. When they are pale golden, scatter them over the yogurt sauce and cover with the lid, or a piece of foil. Cook in a preheated oven at 350°F, allowing 35 minutes if freshly made and still hot, or 50 minutes if you are reheating the casserole.
Serve with a green salad.

BEAN CASSEROLE

Serves 6

1 lb. dried cannellini beans
½ lb. bacon
1 onion, halved
1 carrot, halved
1 stalk celery, halved
2 cloves garlic, peeled
1 bay leaf
3 stalks parsley
salt and black pepper

Soak the bean overnight, or for several hours, in plenty of cold water. Preheat the oven to 300°F, drain the beans, and line a casserole (or earthenware *daubière*) with the bacon strips. Place the drained beans on top, lay the flavoring vegetables among them, and pour over 6 cups cold water. Don't add salt yet. Cover and cook in the oven for 5 hours, by which time most of the water will have been absorbed by the beans. Throw away the flavoring vegetables and herbs, and let stand for about 15 minutes before serving.
To serve: this goes well with sausages, or as a hot soupy dish on its own, with a salad to follow, and cheese.

The ingredients for Buckwheat Casserole

—MENUS—

Some suggestions for well balanced meals based on the casserole recipes

SMOKED TROUT
filleted, with cold Scrambled Egg

BEEF CASSEROLE
baked potatoes, green salad

SLICED PEACHES
in Raspberry Sauce

SLICED AVOCADOS
with olive oil, lemon juice and black pepper

GREEK RABBIT STIFADO
noodles, green salad

YOGURT AND HONEY

SALAMI
with black olives and radishes

OSSO BUCO
Saffron Rice, green salad

SLICED PINEAPPLE
with orange juice

Vegetarian Menu

SPINACH AND MOZZARELLA SALAD

BUCKWHEAT CASSEROLE
green salad

MELON WITH LIMES

BRAISING

raising is an unfashionable art, never very
popular in Britain, where people tend to
roast or grill the prime cuts of meat and stew the
cheaper ones. Braising is a delicious compromise
between the two, and produces comforting dishes of
meat and vegetables combined, cooked mostly in a
mixture of stock and wine. It is a technique that
completely transforms the raw ingredients: the
vegetables absorb the flavors of the meat, while the
sauce is a delicate blend of meat plus vegetables.

The main differences between braising and
casseroling are that only a small amount of liquid is
used in braising, and the meat or bird is usually left
whole. It is most successful used with intermediate
cuts of meat, and for cooking birds such as pheasant
and guinea fowl that tend to dryness, while older birds
can be marinated in the braising liquid first to make
them tender.

For elegant dishes, a good cut of meat such as leg of
veal or rump of beef may be used, and the finished dish
glazed with the reduced sauce and garnished with
freshly cooked vegetables incorporated into the glaze.
For more homely dishes, the meat is served simply
sliced, lying on a bed of the braising vegetables and
moistened with the sauce. Braising also produces a fine
range of cold dishes.

Braised vegetables are another of my favorite dishes,
at their best in the autumn when they can be made
with game stock. The use of game stock and good beef
dripping will transform fennel, celery, onions or
chicory into a memorable dish in its own right, or an
accompaniment to game. Small pearl onions can be
glazed after braising for the most exquisite
accompaniment of all to roast and grilled meat.

Oval casserole in
enamelled cast iron:
4 quart size is ideal for
braising a large bird or
rolled meat.

*"Dinner at Haddo
House," 1884, by
A. E. Emslie. By
courtesy of the
National Portrait
Gallery, London.*

TIPS ON BRAISING MEAT AND POULTRY
❋*A good casserole is essential: it must be
heavy, with a well-fitting lid, and the contents
should fit as snugly as possible. As birds and
rolled meat are roughly oval I usually
recommend an oval shape for braising. Since
only a small amount of liquid is used, it must
not be allowed to evaporate, so if the lid does
not fit tightly, put a layer of foil under it.*
❋*Braised dishes reheat well and often benefit*

from being prepared in advance, since this enables you to remove the fat easily and completely, making a lighter dish.

✳Whenever possible, include a calf's foot, split into four, or part of one. This adds immeasurably to the sauce, giving richness to a hot dish and a syrupy quality for glazing when the sauce is reduced. When served cold the sauce sets to a firm jelly without needing gelatine. It is worth asking your butcher to get a supply of calves' feet for you if he does not stock them normally, so you can freeze them and use them as required. As a substitute, if you can't get a calf's foot you can use a pig's trotter or a piece of knuckle of veal.

✳The vegetables used in braised dishes are usually a classic mixture of onion (or leek), carrot and celery.

✳Add some wine, even a drop, whenever possible. The liquid part of a braised dish should be even richer and more subtly flavored than a successful casserole.

✳Little accompaniment is needed since the dishes already incorporate meat, vegetables and sauce. A purée of potatoes, some noodles, or simply fresh crusty bread is good to mop up the sauce, while a green salad to follow cleanses the palate.

✳Any leftovers can be used to make a sauce for spaghetti, or a soup.

51

MASTER RECIPE

COLD BRAISED VEAL WITH A MAYONNAISE SAUCE

Serves 6

*3 lb. rolled shoulder, or leg, of veal (boned
shoulder is much less expensive than leg,
but harder to carve neatly. If you want to
make a really elegant dish, it may be
worth buying leg)*
1 calf's foot (see Tips on previous page)
3 tbsp. butter
1 large onion, sliced
1 large carrot, sliced
1 large leek, sliced
2 stalks celery, sliced
1 bay leaf
⅔ cup chicken stock
⅔ cup white wine
1 cup homemade Mayonnaise (see page 164)
Garnish:
*2 tbsp. chopped dill, chervil, or tarragon
plus a few extra sprigs*

Start a day in advance. Preheat oven to
300°F. Heat the butter in a flameproof
casserole and brown the meat lightly all
over. Remove it and add the vegetables.
Let them sauté gently for 5 minutes, then
replace the meat, adding the calf's foot and
bay leaf. Heat the stock and wine together
and add to the pan, with salt and pepper.
Bring to the boil, cover and cook for 2
hours, or 40 minutes per lb., in the oven.

When the time is up, remove the meat
and leave overnight in a cool place. Strain
the stock, leave to cool, and then refrigerate overnight. Keep the vegetables for
another dish or a soup. Throw away the
calf's foot and bay leaf.

Next day, make the mayonnaise sauce.
First make 1 cup of Mayonnaise. Then
remove the fat from the surface of the veal
stock, which will have set to a firm jelly.
Warm the stock slightly, by standing it in a
sink half full of hot water, until it has
become liquid, then beat it gradually into
the mayonnaise. Stand the mayonnaise
sauce over a bowl of ice cubes to cool
rapidly, while you carve the meat.

Cut the meat in neat slices and lay on a
broad shallow dish so that they do not
overlap too much. Spoon the sauce over
them; by now it should be just starting to
set. As you spread it over the meat, lift up
the overlapping slices of veal so that the
underneath ones also get a coating of
sauce. Then chill in the refrigerator for a
couple of hours, or even overnight, until it
is well set.

To serve: decorate with chopped herbs just
before serving, laying a few whole sprigs
around the edge. Serve with a salad of new
potatoes (dressed with olive oil and
vinegar, not more Mayonnaise) with lots of
chopped chives and parsley, and a green
salad. This makes a particularly good dish
for a hot summer evening.

Jancis Robinson's Wine Choice:
*The wines of Alsace might have been
designed specifically to be drunk with light
meat dishes such as braised veal. They are
dry, white but with much more body and
flavor than most. Named after the grapes
from which they are made, they have
something of the fragrance of fine German
wines too. Gewurztraminer would probably
be just too fragrant, but Riesling or Pinot
Gris (also known as Tokay d'Alsace), or
even a good Pinot Blanc, would provide a
nicely positive accompaniment.*

FAMILY OF RECIPES

VITELLO TONNATO

This classic dish is made in exactly the same
way as Cold Braised Veal (see Master
Recipe above), but with the following
sauce:

1 cup Mayonnaise
3¼ oz. can tuna fish, drained
1 tbsp. lemon juice
1 tbsp. capers, chopped
1 tbsp. green peppercorns, roughly crushed
2 tbsp. strained veal stock, free from all fat

Make the Mayonnaise. Pound the tuna fish
in a mortar until a smooth paste, then add
the Mayonnaise gradually, pounding until
amalgamated. Stir in the lemon juice,
capers and peppercorns (wrap them in the
corner of a dish towel and crush gently with
a rolling pin). Finally, stir in the veal juices.
This makes a thick sauce, but it will not set
like the other. Spoon it over the sliced veal
and chill for a couple of hours.

Cold Braised Veal with Mayonnaise Sauce, new potatoe

nd green salad; with baked apples with cream and redcurrant jelly to follow.

BRAISED SHOULDER OF VEAL

This makes an elegant dish for a dinner party. It involves quite a lot of work at the last moment, so don't cook anything else that needs your attention. It is best to time it so that it is cooked an hour before you want to serve it; this makes the meat easier to carve and the final assembling less hectic.

Serves 6

3 lb. rolled shoulder of veal
3 tbsp. butter
1 large onion, thinly sliced
1 large carrot, thinly sliced
3 stalks celery, thinly sliced
1 calf's foot (see Tips, page 51)
1 cup chicken stock
1 cup dry white wine
salt and black pepper
1 bay leaf
3 sprigs thyme
Garnish:
¼ lb. small carrots, sliced lengthwise ⅛ inch
  thick
¼ lb. celeriac or parsnip
2 tbsp. butter
1 tbsp. sugar

Preheat the oven to 325°F. Heat the butter in an oval flameproof casserole and brown the meat on all sides. Remove it, put in the vegetables and let them sauté gently for 5 minutes, stirring now and then. Make them into an even layer, lay the meat on them, and add as much of the calf's foot as will fit in the pot. Heat the stock and wine and pour over the meat, adding salt, pepper, and herbs. Bring to the boil, cover, and cook in the oven for 2 hours, or 40 minutes per lb. When it is cooked, remove the meat to a carving platter and cover loosely with a piece of foil. Discard the calf's foot and herbs, transfer the vegetables to a flameproof serving dish, and strain the stock into a bowl. It can now be left for up to 1 hour, making the meat easier to carve and allowing the fat to rise to the surface of the stock.

Thirty minutes before serving, turn the oven up to 400°F. Extract the fat-free stock from below the surface using a bulb baster, and put into a small pan.

Prepare the garnish: slice the carrots, leaving on a little of the green ends if you like. Cut the celeriac or parsnip into a square block 1½ inches across, then into slices ⅛ inch thick, then into triangles. Put the carrots and celeriac (or parsnip) into a pan and add enough of the strained stock to cover. Bring to the boil, and cook, covered, for 5–8 minutes, or until the vegetables are soft. In the meantime, boil the rest of the stock to reduce by about

half; this will give an excellent flavor.

When the vegetables are soft, drain off all but 3 tbsp. of the stock (add it to the rest of the stock), and put the butter and sugar in the pan. Cook over a low heat, shaking the pan from time to time, until the sauce has thickened and the vegetables are coated with a light glaze. Set aside.

To serve: carve the meat and lay over the braised vegetables; don't worry if the slices break up, it won't show under the garnish. Brush the surface of the meat with some of the reduced sauce, and lay the glazed vegetable garnish over the top. Put in the oven for 3–4 minutes, then brush with more reduced stock and repeat. Do this a third time, then serve, with the remaining sauce in a separate bowl. Accompany with noodles and a green salad. This can be kept hot successfully, or reheated.

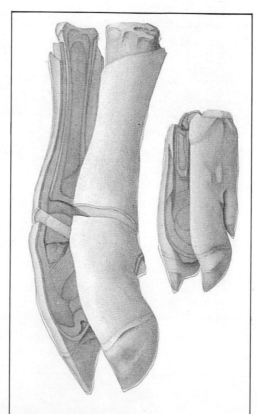

FOR A RICHER DISH
Left: a calf's foot, split in four.
Invaluable for braising, it enriches the sauce and ensures a firm jelly for cold dishes. If unavailable, use a split pig's trotter (right).

BRAISED GUINEA FOWL WITH FIGS AND ORANGES

Serves 6

2 guinea fowl
½ cup olive oil
1 large onion, thinly sliced
1 large carrot, thinly sliced
2 stalks celery, thinly sliced
¾ cup chicken stock
salt and black pepper
1 tsp. flour
1 tsp. butter, at room temperature
3 oranges
2 tbsp. butter, melted
1 tsp. granulated sugar
6 figs

Preheat the oven to 325°F. Heat the oil in an oval flameproof casserole and brown the birds in it, turning them over until they are a pale golden color. Then take them out and set them aside while you cook the vegetables in the same oil. Cook gently, stirring now and then, for 5 minutes, until translucent, then spread them over the bottom of the pan to make an even layer, and lay the birds on, too (on their sides, if possible, but if there isn't enough room, don't worry). Heat the stock and pour it over, adding salt and pepper. Cover and cook in the oven for 1¼ hours.

While the birds are cooking, make a beurre manié with the flour and butter (see Navarin of Lamb, page 46).

Shortly before the birds are finished, peel the oranges and cut them horizontally in 4 thick slices. Brush with melted butter, sprinkle lightly with sugar, and broil gently, allowing 2 minutes per side, until browned in places. Set aside and keep warm. Cut the figs in quarters without quite cutting them through completely, open out gently to form a star shape, and place them under the broiler for a couple of minutes, not too near the heat, so that they warm gently without cooking. Keep warm along with the oranges.

When the birds have finished cooking, lift them on to a carving platter and keep warm. Lift the braised vegetables out with a slotted spoon, and lay them on a shallow serving dish; keep warm. Strain the liquid into a pitcher and let stand for a minute or two to allow the fat to rise to the surface, then extract the fat-free stock from underneath. Reheat the stock in a small pan; as it approaches boiling point gradually add the beurre manié, beating with a wire whisk. When all is smooth, simmer gently for 2–3 minutes to cook the flour, then pour into a warm sauceboat.

To serve: carve the birds into neat pieces.

Lay them over the vegetables, and garnish with the figs and oranges. If you like, you can dribble a little of the sauce over them, serving the rest separately, or keep all the sauce apart. This dish is excellent served with an unusual, nutty-flavored grain, to blend with the fruit: cracked wheat, couscous, buckwheat, brown rice, or a mixture of brown and wild rice are all eminently suitable; wild rice alone would be best of all, were it not so expensive. In any event avoid potatoes, which do not complement fruit. A green salad is the only vegetable needed.

BRAISED SHOULDER OF LAMB

Serves 6

1 shoulder of lamb, boned and rolled (if
    possible, get your butcher to bone and roll
    the lamb, leaving the knuckle bone on; do
    not let him stuff it)
1 large onion, sliced
$\frac{3}{4}$ lb. carrots
$1\frac{1}{4}$ lb. leeks (trimmed down to the white
    parts only, about $\frac{3}{4}$ lb.)
$\frac{3}{4}$ lb. turnips
$\frac{1}{2}$ lb. celeriac, or 3 stalks celery
4 tbsp. butter
4 tbsp. olive oil
$\frac{1}{2}$ calf's foot (see Tips, page 51)
$\frac{1}{2}$ bottle dry white wine
1 cup veal or chicken stock
salt and black pepper
1 bay leaf

Preheat oven (if using oven) to 325°F. Find a casserole which fits the meat nicely. Slice carrots and leeks about $\frac{1}{4}$ inch thick; if they are very large, cut them in half lengthwise first to make semicircular slices. Cut the turnips and celeriac (or celery) into slices $\frac{1}{4}$ inch thick, then across into squares. Heat half the butter and half the olive oil in the casserole and cook the onion for 2–3 minutes, then add all the other vegetables and cook for 5 minutes, stirring often. Then lift them out with a slotted spoon.

Add the remaining oil, put the rolled shoulder in the pan and brown it gently on all sides. Lift out the meat for a moment when it has browned and replace the vegetables. Season well with salt and pepper, then lay the meat on top of them, with the halved calf's foot or knuckle.

Heat wine and stock together and pour over the meat, add the bay leaf, and bring to the boil. Cover the pan and cook gently, on top of the stove or in a preheated oven, for 2 hours.

To serve: take out the lamb and keep hot; discard the calf's foot and bay leaf, lift out the vegetables with a slotted spoon, strain the stock, and leave it to cool in a bowl

Braised Guinea Fowl with Figs and Oranges

while you carve the meat. Make a layer of the vegetables in a shallow dish, lay the slices of lamb on top, and keep warm while you make the sauce. Skim off as much fat as possible from the surface of the stock, then boil it in a small pan to reduce the quantity and concentrate the flavor. When reduced to about 1 cup taste and adjust seasoning, then drop in the rest of the butter in small bits and whisk until melted and glossy. Either pour the sauce over the meat or

serve it separately, with a Potato Purée, and a green vegetable, or a salad to follow.

A simpler and more economical version of this dish can be made by omitting the calf's foot and substituting water for the wine and stock. The sauce will be less rich but it will still be good. When making it this way, I enrich the sauce at the end of the cooking by adding a little beurre manié (see page 46), an egg yolk, a little cream, and some chopped parsley.

Rolling and tying boned breast of veal or lamb

1 Lay the meat skin side down and spread with stuffing.

2 Roll the meat around the stuffing and tie with separate pieces of string, using a slip knot.

3 When one half is tied, start again from the other end.

4 When first tying is complete, start to link the separate ties together with one long piece of string.

5 Turn the rolled meat right side up and continue.

6 Finished roll: remove string as you carve.

BRAISED BREAST OF LAMB

Serves 3–4

1 breast of lamb, boned
3 tbsp. butter
1 large onion, sliced
1 large carrot, sliced
1 large leek, sliced
2 stalks celery, sliced
1 bay leaf
½ cup chicken stock
½ cup white wine
Stuffing:
4 slices dry bread, crusts removed
½ cup milk
½ lb. spinach (fresh), or ¼ lb. frozen leaf
  spinach
salt and black pepper
¼ tsp. mace, or nutmeg
1 egg yolk

Preheat the oven to 300°F. To make the stuffing: soak the bread in the milk for 10 minutes, then squeeze dry. If using fresh spinach, drop into lightly salted boiling water and cook, 4–5 minutes. (If using frozen spinach, cook according to directions on the package.) Transfer to a colander and run cold water over it for a few seconds, to refresh it. Drain, and when cool enough to handle, squeeze out all the moisture using your hands. Lay on a board and chop, then mix with the bread in a bowl with your hands, adding salt and pepper, mace or nutmeg, and the egg yolk. Open out the breast of lamb and spread the stuffing over it. Roll up and tie with string.

Heat the butter in a flameproof casserole and cook the sliced vegetables gently for 5 minutes, stirring now and then. Remove them, put in the meat and brown lightly all over. Then surround the meat with the vegetables, adding the bay leaf. Heat the stock and wine together and pour over the meat. Bring to the boil, cover, and cook in the oven for 2 hours.

To serve: lift out the meat and carve in thick slices. Transfer the vegetables to a shallow serving dish, lay the sliced meat over them, and keep warm. Strain the stock into a bowl and stand for a few minutes. When the fat has risen to the surface, extract the fat-free stock from below and serve in a small pitcher, with the meat. Accompany with noodles and a green salad.

Variation: a more elegant version can be made by using 2 lb. boned breast of veal, and substituting a sliced head of fennel and a sliced green pepper for the leek and celery. Cook exactly as for the lamb; this will serve 6.

BRAISED BEEF

Serves 6

3 lb. chuck steak in one piece, or rump end
2 medium onions
2 large carrots
2 leeks
2 stalks celery
1 parsnip
2 cloves garlic
2 bay leaves
sea salt and black peppercorns
a few sprigs thyme
2½ cups red wine
1 calf's foot (see Tips, page 51)
3 tbsp. butter

Start a day in advance. Put the beef in a deep bowl. Slice 1 onion, 1 carrot, 1 leek, 1 stalk celery and 1 clove garlic, and scatter over the meat, with 1 bay leaf, a sprig of thyme, a pinch of salt and 6 peppercorns. Pour in the red wine and leave to marinate for 12–24 hours, basting occasionally.

Next day, preheat the oven to 325°F. Lift the beef out of its marinade, scraping off the vegetables, and pat it dry with paper towels. Strain the marinade and discard the vegetables and herbs. Slice the remaining onion, carrot, leek, celery, and parsnip. Choose a flameproof casserole that fits the meat nicely if possible, and heat the butter in it, putting in the vegetables. Stir them around in the fat and leave to cook gently for 5 minutes, adding the crushed garlic. Then place the meat on top of the bed of vegetables, adding as much of the calf's foot (if you can get one) as will fit in the pan, and pour over the strained marinade. Cover tightly and cook in the oven for 2½ hours.

To serve: transfer the meat to a carving platter, cover with foil, and keep warm. Transfer the vegetables to a shallow serving dish, using a slotted spoon. Keep warm. Strain the stock, discarding the calf's foot, and the herbs, and let stand for 2–3 minutes to allow the fat to rise to the surface. Extract as much fat-free stock as possible from below the surface, and boil up for a few minutes to reduce, and concentrate the flavor, in a small pan. Carve the meat in fairly thick slices and lay over the vegetables. Moisten with a little of the stock, and serve the rest separately. Accompany with noodles and a green salad, and Horse-radish Sauce.

BEEF OLIVES

Serves 6

6 thin slices top round steak
¼ lb. shredded suet
½ cup soft white breadcrumbs
2 strips bacon, chopped
¼ tsp. grated orange rind
1 tbsp. chopped parsley
½ tsp. chopped thyme, or ¼ tsp. dried thyme
salt and black pepper
1 egg, beaten
3 tbsp. butter
1 onion, thinly sliced
1 carrot, thinly sliced
1 leek, thinly sliced
1 stalk celery, thinly sliced
2 tsp. flour
1 cup beef or chicken stock

Preheat the oven to 325°F, if you are going to use it.

Lay the slices of beef on a sheet of plastic wrap, and cover with another sheet, then beat them out with a mallet, or a wooden rolling pin, or handle of a heavy knife, until very thin. Trim edges into a roughly rect-angular shape, chop the trimmings, and put into a bowl with the suet and bread-crumbs. Stir in the bacon, orange rind, parsley, thyme, salt and pepper. Mix with the beaten egg, then divide the stuffing between the slices of beef. Roll up each one and tie with string.

Melt the butter in a flameproof casserole and brown the sliced vegetables quickly, stirring constantly. When they have colored, remove them. Put in the beef olives and brown them on all sides. Remove them, sprinkle the flour into the casserole, and stir into the butter. Heat the stock, add it to the pan, and stir until blended, adding salt and pepper to taste. Put the vegetables back into the casserole, and lay the olives on top. Cover and cook gently for 1½ hours, on top of the stove, or in the oven.

To serve: cut the string and lay the olives on a bed of mashed potatoes. Spoon the vegetables over the top, moistening with the sauce; or, if you prefer, you could serve the sauce separately.

BRAISED RED CABBAGE

Serves 6–8

1 red cabbage, medium to large
6 tbsp. beef dripping, duck or chicken fat, or
*   butter*
1 Spanish onion, chopped
2 tbsp. sugar
1 large cooking apple, chopped (unpeeled)
¼ cup red wine (or cider) vinegar
salt and black pepper
1 cup vegetable stock, or beef stock
assorted smoked sausages: frankfurters,
*   knockwurst, chorizos, etc.*
1 tbsp. flour
⅓ cup sour cream

Preheat the oven to 300°F. Cut the cabbage in quarters, discarding outer leaves and central core, wash and drain. Then lay each quarter flat on a chopping board and cut across into thin strips with a large, sharp knife. Melt the fat in a casserole and cook the chopped onion until it starts to color. Add the sugar, stirring to mix, then the cabbage. Stir around for a few minutes, then add the apple, vinegar, salt and pep-per. Finally, heat the stock and add to the pan. Bring to the boil, cover and cook in the oven for 2 hours.

About 15 minutes before the cabbage is ready, bring a broad pan of unsalted water to the boil, lower the heat so that it is under boiling point, and drop in the sausages. Cover and keep below boiling point (or they will burst) for 5 minutes, then turn off the heat and leave, covered, until ready to serve.

Just before the cabbage has finished cooking, beat the flour and cream to a smooth paste, in a cup. Then transfer the casserole to a low heat on top of the stove and add the paste by degrees, stirring constantly. Cook gently for 3 minutes, to cook the flour.

To serve: transfer the cabbage into a serving dish and lay the hot sausages over it. Accompany with a Potato Purée and a good mustard.

This is even better reheated; allow 35 minutes at 350°F. It is also good with roast or grilled pork, hot ham, ordinary pork sausages, or game; or omit the sausages to make a vegetarian dish.

Note: the cabbage must not be left for any length of time in a metal pan, unless it is stainless steel, or lined with enamel, for the action of vinegar on metal will cause the cabbage to discolor.

CHOUCROUTE GARNIE

Serves 6–8

2½–3 lb. sauerkraut, fresh or canned
6 tbsp. butter
1 Spanish onion, chopped
4 strips bacon
10 juniper berries, or 1 small tsp. caraway
   seeds
2 tbsp. salt
10 black peppercorns
2 tsp. sugar
2 medium potatoes, peeled and coarsely
   grated
16 large frankfurters, or 6–8 pork chops, or
   a mixture of different sausages
1¼ cups sour cream, heavy cream, or yogurt
   (optional)

Lettuces tied up ready for braising

Sauerkraut (or choucroute) is an Alsatian dish, with strong links with German and French cooking. It is a pickled white cabbage, extremely nourishing and easily digested. It can be eaten raw, as a salad, or cooked, and is worth making in large quantities, since it is inexpensive, keeps well, and improves each time it is reheated. Some delicatessens sell their own sauerkraut straight from the barrel.

If you want a mild dish, or if it is the first time you have eaten it, place it in a colander and rinse under cold running water; this gets rid of the brine. But if you like a slightly sour flavor, drain it in a colander without rinsing, breaking it up with the fingers.

Preheat the oven to 300°F. Melt the butter in a casserole and cook the onion until it starts to turn golden, then add the bacon strips. When these have cooked, add the sauerkraut, stirring until well mixed. Pour in enough cold water to barely cover it, adding the juniper berries or caraway seeds, salt, peppercorns and sugar. Bring to the boil, cover, and cook in the oven for 2 hours.

During the last 30 minutes, cook the sausages or pork chops to go with it. Sausages like frankfurters only need reheating; drop them into a pan of hot water for 5–10 minutes, and leave covered until ready to serve. (Keep it well below boiling point, or they will burst.) Pork chops are best broiled, while unsmoked sausages may be broiled or fried, according to choice.

When the sauerkraut is ready, transfer it to the top of the stove, stir in the grated potato, and cook gently, stirring often to prevent it sticking, for 10 minutes. Then add the cream, or yogurt. (If you are serving this with a creamy Potato Purée you may prefer to omit it.)

To serve: transfer to a serving dish, lay the sausages or pork chops on top, and accompany with a Potato Purée, or boiled potatoes, and some good mustard. This makes a wonderful dish for cool evenings, redolent of a Paris brasserie. It can be safely kept for up to a week in the refrigerator, and improves on reheating.

Braised Fennel

BRAISED WHITE CABBAGE

Serves 6

1 large onion, chopped
3 tbsp. dripping, or butter
1 white cabbage, about 3 lb.
1 cup beef or game stock
1 cup white wine
salt and black pepper
15 juniper berries
<u>Creamier version</u>:
3 tsp. flour
½ cup sour cream
1 tsp. Dijon mustard
4 tbsp. lemon juice

Cook the onion in the fat in a heavy casserole until it starts to become translucent. Cut the cabbage in quarters, remove the core, then cut into thin strips. Add these to the pan and stir well to mix with the onion. Cover the pot and simmer gently for 15 minutes, stirring occasionally. Heat the stock and wine together and add to the pot with salt, pepper and juniper berries. Cook either on top of the stove or in a 300°F oven for 1½ hours.

You can stop here and serve as it is, if accompanying a creamy dish, for instance, or proceed as follows: mix the flour into the sour cream, beating until smooth, then add the mustard and lemon juice. Transfer the cabbage to a serving dish and keep warm, stir the cream into the stock, and stir constantly over a low heat until the sauce has thickened. Simmer gently for 3 minutes, then pour over the cabbage and mix well. Add salt and pepper if needed.

BRAISED LETTUCE

Serves 6

3 large heads of lettuce
4 tbsp. butter
1¼ cups homemade chicken stock
salt and black pepper

Tie the lettuce heads with thin string so that they cannot fall apart during the cooking. Melt the butter in a pot large enough to hold them in a single layer. Put in the heads and cook them gently in the butter for 6 minutes – they will shrink considerably. Transfer to a smaller pan. Heat the stock, and pour it over them. Add salt and pepper, cover pan, and simmer for 30–40 minutes.

To serve: untie the string, cut the heads in half, and lay them in a shallow dish. Pour the juices over them, and serve with roast chicken, duck, or veal.

BRAISED FENNEL

Serves 6

3 bulbs fennel
4 tbsp. butter
¾ cup stock: game, beef, or chicken
1 tbsp. lemon juice
salt and black pepper
2 tbsp. chopped parsley
<u>Beurre Manié:</u>
1 tsp. butter
1 tsp. flour

Trim the fennel, removing any discolored leaves, and cut them in half lengthways. Lay them in one layer in a skillet with a lid. Cut the butter into small pieces and dot over the fennel. Pour in the stock, adding lemon juice, salt and pepper. Bring to the boil, cover, and cook for 1–1½ hours, turning the fennel over from time to time, until it is soft when pierced with a skewer. When it is soft, transfer to a serving dish. Make the beurre manié by mixing the butter and flour to a paste in a saucer, then beat gradually into the sauce. Simmer for 3 minutes, and adjust the seasoning.

To serve: pour the sauce over the fennel and sprinkle chopped parsley over all. This makes an excellent accompaniment to game or rabbit.

GLAZED ONIONS

These are quite troublesome to prepare but worth the effort and go very well with braised meat or game.

Serves 6

2 lb. small onions
1 cup beef or game stock
3 tbsp. butter
2 tsp. white wine vinegar
1 tsp. sugar
salt and black pepper

Peel the onions and put them in a pan with the cold stock. Cover, bring to the boil, and simmer gently until they are soft; this will take 15–30 minutes depending on size. Then lift them carefully out of the stock and drain in a colander. Melt the butter in a sauté pan, add the vinegar, sugar, salt and pepper, and the onions. Cook slowly until they are brown on both sides, turning them over carefully to keep them from breaking.

—MENUS—

Some suggestions for well balanced meals based on the braising recipes

ARTICHOKES
served warm, with Salsa Verde

COLD BRAISED VEAL
with a Mayonnaise Sauce
new potatoes, green salad

BAKED APPLES IN TOFFEE SAUCE

FRESH TOMATO SOUP WITH BASIL

BRAISED GUINEA FOWL
with Figs and Oranges
Cracked Wheat Risotto

GREEN SALAD
with cream cheese or goat's cheese

SMOKED MACKEREL
with Horseradish Sauce

CHOUCROUTE GARNIE
Potato Purée

SLICED ORANGE SALAD

Vegetarian Menu
SPAGHETTI CARBONARA
(omitting bacon)

BRAISED RED CABBAGE
(omitting sausages)
glazed celeriac, fried potatoes

MIXED MELON SALAD

Glazed onions: an excellent accompaniment for braised dishes

ROASTING

Roasting is one of the few kitchen processes which has suffered, rather than gained, from modern technology. In the past, meat was roasted on a horizontal spit over an open fire. In the 19th century, as wood fires gave way to coal, the fireplace changed its shape and the spit became perpendicular so the meat hung in front of rather than over the fire. The invention of the clockwork jack ensured constant self-basting, since fat clings to a rotating joint instead of dripping off, and the introduction of a screen, which protected the meat and reflected the heat of the fire, probably brought the art of roasting to its height.

True roasting is like grilling, since the meat cooks by direct exposure to radiant heat rather than being enclosed in hot air as in the modern oven. Unless we use a rotisserie which is closer to the old method, we are really subjecting our meat to a combination of baking and steaming. But we can still produce good, well-cooked dishes if we choose our meat carefully and use our ovens to their best advantage.

Only good cuts are suitable for roasting, and on a fairly large scale. The only small meats worth roasting are those that are an entity in themselves such as a rack of lamb, or a bird. Since most meats for roasting are covered with fat, either its own natural casing or a layer added by the butcher, I rarely add fat of any sort (except for poultry and game), nor do I even baste it much, unless using a marinade. If cooked correctly, briefly and sharply, the meat develops a crust which protects the inner part from drying.

I suggest the learner cook should not feel obliged to make all the traditional accompaniments for roast meat, especially to start with. While roast potatoes, horseradish sauce, gravy and Yorkshire pudding are all good in their own right, they are demanding to prepare, and can even overshadow a good piece of meat. Try serving roast meat simply for a change, at least until you have familiarized yourself with the process, and with the carving. A medium rare roast beef can be indescribably delicious, served simply with its own juices, and a purée of mixed root vegetables, or with baked potatoes and a mixed salad.

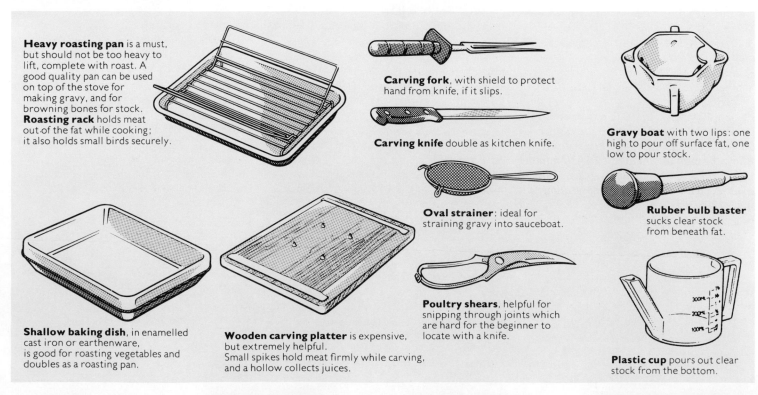

Heavy roasting pan is a must, but should not be too heavy to lift, complete with roast. A good quality pan can be used on top of the stove for making gravy, and for browning bones for stock.
Roasting rack holds meat out of the fat while cooking; it also holds small birds securely.

Carving fork, with shield to protect hand from knife, if it slips.

Carving knife double as kitchen knife.

Gravy boat with two lips: one high to pour off surface fat, one low to pour stock.

Oval strainer: ideal for straining gravy into sauceboat.

Rubber bulb baster sucks clear stock from beneath fat.

Shallow baking dish, in enamelled cast iron or earthenware, is good for roasting vegetables and doubles as a roasting pan.

Wooden carving platter is expensive, but extremely helpful.
Small spikes hold meat firmly while carving, and a hollow collects juices.

Poultry shears, helpful for snipping through joints which are hard for the beginner to locate with a knife.

Plastic cup pours out clear stock from the bottom.

"Many Happy Returns of the day," 1856, by W. P. Frith. By Courtesy of the Harrogate Art Gallery.

TIPS ON ROASTING

✳ *Always preheat the oven before putting in the meat.*

✳ *Use a roasting pan with a grid or rack if you have one; meat should not roast sitting in a puddle of fat.*

✳ *Never attempt to carve meat straight from the oven as the juices will have been drawn to the surface by the heat and will spit and drip. Allow the meat or bird to rest 15–30 minutes in a warm place, ideally uncovered, or loosely covered. (If it is airtight the condensation spoils the crisp surface.)*

✳ *If roasting meat to eat cold, it is immeasurably better if left to cool before carving. Cook the day before and leave overnight in a cool place; do not chill.*

✳ *Keep fat from roasting beef, ducks, chickens and, best of all, geese. Strain it into a bowl, leave to cool and chill overnight. The next day lift the block of fat out and scrape off the sediment and juices that cling to the bottom. These are pure meat juices, delicious for adding to baked eggs, braised vegetables, sauces, or simply eaten with a spoon or given*

to babies. They do not keep, however. The fat will keep for a few weeks in a fridge. Store different fats separately, labelled, and use them for frying and roasting potatoes, braising vegetables, and making vegetable soups. The fat from mutton, lamb or pork is less good because it has a strong flavor.

✳ *In my opinion, roast chicken is only worth making with a farm-bred bird which should have some intrinsic flavor. Factory-raised chickens are better treated in other ways: poached in a sauce, fried or broiled with garlic, herbs or spices to lend flavor. Always remember to remove any plastic bag of innards from oven-ready poultry before roasting.*

✳ *I see no point in making recooked dishes with roast meat; few things are as good as the best cold cuts, while dishes like shepherds pie are better made with cheaper cuts of raw meat.*

✳ *Don't hesitate to ask your butcher's advice about which cuts of meat are suitable for roasting. But don't ask about timing: most butchers seem to like meat very well done indeed.*

TIPS ON GRAVY

Opinions differ about gravy. I can't abide gravy made with flour, browning and other additives. The juice that runs from the meat makes the best sauce of all, though admittedly there is not much of it. I usually just serve the natural pan juices.

✳ *Pour off most of the fat from the roasting pan after the roast has been removed, and boil the pan juices over a moderate flame for a couple of minutes. The important thing is not to waste a scrap of the caramelized meat juices that stick to the bottom of the pan. Scrape away at them with a wooden spoon so they blend into the liquid in the pan to make a good thin, natural gravy.*

✳ *With a dry bird like turkey I make a small amount of stock from the giblets (not the liver) and add it to the juices. The same can be done with a piece of meat, using stock made from the trimmings or a mixture of stock and wine. With roast beef or lamb, the removal of the fat halfway through the roasting and the addition of a glass of wine provides a ready-made gravy. Strain before serving.*

MASTER RECIPE

ROAST SHORT RIBS OF BEEF

Serves 6

3 ribs of beef, weighing about 6 lb. total
1 tbsp. flour
1 tsp. dry mustard
black pepper
¾ cup red wine, heated

Preheat the oven to 450°F. Allow 20 minutes per lb. for medium rare beef. Subtract 15 minutes from the total for rare beef, add 15 minutes for well done.

Mix the mustard and flour, rub over the beef, and sprinkle with pepper. Stand it on a rack in the roasting pan and roast for 20 minutes. Then turn the oven down to 375°F and time the meat from this point. Baste the cut surfaces of the meat once or twice with the fat that runs off. Halfway through, pour off the fat from the pan and pour the wine over the meat. Baste two or three times during the remainder of the cooking time. (The dripping you have poured off can be used for roasting potatoes, or making Yorkshire Pudding.)

When the time is up, transfer the meat to a carving platter and stand in a warm place for 30 minutes, to allow the meat to settle. (The oven can now be turned up and the Yorkshire pudding and/or roast potatoes cooked while the beef stands.) Remove the rack and set the roasting pan over a moderate flame. Scrape the juices and sediment together, let them bubble for a moment or two, then pour through a strainer into a hot gravyboat.

To serve: for the traditional Sunday lunch, serve the roasted beef with Yorkshire Pudding, gravy, Horseradish Sauce, Roast Potatoes, and a green vegetable. Alternatively, serve it with baked potatoes, a Root Vegetable Purée, and a mixed salad.

YORKSHIRE PUDDING

1 cup all-purpose flour, sifted
½ tsp. salt
1 egg
⅔ cup milk
⅔ cup water

If making by hand, try to allow a rest of 30–60 minutes between making the batter and baking it. If making in a food processor, this doesn't seem to matter.

By hand: sift flour and salt into a large bowl, make a well in the center, and break in the egg. Have the milk and water mixed in a cup, in one hand, and a whisk in the other. Start to beat the egg, gradually incorporating the flour from around the edges. Pour in the milk and water slowly as you beat, so that all are incorporated. By the time the milk and water are used up, all the flour should have been drawn in. Continue to beat for 1½–2 minutes, then set aside to allow it to rest. Beat again thoroughly before using.

In a food processor: put flour and salt into the container, add the egg, process briefly, then add the milk and water slowly through the lid while continuing to process. If left to rest, process again before baking.

Pour a very little beef dripping into an ovenproof dish, rectangular if possible. Five minutes before the beef finishes cooking, heat the dish in the oven. When the beef is removed, turn the oven up to its highest. Pour the freshly beaten batter into the hot dish and place on a high rack in the oven for 25–30 minutes. It should be golden brown and puffed up round the edges. Cut in broad strips and serve with the beef.

Jancis Robinson's wine choice:
One classic deserves another, and claret would be the perfect partner for the roast beef. We British have always thought of claret, the red wine of Bordeaux, as our own, and for centuries have imported a wide range from which to choose. The cost of a bottle of claret can vary from about $5.00 to $500 and you know better than I what price bracket you can choose from. Whatever the price, I would suggest that, for current drinking, the vintages 1980 and 1979 (for cheaper wines) and 1976, 1971 and 1970 should prove particularly suitable.

FAMILY OF RECIPES

ROAST LEG OF SPRING LAMB

Serves 4–5

a small leg of spring lamb
4 tbsp. olive oil
4 tbsp. lemon juice
black pepper

Start a day in advance for lunch, or early morning for the evening. Lay the lamb in a dish and pour on the oil and lemon juice. Sprinkle with black pepper and leave for several hours, turning from time to time.

Preheat the oven to 350°F. Lay the leg on a rack in a roasting pan and pour the marinade over it. Roast for 25–30 minutes per lb. The former gives lamb that is still pink in the center, the latter lamb that is just cooked right through.

Serve simply with new potatoes and peas or broad beans.

ROAST LEG OF MATURE LAMB

Serves 6–8

1 large leg of lamb
1 large clove garlic
1 sprig rosemary
black pepper
½ cup red wine, heated

Preheat oven to 350°F. Cut the garlic into slivers and insert into small slits made in the meat. Put the lamb on a rack in a roasting pan and roast for 30 minutes per lb. Halfway through, pour off the fat in the pan and pour the wine over the meat. Baste two or three times during the rest of the cooking. Move to a carving platter, or serving dish, and keep warm for 15–20 minutes before carving. Remove the rack and place the pan over a low flame. Scrape the juices together and let them bubble for a moment or two, then strain into a sauceboat.

Serve the meat with its gravy, redcurrant jelly, a gratin of potatoes (Gratin Dauphinoise), and one or two vegetables, or with a Cucumber and Yogurt Salad.

CROWN ROAST OF LAMB

Serves 7–8

*1 crown roast of lamb, plus trimmings (each
   butcher trims his crown differently. Tell
   him you want the center left hollow, or he
   may fill it with ground meat)*
1 small onion, halved
1 carrot, halved
1 stalk celery, halved
a pinch of salt and 5 black peppercorns
*⅔ cup red or white wine, or 3 tbsp. red wine
vinegar*
Garnish:
½ lb. shelled peas, fresh or frozen
¾ lb. young carrots, thickly sliced
1 tbsp. butter

Start in the morning, or a few hours in
advance. Put the meat trimmings in a
pressure cooker with the flavoring vegetables, salt and peppercorns. Add the
wine, if you have any, and 1 cup cold water
(or use vinegar and 2 cups water). Cook for
30–40 minutes under pressure, strain and
cool. If you do not have a pressure cooker,
a large saucepan or stock pot will do, but
you will have to allow a couple of hours'
simmering to produce a good stock.

Preheat the oven to 425°F. Put the roast
on a rack in a roasting pan, and wrap the
end of each bone with a tiny cap of foil, to
prevent it burning. Roast for 15 minutes,
then turn down the heat to 350°F and pour
off the fat in the roasting pan. Let it stand a
moment or two to allow the fat to rise to the
top, then take the fat from the surface of
the stock and baste the meat with some of
the clear stock, warmed. Return the meat
to the oven and cook another 45–50
minutes, basting two or three times.

In the meantime, cook the peas and
carrots separately, drain, and mix, adding
the butter, salt and pepper, and keep hot.
To serve: when the meat is ready, transfer
it to a dish and fill the center with the peas
and carrots. Remove the foil, and add
paper frills if you like. (These are supplied
by the butcher, but I don't bother as they
fall off anyway, when carving.) Put the
roasting pan over a moderate heat, and add
any remaining stock. Scrape all together
and boil for a minute or two, then pour into
a small pitcher and serve with the meat.
Accompany with new potatoes sprinkled
with chives and redcurrant jelly.

Crown Roast of Lamb

CARRE D'AGNEAU

This makes a delicious meal for 2–3 people,
and is quickly cooked.

*1 carré d'agneau, or rack of lamb, or best
   end of neck, trimmed for roasting,
   consisting of 4–8 bones*

Preheat the oven to its maximum. Lay the
meat on a rack in a roasting pan, and cook
20 minutes for a 4-bone roast, 25 minutes
for a 7–8 bone rack.

To serve: this meat needs no attention
whatsoever, beyond cutting into cutlets to
serve. An elegant way of serving a *carré
d'agneau* for two is to carve the meat
lengthwise, parallel to the chine bone, in
thin strips. Divide them between two hot
plates, then cut up the bones and lay
alongside, to eat with your fingers. I don't
think this needs a sauce, but a fruit jelly can
be served with no extra trouble. Fried
potatoes go well with this, or a Potato
Purée or a Root Vegetable Purée.

ROAST LOIN OF PORK

Serves 6

3 lb. rolled loin of pork, with crackling (ask the butcher to score it for you)
coarse sea salt
⅔ cup beef stock, or stock and wine mixed, heated

Preheat the oven to 400°F. Rub the skin all over with coarse sea salt and lay the loin on a rack in a roasting pan. Roast 30 minutes, then turn down the oven to 375°F and cook a further 1¼–1½ hours. (Allow 35–40 minutes per lb., depending on the thickness of the joint.) Let it rest on a carving platter 15–20 minutes, in a warm place; this will make it easier to carve.

Once the meat has been transferred, remove the rack and make the gravy while the meat is resting. Pour off almost all of the fat in the roasting pan, leaving the meat juices that lie underneath it. Place the pan over a moderate flame, and pour in a little stock, or stock and wine mixed, scraping all the residue of caramelized juices together. Let it all bubble away for a couple of minutes, then pour it through a strainer into a gravyboat.

Serve the pork with its gravy, a Pear and Potato Purée, and a green salad. For a more traditional meal, serve Apple Sauce and gravy, Roast Potatoes and a green vegetable such as green beans.

ROAST DUCK
WITH BAKED APPLES

Serves 4

1 large duck
1¼ tbsp. sea salt
4 smallish cooking apples
1 cup redcurrant jelly
Celery Stuffing (optional): *see page 67*

Preheat the oven to 400°F. First make the stuffing, if you intend to use one (see page 67).

Stuff the duck, prick the skin all over with a sharp fork or skewer, rub with sea salt, and lay upside down on a rack in a roasting pan. Bake for 45 minutes, then remove and pour off the fat in the pan. Turn the duck breast side up, turn down the oven to 350°F and put back in the oven for 45 minutes, if unstuffed, or 1 hour, if stuffed.

Prepare the apples: remove the cores and the top third of the peel, and lay around the duck, or in a separate dish underneath, for the last 30 minutes of cooking. Baste twice with the duck fat.

To serve: put the duck on a carving platter and surround with the apples, filling the centers with the redcurrant jelly. Serve with Roast Potatoes and an Orange and Watercress Salad.

ROAST CHICKEN

There are many different ways to roast a chicken: this is the one I always use. It is only worth doing with a farm-bred bird with some intrinsic flavor. Factory-bred chickens are better poached, served in a sauce, fried, or grilled.

Serves 4

3¼ lb. roasting chicken, weighed after cleaning
5 tbsp. butter, at room temperature
sea salt and black pepper
2–3 stalks parsley

Preheat the oven to 375°F. Butter a large piece of aluminum foil and lay your chicken on it. Rub the bird all over with the soft butter and sprinkle salt and pepper inside and out. Put a lump of butter and a few stalks of parsley inside it. Wrap loosely in foil (this must not be airtight or it will steam) and lay on its side on a roasting rack. Roast for 20 minutes then turn on the other side for a further 20 minutes. Turn right side up, unwrap the foil, and baste with the butter. Roast another 30 minutes basting two or three times. Test to see if it is cooked by (a) tilting the bird to see the color of the juices that run out (if at all pink, roast a further 10 minutes); (b)

Roast Loin of Pork

pulling a leg gently away from the body (if it shows no resistance it is ready), or (c) pricking a drumstick if you must, to check the juices are no longer pink. For a larger bird, allow 20 minutes per lb. plus 10 minutes, then test.

To serve: this method of roasting a chicken produces no gravy, so just use the buttery juices poured into a small pitcher instead. Serve simply with a Potato Purée or noodles, and a green salad.

Roast Duck with Baked Apples

RUMP ROAST

Less expensive than sirloin, this cut of meat is what the French usually choose for 'le rosbif'.

Serves 4–6

2½–3 lb. rump roast
¼ tsp. dry mustard
black pepper

Heat the oven to 425°F. Rub the fatty surface of the roast with mustard, and sprinkle with black pepper. Stand on a rack in a roasting pan and roast for 15 minutes, then turn down the heat to 350°F. Roast for a further 20 minutes per lb. for medium rare beef, or 15 minutes per lb. for rare beef. Let stand for 15–20 minutes before carving. Pour off the fat in the pan, and reheat the meat juices, adding them to those that run from the meat when carving.
Serve with Horseradish Sauce, Yorkshire Pudding, Roast or Puréed Potatoes, and a selection of vegetables.

ROAST QUAIL

These tiny little birds make a rare treat, quick to cook and needing no carving. They are expensive, and must be served with a substantial grain or rice dish if serving one per person. A preliminary poaching in milk is advisable since it plumps them up remarkably.

Serves 6

6 quail, fresh or frozen
4 cups milk
6 tbsp. butter, melted
sea salt and black pepper

Preheat the oven to 400°F. Put the milk in a large pan and bring almost to boiling point. Drop in the quail and poach gently for 7 minutes, drain and pat dry. Lay them on a rack in a roasting pan, pour over the melted butter, and roast for 8 minutes.
To serve: sprinkle with salt and pepper before serving on a bed of buckwheat or cracked wheat, braised red or white cabbage, or sauerkraut. Alternatively, after poaching bury them in an ovenproof dish half full of grapes, pour over the melted butter, and cook for 8 minutes, as above. Serve garnished with croûtons of fried bread as a light main dish, to follow a substantial soup, such as Mediterranean Fish Soup, or Thick Bean Soup.

ROOT VEGETABLE PUREE

Serves 6

2 lb. celeriac – roughly 1½ lb. after trimming
1½ lb. potatoes, peeled
1 lb. carrots
4 tbsp. butter
⅔ cup heavy cream
sea salt and black pepper

Take three saucepans. Cut the celeriac in chunks, cover with lightly salted cold water, and cook until tender. At the same time cook the potatoes in the second pan and the carrots in the third. Drain each vegetable well, drying out a little in the pan over a gentle heat, then push each through a medium food mill into a clean pan. Dry out the purées carefully, by stirring constantly over a low heat, especially the celeriac and carrot ones, which tend to be watery. Mix all together well in a bowl, then add the butter, in small pieces, and the cream, and season with plenty of salt and pepper. Beat with a wooden spoon until well mixed and smooth. Reheat by placing the bowl over a saucepan of boiling water, stirring now and then.
Serve with any roast meat, game, grilled lamb or sausages.

CELERIAC: boil for purées and soups; roast in bacon fat; grate for salads.

PEAR AND POTATO PUREE

This spicy purée is delicious served with roast pork or duck, instead of the more traditional Apple Sauce and serves the same purpose of offsetting the rich meat.

Serves 6

1½ lb. potatoes, peeled and halved
1½ lb. ripe dessert pears, peeled, cored, and quartered
4 tbsp. butter, cut in bits
salt and black pepper
¼ tsp. freshly grated (or ground) ginger

Put the potatoes in a saucepan, cover with lightly salted cold water, and bring to the boil. Cook until just soft, then transfer to a colander with a slotted spoon. Put the pears into the same cooking water and poach gently for 5 minutes, or until soft, then drain. Push the potatoes and pears through a medium food mill into a clean saucepan. Reheat, stirring well to mix, and dry out the purée a little by stirring constantly over low heat for a few minutes. Then add the butter, salt and pepper, and ginger, and mix thoroughly.

ROAST POTATOES

Since these are usually cooked at the same time as a roast or a bird, they are cooked in the same fat. Most people roast potatoes in the roasting pan around the meat or bird but, as I like to use a rack, I prefer to cook them separately in a baking dish.

Serves 4

1½ lb. potatoes
fat from the roast
sea salt

While the bird or roast is cooking, peel the potatoes and cut them in halves or large chunks, according to size. Put them in a pan, cover with lightly salted cold water, bring to the boil, and cook, uncovered, for 5 minutes. Then drain them in a colander. When they have cooled enough to handle, dry them in a cloth and rough up the cut surfaces with a fork. Lay them in a shallow baking dish. When the bird or meat has half cooked, take it out of the oven and pour the fat from the roasting pan over the potatoes. Put them in the oven for the last 30 minutes or so, basting or turning them over from time to time.
To serve: lift them into a clean dish and sprinkle with sea salt.
Variation: Roast parsnips: make exactly as for Roast Potatoes. Delicious with roast beef or lamb.

STUFFINGS

I use stuffings less as I grow more attached to light, unfatty food, but it's good to have a few recipes on hand to make a bird go further, or to add a sense of occasion.

Potentially dry birds like turkeys and capons benefit from stuffing, but fatty ones like goose and duck are better roasted empty since this allows the fat to drain away. Stuffings based on meat, like the sausage and chestnut one, are also good made into balls and fried, while bread-based ones can be cooked in a covered dish in the oven at the same time as the bird without actually being inside it. Cooking them inside the bird means they gain flavor, but at the same time become enriched by some of the bird's fat.

CELERY STUFFING

Will stuff a small turkey, a duck, a capon or a large chicken

1 head celery, tender parts only, chopped
4 cups soft white breadcrumbs
½ tsp. sea salt
1 tsp. black peppercorns, roughly crushed
¼ tsp. ground mace, or nutmeg
2 eggs, lightly beaten
4 tbsp. butter, softened

Mix the chopped celery and breadcrumbs in a large bowl. Add the salt and peppercorns and the mace or nutmeg. Stir in the eggs and, lastly, the softened butter. Mix well.

SAUSAGE AND CHESTNUT STUFFING

Will stuff a small turkey or capon

1 lb. pure pork sausage meat (alternatively, buy good quality pork sausages and skin them, or finely ground pork, or a mixture of lean and fatty pork, which you can chop in a food processor)
1 lb. chestnuts, shelled
1¼ cup milk
¼ lb. shallots, chopped
1 clove garlic, chopped
4 tbsp. chopped parsley
1 tbsp. brandy
2 tsp. sea salt
¼ tsp. ground mace, or nutmeg

To shell chestnuts: make a nick in the flat end with a sharp knife. Put in a pan, cover with cold water, bring to the boil and remove from the heat. Take 3 or 4 nuts out of the water and remove the shells and inner covering. Keep all the nuts as hot as possible, or they will become very hard to shell. Reheat the water from time to time, and only take out a few at a time.

Put the shelled nuts in a small pan, cover with the milk and bring to the boil. Simmer for 8–10 minutes, until soft, then drain and chop coarsely. Stir them into the sausage meat, add the chopped shallots and garlic, parsley, brandy, salt, pepper, and mace or nutmeg. When all is well seasoned and mixed, stuff the bird. Alternatively, make into small balls and fry, and serve as a garnish for roast turkey, capon or chicken.

BREAD STUFFING

This amount will stuff a 12 lb. turkey; make in half quantities for a capon or large chicken.

¾ lb. shallots, peeled and chopped
½ cup butter
6 cups soft white breadcrumbs
½ cup chopped parsley
sea salt and black pepper

Cook the shallots gently in the butter in a deep frying pan until they turn light golden. Add the crumbs and stir to mix. Remove from the heat, and add the chopped parsley and plenty of salt and pepper. Leave to cool before using.

POTATO STUFFING

2 medium onions, chopped
2 tbsp. beef dripping, or butter
1 lb. pure pork sausage meat, or nearest alternative
1 lb. freshly mashed potatoes
1 small can green peppercorns, roughly crushed
1 tbsp. sea salt
6–8 tbsp. chopped parsley

Cook the chopped onions gently in the fat in a deep frying pan. Add the sausage meat, mix with onions, and cook all together until lightly browned. Remove from the heat and stir in the hot mashed potatoes. Crush the green peppercorns roughly by pounding in a mortar with the salt, and stir into the mixture. Add parsley and leave to cool before using. This goes particularly well with Roast Goose.

— MENUS —

Some suggestions for well balanced meals based on the roasting recipes

---

BAKED EGGS
with tarragon

ROAST SHORT RIBS OF BEEF
with Yorkshire Pudding
Root Vegetable Purée

TARTLETS FILLED WITH CURRANTS
with cream

MIXED SMOKED FISH
trout, salmon, mackerel, eel,
with Horseradish Sauce and lemons

ROAST DUCK WITH BAKED APPLES
Roast Potatoes, green salad

BLACKBERRY JELLY
with Almond Sauce

BEEF CONSOMME
with Ginger Garnish

ROAST LOIN OF PORK
Pear and Potato Purée, broccoli

PLUM ICE CREAM

Vegetarian Menu

THICK BEAN SOUP

ROOT VEGETABLE PUREE
Braised Fennel, broiled tomatoes with
herbs and garlic, Onion Bread

COMPOTE OF APRICOTS
with Vanilla Cream

POACHING, STEAMING, BOILING

The use of water and steam provides one of the purest and healthiest methods of cooking. Few foods are actually boiled, except for root vegetables, pasta and rice. Most dishes that we call boiled, such as boiled beef, are actually poached, since fast boiling would extract all the goodness from the foods, transferring it to the liquid they are cooked in.
Poaching is a delicate art and, once learned, opens the way to a range of light, wholesome dishes. A roast chicken is an excellent dish, but a poached bird lends itself to many variations as well as giving a bonus of first rate stock. Poached chicken is also better than roast for most cold dishes, since it can be left to cool in its stock, which keeps the flesh moist.

Poaching is also one of the best ways of cooking fish so long as you have a suitable pan. For whole fish you will need a fish poacher. But steaks and fillets of fish can also be poached successfully and don't need a big pan.

Poached fruit is a much-loved dish in France. Called a compôte, it is simply a dish of fruit, usually fresh but sometimes dried, stewed in a thin syrup and served cold, often with cream.
Steaming is gentler than poaching, for the food never comes in contact with the water but cooks in the steam. It is particularly suited to fish, as they cook it in China. Whole fish are wrapped in foil, flavored with ginger, garlic and scallions, while fillets may be wrapped in lettuce leaves, or steamed simply as they are. Watery vegetables, like squash pumpkin, are better steamed than cooked in water, while zucchini and snow peas are excellent cooked in this way. The liquid in the steamer will be flavored by the food it has cooked and can be used for stock.

Boiled salt beef is a good, traditional English dish but I prefer boiled fresh beef. Unlike salt beef, it can be used for many different dishes, hot, cold and reheated. The remains can be made into salads, while thin slices of cold boiled beef reheated in a thick onion sauce is one of the most comforting family dishes. And the stock makes a delicious consommé.

I use my **pressure cooker** for the youngest and most tender vegetables, not to save time, but simply because the results are amazing. Small zucchini cooked under pressure for 2 minutes taste literally as if they had jumped straight out of the soil.

The more obvious value of the pressure cooker is in cooking foods such as chick peas and dried beans, and in making stock, since it cuts cooking times by two thirds. I also find it invaluable for cooking chickens and large pieces of meat. The results taste like poached food, not boiled as you might imagine.

Steamer, stainless steel, copper bottom.
Small porcelain pan, useful for sauces.

Wok with metal steaming rack, for whole fish wrapped in foil. Must use lid.

Fish poacher, with a lifting tray made of aluminum. Good for poaching whole fish.

"Adrian Van Huesden and her daughter at the New Fish Market in Amsterdam," 1661–3, by Emanuel de Witte.
By courtesy of the Trustees of the National Gallery, London.

TIPS ON COOKING WITH WATER
Poaching

✳Meat and poultry are cooked in plain water with flavoring vegetables and herbs added. Fish takes a much shorter time to cook, so it is best put into liquid that is already flavored. Salmon, however, and shellfish are traditionally cooked in plain salt water.

✳Keep the temperature for all poached foods, especially delicate ones like eggs, fish and fruit, just below boiling point, so the water shakes and shivers, rather than actually bubbles.

✳When poaching fruit, which often takes only a couple of minutes, boil the water and sugar, until the sugar has dissolved, before adding the fruit. As soon as the fruit is tender, remove, then boil up the syrup until reduced to the right amount for your dish.

Steaming

✳Timing is crucial: overcooked steamed food is uneatable.

✳Steamed food tends to be bland, so added flavorings and/or sauces are important.

✳The food in the steamer must not be allowed to touch the water (or stock) below: this is brought to the boil before the steamer is added and the pot must be kept covered throughout.

✳If you don't have a steamer you can improvise. A colander or strainer, or even a lettuce basket, may be laid over a deep stock pot. If the holes are very large, it can be lined with muslin. A wok makes a practical steamer if it has a lid and steaming rack. Chinese wicker baskets can be piled up inside the wok.

Boiling

✳Use lots of water and keep boiling steadily. Have the pan uncovered, or half covered, to allow the steam to escape.

Pressure cooking

✳Never cook with less than 1 cup water, or with more than is recommended.

✳Experiment with tender vegetables. Use the minimum of water, and bring to the boil before adding the vegetables. Cook for a third of the time used in an ordinary pan.

69

MASTER RECIPE

POACHED CHICKEN WITH WATERCRESS SAUCE

Serves 6

1 large roasting chicken, about $3\frac{1}{2}$–4 lb.
1 onion, halved
2 cloves
1 carrot, halved
1 leek, halved
1 stalk celery, halved
1 small bay leaf
3 stalks parsley
1 sprig thyme
2 tsp. sea salt
8 black peppercorns
Watercress sauce *(see below)*

Put the bird in a flameproof casserole that fits it as closely as possible (an oval one is ideal). Surround it with the onion stock with the cloves, carrot, leek, celery, bay leaf, parsley and thyme. Add salt and peppercorns, and enough hot water to come halfway up the legs. (The chicken breast will cook in the steam, so long as the lid fits tightly.)

Bring to the boil quickly, removing any scum that rises to the surface with a slotted spoon. When this has diminished to a white foam, cover the pot and simmer very gently – the water should only bubble here and there – for 1–$1\frac{1}{4}$ hours. Check to make sure the water is not boiling hard, or the chicken will be tough.

When the time is up, test to see if it is cooked by wiggling one of its legs. There should not be much resistance; you will learn this by practice. Don't pierce a leg unless desperate, for you will lose precious juices in the process. If you must, do it only once; the juice should be absolutely clear and colorless. If at all pink, cook for a further 5–10 minutes. When it is done, use 2 large spoons, one of which should be slotted, to lift it on to the carving platter. Tilt the bird as you lift it so the liquid inside runs back into the pot. Cover with foil and keep warm while you make the sauce.

Strain the stock and stand for 2–3 minutes to allow the fat to settle on the surface. Then draw off $1\frac{1}{4}$ cups fat-free stock from below the surface into a measuring cup to make the sauce.

To serve: when the sauce is made, carve the chicken, removing the skin, and lay the chicken pieces on a serving dish. Pour the sauce over them and serve with new potatoes and one or two fresh vegetables: peas, beans, broccoli, or carrots. For a more elegant dish, take the meat off the bones and cut across in thick diagonal slices. Lay on a shallow serving dish and dribble some of the sauce over them, serving the rest separately.

For a party, make a garnish of very thinly sliced zucchinis and carrots, and whole snow peas, poached for 2–3 minutes in boiling water while the chicken finishes cooking. Drain well, then lay them like a fan on a round platter. Lay the boned sliced chicken over them, and dribble some of the sauce over them.

The skin of a poached chicken is pallid and unappetizing, best discarded and returned to the stockpot. After carving, the bones and skin can be put back in the casserole with the remaining vegetables and herbs, and more water added. Boil steadily for 2 hours; the resulting stock can be strained and frozen for future sauces.

WATERCRESS SAUCE

$1\frac{1}{4}$ cups chicken stock
2 tbsp. butter
$1\frac{1}{2}$ tbsp. flour
salt and black pepper
$\frac{1}{2}$ cup watercress leaves, loosely packed
$\frac{1}{2}$ cup heavy cream
2 tsp. Dijon mustard
2 tsp. lemon juice

Reheat the strained stock in a saucepan with a pouring lip. Melt the butter in a heavy-bottomed saucepan over a low heat. When it has melted, remove the pan from the heat and shake in the flour, stirring constantly until it has blended with the butter. Replace the pan over low heat, and stir steadily for 1 minute to cook the flour. The resulting mixture is called a roux; it should be fairly thick but flowing, so that if you scrape the bottom of the pan with the spoon, the roux closes up after it.

Remove the pan again from the heat, and add the hot stock by degrees, beating until each addition is amalgamated before you add more. When half the stock is added, replace the pan over a very low heat and stir constantly while you slowly pour in the remaining stock. Raise the heat slightly and stir hard as the sauce approaches boiling point. When this is reached, lower the heat and beat very hard for 1 minute; this gives a glossy quality to the finished sauce. Add salt and pepper to taste, and simmer gently another 2–3 minutes, stirring now and then.

Meanwhile, put the watercress leaves into the food processor with the cream and process until finely chopped. Stir the resulting cream into the sauce when it has finished cooking. Reheat, stirring in the mustard and lemon juice.

Jancis Robinson's wine choice:
The convention is that we match wines to food by color but more important is to match weight, or strength of flavor. The poached chicken is a subtle dish that could easily be overwhelmed. For maximum pleasure, serve it with a fairly delicate wine. German wines are very light, but should be called either Trocken, Halbtrocken or Kabinett to be dry enough. Vinho Verde from Portugal and the classic dry French whites Muscadet, Chablis and Sancerre might go perfectly – though light reds, such as Beaujolais, and other Gamay and Loire reds, such as Bourgueil and Chinon would also fill the bill.

FAMILY OF RECIPES

COLD POACHED TROUT WITH HORSERADISH VALOUTÉ

Serves 6

3 lb. rainbow trout
a few extra fish bones, heads, etc.
1 onion, halved
1 carrot, halved
1 stalk celery, halved
1 bay leaf
3 stalks parsley
1 tsp. salt
8 black peppercorns
$\frac{1}{2}$ cup dry white wine, or 4 tbsp. vermouth, or white wine vinegar
Horseradish velouté
2 tbsp. butter
1 tbsp. flour
$\frac{3}{4}$ cup fish stock, heated
$\frac{1}{3}$ cup heavy cream
2 tsp. grated horseradish
2 tsp. Dijon mustard
1 tbsp. orange juice
salt and black pepper
$\frac{1}{3}$ cup yogurt
1 tbsp. finely chopped watercress, leaves only

This is a good way of cooking a large rainbow trout if you have a fish poacher. (If not, wrap the fish in lightly oiled foil and

Poached Chicken with Watercress Sauce

lay on the oven rack; bake in a pre-heated oven at 350°F for 30 minutes.

First make the fish stock. Put the fish bones, heads, etc., in a pan with the flavoring vegetables and herbs, salt and peppercorns, and the wine, vermouth or vinegar. Add 1 quart water and bring slowly to the boil.

Simmer for 30 minutes, half covered then strain and reserve 1 cup. Put the rest in the fish poacher and lay in the trout. (If your poacher has no tray, lay the trout in a cloth, using it to lower it in and out of the water.) Add enough cold water just to cover the fish. Heat the water until it shivers, then cover the pan and cook for 15 minutes.

Make the sauce while the fish is cooking. Melt the butter, stir in the flour, and cook for 1 minute, stirring. Add the fish stock and cream; bring back to the boil and simmer for 3 minutes, stirring often. Then add the horseradish, mustard, and orange juice, and salt and pepper to taste (if the fish stock was well seasoned this may not be necessary). Simmer for another 1–2 minutes.

Then pour into a bowl and place in very cold water. Stir frequently while it cools to prevent a skin forming. When cold, stir in the yogurt, beating with a small whisk until smooth, then the finely chopped watercress. Cover with plastic wrap if making in advance, and store in the refrigerator.

To serve: lay the fish on a flat dish. If it has been in the refrigerator, it must be brought back to room temperature before serving; this takes at least 1 hour. Remove the top skin, and serve the cold sauce in a separate bowl. Accompany with a dish of boiled new potatoes, served warm, without butter.

Variation: to serve the same dish hot, simply double the amount of cream and omit the yogurt. Accompany with boiled new potatoes and snow peas, green beans, or broccoli.

This dish can also be made with 6 smaller rainbow trout. If you are using small fish, drop the trout into boiling fish stock, then adjust the heat so that it barely simmers. Poach for 5–7 minutes, depending on the size of the fish. When they are cooked, remove and leave to cool.

RAIE AU BEURRE NOIR

Serves 6

3 lb. wing(s) of skate, skinned
1 onion, cut in quarters
1 bay leaf
3 stalks parsley, chopped
⅔ cup, white wine vinegar
1 tbsp. capers, drained
½ cup butter

You will need a very broad pan in which to cook this; failing a triangular *turbotière*, a large round casserole is probably the answer. If the wing is too large to fit into it, cut it in two. Put the fish in the pan and add enough cold water to barely cover it. Remove the fish, and put the onion, bay leaf, stalks of parsley (reserving the heads), and ½ cup vinegar into the pan, bring to boil and simmer 30 minutes, half-covered. Then add the skate, bring back to the boil, adjust heat, and poach gently for 20 minutes. Then lift out the skate and remove the bones. Divide into serving pieces and lay on a hot dish, scattering the chopped parsley and capers over it. Keep warm while you make the sauce.

To make the beurre noir: heat the butter in a pan until it is a nut brown, neither golden nor black. Pour it over the fish, then add the remaining vinegar to the pan. Let it bubble and froth for a few seconds, then turn over the skate and serve immediately.

POACHED GOUJONS OF SOLE WITH TARRAGON

Serves 6

2 lb fillets of Dover sole, skinned, with
  bones, etc.
½ small onion
½ small carrot
ends of leek and celery
¼ tsp. salt and 6 black peppercorns
2 tbsp. butter
3 shallots, finely chopped
½ cup dry white wine
⅓ cup heavy cream
⅓ cup chopped tarragon

Cut the fish fillets in diagonal strips, about 2½ × ½ inches. Put the fish bones, skins, etc., in a pan with the onion, carrot, leek and celery, salt and peppercorns. Cover with 2 cups cold water, bring to the boil, and simmer for 25 minutes. Strain, then reduce to ¾ cup by fast boiling.

Melt the butter in a clean pan and cook the shallot until it softens and starts to change color. Then add the fish stock and the wine and bring to the boil, stirring. Drop in the strips of fish, a few at a time, and adjust the heat so that the liquid barely simmers. Poach them for 1–2 minutes, then transfer them to a warm dish, using a slotted spoon. Keep warm while you poach the rest. When all are cooked, measure the sauce; if much more than ¾ cup remains, reduce by fast boiling, then stir in the cream, adding salt and pepper to taste. Put the fish back into the sauce, folding them in gently, with most of the tarragon, reserving a little for the garnish. Remove from the heat and stand, covered, for 2–3 minutes, to infuse the sauce with the flavor of the tarragon, then pour into a clean dish and scatter the reserved tarragon over the top. **Serve** with boiled or new potatoes and a simple green salad.

COLD POACHED SALMON

Salmon is traditionally cooked in plain salt water as opposed to a fish stock. An infallible rule, when cooking salmon to eat cold, is as follows: put the fish in a fish poacher, cover with cold water, add salt, and bring to the boil. When it boils, turn off the heat, cover the pan, and leave it until it is completely cold. Whatever the size of the fish, it will be perfectly cooked, so long as the poacher is roughly the right size. (A tiny fish in an immense pan would be over-cooked by the time the water came to the boil.) The salmon continues cooking while cooling, and this keeps it moist. Take it out of the water just before serving.

Variation: for a change from the usual mayonnaise, try serving a cold curry sauce with salmon. See recipe for Hard-Boiled Eggs in Curry Sauce: substitute fish stock for chicken stock if possible, but it is not essential.

POACHED EGGS ON SPINACH

Serves 6

2 lb fresh spinach, or 1½ lb. frozen chopped
  spinach
2 tbsp. butter
1 tbsp. flour
salt and black pepper
freshly grated nutmeg
6 very fresh eggs
a little paprika
<u>Cream sauce</u>:
2 tbsp. butter
1 tbsp. flour
½ cup chicken stock
½ cup light cream
3 tbsp. grated Gruyère

Bring 1 inch very lightly salted water to the boil in a big pan. Throw in the fresh spinach and cook for 4–5 minutes until tender. (If using frozen spinach, follow instructions on the package.) Drain very

Poaching an egg

To poach an egg, bring lightly-salted water to boil in a broad, shallow pan, then lower heat so water is barely shivering. Break egg in (if nervous, break it into a saucer and slide it in). Only very fresh eggs can be poached successfully; when stale the white spreads all over the pan.

Water should be barely shivering.

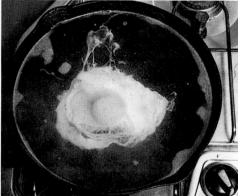

After 30 seconds white becomes opaque.

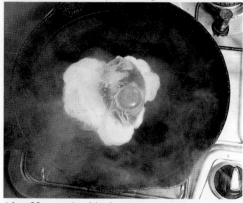

One minute and white is nearly set.

Two minutes: white is set, yolk is soft.

well, forcing out excess water with the back of a wooden spoon. Put it in the food processor and reduce to a purée. (With frozen chopped spinach this is not necessary.)

Melt the butter, add the flour, and cook for 1 minute, stirring. Then add the chopped spinach and cook, stirring often, for 4 minutes. Add salt, pepper and nutmeg, then transfer to a shallow serving dish and keep hot.

Make the cream sauce: melt the butter, add the flour, and cook for 1 minute, stirring. Heat the chicken stock and cream together, then pour on gradually, off the heat, stirring until the sauce thickens. Replace over heat and cook for 3 minutes, stirring often, then add the grated cheese and salt and pepper to taste.

Poach the eggs, drain, and lay them on the spinach. Pour the cream sauce over them – they should not be completely covered – and sprinkle on a little paprika. Serve immediately, as a first course or light main dish. It needs no accompaniment.

STEAMED MEATBALLS

Serves 5–6

¾ lb. ground pork
¾ lb. ground veal
½ bunch scallions, chopped
1½ tsp. ginger root, finely chopped
1 clove garlic, finely chopped
1 small chili pepper, seeded and finely
*   chopped*
5 tsp. light soy sauce
5 tsp. lemon juice
salt and black pepper
1 egg, lightly beaten
2½ cups chicken stock
Dipping Sauce One
¼ cup soy sauce
¼ cup medium dry vermouth
½ tsp. sugar
Dipping Sauce Two
½ cup yogurt
4 tsp. sesame oil
a dash Tabasco

Mix the pork and veal together in a bowl and add the scallions, ginger, garlic, chili pepper, soy sauce, lemon juice, and plenty of salt and pepper. Try out for seasoning by frying a small ball, remembering that steamed food needs to be more highly seasoned than fried food, since steaming makes it bland.

Shape into balls about the size of a pingpong ball and lay them on a small plate that fits inside your steamer. Have the stock boiling away in the bottom part of the steamer, or wok, with the vegetable trimmings for extra flavor. Lay the top part

of steamer, with the meatballs, over it, cover, and cook for 20 minutes, keeping the stock boiling steadily. Check once or twice to see if it needs replenishing.

Serve with some steamed vegetables, cooked separately for 2–5 minutes (snow peas, string beans, broccoli, cauliflower, zucchini or mushrooms) and one or two of the dipping sauces.

STEAMED SCALLOPS

Serves 6 as a first course

18 large scallops, with 6 curved shells
*   (optional)*
a few drops sesame oil, or sunflower seed oil
2 tbsp. ginger root, coarsely grated
2 cloves garlic, very finely chopped
6 large, or 12 small, scallions, cut in 1½ inch
*   lengths*
sea salt and black pepper
2 tsp. soy sauce
Sauce (optional):
2 tbsp. dry vermouth
2 tsp. sunflower seed oil
2 tsp. sesame oil, or sunflower seed oil
4 tsp. soy sauce

Have 6 squares of foil laid out on a flat surface. Rub them with a few drops of

sesame oil, if you have it, or sunflower seed oil. Cut the scallops in quarters, detaching the coral tongues and cutting them in half. Divide them between the foil squares, mixing the ginger and garlic evenly among them. Cut the scallion pieces into very thin slivers, and mix half of them with the scallops. Sprinkle with salt, pepper, and soy sauce. Wrap up the foil packages, sealing the edges tightly.

Have a large pan of boiling water with a rack lying over the surface of the water; a wok with steaming rack is ideal. Lay the packages on the rack, cover with a lid, and steam for 8 minutes. In the meantime, mix together all the ingredients for the sauce and warm the shells. When the scallops are cooked, unwrap the packages and pour the juices into the sauce.

To serve: tip the contents of the packages into the shells, give the sauce a final whisk, and pour it over them. Scatter the reserved sliced scallions over the top, and serve, as a first course.

If you prefer, the scallops can be served still wrapped up in their packages, on small plates. Omit the sauce if you like – it is not essential – or serve it separately.

Steamed Meatballs with vegetables and dipping sauces

73

STEAMED FISH A LA CHINOISE

Serves 3–4 as a first course, 2–3 as a main dish

1 large rainbow trout, or a bass weighing
    1½ –1¾ lb.
1 tsp. sugar
1 tsp. sea salt
2 tsp. sesame oil
2 tsp. light soy sauce
8 thin slices fresh ginger root
2 large cloves garlic, sliced
2 large or 4 medium scallions, sliced
<u>Sauce:</u>
2 tbsp. dry vermouth
2 tbsp. sunflower seed oil
1 tbsp. sesame oil
1 tbsp. light soy sauce
<u>Garnish</u>:
2 large or 4 medium spring onions

To make this dish you need a large wok with steaming rack and lid, or a fish poacher with a perforated tray that can be adjusted so the fish lies above the surface of the water. Or you can make it by baking the foil-wrapped fish, allowing 20 minutes, though then it will not be steamed.

Rub the fish inside and out with the sugar, salt, sesame oil and soy sauce. Oil a piece of foil and lay half the sliced ginger, garlic, and scallions on it. Lay the fish on these and cover with the remaining ginger, garlic and scallions. Wrap the foil around the fish and seal it tightly.

Have some water boiling hard in the wok (or fish poacher). Lay the wrapped fish on the rack, cover with the lid and steam for 25 minutes, keeping the water boiling steadily. Check once or twice that it is not boiling dry: replenish with boiling water.

While it is cooking, mix the sauce ingredients in a small pitcher. Cut the remaining scallions into 2 inch sections, then cut each section into thin strips. When the time is up, unwrap the fish and pour any juices into the sauce. Slide the fish on to a flat dish, discarding the ginger, garlic and scallion. Remove the skin from the top half of the fish and pour the sauce over the fish, after giving it a quick whisk. Then scatter scallions over it, and serve.

To serve: as a first course, this does not need any accompaniment. For a main dish, serve it with steamed zucchinis. Have them waiting in a bamboo steamer while the fish cooks, unpeeled and cut in long thin strips. When the fish is ready, remove it and leave it wrapped in foil while you replace the steaming rack with the bamboo steamer. The squash will only take 3 minutes to cook, and will be ready almost as soon as you have prepared the fish.

Steamed Fish à la Chinoise

STEAMED VEGETABLE MOLD

Serves 4

1 lb. zucchini
4 tbsp. butter
3 tbsp. flour
1 cup milk
½ cup grated Gruyère
salt and pepper
4 eggs, beaten

Butter a bowl and find a saucepan broad enough to lower it in and out easily; if it is a tight fit, find a piece of cloth to stand it on, using the edges of the cloth to lower it in and out of the pan. Stand a small saucer upside down in the pan, and stand the bowl on that. Add enough water to reach halfway up the sides, then remove the bowl. Bring the water to the boil.

Drop the zucchini into lightly salted boiling water and poach for 10 minutes, drain and cool. Chop coarsely: they must not be too fine, nor reduced to a mushy purée. Melt the butter, add the flour, and cook for 1 minute, stirring. Heat the milk and add; stir until blended and simmer for 3 minutes. Stir in the grated cheese, and salt and pepper to taste. Remove from the heat and stir in the chopped zucchini, then fold in the beaten eggs.

Transfer the mixture to the bowl and cover it with foil, tying it around the edges with string. Once the water is boiling fast,

lower the bowl in, cover the pan, and boil steadily for 1½ hours, replenishing the water now and then from a boiling kettle. (Always use boiling water so that the temperature does not drop.)

When the time is up, remove the bowl, unwrap, and run a knife carefully around the edges to loosen them a little. Lay a warm plate over the bowl, and invert both together. Shake hard once or twice, and the mold should fall out of the bowl.

Serve at once with Tomato Coulis. If you prefer, the mold can be cooked in the oven, standing in a roasting pan or bain marie half full of water. Allow 45 minutes in an oven preheated to 325°F. It can also be baked in a ring mold. If a soufflé dish is used, it does not have to be turned out.

Variations: instead of the zucchinis, try using: 1 lb. broccoli, poached until just tender, drained, and coarsely chopped; 1 lb. string beans, poached, drained, and chopped; 1½ lb. green peas or broad beans, shelled, poached and pushed through a medium food mill, or 1½ lb. spinach, boiled, drained, and chopped.

A good dish can be made by making a ring mold of peas, broad beans, or spinach, and filling the center with tiny meatballs (see Steamed Meatballs, page 73) and handing Tomato Coulis separately.

ZUCCHINI
WITH ICED TOMATO SAUCE

Serves 6

12 small zucchini, trimmed but unpeeled
salt
Tomato Sauce:
1 lb. tomatoes, skinned and quartered
1 bunch scallions, sliced
3 tbsp. sunflower seed oil
1 tsp. chopped fresh ginger root
3 tbsp. orange juice
3 tbsp. lemon juice
Garnish:
4 scallions, chopped

Make the tomato sauce in advance. Put the tomatoes in the food processor and process briefly. Cook the sliced scallions in half the oil for 2 minutes, then add to the tomatoes, leaving the oil behind. Add the ginger and process again. Add the remaining oil, orange and lemon juice, and process once more very briefly, then pour into a bowl and chill in the refrigerator for 1–2 hours.

Bring a little water to the boil in a pressure cooker, add a pinch of salt, and put in the whole zucchini. Cook under pressure for 3 minutes, or 4 if they are on the large side. With practice, you will soon be able to guess accurately how long to allow. (If you don't have a pressure cooker they can be poached or steamed.) Test them after 3 or 4 minutes: they need to be only just cooked, still on the crisp side. Lift them out, reserving the water for a vegetable bouillon, and leave to cool for a little.

Zucchini with Iced Tomato Sauce

Serve when they are still warm (after about 20 minutes); cut them in quarters lengthwise and lay on a flat dish. Spoon the chilled tomato sauce over them, and sprinkle with scallions. Serve as a first course, or as an accompaniment to tandoori chicken, or poached or steamed fish. I find this best when the zucchini are still warm, and the sauce very cold. It is also good made with small leeks cut in thick slices instead of the zucchini.

BOILED FRESH BEEF
WITH SALSA VERDE

Serves 4–6

3–4 lb. beef brisket (unsalted)
1 tsp. coarse salt
12 black peppercorns
1 large onion, halved
3 cloves
1 large carrot, halved
1 leek, halved
1 stalk celery, halved
1 bay leaf
3 stalks parsley
1 lb. small onions, peeled
1 lb. small carrots, scrubbed
Salsa Verde: *(see right)*

Put the beef in a casserole or stock pot, cover with very hot water, and bring quickly to the boil, skimming off the scum that rises to the surface. When nothing more remains than a few white bubbles, add salt and peppercorns, an onion stuck with 3 cloves, carrot, leek, celery, bay leaf and parsley. Bring back to the boil, then cover and simmer gently for 1½–2 hours, allowing 30 minutes per lb. Thirty minutes before the time is up, remove the flavoring vegetables and put in the whole onions and carrots.

To cook in a pressure cooker, bring to the boiling point and skim as above, then add vegetables and screw down the lid. Cook under pressure for 30–45 minutes, or 10 minutes per lb. Ten minutes before the time is up, reduce pressure, removed lid, and substitute fresh vegetables for the old ones. Screw down the lid and cook for another 10 minutes under pressure.

To serve: when the time is up, remove the beef and carve some of it. Lay it on a platter, surrounded by the vegetables. Strain the stock, moisten the meat with a little of it, and serve some in a small pitcher (keep the rest for other dishes). Accompany the beef with a Salsa Verde (see right) and some boiled potatoes.

SALSA VERDE

1 egg yolk
1 tbsp. Dijon mustard
1 tsp. sugar
salt and black pepper
2 cloves garlic, crushed
½ large mild Spanish onion, finely chopped
1 cup chopped fresh herbs (parsley, chives, chervil, tarragon, dill)
¼ cup white wine vinegar
⅔ cup olive oil
2 hard-boiled eggs, chopped

This may be made by hand or in the food processor. The results are quite different, but equally good.

By hand: break the egg yolk into a large bowl and stir in the mustard, sugar, salt, and pepper. When smooth, add the garlic, onion, and herbs. Then stir in the vinegar, the olive oil, and, finally, the chopped eggs.

In a food processor: first put in the herbs and chop, then empty them out and chop the onions. Take them out also, and process the egg yolk with the mustard, sugar, salt and pepper. Then add the garlic, chopped onion and herbs, and process all together for a minute. Then pour in the vinegar and oil through the lid while processing. Finally, add the roughly chopped hard-boiled eggs and process briefly. This gives a softer, smoother sauce, while the first version is more separate and distinct. Serve with hot or cold unsalted boiled beef.

MIROTON OF BEEF

Serves 4

About 1 lb. cold boiled beef (unsalted)
1 lb. onions, thinly sliced
4 tbsp. butter
¼ cup flour
2 cups beef stock (homemade, from boiling the beef)
salt and black pepper

Cut the beef in small, neat slices, removing all fat. Cook the onions slowly in the butter, until they are soft and transparent but not brown. Add the flour and stir for 1 minute. Pour in the heated stock gradually, stirring until it has blended. Add salt and pepper, and simmer for 15 minutes, covered. Stir occasionally to prevent sticking. Finally, add the little slices of beef, folding them gently into the sauce, and let stand for 5 minutes to heat through, without allowing it to boil.

To serve: transfer to a dish to serve, or serve straight from the pan, with boiled potatoes. This is a simple dish for family meals, and needs no other vegetables.

COLD BEEF VINAIGRETTE

Serves 4

about 1 lb. cold boiled beef (unsalted)
about 1 lb. waxy potatoes
about ¾ lb. tomatoes, sliced
sea salt and black pepper
½ cup olive oil
3 tbsp. white wine vinegar
3 tbsp. chopped parsley
3 tbsp. chopped chives
½ bunch scallions, sliced

Cut the beef in neat slices, removing all fat. Boil the potatoes in their skins; drain. After they have cooled for a few minutes, peel and cut in thick slices. Lay them on a flat dish and pour 3 tbsp. olive oil over them. Sprinkle with salt and pepper, and half the parsley and chives, and leave to cool completely.

Lay the sliced beef over the potatoes, and sprinkle with salt and pepper. Mix the remaining oil with the vinegar and pour some of it over the beef. Sprinkle with the remaining parsley and chives. Cover with a layer of sliced tomatoes, and pour the rest of the vinaigrette over them. Scatter the sliced scallions over the top, and let stand for an hour or so before serving.

To serve: this needs no accompaniment, although it can be served with a green salad, if you like. It goes well after a hot soup, or before a hot pudding.

BOILED SALT BEEF

Serves 6

3 lb. corned brisket
12 black peppercorns
1 large onion, halved
3 cloves
1 large carrot, halved
1 leek, halved
1 stalk celery, halved
1 bay leaf
3 stalks parsley

Follow the instructions for Boiled Beef with Salsa Verde, page 75, with these minor differences. Cover the beef with cold water instead of hot, and bring slowly to the boil, skimming. Don't add salt. Instead of the salsa verde, serve with mustard, and accompany with a selection of boiled root vegetables (potatoes, turnips, swedes, parsnips, etc.). Throw away the stock afterwards, as it is usually too salty to use. Corned beef is less adaptable than fresh, so it is better to cook a smaller piece. Any remains are best eaten simply, cold with salad.

A SIMPLE POT-AU-FEU

Serves 4–5

2½ lb. cheap stewing beef – chuck, brisket, or skirt
1 onion, halved
1 stalk celery, halved
1 bay leaf
1 tsp. sea salt
8 black peppercorns
3 leeks, thickly sliced
3 large carrots, thickly sliced

Preheat oven to 300°F. Cut the beef in large pieces and put in a casserole. Cover with 2

Cold Beef Vinaigrette

quarts cold water and bring very slowly to the boil. As it approaches boiling point, skim the surface until no more scum forms. Then add the onion, celery stalk, bay leaf, salt, and peppercorns. Cover and cook in a very low oven for 4 hours. After 3 hours add the carrots and leeks.

Serve the meat, carrots and leeks in soup plates, with a little of the broth poured over them. Discard the onion, celery, and bay leaf, which were used for flavoring.

Accompany with fresh brown bread and butter. This is a very simple dish, but comforting and delicious, especially when one is tired. It also leaves a residue of first-rate beef stock, ideal for braising vegetables the following day.

Boiling leaf vegetables

Leaf vegetables need a minimum of cooking if they are not to become soggy; putting them straight into boiling water conserves the nutritional elements that water dissolves, and the color.

GREEN VEGETABLES: drop prepared vegetables into a little boiling salted water.

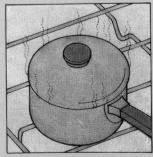

Bring back to the boil as quickly as possible, cover pan and cook steadily.

Boiling root vegetables

Root vegetables, on the other hand, must be cooked right through to break up the plant cells. Starting from cold helps to ensure that the center is cooked.

ROOT VEGETABLES: cover the prepared vegetables with plenty of cold water; add salt.

Bring water to the boil, and boil steadily, uncovered, until cooked through but not mushy.

AMERICAN BOILED DINNER

Serves 6

1 lb. bacon unsliced, if possible
1 boiling fowl, cut into pieces
1 large onion, halved
1 stalk celery, halved
1 bay leaf
2 sprigs thyme
1 tsp. coarse salt
8 black peppercorns
2 leeks, cut in thick slices
2 large carrots, cut in slices
1 cabbage, cut in quarters

Put the bacon and chicken pieces in a flameproof casserole, cover with cold water and bring to the boil, skimming as it approaches boiling point, until the surface is clear. Then add the halved onion and celery, bay leaf, thyme, salt and peppercorns. Simmer for 1¾ hours, then add leeks, carrots and cabbage. Bring back to the boil and simmer another 45 minutes.

To serve: take out the bacon, remove rind, and cut in fairly thick slices. Have some soup plates heated, and put some bacon and chicken in each one. (It looks more appetizing if the chicken is cut off the bone, but this is optional.) Add some leeks, carrots and cabbage (discarding the onion, celery, and herbs), and pour the soup over them. Eat with knife, fork, and spoon. For a more substantial meal, this can be served with a bowl of plain boiled potatoes on the table. This is a simple version of the traditional New England boiled dinner, a family dish that needs nothing before or afterwards.

HARD-BOILED EGGS IN CURRY SAUCE

Serves 3–4

6–8 eggs
Curry Sauce:
2 tbsp. butter
1½ tsp. light curry powder
2 tbsp. flour
1 cup chicken stock (preferably homemade)
½ cup light cream
1 tbsp. lemon juice
salt and black pepper

Take eggs out of the refrigerator at least 1 hour before using them to bring them to room temperature. Put them in a pan, cover with cold water, add a little salt, and bring to the boil. Adjust the heat so that the water boils gently and cook for 12 minutes from the moment it reaches boiling point. Take them out with a slotted spoon and plunge into a bowl of cold water. Shell them carefully; very fresh eggs are hard to shell. It helps to tap them all over first, so that the shell is broken into quite small fragments. When they are shelled, drop them into a bowl of very hot water while you make the sauce. If making in advance, they can be reheated later.

Melt the butter, add the curry powder and the flour, and cook for 1 minute, stirring. Then add the heated stock gradually, stirring until blended. Simmer for 3 minutes, stirring now and then, before adding the cream, lemon juice, and salt and pepper to taste. Lift the eggs out of the hot water and put them in a bowl. Pour over the sauce.

Serve hot with rice. If making in advance, pour the sauce over the eggs in their bowl and leave to cool. Later, stand the bowl over a saucepan of boiling water to reheat. For a cold dish, cool the sauce quickly by standing in a sink half full of very cold water, stirring the sauce to prevent a skin forming. Pour it over the eggs just before serving; do not chill. Serve with rice and a green salad. It goes well with vegetable curries, curried lentils, etc., in which case it will serve 6–8.

GAMMON OR HAM WITH EGG AND PARSLEY SAUCE

Serves 6

3½–4 lb. rolled gammon or ham, smoked or unsmoked
1 large onion, halved
1 large carrot, halved
1 stalk celery, halved
3 cloves
1 bay leaf
3 stalks parsley
10 black peppercorns
Egg and Parsley Sauce:
2 tbsp. butter
2 tbsp. flour
1 cup of gammon or ham stock
⅓ cup light cream
black pepper
ground mace, or nutmeg
¼ cup parsley
2 hard-boiled eggs, chopped

Soak smoked ham for a few hours before cooking, but not unsmoked ham, which is less salty. When ready to cook, put the drained ham in a flameproof casserole or pressure cooker and cover with cold water. Bring slowly towards boiling point, stopping when the bubbles start to rise to the surface. Skim until no more scum rises to the surface, then add the halved vegetables, cloves, herbs and peppercorns.

If using an ordinary pot adjust the heat so the water barely simmers, cover and cook for 1½–1¾ hours. If using a pressure cooker, cover and screw down the lid after skimming, bring to the boil, and cook under pressure for 30–35 minutes. Lift out the ham and keep warm.

Strain the stock and measure 1 cup for the sauce. Melt the butter, add the flour, and cook for 1 minute, stirring. Pour in the hot stock gradually, stirring till blended, and simmer gently for 3 minutes. Then add the cream, black pepper, and a little mace or nutmeg. (If the stock is too salty, use half stock and half milk and omit the cream.) Stir in the chopped parsley and eggs, and pour into a sauceboat or bowl.

To serve: carve the ham and serve with the sauce, boiled potatoes, and boiled leeks or carrots. If the stock is not too salty, keep it for making soup; Corn Chowder, Lentil, Cabbage and split pea soup are all good made with ham stock.

BEEFSTEAK PIE

Serves 4

2 lb. chuck steak
2 medium onions, thinly sliced
2 medium carrots, thinly sliced
salt and black pepper
Suet Dough:
2 cups self-raising flour
½ tsp salt
¼ lb. shredded suet or lard
little iced water

Cut meat into pieces about 2 inches square. Lay them in a sauté pan with a lid, or a broad saucepan with a heavy base. Cover with the onions and carrots, pour in enough boiling water to just barely cover the contents, add salt and pepper and bring to the boil. Skim once or twice, cover the pan, and simmer for 30 minutes.

Towards the end of the time, make suet dough: mix suet or lard with flour and salt. Rub in lightly with fingertips. Add water, mix with a knife blade until it holds together, and use right away. Roll out quite thickly into a circle slightly smaller than circumference of the pan, using the lid as a guide. Lay carefully over the meat, cover with the lid and cook another 1½ hours.

To serve: cut the pastry in quarters and lift on to a plate. Transfer the stew to a shallow dish and lay the pastry triangles on top. Accompany with boiled potatoes and a green vegetable. This is an old fashioned English dish, simple in the extreme but very good. I prefer it to a steak pudding since it is much quicker to make, and not as heavy.

Variation: for steak and Kidney Pie, add ½ lb. ox kidney, cut in cubes, at the same time as the meat.

SUET DUMPLINGS

Serves 6

1½ cups self-rising flour
3 oz. shredded suet
¼ tsp. salt
a little water

Mix suet with flour and salt. Rub in lightly with fingertips. Add water and mix with a knife blade until it holds together. Form into balls, slightly smaller than a ping-pong ball (it should make about 15), and drop into a pan of simmering stock. Cook for 20 minutes. Although it would seem logical to cook the dumplings in the dish they are to accompany, this is tricky since they must boil gently in order to be light, while the meat should be just *below* boiling point so as not to become tough; so cook them in the stock after the beef has been removed.

MARROW DUMPLINGS

Serves 4

6 large marrow bones
1 egg
a pinch of salt
about 2 cups soft white breadcrumbs
1 tbsp. finely chopped chervil

Scoop out the marrow and weigh it; you should have about 1½ oz. Warm it gently in a small pan. When half melted, remove from heat and beat with a wooden spoon. Add beaten egg and salt and beat again. Stir in chervil and breadcrumbs, stopping when you have a soft, firm dough. Leave 30 minutes, then divide into balls not much bigger than your thumbnail, rolling them between your palms. Have a pan of lightly salted water or stock on the boil. Drop in the little dumplings, cover, simmer for 4–5 minutes, then drain.

Serve in a chicken or game consommé. They are particularly light and delicious.

78 *Compôte of Apricots with Vanilla Cream*

HERB DUMPLINGS

Serves 4

½ cup self-rising flour
a pinch of salt
1 tbsp. butter
1 large egg
1 tbsp. finely chopped parsley

Sift the flour and salt into a food processor, or bowl. Using a food processor add the other ingredients and process until smooth. If making by hand, cut in the butter in small bits. Then beat the egg, add the chopped parsley, and beat again, then stir into the flour. Beat until smooth.

Have a broad pan of lightly salted boiling water, or stock. Drop in small teaspoonfuls of the dough and boil gently, covered, for 12 minutes, turning them over halfway through. Lift out with a slotted spoon and drain.

Serve in a beef consommé, or on top of a beef casserole. These are much smaller and lighter than suet dumplings.

Variation: use chervil or dill instead of parsley for serving in a chicken or game stock, or with a chicken casserole. Use fennel for fish soups.

VEGETABLE PUDDING

Serves 4–6

6 large leeks, cut in 1 inch slices, or ¾ lb.
*   large mushrooms, halved and thickly*
*   sliced*
2 tbsp. butter
salt and black pepper
¼ cup beef or chicken stock
1 tbsp. lemon juice (for mushrooms only)
<u>Suet Dough</u>:
3 cups self-rising flour, sifted
¾ tsp. salt
6 oz. shredded suet
little iced water

Grease a 4 cup bowl. Mix suet with flour and salt. Rub in lightly with fingertips. Add water and mix with a knife blade until it holds together. Divide in two pieces, one roughly twice the size of the other. Roll out the large piece thinly into a large circle. Sprinkle with flour and fold in half, to make a semi-circle. Roll the straight edge gently, stretching it slightly to form a pouch, then open out the pastry and drop into the greased bowl.

Fill with leeks or mushrooms, dot with butter, and sprinkle with salt and pepper. Pour in the stock, and lemon juice, if used. Roll out the rest of the pastry. Dampen the edges of the pastry around the rim of the bowl and lay the rest of the crust over it.

Trim the edges, and press together to seal. Cover loosely with a buttered piece of foil, tied around the edge with string.

Find a saucepan large enough to hold the pudding easily: it will be boiling hot when you have to lift it out so if there is not much room for your fingers to get around the bowl, stand it in a square of cloth and use the edges to lift it in and out. Put an old saucer, inverted, on the bottom of the pan. Stand the bowl on it and pour in water until it comes halfway up the sides of the bowl. Remove bowl, bring the water to a fast boil, then replace in pan, cover and boil steadily for 2½ hours, checking now and then to see if the water needs replenishing. (Use boiling water so as not to lower the temperature for a moment.)

To serve: lift out and remove the foil. Serve with a beef casserole, or boiled beef.

COMPOTE OF APRICOTS WITH VANILLA CREAM

Serves 5–6

1½–2 lb. fresh apricots, halved and pitted
5 tbsp. homemade vanilla sugar, or
*   superfine sugar*
<u>Vanilla Cream</u>: *(see below)*

Choose a broad saucepan with a heavy bottom. Put in ¾ inch water, add the vanilla sugar (or superfine sugar and ¼ vanilla pod), and bring slowly to the boil. Cook until sugar has melted, then put in as many halved apricots as will fit in one layer. Cover and poach gently until they are soft when pierced with a fork (2–6 minutes, depending on their ripeness). Then remove them to a serving dish and cook another layer. When all are cooked, remove the apricots (and vanilla pod), and boil up the syrup for a few minutes to reduce. Pour it over the apricots and leave to cool but do not chill; serve at room temperature.

VANILLA CREAM

½ cup whipping cream
½ cup yogurt
1 egg white, stiffly beaten
2 tbsp. homemade vanilla sugar, or
*   superfine sugar*

Whip the cream, beat the yogurt until smooth, and mix together lightly. Fold in the beaten egg white, and the sugar. If you don't have any homemade vanilla sugar, use superfine sugar, and a few drops of vanilla extract, if you wish. Serve in a bowl.

—MENUS—

Some suggestions for well balanced meals based on the poaching recipes

PARMA HAM
or Serrano ham, or coppa,
with ricotta

POACHED CHICKEN
with Watercress Sauce
new potatoes, carrots and snow peas

COMPOTE OF PEARS
served cold with cream

WATERCRESS SOUP

COLD POACHED SALMON
with Mayonnaise
new potatoes, lettuce salad

SMALL PLUM TARTS
served warm, with cream

SPINACH AND MOZZARELLA SALAD

HAM
WITH EGG AND PARSLEY SAUCE
boiled potatoes, carrots and leeks

MIXED GREEN AND PURPLE
GRAPES, ICED

Vegetarian Menu

SIMPLE BORSCHT
(made with vegetable stock)

STEAMED VEGETABLE MOLD
with Tomato Coulis

ORANGE JELLY

FRYING

Fried food can be the best or worst of dishes, depending on the quality of the ingredients and the skill – or care – of the cook. Well-fried food is light and delicious, and absorbs a surprisingly small amount of oil. (This can be tested by measuring the amount of oil before and after frying.) If the oil is brought to the correct temperature before adding the food, a crust forms almost immediately on the outside, so that the minimum of oil is absorbed.

There are three basic forms of frying in general use: deep frying, shallow frying (or sautéing) and stir-frying. (The latter has only become popular in the West over the past ten or twelve years, but I believe it is here to stay.)

Deep frying All food must be given a protective coating before deep frying. This is done for a number of reasons: (a) to protect it from the heat of the oil; (b) to prevent any moisture in the food itself coming in contact with the oil, which would cause it to spit dangerously, and (c) to prevent the flavor of the food contaminating the oil. A skilled chef can fry fish and sweet fritters in succession without any hangover of flavors, but I would not advise this for beginners. It is safest to keep oil for frying fish separate.

The coating may be a simple one of milk and flour, or beaten egg and breadcrumbs, or batter. There are many different batters; I generally use a light all-purpose one, equally good for savory or sweet foods, except for tempura, which demands a special treatment.

Much as I love tempura, fritters, and croquettes, I am not a great advocate of deep frying. It makes the house smell, it is potentially dangerous, and it is uneconomical, unless done frequently. None the less, it is worth mastering, for it embodies the principles of frying, and once learned it may be kept for special occasions. I often cook foods that should really be deep fried in a $\frac{1}{2}$ inch layer of oil in a deep frying pan. This works fairly well with goujons of fish and croquettes, although the finished appearance of the dish is not perfect. Only foods encased in batter absolutely *have* to be deep fried.

Deep frying is usually done in a deep straight-sided pan with a wire basket. I prefer to use a wok, however,

since its shape is so economical of oil, which is important if you fry rarely. Neither is the basket essential; a Chinese mesh scoop is just as useful. The only danger of deep frying in a wok is that the oil may overheat, since the metal is thin, so you must watch it carefully.

Shallow frying, or sautéing Compared to deep frying, this is child's play. The French word *sauter* means to jump; this process involves shaking the pan backwards and forwards, so that the food does, literally, jump about. For this reason, it is best done in a deep frying pan. The choice of fat, or oil, is a personal one; there are a number of different ones, each with their own characteristic. I use a mixture of butter and oil for the most part, since the butter gives a good flavor, while the oil prevents it burning. For light dishes I use sunflower seed oil, alone or mixed with a little butter. For foods that absorb a lot of oil, such as sliced eggplant, I use peanut oil, which is slightly cheaper.

First warm the pan, then add the butter or oil and heat to the desired temperature before putting in the food. Make sure this is well dried, for any moisture will make the fat spit. The oil should never reach more than halfway up the sides of the food. Have plenty of paper towels ready, for all fried foods should be drained before serving, and make sure that plates and dishes are hot.

Stir-frying This is quick and adaptable, ideal for throwing together a meal at a moment's notice for one or two friends. It is not suitable for a larger number of people, however, unless you are experienced, nor for a formal occasion; since it has to be done at the last moment, and with fierce heat, it tends to produce a somewhat hectic atmosphere. I never do it for more than three people, nor do I ever attempt more than two hot dishes. One of these, a basic fried rice or noodles, can be made slightly in advance and kept hot, while the main dish demands your whole attention.

Although the Chinese often use lard for stir-frying, I like to use sunflower seed oil. It is helpful to have a few Chinese sauces and seasonings to add the appropriate flavors; sesame oil and a good soy sauce are almost essential, while oyster sauce, plum sauce and hoisin sauce are fun to have around.

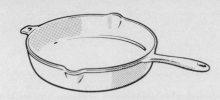

Sauté pan with lid on its own, useful for frying chicken and other bulky items. With lid, invaluable for frying onions without browning, braising small items, and doubles as a casserole.

Crèpe pan for crèpes and pancakes: it can double as a griddle.

Flat whisk, handy for beating a sauce in a frying pan where a balloon whisk won't work.

Griddle: the traditional shape for making drop scones, frying potato cakes, chapatis and any food needing minimum fat eg. hamburgers.

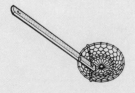

Wire mesh scoop for lifting food out of hot oil.

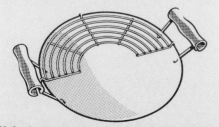

Wok, the most economical shape for deep frying. Clip-on wire rack drains food after cooking.

"The Shikian restaurant on the Sumida River," by Kubo Shumman, 1757–1820. By courtesy of the British Museum.

MASTER RECIPE

TEMPURA

This Japanese dish is a good example of deep frying at its most spectacular, and makes a fabulous dish for an informal supper party. Don't try to make it for too many people, however, or do anything else at the same time, as it demands your whole attention. It needs nothing else, either before or after, except fresh fruit salad.

Serves 4

12 jumbo shrimp, uncooked
½ lb. monkfish, filleted
1 eggplant
1 green pepper
1 Spanish onion
4 small zucchini
4 flowers broccoli, or parsley
¼ lb. small mushrooms
1 lotus root, canned
frying oil
Dipping Sauce:
½ cup chicken stock
⅓ cup soy sauce
⅓ cup sweet vermouth, or sweet sherry, or
   mirin (Japanese rice wine)
1 tbsp. grated daikon (Japanese radish), or
   horseradish
1 tbsp. grated fresh ginger root
Batter:
1 egg
1 cup iced water
1 cup all-purpose flour

First prepare the main ingredients: shell the shrimp, leaving on the tails and the last joint, and discard the vein that runs down the center of the back. Cut the monkfish in strips about 2 × ¾ inches and ½ inch thick. Cut the eggplant in half, cut most of the flesh away leaving about ⅛ inch layer clinging to the skin, then cut the skin in fan shapes, about 1½ inches long. Cut the pepper in strips 2 × ¾ inches. Slice the fattest part of the onion ⅛ inch thick, and separate it into rings; use 8 large rings. Cut the zucchini in half lengthwise, then across in half. Divide the broccoli into sprigs, or the parsley into large clumps. Cut the mushrooms in half, and cut 8 slices of lotus root ⅛ inch thick.
Make the dipping sauce: mix the stock, soy sauce, and vermouth, sherry, or mirin. Pour into 4 small bowls, and divide the grated radish and ginger between them. Set one by each place.
82 *Make the batter:* beat the egg in a large

bowl, and add the iced water, continuing to beat. When all is mixed, fold in sifted flour, being careful not to mix it too well. It should not be thoroughly blended and must be used at once.

Meanwhile, heat the oil in a wok, or deep fryer, to 360–380°F. If you do not have a thermometer, test by dropping in a small cube of dry bread: it should start to sizzle and brown immediately.

Dip each ingredient in the batter, starting with the shrimp; shake off excess, and drop into the hot oil. Don't do too many at once, and only cook one ingredient at a time. Drain on paper towels as soon as they are done; they will take about 2 minutes to become crisp, but do not expect them to brown much. They should stay quite pale, with the batter rather patchy, not quite covering them totally. Ideally the batter should form an uneven coating on emerging from the oil, incorporating a few bubbles, and be crisp and very pale.

As each batch is cooked, transfer them to a hot dish, and serve as soon as possible. Alternatively, cook all the shrimp and half the vegetables and serve, then fry the fish and remaining vegetables for second helpings.
To serve: this should really be eaten with chopsticks, but fingers do very well. Dip each food in sauce before eating.
Variation: tempura is a very adaptable dish, and the ingredients can vary according to availability. Shrimp can be replaced by small squid, while any of the vegetables can be replaced by strips of carrot, snow peas, whole scallions, etc.

Jancis Robinson's wine choice:
It seems sensible when eating Japanese to drink Japanese too. Saké (pronounced something like "sah-kay") is made by steaming and fermenting rice and is usually stronger than table wine but less alcoholic than port and sherry. It is traditionally served warm in little china cups and tastes slightly sweet and oily to my western palate, but seems to go well with tempura. At home you could always serve saké in coffee cups (though not to Japanese purists).

Tempura: top left, the raw ingredients;
right, prepared for dipping;
foreground, battered and fried.

TIPS ON DEEP FRYING

✳ *A thermometer is valuable for beginners: it minimizes the risks of overheating the oil, which is both dangerous and detrimental to the oil, and avoids underheating it, which spoils the food. Most foods cook best at temperatures ranging from 360°F to 380°F.*

✳ *All food needs a protective coating of flour, breadcrumbs or batter before being deep fried.*

✳ *Have food prepared beforehand, and well dried; but only dip in coating while oil heats.*

✳ *Don't leave the kitchen at any stage, either while the oil is heating, or during the actual frying. It may overheat and catch alight while you are out of the room.*

✳ *Don't use stale oil. Allow to cool after frying, then strain into a pitcher. When cold, pour into a wide-mouthed jar with lid and cover. Don't use more than three or four times; throw it away if it becomes dark.*

✳ *Use a wire or mesh scoop, or frying basket, for lifting food in and out of the hot oil. Don't*

use a basket for foods encased in batter, since the wire will cut through the coating and stick to the food.

✳ *Have plenty of paper towels ready, laid out for draining; all fried food should be drained before serving.*

✳ *Have very hot plates and dishes.*

✳ *Sprinkle desserts (i.e. sweet fritters) with granulated or confectioner's sugar after draining.*

FAMILY OF RECIPES

GOUJONS OF SOLE

Serves 6

3 Dover sole, skinned and filleted
2 large egg yolks
2 tbsp. olive oil
2 tbsp. water
dry breadcrumbs
frying oil

Cut the skinned fillets in diagonal strips about ¾ inch wide. Beat the egg yolks with the olive oil and water. Dip the strips of fish in the egg mixture, then in breadcrumbs, shaking off any excess. Have a wok or large pan with oil heated to approx. 360°F. If you do not have a thermometer, test by dropping in a small cube of dry bread. It should start to sizzle immediately, and turn golden brown quite quickly. Cook the goujons quickly, turning them once or twice with a slotted spoon. Do not do too many at once as they must be able to float freely. They will take 2½–3 minutes altogether. Drain while you fry the next batch, then transfer to a hot dish.
Serve immediately, with Fried Parsley (see following recipe) and lemon quarters.

Goujons of Sole with Fried Parsley

FRIED PARSLEY

Serves 6

12 large sprigs parsley
frying oil

If it is necessary to wash the parsley, shake it well, and pat dry in a cloth. Heat some oil in a wok or deep pan to approx. 325°F: it must not be much hotter or the parsley will burn. Drop in the parsley, a few sprigs at a time, and cook for about 30 seconds on each side. It will turn bright emerald green and become very crisp, almost brittle. Drain on paper towels, and serve with fried fish. This is a pretty garnish that is rarely seen nowadays.

ZUCCHINI FRITTERS WITH GARLIC SAUCE

Serves 6 as a first course

6 small to medium zucchini
frying oil
Batter:
1 cup flour, sifted
a pinch of salt
3 tbsp. sunflower seed oil
¾ cup warm water
1 egg white
Garlic Sauce: *(see below)*

Make the batter in advance. Sift flour and salt into food processor or a large bowl. Add the oil and process or beat by hand, then add the water gradually, continuing to beat or process until a smooth cream. Let stand for 1 hour, then process or beat again. Beat the egg white until thick, and fold in.

Cut the unpeeled zucchini in diagonal slices about ¼ inch thick. Dip them in the batter, scraping off any excess on the side of the bowl. Drop into hot oil and fry 2 minutes on each side. Do not crowd them. Drain on paper towels while the next batch cooks, then transfer to a hot dish, and serve with the Garlic Sauce (see below).
Variation: substitute slices of eggplant, or of large firm tomatoes, for the zucchini, or have a mixture of all three. Eggplant slices should be sprinkled with salt and left to drain for 30 minutes, then dried, before frying.

GARLIC SAUCE

1 cup yogurt
2 cloves garlic, crushed
½ tsp. sea salt

Beat yogurt until smooth, then stir in the garlic and salt. Chill, before serving.

STUFFED SQUASH FLOWERS

These are made with the flowers of the zucchini, or other squash. In Italy and the south of France, these are sold in the markets, in sacks; in England, this recipe will only be of practical interest to gardeners. Be careful to pick only the male flowers until the fruit has formed; once the zucchini is big enough to be eaten, the female flowers may also be cut.

Serves 4 as a first course

24 zucchini flowers
frying oil
2 lemons, cut in quarters
Stuffing:
1 medium onion, chopped
2 tbsp. sunflower seed oil
1 small clove garlic, finely chopped
¼ cup rice
½ lb. spinach, or ¼ lb. frozen leaf spinach
salt and black pepper
⅓ cup grated Parmesan
1 egg, beaten with 1 egg yolk
Batter:
1 cup flour, sifted
a pinch of salt
3 tbsp. sunflower seed oil
½ cup tepid water
1 egg white, beaten

First make the stuffing: cook the onion in the oil, adding the garlic halfway through. Set aside. Cook the rice as usual in lightly salted boiling water; drain well. If using fresh spinach, drop into lightly salted boiling water and cook for 4–5 minutes, then drain. When cool enough to handle, squeeze out excess water and chop. If using frozen spinach, cook according to instructions, drain, squeeze out water, and chop. Reheat onion and garlic, stir in the rice and cook for a moment or two, then remove from the heat and stir in the chopped spinach. Add salt and pepper to taste, Parmesan, and beaten egg and egg yolk. Leave to cool.
Make the batter following the recipe for Zucchini Fritters (see above left). Set aside to rest for 1 hour.

When the stuffing is cool, spoon it carefully into the flowers, folding over the petals to enclose it. Have a wok or deep pan with oil heated to 360°F. Beat the batter, fold in the beaten egg white, then dip each stuffed flower in it, scraping off excess on the side of the bowl. Drop them a few at a time into the hot oil, and cook for about 4 minutes, turning once. Lift out and drain on paper towels, then transfer to a hot dish while you fry the rest.
Serve immediately, with lemon quarters.

Common elder flower makes delicious fritters

ELDER FLOWER FRITTERS

This delicate dish can only be made in early summer, when the elder is in flower. Pick the young heads only. These fritters are very popular in the countries of central Europe, in Austria, Czechoslovakia, and Poland, where they are served both as a vegetable dish and as a dessert.

Serves 6

18 elder flower heads
frying oil
superfine sugar, if serving as a dessert
Batter:
1 cup flour, sifted
a pinch of salt
3 tbsp. sunflower seed oil
¼ cup tepid water
1 egg white, beaten

Make the batter an hour beforehand (see recipe for Zucchini Fritters opposite). Have a wok or deep pan with oil heated to approximately 360°F. Beat the batter once more and fold in the beaten egg white. Dip each flower head in the batter, shaking off the excess, and drop into the hot oil. Do not crowd them. Cook for 2–3 minutes, turning once, then lift out and drain on paper towels. Put another batch into the oil, and transfer the first batch to a hot dish.
To serve: when all are done, serve immediately, as a vegetable. They go well with dry dishes of veal or chicken, roast, grilled or fried, as long as there is no sauce. To serve as a dessert, sprinkle with superfine sugar just before serving, and garnish with lemon quarters.
Variation: this can also be made with zucchini flowers, but omitting the sugar. It can then be served with lemon quarters as a first course.

CROQUETTES

These should be very crisp outside, and soft and melting within. They must be served as soon as made, either as a first course, or as a light main dish served with a sauce and a green salad, or in extra small sizes, for nibbling with drinks.

Serves 6

Egg Croquettes:
6 hard-boiled eggs, finely chopped
½ bunch scallions, finely chopped
salt and black pepper
2 tbsp. finely chopped parsley
Spinach Croquettes:
½ lb. finely chopped cooked spinach (start
    with 1 lb. fresh or 14 oz. frozen leaf
    spinach)
6 oz. mozzarella, cut in ¼ inch cubes
salt and black pepper
⅓ cup grated Parmesan
Fish Croquettes:
½ lb. finely chopped cooked haddock, fresh
    or smoked, or a mixture of both
1 cup milk
¾ cup grated Gruyère
salt and black pepper
2 tbsp. finely chopped parsley
Binding Sauce:
1½ cups milk (for egg and spinach
    croquettes only)
¼ small onion
¼ bay leaf
salt and black pepper
a pinch of mace, or nutmeg
3 tbsp. butter
3 tbsp. flour
Coating:
2 egg yolks, beaten with 2 tbsp. milk
flour
dry breadcrumbs

Start a day, or a few hours, in advance.
Egg Croquettes: hard boil the eggs, then, shell and chop finely. Chop the scallions and the parsley, and mix all together, seasoning well.
Spinach Croquettes: drop fresh spinach into lightly salted boiling water and cook 4–5 minutes. (If using frozen spinach, heat slowly until soft, without adding any liquid at all.) Drain in a colander, refresh under cold running water, and leave to cool. Then squeeze out excess moisture between the hands and chop finely by hand. Turn into a bowl, stir in the mozzarella, and add salt and pepper, and Parmesan, to taste.
Fish Croquettes: best made with a mixture of fresh and smoked haddock. Put the fish into a broad pan and cover with a mixture of milk and water. If using any smoked fish, don't add salt. Bring to the boil, turn off the heat, cover, and let stand for 10 minutes, then drain, reserving the stock. Strain, measure 1½ cups and use to make the sauce. When the fish is cool enough to handle, flake it, discarding all skin and bone, then chop quite finely. Place in a bowl, add salt (if needed), pepper, cheese and parsley.
Make the sauce: for egg and spinach croquettes, put the milk in a small pan with the onion, bay leaf, salt, pepper, and mace or nutmeg. Bring slowly to the boil, turn off the heat, and leave, covered, for 20 minutes. Then strain the milk and reheat. For fish croquettes, use the fish stock. Melt the butter in a clean pan, add the flour, and cook for 1 minute, stirring. Add the hot milk or stock, stir until blended, then simmer for 3 minutes, adding salt and pepper to taste, and stirring often. Remove from the heat, and stir in the prepared ingredient, eggs, spinach, or fish.

Place in a shallow dish or metal tray and chill for a few hours, or overnight, in the refrigerator. This will firm up the mixture enough to handle easily, but if you don't have time, you can chill it for 20–30 minutes in the freezer.

When ready to cook, form the mixture into small ovals, or whatever shape you like. Dip them first in flour, then in egg beaten with a little milk, then in breadcrumbs. Have a pan of hot oil ready; it should be about 360°F. Drop in the croquettes, a few at a time, and fry for 2–3 minutes, turning over once, until golden brown. Remember that the inside is already cooked, so they just need long enough to brown the outside and heat through. Drain on paper towels while you fry the next batch, then transfer to a hot dish.

Serve as soon as all are cooked. All three are good served with spicy Tomato and Pepper Sauce, or simply on their own.

TIPS ON SHALLOW FRYING

✳*Good quality frying pans with thick bases are essential; one with a thin, uneven base will cause food to stick and burn. Ideally, you should have several; one large shallow frying pan for things that take up space, such as sliced eggplant; a small one for frying an egg; a deep frying pan, or sauté pan, for frying chicken, onions, etc., and an oval one kept especially for fish as fish, particularly some oily ones, have a peculiarly tenacious smell which could taint other types of food.*

✳*Have a choice of different fats and oils for frying different foods. I mostly use butter mixed with olive oil, or sunflower seed oil or peanut oil. Save every speck of fat from roasting beef, goose, duck, or chicken, store in the refrigerator carefully labeled, and use within ten days for frying potatoes, braising vegetables, and making soups of fresh or fried vegetables.*

✳*Don't keep a frying pan half full of oil on the back of the stove. This is both visually unappealing and unhygienic.*

CHICKEN MARYLAND

Serves 4

3–3½ lb. roasting chicken, cut in quarters, or
    4 lb. chicken, cut in serving pieces
6 tbsp. flour
salt
1 tsp. paprika
1 tsp. ground black pepper
a pinch of cayenne
2 eggs, beaten with ¼ cup milk
about ⅔ cup frying oil

I leave the skin on the chicken pieces, but it may be removed, if preferred. Dip the pieces in the flour, mixed with the salt, paprika, pepper, and cayenne. Then dip them in the beaten eggs and milk, then again in the seasoned flour. Heat some oil in a deep frying pan, or sauté pan. When it is hot, put in the legs and thighs, adding the breasts and wings 5 minutes later. Turn them once during the frying, allowing 20 minutes for the dark meat and 15 minutes for the white. Drain on paper towels and serve with Corn Fritters.

CORN FRITTERS

Serves 4

½ lb. corn kernels, preferably fresh, cut off
    the cob, but frozen will do (allow 2–3
    ears corn)
⅓ cup heavy cream
3 tbsp. flour
½ tsp. baking powder
salt and black pepper
½ tsp. sugar

Cut the kernels off the corn (see step-by-step instructions, opposite). Put them in a mixing bowl and stir in the cream, then add the flour, baking powder, salt, pepper and sugar. Mix well. Heat a griddle or large frying pan and grease it lightly with a small bit of butter. Drop spoonfuls of the corn batter into it, flattening them slightly with a spatula and trying to allow a few holes to develop, giving a lacy effect. Cook until golden brown, turning once, about 4 minutes on each side.

    This is the traditional accompaniment to Chicken Maryland, but is delicious with almost any fried or grilled food, especially ham, bacon, and chicken.

Chicken Maryland with Corn Fritters

*Cooking oils come in many different flavors, strengths and prices
and it is worth experimenting to find one you like.
These are some of my favorites.*

CALF'S LIVER WITH ORANGE JUICE

Serves 6

*6 thin slices calf's liver
4 tbsp. butter
¼ cup sunflower seed oil
6 shallots, finely chopped
½ cup chopped parsley
½ cup orange juice
salt and black pepper*

Heat the butter in a frying pan, add the liver, 2 slices at a time, and cook briefly on each side. It only takes about 1 minute on each side if really thin; it should still be faintly pink in the center. Remove to a hot dish and cook the rest of the liver, adding more butter if needed. When all the liver is cooked, add the oil to the pan, reheat, and fry the chopped shallots for about 2 minutes, until golden. Add the parsley, salt and pepper and mix, then stir in the orange juice. Swirl around a couple of times, then spoon carefully over the slices of liver.
Serve immediately, with broccoli.

FRIED POTATOES

Serves 3–4

The best fried potatoes are thinly sliced when raw, and fried in goose fat. Whole cloves of unpeeled garlic can be added for those who like it. Duck or chicken fat, or oil, can be used instead of goose fat.

*1 lb. potatoes, peeled and thinly sliced
6 tbsp. goose, duck, or chicken fat, or oil
1–3 large cloves garlic, unpeeled
sea salt and black pepper*

The potatoes can be sliced in a food processor, or with a mandoline, or by hand. Wash them well in a large bowl of cold water to get rid of excess starch, then drain them in a colander, and pat dry in a cloth. Heat the fat (or oil) in a deep frying pan, or sauté pan. Put in the sliced potatoes, adding the garlic if used. Cook gently for 15–20 minutes, turning them over from time to time with a spatula. They will break up a bit, but it doesn't matter. Drain on paper towels before serving; they

should be very brown and crisp.
To serve: they are absolutely delicious with broiled, fried, or roast meat or poultry, but would not go well with anything that has a sauce, such as a casserole.

SOLE MEUNIÈRE

Serves 2

*2 Dover sole (or lemon sole), head, tail and
    side fins removed
a little milk
seasoned flour
4 tbsp. butter
chopped parsley
1 tbsp. lemon juice*

I leave the skin on, since it protects the flesh from drying out, and the pale skin becomes crisp and delicious, while the black skin may be left uneaten on the plate, but you may prefer it skinned. Wash fish and pat dry in paper towels. Dip them first in milk, and then in seasoned flour. Heat half the butter in a frying pan (an oval one, if possible) and put in the sole, pale side down. Cook for 5 minutes, then turn and cook for another 5 minutes.

When they are done, transfer them to a hot dish, pale side up, and keep warm. Add the remaining butter to the pan (if the first lot has blackened, throw it out and start again with 4 tbsp. fresh butter). When it is hot, add the parsley and lemon juice and swirl around for a minute or two, then pour over the fish.
Serve with boiled or steamed potatoes. No other vegetable is necessary, although you can have broccoli, leaf spinach, or green beans if you like.

Cutting corn off a cob

After removing the outer leaves, pull away the silky hairs.

Slice kernels off cob on to a flat surface, using a sharp knife.

Transfer to bowl. Using back of knife, scrape cob so the milky juice runs into bowl.

HUEVOS CUBANOS (CUBAN FRIED EGGS)

Serves 4

$\frac{3}{4}$ cup rice
1 large onion, chopped
about 6 tbsp. butter
salt and black pepper
4 strips thick-sliced bacon
2 bananas
4 large eggs

Cook the rice in lightly salted boiling water until just tender; drain in a colander. Cook the onion in about half the butter until pale golden, then add the rice and stir around to coat with fat. When well mixed, turn into a greased 2 cup ring mold. (If you don't have a ring mold, simply make a bed of rice in a shallow dish.) Keep it warm while you cook the other things.

Cut each bacon strip into three and fry in a very little butter until crisp and golden. Drain on paper towels, then keep warm. Cut the bananas in half, then split each half lengthwise. Fry them also in the butter, adding more if required, until lightly browned. Finally, fry the eggs in fresh butter.

To serve: invert the ring mold on to a flat dish. Lay the bacon and banana strips over it diagonally, and the eggs around it. Fill the center with Tomato and Pepper Sauce or Ragú. Serve, as a light main dish, with a green salad.

Variation: to make a vegetarian dish, simply omit the bacon.

SHRIMP WITH GARLIC

Serves 3

$\frac{1}{3}$ cup olive oil
3 cloves garlic, finely chopped
1 lb. shelled shrimp, uncooked if possible
salt and black pepper
2 tbsp. finely chopped parsley

Heat the oil in a frying pan, add the garlic, and cook gently for about 2 minutes, until it starts to color. Watch it all the time; if it burns you must throw it away and start again. Once it starts to brown, add the shrimp and cook gently 5–6 minutes (for uncooked shrimp), or 2 minutes for cooked ones. When they are done, add salt and pepper and stir in the parsley.

Serve immediately, with bread and butter for a first course, or with boiled rice and a green salad as a light main dish.

Cleaning and preparing squid

1 Whole squid, may be fresh or frozen.

2 Pull head and its attachments out of body sac.

3 Cut across head just above eyes, discarding all below that line.

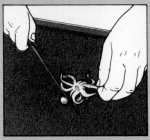
4 Squeeze out small polyp in center of head and discard.

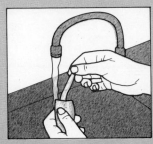
5 Wash sac under cold running water; pull out and discard transparent fin.

6 Squeeze out any odd bits and pieces inside body sac and discard.

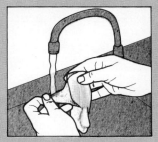
7 Pull away and discard mottled pink skin which covers body.

8 Cut off triangular side fins and keep.

9 Cut sac in $\frac{1}{4}$ inch rings; leave tentacles whole if small, or halve or cut into pairs.

TIPS ON STIR-FRYING

＊Best done in a wok, but a round flameproof casserole or deep frying pan will do in a pinch. The advantages of the wok are (a) it heats up very quickly, (b) its shape enables the cook to fling the food about without running the risk of tossing it over the edge, and (c) it is very economical in terms of oil.

＊I prefer to use a flat-bottomed wok over a gas flame. Although not strictly authentic, the flat bottom allows it to sit firmly on the flame without tipping. Even if you have a round-bottomed wok, learn to use it without the ring, for this lifts it too high from the flame. Ideally, the flames should sweep up the sides of the pan, as if cooking in a brazier, as many of the Chinese do.

＊When starting to cook, have everything prepared beforehand, but only start to cook at the last moment. Most stir-fried dishes only take 2–3 minutes, and can even be made during a commercial break on TV. Serve immediately, straight from the wok, or pan.

STIR-FRIED SQUID WITH GINGER

Serves 3–4

1 lb. small squid, fresh or frozen
$\frac{1}{4}$ cup sunflower seed oil
4 scallions, chopped
1 tbsp. ginger root, finely chopped
1 tsp. sugar
$\frac{1}{2}$ tsp. sea salt
1 tbsp. dry vermouth, or sherry

Prepare the squid (see step-by-step instructions), cutting the sac in rings about $\frac{1}{4}$ inch wide, and leaving the tentacles in clumps. Heat a wok or deep frying pan, add the oil, and heat again. Put in the squid and stir-fry furiously for 2–3 minutes, adding the scallions and ginger halfway through. When the time is up, add the sugar, salt, and vermouth (or sherry). Toss all together for another minute.

Serve with fried rice.

STIR-FRIED SCALLOPS

Serves 2–3

12 large fresh scallops, or 1 lb. frozen
*   scallops*
2 tbsp. sunflower seed oil
¼ small onion, finely chopped
1 tsp. ginger root, finely chopped
1 small green chili, seeded and finely
*   chopped*
juice of 1 orange
juice of 1 lime, or ½ lemon
a few drops soy sauce
2 tbsp. chopped parsley

Cut the scallops in quarters, discarding the orange part. (If using frozen scallops, thaw them first.) Heat a wok or deep frying pan, add the oil, and heat again. Put in the onion and toss for 1 minute, then add the ginger and chili and toss for a further 30 seconds. Put in the scallops, and stir-fry for 2–3 minutes. Then add the fruit juice and soy sauce and stir for another minute. Finally, stir in the chopped parsley.

Serve accompanied with fried rice or noodles as a light main dish, followed by a green or mixed salad.

Variation: this is especially good when made with tiny bay scallops. In which case, leave them whole.

STIR-FRIED RICE

Serves 4

¾ cup uncooked rice, or about 2 cups cooked
*   rice*
2 tbsp. sunflower seed oil
½ medium onion, thinly sliced
2 strips thick-sliced bacon, cut in thin strips
a few shakes soy sauce

This is often made with left over boiled rice, but is best done with rice cooked specially, 2–3 hours beforehand. Whichever you use, make sure it is well drained. Heat the oil in a wok or deep frying pan; do not let it get too hot, or the onion will burn. Put in the onion and toss until it starts to change color, then add the bacon strips and continue to stir-fry until all is light golden. Add the cooked rice and toss continuously for 2–3 minutes, until well mixed and reheated. Sprinkle with soy sauce. A few cooked green peas, or a small omelette cut in shreds, may also be added.

Serve as an accompaniment to other stir-fried dishes.

It is one of the few stir-fried dishes that can be made a little in advance and kept hot without spoiling.

Variation: substitute 6 oz. thin noodles, cooked, for the rice.

—MENUS—

**Some suggestions for well balanced meals
based on the poaching recipes**

TEMPURA

LETTUCE, ORANGE AND ALMOND
SALAD

PETITS POTS DE CREME AU CAFE

POACHING SAUSAGE EN CROÛTE
with Mustard and Horseradish Sauce

GOUJONS OF SOLE
with Fried Parsley

WALNUT AND CHICORY SALAD
with goat's cheese

ORIENTAL SALAD
with toasted pitta bread

CHICKEN MARYLAND
with Corn Fritters

SLICED PEACHES, STRAWBERRIES
AND MELONS
with lime juice

Vegetarian Menu

STUFFED ZUCCHINI FLOWERS

ONION TART
made with yeast pastry
green salad

APPLES, CELERY AND
ENGLISH CHEESES

Stir-fried Squid with Ginger

GRILLING & BROILING

Grilling is a fierce and uncompromising technique, since the food is cooked by direct exposure to intense heat. Only prime cuts of meat can stand up to this barrage of heat and still emerge tender and juicy. Thus steaks, chops and cutlets are the obvious choice, although a cheaper cut like breast of lamb can be braised first, then grilled, to give a crisp exterior.

Fish presents no such problems, however, since it is never tough. Even the cheaper, oily fish such as sardines and mackerel are good cooked in this way. White fish needs careful basting to prevent it drying out, however, especially when cut into steaks, without the protection of its skin.

Marinades can be used with fish and meat, both to keep them moist while cooking, and to introduce other flavors. Grilled food is invariably appetizing, with its crisp golden finish. The smell of meat grilling over wood or charcoal must be one of the most evocative in the whole range of kitchen processes.

Methods of Grilling

Over wood Wood is just as good, if not better, than charcoal for grilling. Some woods, like apple and other fruit woods, impart their own special flavor, but any good hard wood is satisfactory. Lime or any sort of fir, however, give off an acrid smoke. Any keen cook who has an open fire in their house should experiment with this form of cooking, since it is both delicious and appealing. It is not hard to contrive a homemade grill over the fire. Try an old oven rack, supported by bricks. Remember that it is a messy business however, one that is better suited to a cottage than to a smart living room.

Over charcoal This is usually associated with open-air cooking, but a few lucky cooks have barbecues built into their kitchen. This is not hard to do if you have a disused fireplace, or at least a flue. (Charcoal must have ventilation, as the fumes are poisonous.) Those with a garden can build their own barbecue, using a few bricks and a metal rack. This may be one made especially for this purpose or a sturdy wire cake rack which is cheaper and works equally well. If this seems a bit informal for a dinner party, remember that some grilled food is just as good cold as hot, and can be cooked in advance.

Domestic Broilers Broilers today are usually placed in the top part of the oven, allowing you to adjust the distance between the food and the heating element, which I find more important than adjusting the heat of the broiler. I always use the broiler at its hottest; almost all food wants an initial period of intense heat, to form a crust that seals the surface and prevents the inside drying. If the food needs longer cooking, it can then be moved further away from the heat. Broiled food must be served immediately, or left to get cold; it cannot be kept hot or reheated, without becoming tough and dry.

Cast iron grill pans These are a relatively new development. They are made of black cast iron, with ridges running across their entire surface, so the food cooks by contact with raised bars of hot iron. It is more like dry-frying than grilling, but the results are delicious; in fact, this may be the answer for cooks with unsatisfactory broilers and no space for barbecues.

Cast-iron grill pan Excellent for steaks, and for toasting French bread.

Stainless steel and wood skewers: steel skewers should be flat, as cooked food slips while round skewers turn within it. Wooden skewers are also useful for serving food at buffets.

Tongs are useful for turning food while cooking.

Baskets for barbecuing or grilling over the open fire. The large one, in tinned metal, is useful for meat: the fish-shaped one is ideal for grilling trout.

"Girl with Green and Red Jacket" 1939, by Balthus. Collection, The Museum of Modern Art, New York. Helen Acheson Bequest.

TIPS ON BROILING AND GRILLING
❊*Always have the broiler very hot before starting to cook.*
❊*Never season meat before broiling; the salt will draw out the juices.*
❊*Only start to cook at the last moment; broiled food becomes tough and dry if is is kept waiting or – worse still – reheated. It can be cooked ahead, however, and served cold.*

❊*If possible, have a separate grid for cooking fish, and always line the broiling pan with foil. If you don't have a separate grid, lay the fish directly on the foil, or the grid will smell of fish forever.*
❊*Oily fish like sardines and mackerel make the whole house smell when grilling or broiling. Have the kitchen well-ventilated, and shut the door to the rest of the house.*

❊*Fish, especially white fish cut into steaks, needs constant basting while cooking; this can be done with melted butter or a light oil such as sunflower seed oil.*
❊*In general, don't serve the basting juices from fish with the food; they are best discarded.*
❊*Serve on very hot plates, and have sharp knives for eating grilled or broiled meat.*

91

92   Boned Leg of Lamb grilled over the fire, with a Potato Cake and a mixed salad; and, to start, toasted slices of French bread with savory spreads.

MASTER RECIPE

BONED LEG OF LAMB GRILLED OVER THE FIRE

Serves 6

One 4½ lb. leg of lamb (ask your butcher to bone the lamb and open it out into a flat, rectangular shape – you don't want it rolled and tied. Alternatively you can bone it yourself using our step-by-step guide, page 94. If cooking over the fire buy New Zealand lamb for tender domestic lamb is wasted on such a fierce heat)

Light the fire at least an hour in advance and tend it carefully so that it is really hot in the center with a good area of glowing heat. Have a rack arranged in advance, lying over the fire a few inches above the flames, supported on each side by bricks or square-cut logs.

Lay the lamb on this, skin side down. Don't bother with seasonings, herbs or marinades. The fat will drip down, causing the flames to flare up and envelop the meat. Don't panic: this is meant to happen. They will eventually die down. Cook for 7 to 8 minutes, then turn and cook another 7 to 8 minutes on the other side. The meat should now be ready.

To serve: lay on a wooden platter, cut in fairly thick slices, and serve with fruit jelly (rowan, crab apple or redcurrant), a Potato Cake or a Potato Purée, and a green, or mixed salad.

This method of cooking demands total confidence on the part of the cook. Guests are appalled as they see a perfectly good looking piece of meat reduced to a charred and blackened object, one third smaller than it was and looking more like an old boot than the main course. Faint-hearted cooks sometimes wrap the meat in foil after a preliminary browning but there is no need. I have cooked lamb this way for years and it is never less than delicious. However it does impose its own style on the occasion: since the meat must not be left, a first course is ruled out and it is better to nibble something with drinks while watching the meat cook. This might be small squares of pizza or quiche; crudités with a dip; little sausages or prunes wrapped in bacon and then grilled; toasted French bread with a Provençal spread such as Tapénade or Anchoïade; or toasted cheese topped with anchovy.

Variation (if cooking under an oven broiler, the lamb should be marinated):
Marinade:
¼ cup olive oil
juice of ½ lemon
black pepper
a few sprigs thyme, rosemary and marjoram, or 1 tsp. dried oregano

About 2 hours before cooking, lay the lamb, skin side down, in a dish, dribble the oil and lemon juice over it, and sprinkle with pepper and herbs. leave for 2 hours.

Preheat the broiler as hot as possible. Lay the lamb under it, still skin side down, and broil for about 12 minutes. Turn and broil another 12 minutes. (The turning depends on the heat of the broiler and the thickness of the meat; it is soon learned with practice.)

Serve as for lamb cooked over the fire. Although less delicious than meat cooked over wood or charcoal, this still makes a good dish and one that is easy to cook. There is also less shrinkage than when the meat is subjected to the very fierce heat of the open fire.

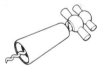

Jancis Robinson's wine choice:
For this Master Recipe, it makes sense to go to the respective lands of the "bar-B-Q" and "barbie" for red wine ripe enough to complement the fruit jelly. The more sunshine the grapes get, the sweeter even a red wine will taste, and this is evident in those from California and Australia. California's native grape Zinfandel would, with its warm berry flavor, be perfect. Australia's equivalent is the Shiraz, a grape producing powerful, earthy wines.

Boning a leg of lamb

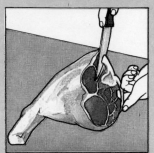

There are three bones to be extracted: the pelvic bone, the middle bone and the shank bone. First cut around and pull out the pelvic bone which sticks out at the wide end.

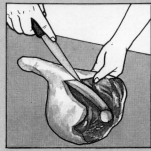

Feel for the middle bone with your fingers. Slit leg above it and cut it out, easing around the joint where it meets the shank bone. Remove the shank bone in the same way.

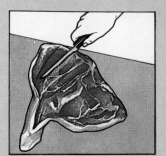

To open out the meat as flat as possible, make two further parallel cuts through the two thickest seams of meat, one on either side of the space left by the middle bone.

Cut off pointed narrow end, and beat the meat once or twice with a wooden mallet, to even out the thickness. It should be roughly rectangular in shape.

FAMILY OF RECIPES

GRILLED BREAST OF LAMB

Serves 3–4

1 breast of lamb
1 onion, sliced
1 leek, sliced
1 large carrot, sliced
2 tbsp. dripping, or butter
2 cups beef stock
salt and black pepper
1 large egg, beaten
½–¾ cup dry breadcrumbs
4 tbsp. butter, melted
2 tbsp. olive oil

Cook the sliced vegetables for 5 minutes in the fat, in a large saucepan. Then pour over the stock, and lay the breast of lamb, folded over, on top. Add salt and pepper, bring to the boil, and simmer 1 hour 45 minutes. Remove the lamb, and leave to cool a little.

When the meat is cool enough to handle, slide out the bones, using a small knife to help loosen them. Cut the meat in strips about 1 inch wide, and dip them first in beaten egg and then in breadcrumbs. Lay them on the rack of the broiling pan, baste with melted butter and oil, and broil for 5 minutes. They should be brown and crisp all over. Turn them, baste again, and broil for another 5 minutes.

Serve on a flat plate, with a Mustard and Horseradish Sauce. This makes a good and very inexpensive dish as a first course, or a light main dish. It needs no other accompaniment, and is a good dish to serve after a hearty soup, such as minestrone.

GRILLED SKEWERS OF LAMB

Serves 4–5

½ boned leg, or shoulder, of lamb
Marinade:
2 tbsp. onion, finely chopped
2 tbsp. parsley, chopped
coarsely ground black pepper
4 tbsp. lemon juice
½ cup olive oil

Start well in advance. Cut the lamb in neat cubes, quite small. Put them in a bowl. Make the marinade: beat all the ingredients together and pour over the lamb. Leave for several hours, or overnight, turning over once or twice, if possible.

When ready to cook, thread the pieces of meat on to skewers, being careful not to crowd them. Preheat the broiler, then lay the skewers on the broiling pan and cook them briskly, turning over and over and basting with the marinade. They should be well browned on the outside and still very slightly pink in the center. Test one to see when they are cooked.

Serve still on the skewers, with rice, or noodles, or hot flat bread. Accompany them with a mixed salad, and a Cucumber and Yogurt Salad.

VEAL CHOPS WITH GINGER

Serves 6

6 veal chops
Marinade:
¼ cup soy sauce
¼ cup moist brown sugar, packed
2 tbsp. olive oil
2 cloves garlic, finely chopped
2 tsp. ginger, peeled and finely chopped
a little black pepper

A few hours in advance, make the marinade, mixing all the ingredients together in a bowl. Lay the veal chops in a shallow dish and spoon some of the marinade over them. Leave for an hour, then turn them and baste on the other side with more of the marinade. Leave for 2–4 hours before cooking. Then heat the broiler to its hottest, lay the chops on the rack of the broiling pan, and cook for 10 minutes, basting with more of the marinade halfway through. Turn them over and repeat the process, cooking for another 10 minutes, basting once or twice, and watching that they do not burn. They should be nicely browned without being blackened. It may be necessary to move them around once or twice, so that they cook evenly.

Serve with noodles and a green salad. Pork chops may be used instead of veal.

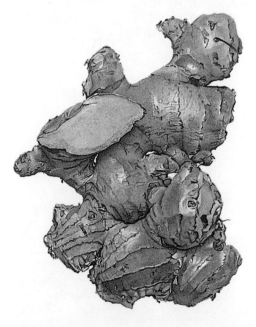

GINGER ROOT is useful for marinades, and for giving an oriental flavor. Keeps for a week or two in the refrigerator.

BROILED PORK LOIN WITH SESAME SEEDS

Serves 6

3½ lb. loin of pork, boned but not rolled, without kidney
2 tsp. sesame seeds
Marinade:
¼ cup light soy sauce
¼ cup dry vermouth
2 tbsp. finely chopped shallots
coarsely ground black pepper

Remove the crackling and cut the pork in slices ½ inch thick. Lay them in a shallow dish. Mix the marinade and paint the meat with it on both sides. Leave for 1–2 hours, then heat the broiler. Lay the pork slices on the broiling pan and scatter half the sesame seeds over them. Place the pan some distance from the broiler, and cook gently for about 3 minutes, until nicely browned. Then turn them over, scatter with the remaining sesame seeds, and cook another 3–4 minutes, turning them around if necessary, to cook evenly all over.
Serve with steamed (or poached) snow peas, and noodles, rice, or new potatoes.

BARBECUED SPARERIBS

Serves 6 as a first course

3 lb. spareribs (make sure your butcher understands you want spareribs for barbecuing. You can buy them either in racks, or cut up by the butcher)
Marinade One:
½ cup grapefruit juice
⅓ cup white wine vinegar
⅓ cup moist brown sugar, packed
2 tbsp. Dijon mustard
or Marinade Two:
1 medium onion, chopped
¼ cup olive oil
¼ cup tomato paste
⅓ cup white wine vinegar
¾ cup chicken stock
2 tbsp. honey
1 tsp. Dijon mustard
1 large clove garlic, crushed
½ bay leaf, crumbled
1 tsp. dried oregano
salt and black pepper
a dash Tabasco

Start the day before, or several hours in advance. Choose your marinade; the first is very simple and quick to make, but the second repays the effort if you can spare the time. To make the first: simply mix the ingredients together in a bowl 3–4 hours before cooking, lay the ribs in a shallow dish, and spoon some of the marinade over them. Leave for a few hours, turning and basting now and then. To make the second: cook the onion slowly in the oil until soft, then mix the tomato purée and vinegar to a paste and stir into the onion. Add the heated stock, then stir in the honey, mustard, garlic, and herbs. Cover, and simmer for 15 minutes, stirring often. If it gets too thick add a little extra stock. Add the dash of Tabasco and leave to cool before using.

Heat the broiler to its hottest, and line the broiling pan with foil. (This is essential, otherwise you will ruin your pan.) Lay the ribs on the foil, using the rack. Cook them 15 minutes on each side, basting now and then with the marinade. They need to be well browned, almost black in places, without being actually burned. Move them around as well as turning them, so they brown evenly.
Serve on a flat dish. If you use the second, tomato-based marinade, there may be enough left over to use as a dripping sauce. If so, purée it briefly in the food processor, adding a drop of stock to thin it if necessary, and serve in a small bowl.
For a main course: allow 1 lb. per head, but it is impossible to fit more than 2½–3 lb. in the average broiling pan. They can be cooked in the oven, in two roasting pans, one above the other, for 1 hour at 450°F. In this case, line the oven floor as well as the pans with foil, and switch the pans around half-way through. They can also be cooked on a barbecue, but not over a living room fire as they are too messy.

GRILLED SIRLOIN (ENTRECOTE) STEAKS

Serves 2

2 sirloin steaks

Heat a cast iron grill pan for 2 or 3 minutes until very hot. Lightly grease the ridges with a small piece of fat from the steaks. Lay steaks across the ridges and cook briskly for 2–2½ minutes, then slide a small spatula under them and turn them over. Cook another 2–2½ minutes, depending on their thickness and your taste. (The timing is soon learned by experience.)
Serve immediately on hot plates, either alone or with Parsley Butter. Accompany with a Potato Purée and a salad.

HERB BUTTERS

These delicious accompaniments to grills are very simple to make. Start some hours in advance and make double or triple quantities if you prefer and freeze the remainder in foil. This is a good way of using up small amounts of fresh herbs before the winter comes.

Parsley butter:
6 tbsp. butter
3 tbsp. chopped parsley
1 clove crushed garlic
1 tbsp. lemon juice
sea salt and black pepper

Cream the butter in a food processor, adding parsley, garlic, lemon juice, and salt and pepper to taste. Wrap in plastic wrap and chill for 20–30 minutes until firm. Then form into an even roll about 1 inch across. Chill again until hard, then cut into thick slices to serve. Good with grilled steaks, sole or cod, but omit the garlic when serving with fish.
Mint butter: substitute 2 tbsp. chopped mint for the parsley. Serve with lamb chops and cutlets, or broiled tomatoes.
Sage butter: substitute 1 tbsp. chopped sage for the parsley. Serve with veal or lamb chops or whole baked onions.
Mixed herb butter: substitute 2 tsp. chopped mixed herbs: (2 tsp. each tarragon, chervil, dill, mint and chives for the parsley. Serve with grilled meat or fish, or grilled tomatoes.

THE VERSATILE POTATO

Potato cake

Potato purée

Baked potatoes
in their jackets

Waffle-cut chips

French fried,
or shoestring potatoes

New potatoes,
boiled in their skins

Potato salad,
with chopped chives

Roast potatoes

Potato gratin

POTATO PUREE

A creamy purée of potatoes is the best possible accompaniment for grilled or boiled food, since it provides a good contrast.

Serves 6

2 lb. potatoes
sea salt and black pepper
1 cup milk
½ cup butter

Boil the potatoes until tender, but be careful not to overcook them. Drain well, then return to the pan and shake over a very low heat for a moment or two, to drive off excess moisture. Push through a medium food mill into the cleaned pan, and stir for another minute or two over a low heat. Warm the milk and butter in a small pan, adding lots of salt and black pepper. When the butter has melted, beat it into the potatoes with a wooden spoon. The consistency of the purée can be adjusted by altering the amount of milk. Transfer to a hot dish to serve.

POTATO CAKE

This is particularly good served with broiled or roast meat, or with fried bacon and eggs, or cold meat.

2 lb. poatoes, peeled and cut in half
2 large leeks, or 1 large onion, sliced
4 tbsp. butter
salt and black pepper

Boil the potatoes until tender. Meanwhile, cook the sliced leeks or onion slowly in 3 tbsp. butter in a deep frying pan or sauté pan until browned. When the potatoes are ready, drain them in a colander, then push through a medium food mill. Stir in the browned leeks (or onions) and their fat, adding lots of salt and black pepper. Melt the remaining butter in a shallow frying pan or crêpe pan with a heavy bottom. (Make sure that the pan is not too heavy to lift, for it has to be inverted at the end.) Swirl the butter around so that the entire surface of the pan is greased, including the sides. Turn the potato mixture into the pan, spreading it evenly with a spatula. Cook over low heat for about 25 minutes (30 minutes if reheating from cold).
To serve: turn out on to a flat dish, cutting in wedges like a cake. It should make a flat cake about 1–1½ inches thick, with a crisp brown casing. Don't worry if the brown part sticks to the pan, simply lift it out with a spatula and lay it over the potato cake.

Potato cake, for serving with roast, grilled or broiled or cold meats (see right).
Creamy potato purée, for serving with roasts and grills, and casseroles (see right).
Baked potatoes, with butter or sour cream: serve with grills, roasts, casseroles and cold meat.
Waffle-cut chips, cut with a mandoline; good with grilled steaks.
French fries, for serving with grilled steaks.
New potatoes, boiled in their skins: serve

with broiled or roast meat. With fish they are better peeled.
Potato salad, dressed while still warm with olive oil and vinegar (or with yogurt and mayonnaise), chopped spring onions or chives and parsley. Serve with cold meats.
Roast potatoes, best made with duck or goose fat, or beef dripping.
Potato gratin, thinly sliced potatoes baked in egg and milk (or stock). Excellent with roast lamb or game.

TANDOORI CHICKEN

Serves 6

*One and a half 3½ lb. roasting chickens, cut
   into serving pieces*
Marinade:
*1 tbsp. Dijon mustard
½ cup sunflower seed oil
½ cup yogurt
1 tbsp. fresh ginger, chopped
½ tsp. cumin seeds
½ tsp. coriander seeds
½ tsp. ground turmeric
juice of 1 lemon
1 green chili, seeded and finely minced*

Start well in advance. Put the mustard in a
bowl and add the oil, drop by drop, as if
making a mayonnaise. When all is absorbed, stir in the yogurt, which you have
beaten until smooth. Put the ginger into a
mortar with the cumin and coriander seeds
and the ground turmeric. Pound until
reduced to a powder, then add the lemon
juice to make a paste. Stir into the yogurt
mixture, adding the chili.

Take the skin off the chicken pieces and
make small diagonal cuts in them here and
there with the point of a sharp knife. Rub
the marinade all over the chicken and leave
for 6 to 24 hours. (If leaving it overnight it
is best to put it in the refrigerator.)

When ready to cook, preheat the broiler,
lay the chicken pieces in the broiling pan,
and cook for about 15 minutes on each
side. Watch them carefully, and turn them
around giving them a chance to brown
evenly all over.

To serve: lay on a bed of lettuce leaves and
serve with *nan* (flat unleavened bread which
can be bought from an Indian restaurant),
or with Saffron Rice, and an Avocado and
Tomato Salad. A dish of chopped
cucumber in garlic-flavored yogurt goes
well with tandoori chicken.

BROILED SPRING CHICKENS

Serves 4–6

*2 spring chickens, cut in quarters
2 bunches watercess*
Marinade:
*Dijon mustard
olive oil
juice of 1 or 2 lemons
black pepper*

Start about 2 hours before cooking. Paint
the chicken pieces on the skin side with
Dijon mustard, lay them in a dish, and
dribble olive oil and lemon juice all over
them, on both sides. Grind some black
pepper over them and leave for 2 hours.

Preheat the broiler until very hot, then

Tandoori Chicken

broil the chicken, skin side up, for 8–10
minutes, until very brown and half cooked.
Turn the pieces over, dribble over more oil
and lemon juice, and broil for another 8–10
minutes. The chicken should be deep
brown, almost charred, on the outside and
just cooked in the center.

Serve on a bed of watercress, with new
potatoes and a mixed salad. This marinade
can be used for spit-roasting a whole
chicken, or for barbecuing chicken pieces.
The dish is also good eaten cold.

SHRIMP GRILLED IN BACON

Serves 4

*16 jumbo shrimp, cooked (4 per person)
16 strips bacon
2–3 tbsp. olive oil*

Wrap each shelled shrimp in a strip of
bacon and thread on skewers. Brush them
with oil and grill gently for about 2 minutes
on each side, just long enough to cook the
bacon and heat the shrimp.

Serve with cut lemons, as a first course, or
on a bed of rice, accompanied by a green
salad, as a light main course.

Shrimp Grilled in Bacon

BROILED DUCK
WITH ORANGE JUICE

Serves 2

half a 5 lb. duck (ask the butcher to cut the
*   duck in half for you, and freeze the*
*   second half for another meal)*
Marinade:
1 tbsp. dark brown sugar
2 tsp. soy sauce
1 tbsp. cider vinegar
juice of 1 large orange

One or two hours before serving, heat the
oven to 400°F. Prick the skin all over with a
sharp skewer, lay the duck skin side down
on a rack in a roasting pan and roast for 20
minutes. Take out of the oven and leave for
30–45 minutes to cool. (This preliminary
roasting gets rid of most of the fat; reserve
it for frying potatoes.)

   When the duck has cooled, mix the sugar
with the soy sauce and vinegar to make a
paste, and paint it all over the skin of the
duck. Heat the broiler, then broil the duck
for 30 minutes, basting after the first 10
minutes with the orange juice, turning it
over halfway through and basting again.
Serve on a flat dish, garnished with watercress. Accompany with rice or noodles, and
a green salad.

GRILLED SHRIMP

Serves 4 as a first course

16 jumbo shrimp (4 per person), uncooked
½ cup butter
3 tbsp. lemon juice
freshly ground black pepper

Thread the shrimp on small skewers. Melt
the butter, adding lemon juice and pepper.
Grill the shrimp, basting with the melted
butter and lemon juice, allowing about 2
minutes on each side.
Serve with lemon quarters.

GRILLED SALMON STEAKS
WITH PARSLEY BUTTER

Serves 6

6 salmon steaks, about ¾ inch thick
4 tbsp. butter, melted
Parsley Butter *(see page 95)*

Melt the butter while you heat the broiler.
Then brush the salmon steaks with melted
butter and broil slowly, not too close to the
heat, about 6 minutes on the first side and 4
minutes on the other, basting once or twice.
Serve on a flat dish, with a piece of Parsley
Butter on each steak, and accompany with
new potatoes and green beans or broccoli.

BROILED TROUT

Serves 6

6 rainbow trout
salt and black pepper
6 tbsp. butter
3 tbsp. lemon juice
2 lemons

Make 2 or 3 small diagonal cuts on each
side of the trout, using a small knife with a
sharp point. Sprinkle the fish with salt and
pepper. Warm the butter in a small pan
with the lemon juice, then set aside. Heat
the broiler. When it is very hot, lay the fish
on the broiling pan and brush with some of
the butter and lemon juice. Broil them quite
close to the heat for 5 minutes, basting with
butter, then move further away for another
4 minutes. Turn them, baste again, and
repeat the process. The skins should be
brown and speckled, and the flesh tender
but still firm.
Serve on a flat dish with the remaining
butter and lemon juice poured over them,
and lemon quarters. Accompany them
with boiled or steamed potatoes. No other
vegetable is necessary, but you can serve a
green vegetable if you like, or a green salad.

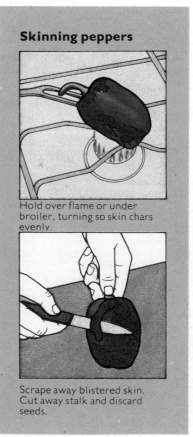

Skinning peppers

Hold over flame or under
broiler, turning so skin chars
evenly.

Scrape away blistered skin.
Cut away stalk and discard
seeds.

Green, yellow and red peppers (yellow and red are sweeter than green).
Skinning them makes them sweet and melting, and easily digested.

Grilled Pepper Salad with anchovies
and hard-boiled eggs

GRILLED HERRINGS IN OATMEAL

herrings, filleted, 2 per person
salt and black pepper
a little milk
coarse oatmeal
4–6 tbsp. butter, cut in small bits
2 lemons

Ask the fish store to fillet the herrings for you. When you get them home, wash them and dry in paper towels, removing any odd bones that have been left behind (herrings are very bony fish). Sprinkle them with salt and black pepper.

Have two shallow dishes, one half filled with milk and the other with coarse oatmeal. Dip the filleted fish first in the milk, then in oatmeal, then lay them on the broiling pan. They will probably have to be done in two batches, and kept hot. Dot them with butter and grill or broil, quite close to the heat for 4–5 minutes, until they are nicely browned, almost burned in places. Then turn them carefully, trying not to knock of the oatmeal casing, dot with more butter, and grill a minute or two less than the first side.
Serve on a flat dish, garnished with lemon quarters. Serve alone, or with boiled potatoes and sliced leeks.

BROILED DOVER SOLE, OR LEMON SOLE

1 sole per person
2 tbsp. butter and 2 tsp. lemon juice per fish
½ extra lemon per person

Ask the fish store to remove the black skin for you and to scale the white skin. Get them to trim the side fins, and remove the head and tail. (This is optional; you may keep them on if you prefer.) Melt the butter while the broiler is heating, and mix with the lemon juice. Brush the fish on both sides with the melted butter and lay on the broiling pan, skin side up. Broil them quite close to the heat for 6 minutes, basting once. Then turn them over, baste again and cook another 6 minutes, basting twice.
Serve on a flat dish, with lemon quarters (the basting juices are best discarded). Parsley butter can be served with them, and a few boiled or steamed potatoes. No other vegetable is necessary.

BROILED GRAPEFRUIT

Serves 6

3 pink grapefruit, halved
granulated sugar
6 tsp. kirsch, cointreau, calvados, or brandy

Prepare the grapefruit in advance, cutting around each section. While the grill is heating, sprinkle with sugar and pour 1 tsp. liqueur over each. Broil for 5 minutes, until the sugar has caramelized slightly.
Serve immediately, as a dessert.

GRILLED PEPPER SALAD

Serves 4 as a first course

6 large peppers (red, yellow and green when
  available, or red and green)
3 hard boiled eggs
6 anchovy fillets
2 tbsp. olive oil
freshly ground black pepper

Skin the whole peppers by grilling them over an open flame, or under the broiler, turning them constantly until the skin has blistered and blackened evenly all over. Leave to cool for a little, then scrape off skin with a knife. Cut away the stalks and inner membrane, and wash away the seeds. Cut the flesh into shapes like petals, and arrange them like a flower on a flat round dish, garnishing with the hard boiled eggs, cut into quarters, and the anchovy fillets. Pour over the olive oil and sprinkle with a little black pepper.

—MENUS—

Some suggestions for well balanced meals based on the poaching recipes

TAPENADE, OR ANCHOIADE
on lightly toasted French bread

BONED LEG OF LAMB
GRILLED OVER THE FIRE
fruit jelly, Potato Cake, green salad

COMPOTE OF PEACHES
with Vanilla Cream

VICHYSSOISE

SHRIMP GRILLED IN BACON
boiled rice, green salad

CUBED MELON, SECTIONS OF PINK
GRAPEFRUIT AND SLICED KIWI FRUIT
with fresh lime juice

SCALLOP, ARTICHOKE AND
AVOCADO SALAD

TANDOORI CHICKEN
Saffron Rice
Watercress and Orange Salad

CITRUS FRUIT SORBET

Vegetarian Menu

ARTICHOKES
served hot, with melted butter

GRILLED PEPPER SALAD
(omitting anchovies) Spinach and
Mozzarella Salad, Potato Bread

CREAM CHEESE AND WATER BISCUITS

PASTA

Quite apart from an endless variety of shapes, pasta is now available – at least to those of us lucky enough to be able to find it – in three different forms: dried; bought freshly made; and homemade – freshest of all.

Dried pasta

This can be kept for months, but not indefinitely or it will become stale. Although spaghetti and noodles are the most useful, I try to keep a few more unusual shapes as well for special dishes. Buckwheat spaghetti, bought in health food stores and eastern stores, makes excellent vegetarian dishes, and a good variation of spaghetti carbonara.

Hollow shapes such as *penne* (quills) and shells are good for serving with meat sauces, since they catch the sauce within their shape. Spaghettini (extra-thin spaghetti) is the usual shape for serving with shellfish sauces, and a quick one can be made with canned clams. Macaroni, either plain or wholewheat, is always useful for adding to thick vegetable soups like minestrone.

I usually keep two or three shapes of soup pasta, although ordinary noodles can be broken up and used for this. One of my favorites is called *risoni* and is much used in the Middle East and North Africa. This looks like rice or pine nuts, but swells to four or five times its size on cooking. I use it exactly like barley, adding it to soups or stews, with lots of chopped parsley added at the end.

If, like me, you rely on dried pasta for impromptu and inexpensive meals, it is worth devoting a corner of the store cupboard to the relevant ingredients. With a few cans of tomatoes, tomato paste, red peppers, clams, anchovies, tuna and black olives, a wide range of dishes immediately presents itself.

If you have fresh eggs, butter and cream, onions, garlic and olive oil on hand, yet more possibilities spring to mind. Chopped nuts can be combined with garlic and herbs for unusual sauces, while a small package of ground chuck steak in the freezer gives the basis of a good *ragú* at any time. Ham is always useful for pasta, as are mushrooms and herbs, dried or fresh, and Parmesan cheese.

Bought, freshly made pasta

Many shops now have deliveries of freshly made pasta two or three times a week, and it is extremely good, although expensive. Perhaps the nicest of the fresh pasta varieties are the filled ones, such as ravioli and tortellini.

Homemade pasta

Pasta is time-consuming to make, even with the help of a food processor to make the dough and a pasta machine to roll it. I would not recommend making it without, unless you have an Italian friend to advise. Even with the help of a processor and machine, it needs time and patience and enthusiasm. However, it is fun to do, and the results are worth the effort.

I find the flat pasta sheets are the most useful, but they do involve a lot of extra work in the form of fillings, sauces etc. They freeze well, though, so two or three dishes of cannelloni or lasagne can be made and frozen for a short time.

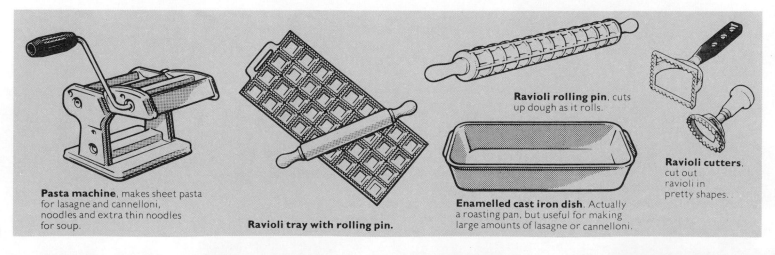

Pasta machine, makes sheet pasta for lasagne and cannelloni, noodles and extra thin noodles for soup.

Ravioli tray with rolling pin.

Ravioli rolling pin, cuts up dough as it rolls.

Enamelled cast iron dish. Actually a roasting pan, but useful for making large amounts of lasagne or cannelloni.

Ravioli cutters, cut out ravioli in pretty shapes.

"Le Déjeuner," by Édouard Vuillard, 1868–1940. Picture from Scala/Vision International. Courtesy Musée de Grenoble.

TIPS ON PREPARING PASTA

✳ *Don't keep dried pasta too long or it will become stale and tasteless.*

✳ *Bought fresh pasta can be kept in the refrigerator for up to a week, but is best the day it is made. (It can also be frozen.)*

✳ *Perfect pasta should be soft when cooked but still have bite ("al dente," as the Italians say).*

✳ *Have a supply of clean cloths for drying the cooked pasta.*

✳ *Don't buy grated Parmesan unless you have no choice. It is best bought in the piece and kept in a cool place (although, grated, it can be frozen). Bought grated, Parmesan is often not worth its price, unless it has been freshly grated in a reliable shop.*

✳ *Always have some dried oregano and thyme for adding to pasta sauces; these also get stale quickly and should be replaced twice a year. When possible, have a supply of fresh basil, marjoram, thyme and sage on hand.*

✳ *Prepare the kitchen before starting to make your own pasta. Put the pasta machine in a suitable place: the end of an empty table is ideal. Sprinkle table all over with flour to lay the strips of pasta on. If possible, put a narrow board under your pasta machine: it's a great help in catching and moving the pasta as it emerges from the mill. The first time you use the mill, it's useful to have a friend to help you. One person can turn the handle while the other feeds in the pasta.*

MASTER RECIPE

RAVIOLI WITH SPINACH FILLING AND PIZZAIOLA SAUCE

Serves 6 as a first course

Filling:
½ lb. spinach
1½ cups ricotta, or cottage cheese
1 egg yolk
½ cup grated Parmesan
freshly grated nutmeg
salt and black pepper
Pizzaiola Sauce: (see below)
Pasta Dough:
2 eggs plus 2 egg whites
4 tsp. olive oil
2 tsp. water
a pinch of salt
3 cups flour
Garnish:
freshly grated Parmesan

Make the filling: wash the spinach, pinching off the stalks. Bring 1 inch lightly salted water to the boil in a broad pan, throw in the spinach, and boil 4–5 minutes, depending on its quality. Drain and leave to cool. When cool enough to handle, squeeze out all the moisture between the hands, and chop roughly. Put in a food processor with the ricotta (or cottage cheese), egg yolk, Parmesan, nutmeg, salt and pepper. Process to a smooth paste, then turn into a bowl and chill for 30 minutes or so to firm.
Make the sauce (see next recipe).
Make the dough while the sauce is cooking, following step-by-step instructions 1–14 on page 104. I find it easier to make the dough in two parts. Put 1 egg and 1 egg white, 2 tsp. olive oil, 1 tsp. water, and a pinch of salt in the food processor and process for 30 seconds. Then add half the flour and process for another 30 seconds. Turn out on to a floured piece of plastic wrap, form into a ball and wrap, then rest for 5 minutes. When the time is almost up, make the second half, and wrap; this can then be left until the first batch is rolled out.

Have the pasta machine set to the broadest setting. Flatten the dough with the heel of the hand, and feed through the mill. A rather raggedy strip will emerge, but don't panic. Fold into three, making a shorter strip. Trim off any very raggedy edges and feed through again. Let it go through the broadest roller 3 times. This process takes the place of kneading, when made by hand.

Then start to move the rollers closer together, feeding the dough through each

setting once, until you are one away from the very thinnest. This is thin enough for most purposes, and not too delicate to handle. Halfway through the operation, cut the dough in half. When all is rolled out, lay the strips on a flat surface and cover with a damp cloth to prevent them drying out as that would make them brittle. Roll out the second half in the same way, and proceed to make the ravioli according to the method you are using.

Using a ravioli tray (see step-by-step instructions 15–18 on page 104): lay one strip of pasta over the tray, pushing down gently into the hollows. Using 2 teaspoons, put a tiny mound of filling – about ½ tsp. – into the center of each hollow, then cover with a second sheet of pasta. Roll up and down firmly with the small rolling pin, and tip the ravioli out of the tray on to a floured board. Separate the little envelopes by hand or by running a pastry wheel between them.
Using a special rolling pin: lay one strip of pasta on a flat surface and mark lightly with the rolling pin as a guide. Put a little mound of filling in each square, cover with a second sheet of pasta, and roll firmly.
Using a ravioli cutter: mark the first sheet of pasta lightly as a guide, then fill and cover. Cut out, separating by hand, and saving the trimmings (if using a round cutter there will be quite a lot) for soup.

When all are made, bring a broad pan of lightly salted water to the boil, and drop in the ravioli a few at a time. They must have room to float freely. Keep the water boiling steadily, allowing 2 minutes for freshly made ravioli. If made the day before and kept in the refrigerator, allow 3 minutes. While they are cooking, reheat the sauce gently, removing from the heat as soon as the butter has melted; do not allow to boil. Pile the ravioli in a warm bowl and pour the sauce over them.
Serve with a bowl of grated Parmesan.

PIZZAIOLA SAUCE

This is a good basic tomato sauce for serving with pasta or with grilled steaks.

Makes about 1 pint

1 large onion, chopped
2 tbsp. olive oil
2 large cloves garlic, crushed
2 14 oz. cans tomatoes, or 2 lb. fresh tomatoes, skinned, plus 2 tbsp. tomato paste
1 small bay leaf
1½ tsp. dried oregano
1½ tsp. sugar
salt and black pepper

Cook the onion slowly in the oil in a sauté pan or deep frying pan. Do not let it get brown. When it has softened, add the garlic and cook a few minutes longer. Then add the roughly chopped tomatoes (if using fresh tomatoes, which often have less flavor than canned ones, add the tomato paste), and the herbs and seasonings. Bring to the boil and simmer, partly covered, for 1 hour, stirring occasionally.

When it is cooked, remove the bay leaf and adjust the seasoning, purée the tomato sauce briefly – it should not be too smooth – either in the food processor, or by pushing it through a medium food mill. Reheat gently in a saucepan.
Serve in a warm bowl with the ravioli (or other pasta), and a smaller bowl of grated Parmesan.

Jancis Robinson's wine choice:
Good quality Italian reds are made to be drunk with food, especially with Italian food like pasta and a sauce as forceful as pizzaiola (see our Master Recipe). A full-bodied wine is called for, and you can't get much fuller-bodied than Amarone, the strong dry curiosity from dried Valpolicella grapes; Barolo, the great Piedmont wine made from dark, concentrated Nebbiolo grapes; and Brunello di Montalcino from Tuscany, which can cost hundreds of dollars per bottle. You can get the same effect, for less money, with a wine called Nebbiolo, or Spanna, Garrinăra or Ghemme.

The ingredients for Ravioli with Spinach filling and Pizzaiola Sauce

Making your own ravioli

1 Assemble the ingredients for the pasta: flour and salt, eggs, olive oil and water.

2 Put eggs and egg whites into the food processor.

3 Add olive oil, water and a pinch of salt.

4 Process 30 seconds.

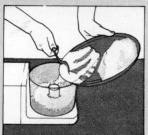

5 Add the flour and process another 30 seconds.

6 Turn out on to floured plastic wrap, form into a ball, wrap and rest 5 minutes.

7 Turn out dough on to floured table and flatten slightly.

8 Feed dough through the widest gauge roller of pasta machine.

9 Fold the pasta strip in three, trimming ragged edges; repeat stages **8** and **9** twice more.

10 Move the rollers a notch closer together; feed dough through, then fold in three.

11 Continue passing dough through, moving rollers closer each time and folding in three.

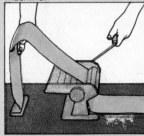

12 Use board to support strip. As dough lengthens, cut it in half for easier handling.

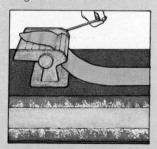

13 Feed through last time one notch from thinnest setting. Cover with a damp cloth.

14 Lay one strip of pasta over the ravioli tray, pushing it gently into the hollows.

15 Put a little mound of filling into each hollow.

16 Cover with second sheet of pasta and roll up and down firmly with the small rolling pin.

17 Turn out on to a floured table.

18 Run pastry wheel up and down to cut dough into separate little envelopes.

19 Drop the ravioli, a few at a time, into lightly salted boiling water.

20 Allow ravioli room to float freely, and cook for 2–3 minutes.

FAMILY OF RECIPES

LASAGNE

Serves 6

½ lb. fresh lasagne
1 tbsp. olive oil
Ragú *(see following recipe)*
¼ cup grated Parmesan
Béchamel Sauce:
4 tbsp. butter
5 tbsp. flour
2 cups chicken stock
1¼ cup light cream
salt and black pepper
grated nutmeg

Preheat the oven to 350°F, unless making in advance. Bring a broad pan of lightly salted water to the boil: the sheets need lots of room to float about. Drop in a few at a time, and boil steadily until they float to the top. Then test one to make sure it is cooked. If made the same day, they need only 2 minutes, but bought lasagne will probably take longer. Dried lasagne, which I don't recommend as it is often stale, can take 20 minutes to become soft. After cooking, lift them out and drop into a large bowl of cold water with 1 tbsp. olive oil in it. After a minute, lift them out and drain on a cloth. (You will need 2 or 3 clean dish towels laid out on flat surfaces around the kitchen.)

Have the ragú made in advance, and make the béchamel as usual. (Heat the butter, stir in the flour, and cook for 1 minute, stirring. Heat the stock and cream together and add gradually to the pan, stirring until blended. Simmer for 3 minutes, stirring often, then add the salt and black pepper to taste, and a pinch of nutmeg.)

To assemble: butter a shallow ovenproof dish, rectangular if possible. Make alternating layers of sauce and pasta as follows:

1 A thin layer ragú
2 A layer of lasagne, overlapping
3 A layer ragú
4 A thin layer béchamel, dribbled over the ragú
5 More lasagne
6 More ragú
7 More béchamel
8 Remaining lasagne
9 A layer béchamel covering all
10 Grated Parmesan sprinkled over the béchamel.

Spaghetti Carbonara

You can make the lasagne in advance up to this point if you wish. It can be kept in the refrigerator for a few hours, or frozen. When you are ready to cook it, bake for 35 minutes, if already warm (or 45 minutes if made in advance and reheating from cold), in a preheated 350°F oven.
Serve with a green salad.

RAGU (SAUCE BOLOGNESE)

Serves 6 with pasta

4 tbsp. butter
3 tbsp. olive oil
1 medium onion, chopped
2 ribs celery, chopped
½ lb. bacon, chopped
1½ lb. chuck steak, finely chopped (or ground)
1 tbsp. flour
2 tbsp. tomato paste
2 cups beef stock
½ cup white wine
salt and black pepper
½ tsp. dried oregano

Heat the butter and olive oil in a deep frying pan. Put in the onion, celery and bacon, and cook 5 minutes, until starting to brown. Add the chopped steak; I usually buy this in one piece and chop it in the food processor. If using ground meat, break it up with a wooden spoon, and mix with the onion, etc. Stir until lightly browned all over, then leave to cook gently for 12 minutes, stirring now and then. Then add the flour, tomato paste, stock and wine, heated together. Bring to the boil, stirring,

add salt, pepper and oregano, and simmer gently for 60 minutes, stirring occasionally, until thick. Use as directed for lasagne.
Variation: this can also be used as a sauce for spaghetti, noodles or *penne* (quills), with a green salad. In this case, do not let it get too thick: simmer about 45 minutes and add extra stock if necessary. Just before serving, stir in an extra 2 tablespoons of butter.

SPAGHETTI CARBONARA

Serves 6

⅓ lb. bacon
2 tbsp. butter
1 tbsp. olive oil
1 whole clove garlic, peeled and roughly crushed
1 medium onion, chopped
3 medium eggs
1 cup heavy cream
1 cup grated Parmesan
sea salt and black pepper
1¼ lb. spaghetti, or spaghettini

Heat a large bowl in a very low oven. Cut the bacon into thin strips. Heat the butter and oil in a deep frying pan, or sauté pan, with the garlic. When it is hot, remove the garlic and put in the chopped onion. Cook until it is pale golden, then add the bacon strips and fry until crisp. Put aside and keep warm.

Beat the eggs and mix with the cream. When blended, stir in the grated Parmesan, and salt and pepper to taste. Cook the spaghetti in plenty of salted water until tender, drain quickly in a colander, and turn into the hot bowl. Stir in the bacon and onion mixture, and immediately pour in the beaten eggs, cheese, and cream. Using two large forks, lift the spaghetti to mix, and serve immediately. Everything must be as hot as possible, and the mixing done speedily, otherwise there will not be enough heat to cook the eggs.
Serve alone, followed by a green salad.
Variation: this is also excellent made with buckwheat spaghetti, omitting the bacon and adding mushrooms: slice 6 oz. mushrooms and cook until soft in an extra 2 tablespoons of butter, then drain off their juices and mix with the onions after they have cooked. This makes a good vegetarian dish.

SPAGHETTI WITH TUNA AND OLIVES

Serves 6

14 oz. can tomatoes
1¼ lb. spaghetti
1 cup olive oil
sea salt and black pepper
⅓ cup basil, when available, cut in strips
3½–4 oz. can tuna fish, flaked
12 black olives

Put the tomatoes in the food processor with their juice and process briefly. Cook the sphaghetti in plenty of boiling salted water until it is tender. Drain quickly in a colander and turn into a large bowl. Pour over the oil and the tomato sauce, adding plenty of salt and pepper, and the chopped basil. Mix well, then scatter the flaked tuna fish and the black olives over the top.
Serve hot, warm, or cool, but not chilled. This is a useful holiday dish in that it can be served hot one evening, and cold the following day for lunch. Leave in a cool place overnight, but not in the refrigerator or the spaghetti will become tough.

SPAGHETTINI WITH SHELLFISH SAUCE

Serves 6

1 lb. mussels
1 lb. small clams, or 10–12 large clams, or
  7–8 oz. canned clams
⅓ cup olive oil
2 cloves garlic, finely chopped
¾ cup dry white wine
¼ cup finely chopped parsley
1 lb spaghettini (thin spaghetti), or
  spaghetti

Put the shellfish into a sink full of cold water and leave for 5 minutes. Discard any that are not tightly closed, or have broken shells. Clean the others very well, scraping off any barnacles with a knife, pulling away the 'beard' that protrudes from the mussels, and scrubbing with a stiff brush under cold running water. Leave in a basin of cold water until ready to use.

Heat half the oil in a flameproof casserole and put in the shellfish. (If they are very unequal in size put in the bigger ones first and add the others after 2 minutes.) Cover and cook over moderate heat for about 4 minutes, until they have opened. Watch them, taking them out as they open. Really large clams may need as much as 10 minutes, with a little boiling water added to prevent them burning. Leave the juices in the pan, while the shellfish cool in a colander.

When they are just cool enough to handle, shell the large ones. (This dish looks prettiest if some are left in their shells, but this is only practical if they are small.) Large clams should be shelled and

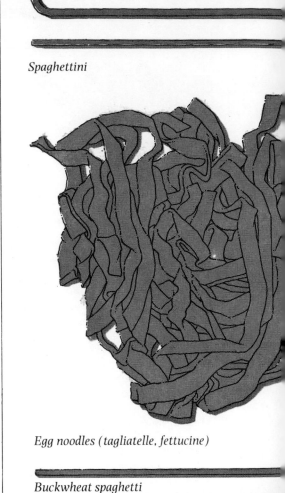

Spaghettini

Egg noodles (tagliatelle, fettucine)

Buckwheat spaghetti

Japanese noodles

chopped, while very small ones can be left in the shells. Mussels should be shelled and left whole; a few can be left in their shells to decorate the dish.

Strain the juice. Clean the pan and heat the remaining oil in it; cook the garlic for 1½–2 minutes, watching like a hawk to make sure it doesn't burn. If it does, throw it away and start again. Then add the wine and the strained fish stock and boil gently, uncovered, until reduced to about ½ cup. Add the shellfish and the parsley, cover, and remove from the heat. If using canned clams, drain them and add at this stage; they only need reheating.

Cook the pasta in plenty of boiling salted water and drain well.
To serve: turn the pasta into a large hot bowl. Pour the shellfish sauce over the spaghetti and mix, arranging a few unshelled mussels or clams over the top. Stand in a warm place, covered, for 3–4 minutes before serving.

Clams and mussels being cooked for Shellfish Sauce

VARIOUS FORMS OF PASTA (to scale)

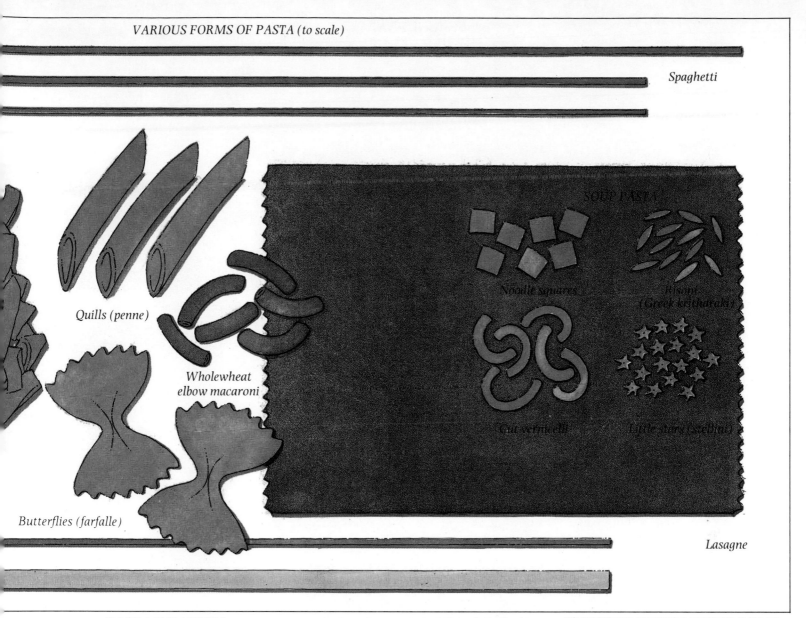

Spaghetti

Quills (penne)

Wholewheat elbow macaroni

Butterflies (farfalle)

SOUP PASTA

Noodle squares

Risoni (Greek kritharaki)

Cut vermicelli

Little stars (stellini)

Lasagne

PASTA E FAGIOLI

Serves 4–5

½ lb. dried Italian cannellini beans
1 small onion, chopped
¼ cup olive oil
⅛ lb. bacon or pancetta chopped
1 carrot, chopped
1 clove garlic, crushed
1 stalk celery, chopped
black pepper
¼ lb. fatty salt pork, or unsmoked bacon, in the piece
5 cups light chicken stock
¼ lb. spaghetti, broken into short lengths
⅓ cup parsley, chopped

Soak beans for 3–4 hours, then drain. Fry the onion in the oil for 5 minutes, then add the bacon or pancetta and cook another 2–3 minutes. Add garlic, celery and carrot, and cook all together for 5 minutes. Add the drained beans, pepper (no salt), and the salt pork or bacon. Heat the stock and pour on. Bring to the boil, skimming until the surface is clear, then cover the pan and simmer until the beans are soft, about 50 minutes.

Using a slotted spoon, lift out about one-third of the beans and purée in the food processor with a little of the liquid. Then stir the purée back into the soup. Bring back to the boil, stirring to mix well, and add the pasta. Cook gently, stirring often, for 15 minutes, or until the spaghetti is tender. If it gets too thick and starts to stick, simply cover the pan and turn off the heat. Leave for 10 minutes and the pasta will finish cooking in the heat of the soup. Remove the salt pork or bacon.
To serve: pour into a bowl and sprinkle with chopped parsley. This is like a cross between a thick soup and a creamy stew. In Italy it is often eaten with grated Parmesan, but I prefer it with parsley.

NOODLES WITH MUSHROOMS

Serves 6

¾ lb. mushrooms, sliced
¾ cup butter
1 lb. noodles
sea salt and black pepper

Cook the sliced mushrooms gently in half the butter until softened; set aside. Cook the noodles in plenty of boiling salted water, drain, and return to the pan. Stir in the remaining butter, and salt and pepper to taste, and mix in the mushrooms and their juices.
Serve with a green salad.

NOODLES WITH POPPY SEEDS

Serves 6

½ cup butter
¾ cup dry breadcrumbs
2 tbsp. poppy seeds
1 lb. noodles
sea salt and black pepper

Heat 6 tbsp. butter in a heavy frying pan. When very hot, add breadcrumbs and cook until pale golden, stirring often. When they are almost done, add poppy seeds and stir around for the last moment or two. Set aside. Cook the noodles in plenty of boiling salted water until tender, drain and return to pan. Stir in the remaining butter, salt and pepper, and mix with the crumbs and poppy seeds, tossing well.
Serve with a green salad.

NOODLES WITH SALAMI

Serves 6

¼ lb. Italian salami
¾ cup frozen Petits Pois
1 lb. noodles
3 tbsp. butter
¾ cup light cream
sea salt and black pepper

Take rind off the salami and dice small. Cook the peas and keep warm. Cook the noodles in plenty of boiling salted water until tender, drain, and return to pan. Stir in the butter, cream, chopped salami, peas, salt and pepper, and serve.

COLD ALMOND SAUCE

Serves 6 with 1¼ lb. pasta

¼ lb. almonds, blanched and skinned
3 large cloves garlic, peeled and crushed
¾ cup parsley, coarsely chopped
1 cup olive oil
sea salt and black pepper

If your almonds are still in their brown skins, you must blanch them. Pour boiling water over them and leave for a couple of minutes; then drain them, a few at a time, by lifting out with a slotted spoon, and rub the skins off between the fingers.

Put the skinned almonds into the food processor with the crushed garlic and the parsley (heads only). Process until all is evenly chopped, without being reduced to a purée. Transfer to a bowl and stir in the olive oil, adding lots of salt and pepper. Remember that salt does not dissolve in oil, so mix thoroughly and taste carefully. Set aside until ready to serve. Cook the pasta in lots of boiling water, lightly salted, and drain well.
To serve: turn pasta into a hot bowl, and pour the almond sauce over the top. Toss at the table, just before serving. This is a sauce for garlic addicts, which has the advantage of being very quickly made. Since it is served cold, over the hot pasta, it can be made a day in advance, but be sure to have really hot plates and serving dishes. Do not serve cheese with this sauce as the flavors are not complementary.

EGGPLANT AND PEPPER SAUCE

Serves 4 with ¾ lb. pasta

¾ lb. small eggplants
salt
peanut oil, for frying
1 large green, 1 large yellow, and 1 large
    red pepper, or 2 medium red and 2
    medium green peppers
¼ cup olive oil
1 large clove garlic, crushed
6 black olives, pitted
1 tbsp. capers, drained
black pepper

Cut the eggplants in slices about ½ inch thick. Sprinkle them with salt and leave to drain for an hour, then pat dry. Heat ¾ inch frying oil in a broad frying pan. When it is very hot, put in just enough eggplant slices to cover the bottom of the pan. Cook until they are golden on both sides, turning once, then drain on paper towels while you cook the next batch.

Cut the peppers in strips about 1 × ½ inch, discarding interior membranes and seeds. Heat the olive oil in a deep frying pan with lid, or sauté pan, and cook the peppers slowly, covered, for 20 minutes, adding the garlic halfway through and stirring every now and then. When the time is up, add the olives and capers and cook for another 5 minutes. Cut the fried and drained eggplant slices in broad strips and add to the pan, mixing gently so as not to break them up. Add salt and pepper, and cook gently for a final 5 minutes.

CHICKEN SAUCE

Serves 6 with 1¼ lb. pasta

3½ lb. roasting chicken
2 onions
3 carrots
3 leeks
3 stalks celery
2 cloves garlic
14 oz. can tomatoes
salt and black pepper
½ lb. mushrooms, small
4 tbsp. butter
¼ cup olive oil

Put the chicken in a casserole with a halved onion, leek, carrot, and celery stalk. Half-cover with hot water, add a little salt, and bring to the boil. Lower the heat, cover the pan, and simmer gently for 1 hour. This may be done in advance, and the bird left to cool in the stock.

Later, remove the chicken and strain the stock. Measure 1 cup, leaving behind the fat. Chop the remaining onion coarsely; cut the carrots, leeks, and celery in slices

Tagliatelle (on the scales) with the raw ingredients for Eggplant and Pepper Sauce

about ¼ inch thick, keeping them in separate piles. Crush the garlic, drain the tomatoes, and chop them roughly. Cut the mushrooms in halves or quarters according to size, or leave them whole if very small. Cut the flesh off the chicken, discarding the skin, and chop in pieces about ½ inch square.

Melt half the butter with all the oil in a deep frying pan and cook the onion and leeks for 6–8 minutes, stirring often, until they start to soften. Put the sliced carrots in a small pan, cover with lightly salted cold water, bring to the boil, and cook for 5 minutes, then drain. Add the carrots to the onion and leeks, then add the celery and cook for 5 minutes. Add the garlic and the tomatoes and cook for another 3 minutes, then add the heated stock. Bring to the boil and simmer for 20 minutes, adding salt and black pepper.

Toss the mushrooms in the remaining butter until soft, then drain and reserve. When the sauce is ready, stir in the chopped chicken and reheat, stirring, for 2–3 minutes, then add the mushrooms.
Serve with the pasta, in a separate bowl, and a green salad.
Variation: to make a vegetarian sauce for pasta simply omit the chicken, and add ⅓ lb. thickly-sliced zucchini, and ⅓ lb. green beans, cut in chunks, at the same time as the tomatoes.

TOMATO COULIS

A simple tomato sauce, good for serving with pasta of all sorts.

Serves 6 with 1½ lb. pasta

1 small onion, finely chopped
2 tbsp. butter
1 tbsp. olive oil
1 clove garlic, crushed
1¼ lb. tomatoes, fresh or canned
salt and black pepper
¼ tsp. sugar
½ small bay leaf
½ tsp. dried oregano, or 3 tbsp. fresh basil, cut in strips

Cook the onion gently in half the butter and the oil in a heavy pan. After 5 minutes, add the garlic and cook 2 minutes more. Then add the tomatoes, skinned and roughly chopped (or pulped by squeezing in the hand, if canned). Add salt and pepper, sugar, bay leaf, and dried oregano but not fresh basil. Simmer for 20–25 minutes, stirring occasionally, until it reaches the right consistency. For a thick tomato coulis, leave as it is; if a smoother version is required, purée briefly in the food processor, or push through a food mill.
To serve: a few minutes before serving, reheat, adding the remaining butter and the fresh basil, when used.

—MENUS—
Some suggestions for well balanced meals based on the pasta recipes

RAVIOLI WITH SPINACH FILLING
and Pizzaiola Sauce

COLD POACHED TROUT
WITH HORSERADISH VELOUTE
lettuce salad

MANGOES WITH LIMES

SPAGHETTINI WITH SHELLFISH
SAUCE

COLD BOILED BEEF
with Salsa Verde
mixed lettuce and tomato salad

FLOATING ISLANDS

MIXED SALAMI AND OTHER
SMOKED MEATS

LASAGNE
green salad

CITRUS FRUIT SALAD
with lime juice

Vegetarian Menu
CARROT AND TOMATO SOUP

SPAGHETTI
with Eggplant and Pepper Sauce
green salad

YOGURT
with toasted hazelnuts and honey

Peppers being cooked for Eggplant and Pepper Sauce

BAKING

In baking, food is cooked in the heat of the oven, enclosed, and without liquid. With modern ovens it is often hard to distinguish between baking and roasting: purists claim that oven-cooked meat is baked rather than roasted, but in fact, the basting that usually accompanies roasting meat makes it a sort of compromise between baking and steaming.

On the Continent, many families still use a bread oven, heated from within by burning charcoal or wood for an hour or two before baking. The ashes are then swept out, and the floor washed with a damp mop. This goes on especially in Italy, while in Greece and the Middle East few village houses have an oven at all, and dishes are still sent to the local baker's for cooking, just as they once were in England. These charcoal-fired ovens are hotter than our domestic ones, and the falling heat, combined with the steam caused by mopping the floor, suits bread perfectly. Hotter still are the Indian *tandoor* ovens, also made of clay and heated by charcoal. Their heat is so intense that a whole chicken can be cooked in ten minutes.

Domestic ovens are changing all the time, but not necessarily for the better. Some are fan-heated, with convected hot air constantly on the move, microwave ovens have their advocates. This makes it almost impossible to give exact baking times. Everything depends on the individual stove, and I strongly recommend buying an oven thermometer, and using it constantly for a few weeks.

A whole chapter could be dedicated to pastry alone, for there are so many different sorts. Since puff pastry and *filo* (or strudel leaves) can be bought, I have restricted myself to a few others, easy to make and slightly unusual. A creamy filling of leeks in a cheese pastry shell has more to offer than an ordinary quiche, while yeast pastry adds a totally different character to an onion tart, or sausage rolls.

Cakes and cookies are fun to make, and perhaps the most rewarding of all for the beginner cook. The use of food processors has transformed the creaming of butter and sugar – formerly a laborious process – into the work of minutes. I particularly like the habit of storing cookie dough in the refrigerator, only baking a little at a time, as needed.

A particularly useful branch of vegetable cookery are the baked dishes called gratins. The word gratin means a crust, which is formed on the surface of the dish by a hot oven or broiler. Although over-used in recent years by restaurants, who send dish after dish to the table, red-hot and bubbling under an identical cheese sauce, it can be used with greater subtlety. There are few more appetizing sights than a gratin of potatoes, with its crisp golden surface contrasting with the melting layers beneath. In most cases, the sliced vegetables are baked in a mixture of eggs and cream; in others, this is replaced by stock or olive oil, with onion, garlic, and herbs to flavor it.

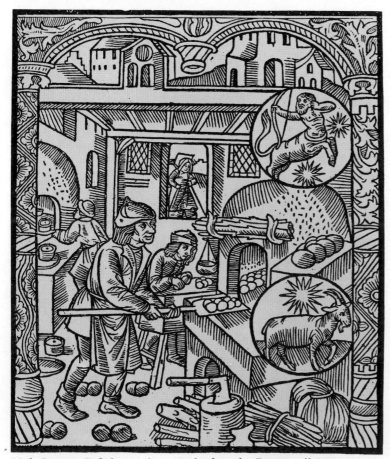

15th Century Bakehouse, from "Kalendrier des Bergeres," 1499.
with woodcuts by Pierre le Rouge. Mansell Collection, London.

"Women planting corn," 1894–6, by Olaf Krans. Courtesy Illinois Department of Conservation.

TIPS ON MAKING PASTRY

✻*For short pastry, use butter mixed with lard or vegetable shortening for an economical pastry, or butter alone if you prefer it.*

✻*Have everything very cool. Take fat out of refrigerator 30 minutes beforehand if using a food processor, or one hour if making by hand. (Some people use butter straight from the freezer and grate it coarsely.) Put water in a small pitcher with an ice cube.*

✻*The less pastry is handled the cooler – and therefore the better – it will be. For this reason it is usually better made in a food processor than by hand.*

✻*Use a cool surface for rolling: slate or marble is ideal.*

✻*Before starting to make yeast pastry, find a place slightly above room temperature where the dough can rise: for instance in the main oven with the second oven on its lowest heat.*

✻*All pastry except that made with suet is best chilled before rolling. Pastry cases should be chilled again whenever possible just before baking. This prevents shrinkage. (Suet pastry is made with self-rising flour which must be baked as soon as possible after mixing, since the rising agent in the flour starts to operate within minutes.)*

✻*If your pastry is hard and tough, you have used too much water.*

✻*If it is too soft and tears when lifted, you have used too little water, or too much fat, or soft shortening.*

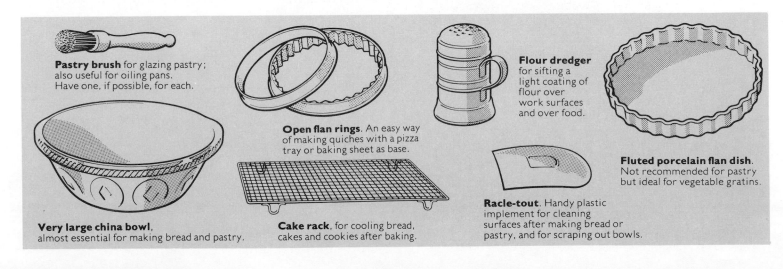

Pastry brush for glazing pastry; also useful for oiling pans. Have one, if possible, for each.

Open flan rings. An easy way of making quiches with a pizza tray or baking sheet as base.

Flour dredger for sifting a light coating of flour over work surfaces and over food.

Fluted porcelain flan dish. Not recommended for pastry but ideal for vegetable gratins.

Very large china bowl, almost essential for making bread and pastry.

Cake rack, for cooling bread, cakes and cookies after baking.

Racle-tout. Handy plastic implement for cleaning surfaces after making bread or pastry, and for scraping out bowls.

MASTER RECIPE

APPLE TART

Serves 6–8

Rich Sweet Pastry:
2 cups all-purpose flour, sifted
a pinch of salt
2 tsp. confectioner's sugar
10 tbsp. very cold butter
1 egg yolk
1 tsp. lemon juice (optional)
a few drops iced water
Glaze:
1 egg yolk, beaten with 1 tbsp. milk
Filling:
4–5 dessert apples
$\frac{1}{4}$ cup superfine sugar
2 tbsp. butter, cut in small pieces
1 cup quince or apple jelly

Make the pastry by hand or in the food processor, following step-by-step instructions overleaf. (I was taught to make pastry by an Austrian, who always added 1 or 2 tsp. of lemon juice to sweet pastry and you might like to try it: add it with the water.) Chill for 20 minutes, then roll out to line a buttered jelly roll pan measuring 12×8 inches. Chill again for 15–20 minutes before baking. Preheat oven to 400°F. Bake blind for 10 minutes (see step-by-step instructions overleaf), remove foil or beans and brush tart with the glaze. Bake another 8 minutes, then remove from the oven and leave to cool.

Core the apples, peel them and cut in half. Slice each half, fanning out the slices between the hands to make an even layer across the short width of the pan. Repeat this process until the tart is filled with parallel rows of sliced apples. Sprinkle with superfine sugar and dot with butter. Bake for 10 minutes, then lower the heat to 350°F and bake another 45 minutes. Remove from the oven. Warm the jelly in a small pan and brush over the apples. Leave to cool, but do not chill.
Serve at room temperature, with a pitcher of heavy cream.

Jancis Robinson's wine choice:
Something sweet, white and luscious is the obvious choice for a wine to savor with the apple tart. It's a shame that memories of the over-sulphured, cheap Sauternes that has been many people's introduction to wine drinking may have put them off the delicious bottles that are available from this old-fashioned area near Bordeaux. Most Sauternes with a Chateau name on the label provide superior drinking and come in clear glass bottles which allow you to judge how rich the wine is by how golden. The lighter the color, the lighter the wine usually is – and wine that looks distastefully brown can be wonderful.

FAMILY OF RECIPES

SMALL PLUM TARTS

Makes 10–12

Rich Sweet Pastry: *see Master Recipe*
Glaze:
1 egg yolk beaten with 1 tbsp. milk
Filling:
$\frac{1}{2}$ lb. dessert plums
about 2 tbsp. granulated sugar
$\frac{3}{4}$ cup apricot or apple jelly

Make the pastry following step-by-step instructions overleaf. After chilling roll out thinly and line 10–12 small pans. Chill again for 15–20 minutes before baking.

Preheat oven to 400°F. Bake the tarts blind for 6 minutes, remove foil or beans, brush with glaze and bake another 6 minutes. Remove from oven and leave to cool.

Turn down the oven to 350°F. Chop the plums into cubes about $\frac{1}{4}$ inch square. Put them in the tarts, sprinkle with sugar, about $\frac{1}{2}$ tsp. to each tart. Bake 15 minutes, then remove from the oven. Warm the jelly and brush the plums with it.
Serve warm, within the hour if possible, with cream. If serving cold, glaze with jelly 2–3 times while cooling.

TARTLETS
FILLED WITH CURRANTS

This recipe is for you if you are lucky enough to have wild currants.

Rich Sweet Pastry: *see Master Recipe, page 113*
Filling:
¾ *lb. red, white or black currants*
¼ *cup superfine sugar*
Glaze:
1 egg yolk, beaten with 1 tbsp. milk

Make pastry following step-by-step instructions opposite. After chilling roll out thinly and line 10–12 small pans. Chill again 15–20 minutes before baking. While the pastry chills, preheat the oven to 400°F, and make the filling. Pick the currants off their stalks – if using a mixture of different colors, keep them separate – and wash in a colander. Put them in a pan with the water that clings to them, and add the sugar. Cook gently for 2–4 minutes (slightly longer for blackcurrants), just until the sugar has melted and the currants start to soften, then set aside.

Take the tarts out of the fridge and bake blind for 5 minutes, then remove beans, brush all over with glaze and bake for 8–10 minutes, until light golden. Remove them and leave to cool slightly.

Just before serving, fill them with the currants. They should be served warm, or at room temperature; never chilled. If made in advance, they will need to go back in the oven at 300°F, to warm through.

BASIC PASTRY RECIPES

Short pastry
2 cups flour, sifted
¼ *tsp. salt*
4 tbsp. cold butter and 4 tbsp. lard, or 8 tbsp. butter, cut in pieces
a little iced water

Using food processor: sift flour and salt into container, add fat, process until blended, add water through lid while processing. Stop when it forms a ball. Wrap in floured plastic wrap, and chill for 20 minutes.
Making by hand: sift flour and salt into bowl, mix in fat with a knife blade, then rub lightly into flour, using fingertips, stopping as soon as mix looks like sugar, with flakes of fat evenly distributed. Add water gradually, using knife to mix. As soon as dough holds together, proceed as above.

Sweet short pastry
As above, substituting 2 tsp. confectioner's sugar for the salt.

Rich short pastry
As for short pastry but adding 1 egg yolk when fat and flour are mixed.

Rich sweet pastry
See Master Recipe, page 113.

Suet pastry
2 cups self-rising flour
½ *tsp. salt*
¼ *lb. shredded suet*
a little iced water

Mix suet with flour and salt. Rub in lightly with fingertips. Add water, mix with a knife blade until it holds together. Turn out, roll and use right away.

Cheese pastry
2 cups flour, sifted
¼ *tsp. salt*
¾ *cup grated cheddar*
6 tbsp. cold butter, diced
about 6 tbsp. iced water

Using food processor: sift flour and salt into container, add cheese and butter, process until blended. Add iced water gradually through lid while processing, stopping as soon as dough forms a ball. Transfer to plastic wrap and chill for 20 minutes.
Making by hand: sift flour and salt into large bowl. Cut in butter and cheese using two knives, one in each hand. Stir in just enough iced water to make it hold together. Proceed as above.

Cream cheese pastry
6 oz. Philadelphia or other firm cream cheese, cut in pieces
¾ *cup cold butter, cut in pieces*
2¼ *cups flour, sifted*
a pinch of salt
¾ *tsp. confectioner's sugar*

This is best made in a food processor. Process the cream cheese and butter until blended, add flour, salt and sugar and process again until mixed. Transfer to plastic wrap, form into a ball, wrap, and chill 45 minutes before using. If too firm to roll, stand the dough at room temperature for 5–10 minutes.

Yeast pastry
2 cups white bread flour
¼ *tsp. salt*
½ *oz. fresh yeast, or 1 package dried yeast*
⅓ *cup tepid water*
6 tbsp. butter, cut in pieces
1 egg, beaten

Using food processor: put flour and salt into container. Crumble yeast (if fresh), or measure out dried yeast, into warm water in a cup and stand for 10 minutes in a warm place to "proof". (It should be starting to bubble slightly, but don't worry if it doesn't.) Add butter to flour and process until blended. Pour yeast mixture and egg through lid while continuing to process. Stop as soon as it forms a ball. Turn into a greased bowl, cover with plastic wrap or a cloth, and stand in a warm place until doubled in size, about 1–1½ hours. Roll out and bake as particular recipes dictate.
Making by hand: put flour into large bowl with salt. "Proof" yeast as above, rub butter into flour, make a well in center and pour in yeast mixture and egg. Beat with a wooden spoon until well mixed and starting to hold together. Using hands, work briefly on floured board until dough forms a ball. Put into a greased bowl and proceed as above.

To make a yeast pastry quiche or pizza, roll out gently and line a flan ring, pizza tray or rectangular baking sheet, pressing gently into place with the fingers. Cover with filling and put back in the warm to rise for another 15–20 minutes before baking.

To make small filled pastries, roll out, cut and fill. Brush with beaten egg and make immediately. These do not need a second rising.

Making rich sweet pastry

By food processor
1 Sift flour into processor, add salt, sugar and butter cut in small bits. Process until mixed.

2 Add a beaten egg yolk through the lid while processing.

3 Add a very little water, first chilled with an ice cube, while processing.

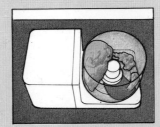

4 Stop processing as soon as the dough forms a ball. Wrap in plastic wrap and chill for 20 minutes in the refrigerator.

By hand
1 Thaw butter and assemble with sifted flour and confectioner's sugar, salt, egg yolk and 2–4 tbsp. iced water in a cup.

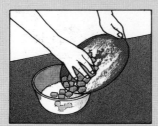

2 Cut the butter in pieces about ¼ inch square, add to the flour, sugar and salt, and mix in with a knife blade.

3 Rub in swiftly with fingertips, lifting and letting it fall back, and squeezing the fat very lightly so it merges into flour in small flakes.

4 Add an egg yolk, then a very small amount of iced water, a little at a time, to achieve the desired consistency.

5 Mix the dough with a knife blade and stop as soon as the mixture will cling together, picking up all the bits from around the sides of the bowl.

6 Form the dough into a ball, wrap in plastic wrap and chill for 20 minutes in the refrigerator. This keeps the fat firm, making light pastry that is easy to roll.

Rolling out pastry and lining a flan ring

1 Sprinkle surface and rolling pin lightly with flour, unwrap the chilled dough and form into an even circle.

2 Roll from the center outwards, away from you, in three different directions, turning the pastry.

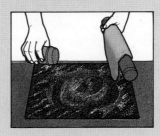

3 As you lift the pastry to turn, sprinkle more flour underneath to encourage it to spread. Don't stretch it.

4 Remember the shape of the dish you intend to line and roll accordingly, ¼ inch thick for quiches, ⅛ inch for small tarts.

5 Have pan well greased. Fold pastry over rolling pin and half lift, half side it over the tin being careful not to stretch it.

6 Allow plenty of leeway when easing the dough into the angles and be careful not to puncture it with a fingernail.

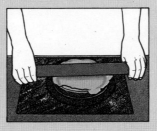

7 Trim the edges of the flan by rolling the rolling pin over the top and then removing any excess that overlaps.

8 Press gently round sides with fingertips, and chill again for 15–20 minutes, if you have time, to reduce shrinkage.

Baking blind

It is always best to bake pastry shells for flans, quiches, and tartlets blind before filling them otherwise the filling makes the base soggy. There are various ways of doing this.
1 Lay a piece of foil loosely inside the pastry shell and bake for 5–10 minutes at 400°F. Remove foil, brush all over with beaten egg and bake another 5–10 minutes. Cool before baking again, or freezing.

2 Line the shell with baking parchment weighed down with ceramic or dried beans, then proceed as in **1** above.
3 Don't use foil or paper but simply lay the ceramic beans directly on the pastry and proceed as in **1** above. This has the advantage of allowing the air to circulate, but it is fiddly removing the hot beans. Then they have to be washed in soapy water as they get greasy, and they leave a dimpled surface on the pastry, though this is hidden by the filling.

Tomato and Mustard Quiche

CHICKEN PIE

Serves 4

$4\frac{1}{2}$ lb. roasting chicken
1 onion, halved
1 carrot, halved
1 stalk celery, halved
1 bay leaf
3 stalks parsley
salt and 6 black peppercorns
6 small leeks, cut in three
6 small carrots, cut in three
$\frac{1}{4}$ lb. shelled peas, fresh or frozen
3 tbsp. butter
2 tbsp. flour
$\frac{1}{2}$ cup light cream
2 tbsp. chopped parsley
Short Pastry: *see Basic Recipe page 114*
Glaze:
1 egg yolk beaten with milk

Start the day before if possible, or in the morning. Put chicken in a casserole with onion, carrot and celery, herbs, salt, and peppercorns. Add enough hot water to cover the legs and bring to the boil. Lower the heat, cover the pot, and simmer for 1 hour 5 minutes. Test (by waggling a leg) to see if chicken is cooked. (If not, cook another 5 minutes.)

Remove it and continue to boil up the stock for 5–10 minutes, uncovered, to reduce to 2 cups. Strain and leave to cool, discarding flavoring vegetables, then chill overnight.

Next day, make the pastry and chill in the refrigerator.

Preheat the oven to 400°F. Cook the leeks and carrots, separately, until just tender; drain well. Cook the peas in a little water for 2 minutes if fresh, or just until thawed if frozen; drain. Cut the chicken off the bone, discarding the skin, and cut in neat pieces. Lay them in a shallow pie-dish with the vegetables over and among them.

Remove the fat from stock and measure 2 cups; heat it. Melt the butter in a pan, add flour, and cook 1 minute, stirring. Pour in the heated stock and stir until smooth; simmer 3 minutes, stirring now and then. Add cream and bring back to boil, stirring. Add salt and pepper to taste and stir in chopped parsley. Pour over chicken in pie dish.

Roll out pastry about $\frac{1}{3}$ inch thick. Cut some long strips from the edges, about $\frac{1}{2}$ inch wide, and stick to the dampened rim of the pie dish. Damp these also and lay the pastry lid over. Press down to seal, then trim with a knife and press up edges with the handle of a wooden spoon. Decorate with pastry trimmings and glaze. Bake for 15 minutes, then turn down heat to 350°F and bake a further 15 minutes.

TOMATO AND MUSTARD QUICHE

Serves 6 as a first course, or 4 as a light main dish with green salad

Short Pastry: *see Basic Recipe page 114*
Glaze:
1 egg yolk, beaten
Filling:
1–2 tbsp. Dijon mustard
4 eggs
$1\frac{1}{4}$ cups heavy cream
salt and black pepper
1 lb tomatoes, peeled, seeded, and coarsely chopped
$\frac{1}{2}$ cup grated Gruyère

Make the pastry and chill, following Basic Recipe.

Preheat oven to 400°F. Roll out the pastry and line a 9–10 inch flan ring or quiche pan and bake blind for 10 minutes, then remove beans, glaze and bake another 5 minutes. Take out and leave to cool. Turn down oven to 325°F.

Later, spread a layer of mustard over the bottom of the pastry shell. Beat the eggs, adding cream, salt and pepper. Mix with the tomatoes and most of the cheese. Pour into the pastry shell and scatter remaining cheese over top. Bake for 35–40 minutes, until golden brown and puffy.

Chicken Pie

Serve hot or cold, or reheated (allow 30 minutes at 350°F, with new potatoes or a potato purée and another vegetable of your choice.

ONION TART

This can be made with short pastry for a conventional quiche, or with yeast pastry for an unusual and delicious dish.

Serves 6 as a first course, or 4–5 as a main course with a green salad

Short Pastry: *see Basic Recipe page 114*
Yeast Pastry: *see Basic Recipe page 114*
Glaze *(for short pastry only)*:
1 egg, beaten
Filling:
1 lb. onions, thinly sliced
3 tbsp. butter
¼ lb. bacon
2 eggs, beaten
½ cup heavy cream
salt and black pepper

Make whichever pastry you prefer, following the Basic Recipe on page 114. Make the filling while the yeast pastry rises, or the short pastry chills. Cook the onions gently in the butter in a deep frying pan for about 10 minutes, until soft and pale golden. Add bacon strips and cook until they, too, are colored. Turn off the heat. The short pastry version can be made in advance to this point, but not the yeast.

Using yeast pastry: roll out and line a 9–10 inch flan ring. Preheat oven to 400°F. Beat eggs with cream, adding salt and pepper (not too much salt because of the bacon), and mix with the onions. Pour into the pastry shell and put in a warm place to rise for another 15 minutes. Bake for 20 minutes; then lower heat to 350°F and bake a further 20 minutes.

Using short pastry: roll out and line a flan ring, and bake blind for 10 minutes at 400°F. Remove beans and bake another 5 minutes, then remove from the oven and leave to cool. Later, beat eggs with cream, add salt and pepper, and mix with the onions. Pour into pastry shell and bake for 30 minutes at 400°F.

SAUSAGE EN CROUTE

Serves 2–3 as a light main course, or 3–4 as a first course

¾ lb. sausage, such as cotechino, in one piece
Short Pastry:
1½ cups flour
¼ tsp. salt
3 tbsp. each, butter and lard or 6 tbsp. butter
a little iced water
Glaze:
1 egg yolk, beaten with 1 tbsp. milk

Find a pan to fit the sausage, where it can lie straight. A fish poacher will probably be best. Cover it with hot water and bring to the boil. Simmer for 50 minutes, then take out and leave to cool. (If it is curved, this is the moment to straighten it, by cooling it under a weight.) When it is completely cold, it will stiffen and be easier to handle.

In the meantime, make pastry following Basic Recipe on page 114, but with these quantities, and chill in the refrigerator.

Preheat the oven to 350°F. Roll out the pastry into a rectangle, lay the sausage on it and wrap the pastry loosely around the sausage, trimming to fit. Seal the edges by moistening the inner surfaces and pinching together. Decorate with pastry trimmings, lift carefully on to a greased baking sheet and brush with beaten egg and milk. Bake for 30 minutes.

Serve hot, cut in thick slices, with a Mustard and Horseradish Sauce as a first course. As a main course, add *cornichons* (small gherkins) and a green salad. If you want to increase the quantities, make two separate sausages, since a very large roll is difficult to manage.

Variation: this is also good made with yeast pastry. Make pastry following Basic Recipe on page 114, and rise until doubled. Punch down, roll out, and wrap around cold cooked sausage. Put back in warm place to rise for 15 minutes, then brush with beaten egg and milk and bake as above.

Sausage en Croûte

PIROSHKIS

These are small filled pastries, traditionally served with *borscht*, made with yeast pastry or one based on cream cheese.

Serves 6–8

Yeast Pastry: *see Basic Recipe page 114*
   or Cream Cheese Pastry: *see Basic*
   Recipe page 114
Minced Meat Filling:
½ lb. ground beef
2 tbsp. chopped onion
1 hard-boiled egg, chopped
2 tbsp. butter, melted
salt and black pepper
Cabbage Filling:
2 cups chopped cabbage
1 small onion, chopped
2 tbsp. butter, melted
1 hard-boiled egg, chopped
salt and black pepper

Either pastry can be used with either filling. The yeast pastry is both crisp and soft; the cream cheese one is rich and light. Make either according to Basic Recipe.

While the yeast pastry is rising, or the cream cheese one is chilling, make the filling of your choice.
For the meat filling: fry the ground beef and onion in a heavy frying pan without any fat, stirring frequently to prevent it sticking. When all is brown, turn into a colander and leave 10 minutes to drain. Then put into food processor, add the egg and process until finely chopped. Tip into a bowl, stir in the butter, salt and pepper, and leave to cool.
For the cabbage filling, follow the recipe for Pirog (right) but using the quantities given here. Leave to cool.

Preheat oven to 400°F. Roll out the pastry until ⅛ inch thick. Cut out circles about 3 inches across, using a cup as a guide. Place a heaped teaspoon filling on one half of the pastry, and dampen the edges. Holding the pastry in the palm of the hand, gather the edges together and pinch to seal. This makes the authentic shape with a raised seam in the center, like a miniature Cornish pasty. Lay on a buttered baking tray and bake for about 15 minutes until golden brown.
Serve with Borscht, Consommé, or with drinks. The yeast recipe makes about 12 Piroshkis, serving 6, while the cream cheese pastry makes about 16.

LEEK AND MUSHROOM TARTS

Serves 6 as a first course

Cheese Pastry: *see Basic Recipe page 114*
Glaze:
1 egg yolk, beaten
Filling:
½ lb. mushrooms, finely chopped
4 tbsp. butter
1 large leek, white part only, chopped
1 tbsp. flour
about ¼ cup milk
salt and black pepper
1 egg, separated

Make pastry following Basic Recipe and chill 20 minutes in refrigerator. Cook the mushrooms in 2 tbsp. butter until soft, then drain in a colander. Bring 1 cup lightly salted water to the boil and cook leek for 5 minutes; drain, reserving the water. Return this to pan and boil up until reduced to about ¼ cup, tasting to make sure it does not get too salty (stop reducing if it does). Measure, and make up to ½ cup with milk.

Preheat oven to 400°F. Roll out pastry thinly and line 6 small flan tins or miniature quiche pans about 4 inches across and 1 inch deep, which sometimes have removable bottoms. Allow the pastry to stick up ¼ inch or so around the edges as it shrinks on baking. (An extra 10 minutes in the refrigerator before baking helps to minimize shrinkage.) Then bake blind for 6 minutes, remove beans, brush tarts with glaze and bake a further 6 minutes. Take out and leave to cool.

Shortly before cooking, melt the remaining butter, stir in the flour and cook 1 minute, stirring. Then add heated leek stock, stir until blended, and simmer 3 minutes, stirring now and then. Add the drained leeks and mix well, reheating at the same time. Remove from the heat and stir in the lightly beaten egg yolk. Allow to cool while you beat the white stiffly, then fold in. Spoon the mushrooms into the tarts and cover completely with a generous dollop of the leek mixture. Bake 15–20 minutes, until golden brown and puffed up.
Serve as soon as possible after baking.

PIROG

This Russian vegetable pie makes an unusual and delicious family meal. For feeding vegetarians omit the chicken broth.

Serves 6

Yeast Pastry:
3 cups white bread flour
1 tsp. salt
1 cake fresh yeast
8 tbsp. butter, cut in small bits
1 large egg, beaten
Filling:
1 small green cabbage, about ¾ lb.
4 tbsp. butter
1 large onion, chopped
salt and black pepper
2 hard boiled eggs, chopped
Glaze:
1 egg, beaten

Make the pastry following Basic Recipe on page 114 but with these quantities. While it is rising, make the filling. Cut cabbage in quarters, remove core and slice up each quarter. Throw into lightly salted boiling water and cook 5 minutes. Drain, run briefly under cold water, and drain again. Melt butter in a deep frying pan and cook onion about 10 minutes until pale golden. Add cabbage, cook another 5 minutes, stirring now and then, adding salt and pepper. Finally, stir in the hard boiled eggs and leave to cool.

When the pastry has finished rising, punch it down, knead briefly, and roll out into a rectangle about ¼ inch thick. Lay the filling on one half of the rectangle, leaving at least ½ inch free around the edges. Moisten the lower edge with water, then fold the pastry over the filling. Squeeze edges together to seal and trim. Lift carefully on to a buttered baking sheet, using two spatulas, and put back in the warm to rise for another 20–30 minutes, until puffy.

Preheat oven to 400°F. When the pie has finished rising for the second time, brush with glaze and prick here and there with a sharp fork. Bake 30–35 minutes until golden brown.
Serve cut in thick slices with a melted butter sauce in a small pitcher, or cups of chicken broth (homemade chicken stock, well strained and seasoned).

KOUBILIAC

This pie is made in exactly the same way as Pirog, but with a fish filling.

Serves 6

Yeast Pastry: *see Pirog*
Filling:
¾ cup freshly boiled rice
6 tbsp. melted butter
¼ cup chopped dill or parsley
salt and black pepper
4 hard-boiled eggs, sliced
*1 lb. poached salmon, free of skin and bone,
   flaked*

Mix the rice with the melted butter, add chopped herb, salt and pepper. Make a layer of half the rice on one half of the pastry, rolled out as for Pirog. Cover with half the eggs, sprinkle with salt and pepper, and lay the flaked salmon over the eggs. Add more salt and pepper, then the remaining eggs, then the rest of the rice. Fold and seal. Rise again, brush with egg, prick, and bake 30–35 minutes.

Serve with small cups of beef or chicken broth, or a melted butter sauce. This can be served as a first course or a main dish and needs no accompaniment.

APPLE CRUMBLE

A crumble is basically a short pastry mixture made without water.

Serves 6

Crumble Topping:
1 cup flour, sifted
¼ tsp. salt
½ cup sugar
6 tbsp. butter, cut in small bits
Filling:
*2 lb cooking apples, peeled, cored and
   quartered*
⅓ cup lemon juice
⅓ cup water
1 tsp. ground cinnamon (optional)
¼ cup sugar

Preheat oven to 375°F.
Make the crumble: sift flour and salt into a bowl, mix in the sugar, then stir in the butter with the blade of a knife. Rub in lightly, as for pastry, until evenly mixed.
Make the filling: slice the apples and put them in a buttered pie dish. Mix the cinnamon with the sugar, and sprinkle over. Mix lemon juice and water and pour over. Spread the crumble topping evenly over the apples, so the dish is completely sealed. Bake for 40 minutes, until golden brown.
Serve hot, or warm, with thick cream.

STRAWBERRY SHORTCAKE

Serves 6

Shortcake:
2 cups flour
2 tsp. baking powder
½ tsp. salt
1 tbsp. sugar
4 tbsp. butter, cut in bits
¾ cup milk and light cream, mixed
Filling:
2 cups whipping cream
¾ lb. strawberries
3 tbsp. sugar

Heat oven to 450°F. Sift flour, baking powder, salt and sugar into food processor and add butter. Blend, then add creamy milk through the lid, continuing to process. Knead once or twice on a lightly floured board. Divide into two slightly unequal pieces. Roll and pat out until you have two circles about ½ inch thick, one a little larger than the other. Lay on greased baking sheets and bake 12–15 minutes until pale golden.

Meanwhile, prepare berries. Reserve a few perfect ones, cut the others in half, and mix with the sugar. When the shortcakes are ready, let them cool for 15 minutes on a wire rack, then lay the larger one on a flat dish and cover with most of the lightly whipped cream. Press halved strawberries into cream, and cover with the smaller circle. Garnish with remaining whipped cream and berries. Serve within the hour if possible, while still warm.

CHEESECAKE

Serves 6

Crust:
1½ cups crushed graham crackers
3 tbsp. butter, melted
1 heaped tbsp. soft brown sugar
Filling:

1 cup sugar
4 tbsp. butter
2 egg yolks
¼ pint heavy cream
1 lb. cottage cheese, or low-fat cream cheese
1½ tbsp. lemon juice

Heat oven to 350°F. Mix the graham cracker crumbs with the melted butter and brown sugar. Use to line a round baking pan, about 2 inches deep. Press it up sides as well as on base. Bake for 8 minutes and leave to cool. Put all filling ingredients in food processor and blend until smooth. Pour into case and chill.

—MENUS—

**Some suggestions for well balanced meals
based on the pastry recipes**

MUSHROOMS STUFFED WITH
EGGPLANT SALAD

GRILLED SIRLOIN STEAK
Potato Purée, Glazed Onions

APPLE TART
served warm, with cream

LEEK AND MUSHROOM
TARTS

STEAMED FISH
A LA CHINOISE

GREEN SALAD,
WITH CHEESES

CAPONATA

CHICKEN PIE
new potatoes, broccoli

RASPBERRY AND PEACH JELLY
with Almond Sauce

Vegetarian Menu
TOMATO AND MUSTARD QUICHE
CARROT SALAD WITH SESAME
SEEDS, DANDELION SALAD
(omitting bacon)
CUCUMBER AND YOGURT SALAD
Saffron Bread
STEAMED LEMON MOUSSE

"La Patisserie Gloppe," 1899, by Béraud. Photo Bulloz. Courtesy Musée Carnavalet, Paris. Copyright SPADEM.

TIPS ON BAKING BREAD, CAKES, BISCUITS, AND GRATINS:

✳ *Invest in good quality baking sheets, and pans and trays in various shapes and sizes.*

✳ *Non-stick baking pans save time and trouble, as do cake pans with removable bottoms, and open flan rings.*

Loaf pans are useful for making patés and terrines as well as bread, and for aspic dishes.

✳ *A jelly roll pan is essential for making roulades, while pizza trays make useful bases for open flan rings, for baking a few rolls or cookies, or for baking simple round loaves, i.e. onion bread.*

✳ *Shallow square pans roughly 8–10 inches across and 1½–2 inches deep are immensely practical for a multitude of things, from chocolate cake to meat loaf.*

✳ *Buy a good oven thermometer and get accustomed to using it. Make a note of how long it takes your oven to heat up. Keep a small note pad near the oven, or note baking times on the recipes you use.*

✳ *Always have a stock of foil and non-stick baking parchment and wax paper. Small rolls*

of foil are the most useful, except for baking large fish.

✳ *Keep paper from sticks of butter in the refrigerator for greasing pans or use a pastry brush and a few drops of oil.*

✳ *Learn to use the heat of the cooling oven for something useful, like drying bread for crumbs, crisping cookies and crackers, or warming plates.*

✳ *Keep some really good chocolate in the refrigerator for making cakes.*

A SIMPLE LOAF

Makes 1 lb. loaf

4 cups white bread flour
½ tsp. sea salt, or to taste
1 cake fresh yeast, or 1 package (1 tbsp.) dried yeast
1 cup lukewarm water

Put the flour into a large bowl with the salt; there is no need to sift it. If you like salty bread, and many people do, you may use more salt, but don't use more than 1½ tsp. or it will slow down the rising. Put 2–3 tbsp. of the warm water into a cup and crumble the yeast into it. Stand in a warm place for 10 minutes; the flour can be put in the same place to warm very slightly. After 10 minutes, the yeast should have started to bubble and froth; this is a sign that it is fresh and active, but don't worry if it doesn't. Have the rest of the tepid water in a measuring cup; the temperature should be slightly warmer than blood temperature.

Make a well in the center of the flour and pour in the yeast mixture. Cover it with flour, and pour most of the water into the bowl, stirring vigorously with a wooden spoon. Continue adding water until the dough starts to cling together; you may not need it all. Knead the dough a few times by hand, while it is still in the bowl, then turn it out on to a floured surface and knead it briskly for 6–8 minutes (this may be done in a food processor if you prefer). Wash and dry the bowl, rub it lightly with oil and put the dough back in, turning it once or twice to coat lightly with oil. Cover with plastic wrap and stand in a warm place for about 1½ hours, or until the dough has doubled in volume.

You may need to experiment once or twice to find the right temperature; it should be slightly warmer than normal room temperature. You may find it near a radiator, in a linen cupboard, or in a warm oven. On a summer day, a sunny window sill will be warm enough. If the dough has doubled in bulk in less than an hour, this shows the temperature is too high.

Once the bread has finished rising, punch it down a few times with your fist and turn it on to a floured surface. Knead for 4–6 minutes, then place in a greased loaf pan ($10 \times 4 \times 3$ inches is the right size for a 1 lb. loaf). If you don't have one you can use a clean clay flowerpot or simply form the dough into a bun shape and lay on a greased baking sheet. Sprinkle a little flour over the top. It should fill the pan by just over half, and not more than two thirds. Put back in the warm, covered lightly with a clean dish towel, and leave to rise again for 45–60 minutes, by which time it will have filled the pan.

Heat the oven to 400°F. When the dough has risen, put the pan in the center of the oven, uncovered, and bake 40 minutes. Test to see if it is cooked by tipping it out of the pan and knocking on the bottom with your knuckle. If it sounds hollow, it is ready. If not, lay it on its side on the oven rack for another 5–10 minutes. Or turn off the oven and simply leave the loaf to cool down in it. Bread likes a brisk oven to start with, but a cooling oven suits it well for the final baking. Lay on a rack to cool, then wrap in a cloth and store in a bread crock, if you have one.

Variation: for a brown loaf, simply substitute wholemeal, wheatmeal or granary flour for the white flour. You can use a mixture of flours if you like, but I prefer to keep them distinct.

POTATO BREAD

Makes two ¾ lb. loaves

1 cake fresh yeast, or 1 package (1 tbsp.)
  dried yeast
½ cup sugar
1 cup milk
12 tbsp. butter
1 tbsp. sea salt
2 eggs, beaten
¾ cup freshly mashed potato
6 cups white bread flour

Crumble the fresh yeast, or shake the dried yeast, into a large bowl. Add 1 tbsp. sugar and ½ cup lukewarm water. Stand in a warm place for 10 minutes. Then warm the milk and add the butter cut in small bits. When warm, with the butter half melted, combine with the yeast and add remaining sugar, salt, and beaten eggs. Stir well, then pour on to the mashed potato in another bowl, beating with a wooden spoon. When smooth, start to add the flour, cupful by cupful. Beat vigorously with a wooden spoon, stopping as soon as the dough clings together. Turn on to a floured surface and knead for 10 minutes, adding some of the remaining flour if necessary, until you have a smooth springy dough. Wash and dry the bowl, rub lightly with oil, and put back the dough. Cover with plastic wrap and stand in a warm place for 1½ hours, or until the dough has doubled in volume.

Heat oven to 375°F. Punch down, turn out, and knead dough for another 5 minutes. Divide in half, form into loaf shapes, and put in two buttered loaf pans. Put back in the warm place, covered with a cloth, for 45–60 minutes, until well risen, then bake for 40–45 minutes, until they sound hollow when tapped on the bottom. Cool completely before eating.

To serve: this bread is delicious with cheese, honey or jam, and makes very good toast. The crumbs are good for making stuffings.

Variation: to make potato rolls, make in half quantities and divide into rolls after the second kneading, before the second rising. Lay them on buttered baking sheets and put back in the warm for 30 minutes to rise, then bake for 20–25 minutes, depending on size. Makes 8 large or 16 small rolls.

BREAD STICKS

Makes 16, serves 5–6

¼ oz. fresh yeast, or ½ package (½ tbsp.)
  dried yeast
1 tsp. honey
about ¼ cup lukewarm water
2 cups white bread flour
1 tsp. sea salt
1 tsp. olive oil
1 egg, beaten
2 tbsp. sesame seeds

Crumble the fresh yeast (or shake the dried yeast) into a cup and add the honey and 3 tbsp. warm water. If using fresh yeast, stand for 10 minutes in a warm place; dried yeast can be used right away. Put the flour into a large bowl and make a well in the center. Dissolve the salt in a little very hot water, then make it up to ½ cup with warm water. Pour the yeast mixture into the center of the flour, cover it with flour, and pour most of the warm salt water on top, stirring vigorously with a wooden spoon. You may not need to use all the water: flours vary in the amount they can absorb. Stop adding water once the dough starts to cling together. Knead once or twice in the bowl, then turn on to a floured surface and knead for 4 minutes, until springy and smooth. Form into a ball, cover with a floured cloth, and rest for 5 minutes.

Heat the oven to 325°F. Oil 2 baking sheets. Divide the dough into 16 pieces and roll each into a sausage shape about as thick as your middle finger. Lay them on oiled baking sheets, not too close together. Stand in a warm place until they start to rise, about 15 minutes. Then brush them with beaten egg and shake the sesame seeds over them. Bake for 35 minutes, until light golden. Take out of the oven and lay on a wire rack to cool for about 10 minutes, then serve as soon as possible, with butter.

To serve: these make the nicest possible accompaniment to a soup or salad.

ONION BREAD

Makes 1 lb. round loaf

4 cups white bread flour
¼ tsp. sea salt
½ oz. fresh yeast, or 1 package (1 tbsp.)
  dried yeast
scant 1 cup lukewarm water
1 lb. Spanish onions, sliced
4 tbsp. butter
salt and black pepper
2 egg yolks, beaten

Make dough as for A Simple Loaf on page 120. After the second kneading, form into a round shape like a large flat bun and lay on a greased baking sheet. Sprinkle with flour. Put back in the warm to rise again for 45 minutes.

Heat the oven to 450°F. Cook the onions slowly in the butter in a covered sauté pan until soft but not browned. Drain them in a colander. When the bread is ready for baking, pile them on top of it. Brush all over with the beaten egg and bake for 15 minutes, then turn the heat down to 425°F and bake a further 30 minutes. Watch that the onions don't burn; if they start to brown lay a sheet of foil over them. Lay on a rack to cool a little.

To serve: try to serve while still warm. This is delicious with patés.

SEED BREAD

Makes 1 lb. loaf

4 cups white, or unbleached, bread flour
¼ tsp. sea salt
½ oz. fresh yeast, or 1 package (1 tbsp.)
  dried yeast
1 tbsp. sugar
1 cup milk
1 egg, beaten
2 tsp. caraway seeds, or anise seeds

Put the flour into a large bowl with the salt. There is no need to sift it. Crumble the fresh yeast into a cup, or shake in the dried yeast, and add the sugar. Warm the milk to body temperature and add 2 tbsp. to the yeast. If using fresh yeast, stand it in a warm place for 10 minutes to prove. Dried yeast can be used right away. Beat the egg in a cup and add the seeds.

Make a well in the center of the flour and pour in the yeast mixture and egg. Cover with flour, and pour most of the milk over it, stirring vigorously with a wooden spoon. Once the dough starts to bind, knead once or twice in the bowl, turn on to a floured surface, and knead vigorously for 6–8 minutes, until smooth and elastic.

Wash the bowl and dry it; rub it with a little oil and put the dough back in it,

Onion Bread

turning it to coat with oil. Cover with plastic wrap and stand in a warm place for 1–1½ hours, until doubled in bulk. Punch down, turn out, and knead for another 4–5 minutes. Form into a loaf shape and put in an oiled loaf pan. Cover with a cloth and leave about 45 minutes, until risen to the top. Heat the oven to 400°F. Bake the loaf for 40 minutes, or until it sounds hollow when tapped on the bottom. (Once tested, it can be returned to oven out of the pan.) Cool on a rack.

To serve: this is an unusual bread, excellent as an accompaniment to cream cheese, paté, or scrambled eggs.

SAFFRON BREAD

Makes 1 lb. loaf

4 cups white bread flour
1½ tsp. sea salt
½ oz. fresh yeast, or 1 package (1 tbsp.)
  dried yeast
¾ cup lukewarm water
½ cup milk
¼ tsp. saffron, preferably powder
2 eggs, beaten

Put flour and salt into a large bowl; do not sift. Crumble the fresh yeast (or shake the dried yeast) into a cup and add the warm water. If using fresh yeast, stand for 10 minutes in a warm place before using. Put milk in a small pan and add the saffron: heat slowly until it reaches boiling point, then remove from heat and leave to cool, stirring occasionally. When it is about 110°F, stir it into the beaten eggs. (If using saffron in stamen form, pour it through a strainer on to the eggs.)

Make a well in the center of the flour and pour in the yeast mixture. Cover with flour, then pour on the saffron colored egg, stirring hard with a wooden spoon. If the dough still seems too dry to cling together, add a few drops more milk or water. Once it starts to hold together, turn it out on to a floured surface and knead vigorously for 5–6 minutes.

Wash and dry bowl, rub with oil and replace the dough. Cover with plastic wrap and stand in a warm place for 1–1½ hours, until doubled in size. Punch down, turn out, and knead another 5 minutes. Then form into a loaf shape and put in a greased loaf pan. Cover with a cloth and put back

in the warm for another 45–60 minutes or until it has risen to the top. Heat the oven to 375°F. Bake 30–40 minutes, until it sounds hollow when tapped on the bottom. Cool on a wire rack.
To serve: this is excellent with fish soups, minestrone, or fish paté. If allowed to get stale, it is delicious cut in thick strips and dried in the oven, or made into croûtons, to serve with a Mediterranean-style fish soup. Saffron breadcrumbs are also good for coating fish or fish cakes for frying.

SPICED FRUIT BREAD

Makes one $\frac{3}{4}$ lb. loaf

$\frac{1}{2}$ oz. fresh yeast, or 1 package (1 tbsp.) dried yeast
$3\frac{1}{2}$ cups white bread flour
3 tbsp. lard or chilled shortening
1 egg, beaten
$\frac{1}{2}$ cup warm milk
$\frac{1}{2}$ tsp. mixed spice: nutmeg, cloves and cinnamon
1 cup raisins
$\frac{1}{2}$ cup currants
$\frac{1}{2}$ cup golden raisins
$\frac{1}{4}$ cup mixed candied peel, chopped
6 tbsp. sugar
2 tsp. molasses

Crumble the fresh yeast (or shake the dried yeast) into a cup, add 3 tbsp. warm water, and stand in a warm place for 10 minutes. Put the flour in a large bowl and rub in the lard or shortening, cut in small bits. Beat the egg in a measuring cup, and add the warm milk, and enough warm water to make up to 1 cup. Make a well in the center of the flour and pour in yeast mixture, cover with flour, then pour on the egg and milk mixture, stirring hard with a wooden spoon. Cover bowl with plastic wrap and stand in a warm place for 30 minutes. Put all the dried fruit and peel in another bowl and stand in the warm place also. When the time is up, turn out the flour and knead for 3–4 minutes, then mix in the dried fruit, sugar, and molasses. Have a large loaf pan greased with butter and lined with grease-proof paper or baking parchment – if using paper, rub it with butter too. Form the dough into a loaf shape and place in the pan. Put back in the warm for 20 minutes, while you heat the oven to 350°F. Bake for $1\frac{1}{4}$ hours, covering the pan loosely with a sheet of foil if it starts to brown. Cool on a wire rack; wrap in a cloth and store in a tin or air-tight bread crock. This keeps well for several days, and can be made well in advance which is useful before a holiday. It is excellent sliced and buttered.

MUFFIN BREAD

Makes one $\frac{3}{4}$ lb. loaf

$\frac{1}{2}$ oz. fresh yeast, or 1 package (1 tbsp.) dried yeast
2 tsp. sugar
$\frac{1}{4}$ cup warm water
$3\frac{1}{2}$ cups white bread flour
1 tsp. sea salt
$\frac{1}{8}$ tsp. baking powder
1 cup milk

Crumble fresh yeast (or shake dried yeast) into a cup, adding sugar and warm water: stand in a warm place for 10 minutes. Put half the flour in a large warm bowl, adding salt and baking powder. Heat milk to about 120°F and set aside. Stir the yeast mixture into the flour, followed by the warm milk, mixing with a wooden spoon. Then stir in remaining flour, cup by cup, until you have a soft dough. (You may not need all the flour.) Form it into a loaf shape and turn into a buttered loaf pan. 9 × 4 × 3 inches. Put in a warm place to rise for about 45 minutes, covered with a cloth, until it has filled the pan. Preheat the oven to 400°F then bake for 45 minutes. Cool on a rack. Eat the same day or, toasted, the next day.
To serve: this makes delicious bread, slightly like a brioche, excellent with paté when toasted. It is ideal for Eggs Benedict: lay a slice of ham on a piece of toasted muffin bread, lay a poached egg on top, and cover with a Sauce Hollandaise.

VANILLA SUGAR
To make vanilla sugar, put 2 or 3 vanilla pods into a screw-top jar, fill it with white sugar, screw on the lid and leave for a week before using. Homemade vanilla sugar adds a delicious flavor to many biscuits, cakes, custards and sweet sauces.

OATMEAL COOKIES

Makes about 30

$\frac{1}{2}$ cup unsalted butter
$\frac{1}{2}$ cup light brown sugar
scant $\frac{1}{2}$ cup sugar
1 egg
1 tbsp. milk
1 cup self-rising flour
a pinch of salt
$1\frac{1}{2}$ cup oatmeal

Put butter and both sugars in the food processor and process until mixed. Add egg and milk and process again. Add flour, sifted with salt, process again, then turn into a bowl and fold in oatmeal. Chill in refrigerator 30 minutes, then form into a fat sausage about 2 inches thick, wrap in plastic wrap and store in refrigerator until needed.

To bake: heat oven to 350°F. Cut dough in thin slices and lay them, not too close together, on an oiled baking sheet. Bake 8–10 minutes, until straw-colored, remove and leave to cool. After a minute or two, lift them with a spatula and cool on a wire rack.

TUILES D'AMANDES

Makes about 16

4 tbsp. unsalted butter
2 egg whites
1 cup sugar or vanilla sugar (see p. 000)
$\frac{1}{2}$ cup flour, sifted
$\frac{1}{2}$ cup sliced almonds

Heat oven to 350°F. Melt butter slowly in a double boiler, without allowing it to get hot. Set aside to cool. Break egg whites into a clean bowl and add sifted sugar, beating it in with a fork. Then beat in the flour, almonds, and melted butter. Using 2 tea-spoons, drop rounds of the mixture on to greased baking sheets, leaving 5 inches between cookies. Bake 6–8 minutes, until spread out and light golden. Remove from oven and leave 30 seconds, then lift off tray with a spatula and lay over oiled wine bottles, or a rolling pin. Later, when cold and crisp, slide them off and lay on a plate.

CHOCOLATE CHIP COOKIES

Makes about 30

6 tbsp. unsalted butter
6 tbsp. sugar
¼ cup light brown sugar
1 egg, beaten
1½ cups flour
a pinch of salt
2 oz. semi-sweet chocolate

Heat oven to 375°F. Put butter in a food processor with both sugars. Process, add beaten egg, sifted flour and salt, and process again. Turn into a bowl and stir in the chocolate, chopped into small bits. Drop little mounds of the mixture on to oiled baking sheets and bake 12–15 minutes until light golden.

ICEBOX COOKIES

Makes about 30

7 tbsp. unsalted butter
½ cup sugar
1 egg
1½ cups self-rising flour
a pinch of salt

Cut butter in bits and put in food processor with sugar. Process until mixed, then add egg and process again. Sift flour with salt and add to butter cream; process until well mixed. Turn out on to plastic wrap, wrap loosely, and chill for 30 minutes to firm up. Then form into a roll, like a fat sausage, about 2 inches thick, wrap and store in refrigerator until needed: it will keep several weeks, or even longer, frozen.

To bake: heat oven to 350°F. Cut dough into thin slices and lay them on an oiled baking sheet, not too close together as they spread on baking. (If frozen, allow the dough to thaw for an hour at room temperature before slicing.) Bake 8–10 minutes until pale golden brown, slightly darker around the edges. Remove and leave on baking sheet a moment or two as they are too soft to lift immediately. If left too long they will become brittle and break as you lift them. If they do, put them back in the oven for a minute or two to soften. Lay them on a wire rack to cool.

Variations: make as above, but add 2 oz. melted chocolate to the butter and egg, before adding the flour.

For Pinwheel Cookies, make Icebox Cookie dough and divide in half. Stir 1 oz. melted chocolate into half the mixture, chill both until firm, then roll out both pieces to about ⅛ inch thick. Lay the chocolate dough over the plain one and roll up like a Swiss roll. Wrap in plastic wrap or foil, chill, then slice and bake.

Chocolate Cake with whipped cream

FRUIT CAKE

This cake can be covered with almond paste and iced for Christmas, birthdays, or weddings, or christenings.

Makes a 4 lb. cake

1 cup unsalted butter
generous 1 cup brown sugar
3 tbsp. molasses, warmed
4 medium eggs
3 cups flour, sifted
1 tsp. baking powder
1½ tsp. ground cloves
1½ tsp. ground cinnamon
1½ tsp. ground nutmeg
¾ cup ground almonds
1½ cups currants
1½ cups raisins
1½ cups golden raisins
½ cup milk
juice of 1 orange

Have the butter at room temperature. Cream it, by hand or in a food processor, and beat in the sugar gradually. Stir in the molasses, mixing well. Beat the eggs one at a time and add to the mixture. Fold in 1 tbsp. flour after each egg, to prevent the mixture separating. When all the eggs are added, stir the baking powder and the spices into the remaining flour and fold into the mixture. Then stir in the ground almonds, currants, raisins, and golden raisins. Finally, stir in the milk and the orange juice.

Preheat the oven to 325°F. Take a large round pan holding about 2 quarts or 2 loaf pans measuring 8 × 4 × 3 inches deep. Butter them, line with buttered wax paper or baking parchment, and pile in the mixture. Bake the large cake 3 hours, the loaf pans 2½ hours. After the first hour, cover the pans with a sheet of foil to prevent the cake burning.

Turn on to a wire rack to cool. If icing, allow it to cool completely, and ice the following day.

CHOCOLATE CAKE

Makes about 12 pieces

4 oz. semi-sweet chocolate
7 tbsp. butter
4 eggs
a pinch of salt
1 cup sugar
1 cup flour, sifted

Break the chocolate into small pieces and put in a small bowl standing over a pan of very hot water. Add butter, cut in small bits. Once they have melted, remove from the heat, stir and leave to cool to room temperature. About 1 hour later, heat the oven to 350°F. Beat the eggs very well and gradually beat in sugar and salt. Stir in the melted chocolate and butter, then fold in the flour. Do not mix too thoroughly; the whole process should be done lightly rather than laboriously.

Have a square pan measuring $10 \times 1\frac{1}{2}$ inches deep, or similar, greased with butter. Pour in the chocolate mixture, spreading it evenly with a spatula. Bake for about 35 minutes, until it begins to brown at the edges and shrink away from the sides of the pan. If you test it by sticking a toothpick in the center, note that it should still be moist; do not go on cooking until it comes out dry, for this cake should be slightly chewy in the center.

Cool in the pan, then cut in pieces. Top each with a spoonful of lightly whipped cream. If you want to keep it for 1–2 days before eating, cover the pan with foil and wrap tightly. This is a good way to carry it on picnics. (Pack cream separately.)

CARROT CAKE

Serves 8

1¼ cups sugar
1 cup sunflower seed oil
3 eggs
1½ cups flour, sifted
1½ tsp. baking powder
1½ tsp. ground cinnamon
¼ tsp. ground cloves
¼ tsp. sea salt
½ lb. carrots, grated finely
¼ lb. walnuts, finely chopped
Cream Cheese Frosting:
1 small package cream cheese
3 tbsp. unsalted butter
¼ cup sugar

Heat oven to 350°F. Put sugar in a large bowl and stir in oil, beating with a wooden spoon. Break in eggs one at a time, beating in each one until it is amalgamated. Sift the flour into another bowl with the baking powder, cinnamon, cloves, and salt. Add these, spoonful by spoonful, to the first mixture, continuing to beat. Finally, stir in the grated carrots and the chopped nuts.

Have a round cake pan lined with buttered wax paper or baking parchment. Spoon the cake mixture into it and bake about 70–80 minutes, or until the top springs back when pressed down with a finger. Cool on a wire rack.
To make the frosting: beat the cream cheese with the back of a wooden spoon until smooth. Add the butter, cut in small bits and at room temperature, mashing it into the cheese until smoothly blended. (This can be quickly done in a food processor.) When blended, stir in the sugar, beating until smooth. When the cake is quite cold,

spread the frosting over the top, smoothing with a spatula dipped in hot water.
Serve the same day, or keep in the refrigerator overnight. This is a useful cake, quite solid, that can be served either as a dessert, or for tea, or taken on a picnic.

SMALL ORANGE CAKES

Makes about 10 small cakes

8 tbsp. unsalted butter
¼ cup sugar
rind of 1 small orange finely grated
¼ cup orange juice
2 eggs, beaten
1 cup all-purpose flour, sifted
a pinch of salt

Heat oven to 375°F. Cream butter, add sugar gradually, continuing to cream until you have a smooth mixture. Stir in orange rind, then juice. Stir in the eggs, then the flour and salt. Have a tray of cupcake tins greased with butter, and divide the mixture between them. Bake for 15 minutes on the top shelf of the oven, or until domed and firm in the center. Take out of the oven and leave to cool for 2–3 minutes, then loosen round the edges with the point of a knife, and lift on to a rack to cool.

SMALL MOCHA CAKES

Makes 6–8 small cakes

1 oz. semi-sweet chocolate
2 tbsp. very strong black coffee
6 tbsp. unsalted butter
6 tbsp. sugar, sifted
¾ cup flour, sifted
1 large egg, beaten
Coffee Frosting: (optional)
8 tbsp. unsalted butter
½ cup superfine sugar
1 large egg yolk, beaten
1 tbsp. extra strong black coffee, cold

Break chocolate into small pieces and melt in the coffee in a small bowl sitting over a pan of very hot water. When the chocolate has melted, stir, remove from heat, and leave to cool to room temperature.

Heat the oven to 375°F. Cream the butter, add the sugar, and cream again. When it is smooth, fold in the flour, then stir in the coffee mixture. Pour into 6 small buttered cupcake tins and bake for about 15 minutes, until puffy and lightly colored. Take out of the oven; a few minutes later, lift out of the tins and cool on a wire rack.
To make the frosting: cream butter, stir in sugar, and beat until smooth. Stir in egg yolk and coffee. Spread over the little cakes once they have cooled.

Carrot Cake with Cream Cheese Frosting

GRATIN DAUPHINOISE

Serves 6

$1\frac{1}{2}$ lb. waxy potatoes, peeled
2–4 tbsp. butter
1 large clove garlic, cut in half
sea salt and black pepper
$\frac{1}{4}$ tsp. grated nutmeg, or $\frac{3}{4}$ cup grated Gruyère, or Emmental
2 cups light cream

Preheat oven to 325°F. The whole point of this dish is to have the potatoes in a thin layer, so choose a broad, shallow flameproof dish. Butter it thickly, and rub all over with a cut clove of garlic. The potatoes should be sliced very thinly and evenly, so they are all cooked at the same time: use a food processor, or mandoline. Wash sliced potatoes in cold water to get rid of excess starch, then drain and dry in a cloth.

Make a layer of them in the dish, using the smaller, uneven slices at the bottom. Sprinkle with salt, pepper and grated nutmeg or cheese. Then make another layer; try not to have more than three in all, and make the top layer very even. Finally, pour over cream, to almost cover the potatoes. Bake $1\frac{1}{4}$–$1\frac{1}{2}$ hours, until top is golden brown and potatoes soft and melting.

Variation: instead of cream, use 2 cups milk beaten with 1 large egg, or 1 cup each, milk and light cream, mixed, or 1 cup homemade beef or chicken stock.

ZUCCHINI GRATIN

Serves 6 as a first course, or 4 as a light main dish

$1\frac{1}{2}$ lb. zucchini, cut in $\frac{1}{2}$ inch slices
3 large eggs
$\frac{3}{4}$ cup heavy cream
salt and black pepper
$\frac{1}{4}$ tsp. grated nutmeg
$\frac{3}{4}$ cup grated Gruyère, or Emmental

Heat oven to 400°F. Boil some lightly salted water, drop in zucchini, and cook 10 minutes, covered. Tip into colander and drain well.

Butter a gratin dish. Beat eggs with cream, adding plenty of salt and pepper and nutmeg. Stir in half the grated cheese and gently fold in the zucchini. Transfer to the gratin dish, sprinkle the remaining cheese on top, and bake for 25 minutes until puffed up and golden brown. (The exact timing will depend on the thickness of the dish.)

To serve: vegetable gratins make good first courses, especially before a cold main dish. They can also be served as a light main dish with a green salad, either as part of a vegetarian meal, or after a substantial soup. Like potato gratin, they must be made in wide, shallow dishes. Glazed brown earthenware dishes are ideal, as are white porcelain flan dishes; enamelled cast iron ones have the advantage of going under the broiler without risk.

Variations:

Leek Gratin: substitute $1\frac{1}{2}$ lb. leeks, weighed after trimming, and cut in $\frac{1}{2}$ inch slices, for zucchini. Cook as for zucchini.

Endive Gratin: substitute $1\frac{1}{2}$ lb. Belgian endive, cut in 1 inch slices, for zucchini. Cook gently in 3 tbsp. butter and 2 tsp. lemon juice for 10 minutes in a covered pan, then drain.

Spinach Gratin: substitute 2 lb. spinach for zucchini. Cook 4–5 minutes in lightly salted boiling water, then drain, cool, squeeze out excess moisture and chop coarsely, by hand.

TOMATO GRATIN

Serves 6 as a first course, or 4 as a light main dish

1 lb. waxy potatoes
$\frac{1}{3}$ cup olive oil
1 lb. onions, thinly sliced
salt and black pepper
$\frac{3}{4}$ cup grated Gruyère, or Emmental
$1\frac{1}{2}$ lb. tomatoes, unpeeled and sliced
1 large clove garlic, finely chopped
1 tsp. fresh thyme, leaves only, or $\frac{1}{2}$ tsp. dried thyme

Boil potatoes in their skins; drain and cool. Preheat oven to 425°F. When potatoes are cool enough to handle, peel and cut in thick slices. Rub a shallow earthenware dish with 2 tsp. olive oil and lay half the potatoes in it. Cover with half the onions and sprinkle with salt, pepper and half the cheese. Lay half the sliced tomatoes over the onions and sprinkle with garlic and half the thyme. Repeat the layers, finishing with tomatoes. Sprinkle with remaining thyme and dribble remaining oil over top.

Serve hot, with crusty French bread. If serving as a main dish, accompany with a green salad.

MEDITERRANEAN BAKED FISH

Serves 4–6

2 medium onions, sliced
$\frac{1}{4}$ cup olive oil
1 carrot, sliced
1 stalk celery, sliced
2 cloves garlic, crushed
$\frac{1}{2}$ cup water
salt and black pepper
2 tomatoes, skinned and chopped
$\frac{1}{2}$ cup dry white wine
2–3 lb. bass, bream, or grey mullet, head and tail severed
2 tbsp. chopped parsley

Cook the onions in the oil until they start to color, then add the carrot and celery. Cook gently for 6–8 minutes, then add the garlic and $\frac{1}{2}$ cup water. Add salt and pepper and cover the pan. Simmer for 10 minutes, then add the chopped tomatoes and cook gently for another 4 minutes. Add the wine and leave to cool.

Heat oven to 350°F. Butter a flameproof dish large enough to hold the fish; if necessary, it can be cut in thick slices, but it will not look so pretty. Lay the fish in it and pour the sauce over it. Cover with a piece of buttered foil and bake 30–45 minutes, until the fish flakes easily from the bone. Remove from the oven and leave to cool for 15 minutes before serving.

To serve: it may be served straight from the dish, sprinkled with parsley, or transferred to a clean dish, the top skin removed, and the sauce poured over it. Serve with boiled potatoes and a lettuce salad to follow. This dish may also be served cold, but not chilled.

Variation: this method of cooking also works well with steaks cut from a large fish like halibut or bonito. (When made with halibut, it cannot, of course, be called Mediterranean.)

FISH BAKED IN FOIL

This is a useful way of cooking a whole fish if you don't have a fish poacher. It works well with small salmon, salmon trout, large rainbow trout, and bass. It gives you a perfectly plain fish, not unlike a poached fish, perfect for eating hot or cold, with mayonnaise or other sauces.

Heat the oven to 350°F. Sprinkle the fish with salt and pepper and wrap in a well buttered piece of foil, sealing the ends tightly. Lay the package on the oven rack, in the center of the oven. Allow 20–25 minutes for a $1\frac{1}{2}$–2 lb. fish, 30–35 minutes for a 2–3 lb. fish, 40 minutes for one weighing up to $3\frac{1}{2}$ lb.

To serve hot, unwrap the fish and slide on

to a warm dish. Remove the top skin if you like, and serve with a Sauce Hollandaise, or a simple sauce of melted butter with chopped herbs. Chervil, dill, and tarragon all go particularly well with fish. To serve cold, leave the fish to cool in its package, but serve the same day. Lay on a large dish, remove the top skin, and serve with a Mayonnaise or Sauce Verte.

I like these sorts of fish dishes served hot with the simplest of accompaniments: just a few boiled or steamed new potatoes, which go well with the sauce, be it Mayonnaise or melted butter, and no other vegetable. If you serve it cold, a cucumber salad would make a nice accompaniment, with a few new potatoes served warm, and a salad of soft lettuce leave sprinkled with young green peas.

STUFFED BAKED POTATOES

Serves 4

4 large floury potatoes
4 small eggs
3 tbsp. butter, in small bits
sea salt and black pepper

Preheat oven to 400°F. Lay potatoes on top rack and bake 1 hour, until soft in the center when pierced with a fork. Remove and cut a slice off the top of each. Scoop out insides and mash with a fork. Stir in butter, in small bits, and add salt and pepper to taste. Pile back into potato skins, making a hollow in the center. Break an egg into each, sprinkle with salt and pepper, return to oven and cook until the whites have set.
Variation: omit the eggs, and add 1 cup grated cheese: Gruyère, Emmental and Cheddar are best. Mix half the cheese with the potato, and scatter the remainder over the tops. Replace in oven until the cheese is melted and brown.

BAKED EGGS

Serves 6

6 eggs, medium to large
sea salt and black pepper
¾ cup light cream

Heat the oven to 325°F. Butter 6 ramekins, break an egg into each and sprinkle with salt and pepper. Stand the dishes in a roasting pan with hot water coming half way up them. Bake in the oven, uncovered, until the whites have become almost opaque. This will take about 8–12 minutes, depending on your oven. Just before the whites have totally set, warm the cream and pour 2 tbsp. over each egg. Return to the oven for another 2 minutes; then serve immediately. This is one of the simplest and

best ways of serving eggs as a first course. If you have enough dishes, you can serve 2 small eggs per person.
Variation: take the leaves off 4 sprigs tarragon and put the stems into the cream in a small pan. Heat until almost boiling, then cover and remove from the heat. Stand for 15–20 minutes to infuse the flavor, then strain. Chop the leaves and stir into the cream. Pour over the eggs just before they finish cooking, as above.

BAKED BANANAS

Serves 6

6 large bananas, or 9 small ones
juice of 1¼ oranges
juice of 1¼ lemons
¼–⅓ cup rum
2 tbsp. sugar
3 tbsp. unsalted butter

Heat the oven to 350°F. Peel the bananas and cut them in half lengthwise. Butter a shallow ovenproof dish and lay the bananas in it. Mix the fruit juices with the rum and pour over them. Sprinkle with sugar, dot with butter, and bake for 20 minutes. Allow to cool for 10–15 minutes before serving with cream.

BAKED APPLES IN TOFFEE SAUCE

Serves 6

6 small cooking apples
3–4 golden plums, when available
6 thick slices dry white bread
4 tbsp. butter at room temperature
⅓ cup soft brown sugar
⅓ cup heavy cream

Heat oven to 400°F. Core the apples and remove the top ⅓ of the peel. Pit the plums and cut into dice. Cut the bread into circles, removing the crusts. Lay them in a buttered roasting pan. Put an apple on each piece and fill the center with chopped plums. Mix the butter and sugar into a paste, and dot around the apples. Bake for 30 minutes, basting now and then with the sauce.

When the apples are cooked, lift on to a serving dish and keep warm. Put the roasting pan over a low flame and stir the cream into the toffee mixture. Let it all bubble together a moment or two, then pour into a small pitcher and serve with the apples. When plums are out of season, fill the apples with the butter and sugar paste.

—MENUS—

Some suggestions for well balanced meals based on the baking recipes

MUSSEL SOUP
with Saffron Bread

GRILLED BREAST OF LAMB
with Mustard and Horseradish Sauce

SOUFFLE OMELETTE

CHICKEN NOODLE SOUP

GRILLED SHRIMP
Saffron Rice, lettuce salad

BAKED BANANAS

LEEK GRATIN

GRILLED DOVER SOLE
or SOLE MEUNIERE
new potatoes

TEA SORBET

Vegetarian Menu

LENTIL SOUP

CHICORY GRATIN
Seed Bread

CARROT CAKE

EGGS

This section is based mainly on the use of egg yolks as a thickening agent and the ways this almost magical substance can be used. Egg yolks with olive oil form the basis of mayonnaise, and the pungent garlic sauces of the Mediterranean, such as aïoli, while cooked sauces and soups may also be thickened with yolks.

The Greeks use a mixture of egg yolks and lemon juice called *avgolemono*, with chicken or lamb stock to make a delicious soup. Much richer is the French *Bourride*, a dish of poached fish with an aïoli and extra yolks incorporated in the broth. One of my favorite dishes is a rich Belgian one called *Waterzoie*: poached chicken and vegetables enriched by generous additions of egg yolks and cream.

A sweet egg-based sauce is *Sauce à la Vanille* (or boiled custard, to use its somewhat unappealing English name). This is one of the few really good English sauces, and has sadly fallen into disrepute. I still make it often, as a base for ice creams, or as an accompaniment to fruit puddings. It is a good way of mastering the technique of thickening with egg yolks.

Whole eggs are used alone in dishes of scrambled eggs and omelettes. It is interesting that only the degree of heat and the speed with which they are made differs between these two dishes. By beating the whites separately, air is incorporated into the dish, causing it to puff up in the heat of the oven. This gives the classic soufflé, while a modified version can be used to add lightness to a sauce, or to make a puffy omelette.

CHOOSING GARLIC. Try to find fat heads of garlic sold loose rather than shrivelled prewrapped bulbs. The pink skinned garlic (right) grown in Italy and Provence is particularly good. In early summer look for fresh garlic, plump and juicy. It is one of the chief ingredients of aïoli (see next page).

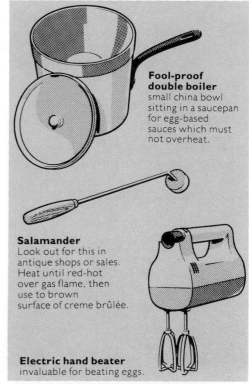

Fool-proof double boiler small china bowl sitting in a saucepan for egg-based sauces which must not overheat.

Salamander Look out for this in antique shops or sales. Heat until red-hot over gas flame, then use to brown surface of creme brûlée.

Electric hand beater invaluable for beating eggs.

TIPS ON USING EGGS

✳ *Since eggs have a lower boiling temperature than almost any other food, they must be handled with extreme care. The degree of heat required to thicken them without making them solid is very precise and a compromise must be reached between speed and safety. While a professional chef will make an egg custard straight over the fire, beginners are advised to use a china bowl standing over, but not touching, simmering water. This demands patience, for the custard may take as long as 10–12 minutes to thicken. Later, you can progress to a metal double boiler, which is faster, but still fairly safe.*

✳ *Good equipment is important when making egg-based sauces: an electric hand beater, rotary hand beater, or balloon whisk, for a start, and preferably a fine strainer and a good double boiler. Alternatively you could use a china bowl sitting over a saucepan (not a Pyrex bowl as glass is a poor conductor of heat and the sauce will never thicken).*

✳ *If an egg-based sauce does overheat and turn into lightly scrambled eggs, it can sometimes be saved by whizzing in a food processor or blender.*

✳ *Make a good supply of vanilla sugar before starting to make custard desserts. Fill a large jar with sugar, bury 3 or 4 vanilla pods in it, cover, and leave for a week.*

✳ *Always rub soufflé dishes with butter before using, or they will be hard to clean.*

*"La Colation." 1868
by Claude Monet.
Photo by Scala/Vision
International.
Courtesy Jeu de Paume,
Louvre, Paris.*

MASTER RECIPE

BOURRIDE

This Mediterranean fish dish is infinitely more delicious than bouillabaisse, in my opinion, and can be made with local fish, unlike bouillabaisse which needs the *poissons des roches* (rock fish) from the area immediately around Marseille.

Serves 6
Aïoli:
4 cloves garlic, peeled and chopped
2 egg yolks
a pinch of salt
1 cup best olive oil
Soup:
3–3½ lb. bass, grey mullet, cod, or end of
hake or halibut. (If using a whole fish,
ask the fish store to cut off the head and
tail and include them. If using a piece of
large fish, ask them to include the tail and
a cod's head, or other bones for stock.)
2 leeks
1 carrot, halved
2 branches fennel
3 stalks parsley
1 bay leaf
½ cup dry white wine
2–2½ quarts water
¼ cup olive oil
2 cloves garlic, chopped
salt and black pepper
⅛ tsp. cayenne
4 egg yolks
1 narrow French loaf, thinly sliced and dried
(not browned) in oven

First make the aïoli: pound garlic to a pulp in a mortar. Or crush in a garlic press and mash with the back of a wooden spoon in a deep bowl. Add egg yolks and salt and beat to a paste. Start adding the oil drop by drop, beating constantly exactly as if you were making Mayonnaise. When one third of the oil has been used up, add the rest more quickly, then set aside.
Make the soup: put the fish head and tail in a fish poacher with the green part of the leeks, the carrot, the fennel, the parsley, and bay leaf. Pour the wine and water over all the ingredients, bring to boil and simmer for 25 minutes.

In the meantime, chop the white part of the leeks and cook them gently in the olive oil in a deep frying pan, adding the garlic

Bourride: some of the fish you can use
and the finished soup, complete with French
bread spread with aïoli and rouille

halfway through, until leeks are golden. Strain the fish stock and pour over the leeks. Discard the fish trimmings, flavoring vegetables, and herbs. Put the whole fish in the poacher, pour stock and fried leeks over, and bring to boil adding salt, pepper and cayenne. Simmer gently, until the fish is just tender, about 20 minutes. Lift out the fish and keep warm.
To thicken the soup: put half the aïoli into a deep china bowl and beat in the remaining 4 egg yolks one by one. Pour the simmering fish stock through a strainer into a bowl or pitcher, then slowly pour it on to the aïoli, beating constantly with a whisk. Stand the bowl over a large pan of gently simmering water, and stir almost continuously for 5–6 minutes, until it lightly coats the back of a spoon. (Don't use a Pyrex bowl or it will never thicken.)
To serve: spread some of the aïoli on the dried bread and keep warm on a plate. Fillet the fish and divide it between 6 soup plates, or simply put in a little and keep the rest for second helpings. Lay 2 slices of bread spread with aïoli in each plate, and spoon some of the soup over it. Serve the extra soup in a tureen, extra bread spread with aïoli on a plate, and any extra aïoli in a small bowl. Give each guest a soup plate with spoon, knife and fork.

If you like, you can also make a Rouille Sauce and then spread some of the bread with aïoli and some with rouille, putting 2 small bowls of the sauces on the table, to add to the soup.

Crayfish, lobster, or giant shrimp may be added for a more luxurious meal, while cod, grey mullet or hake can be used alone for a cheaper dish. This makes a soup and main dish combined, needing nothing before or after, nor any vegetable.

Jancis Robinson's wine choice:
Someone somewhere once wrote that wine cannot be enjoyed with eggs and this diktat has been handed down ever since. Boiled eggs might indeed be slightly ill at ease with great claret, but the egg in any other form – soufflés, quiches, mayonnaise and sauces such as aïoli – shouldn't stop anyone enjoying a glass of wine. Dry rosé from Provence would be a romantic and geographically apt accompaniment to the Bourride. These wines are very pale and often more salmon pink than crimson and they are infinitely more distinguished than most other rosés.

FAMILY OF RECIPES

AÏOLI GARNI

Serves 6

1 large roasting chicken
(4–4½ lb.)
1 onion, halved
1 carrot, halved
1 stalk celery
1 bay leaf
salt and black peppercorns
1½ lb. new potatoes
6 artichokes, trimmed down to the bottom
(see step-by-step instructions overleaf)
¾ lb. broccoli, or 1 cauliflower divided into
florets
¾ lb. green beans
¾ lb. tomatoes
6 eggs
Aïoli:
4 large cloves garlic, chopped
2 egg yolks
a pinch of salt
1½ cups best olive oil
about 1 tbsp. white wine vinegar
about 1 tbsp. lemon juice

Poach the chicken with onion, carrot, celery, bay leaf and seasoning (following the Master Recipe for Poached Chicken on page 70). While it is cooking, boil the potatoes, artichoke bottoms, broccoli or cauliflower, and green beans, separately, until just tender. Drain and keep warm. Skin the tomatoes and cut into quarters. Hard-boil the eggs, shell them and keep warm in hot water.

Make the aïoli (following the Master Recipe, left). When all the oil is added, add vinegar and lemon juice to taste.
To serve: put the chicken on a platter, pile up the hot vegetables on another platter with the eggs, and serve the tomatoes on a separate dish. Carve the chicken at the table, and let the guests help themselves. The plates should be warm but not hot, and the vegetables warm too, rather than scalding.
Variation: a large piece of poached cod can be substituted for the chicken. For a vegetarian meal, omit both and serve the aïoli with a mixture of vegetables and eggs. For a first course, the aïoli can be served with 2 or 3 poached vegetables.

Preparing artichoke bottoms

1 Cut off stem and trim to a flat base. Remove two outer layers of leaves completely.

2 With a stainless steel knife, pare away layers of leaves, leaving only fleshy leaf base.

3 Continue to pare leaves until you have cleared a good inch from the base.

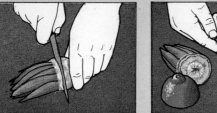

4 Using a sharp knife, cut through the artichoke and discard the top leafy part.

5 Scrape out choke with a teaspoon. (Easier to do after cooking, if recipe permits.)

6 To prevent discoloration, keep in water acidulated with juice of ½ lemon, until needed.

WATERZOÏE

This Belgian dish is made with a large tender chicken, or with a mixture of fresh fish – perch, pike, carp, etc. – like a bland, northern version of a bouillabaisse.

Serves 6

1 large roasting chicken, 4–4½ lb.
6 tbsp. butter
2 lb. leeks, coarsely chopped
1 lb. carrots, coarsely chopped
2 stalks celery, coarsely chopped
¼ lb. mushrooms, coarsely chopped
4 tbsp. chopped parsley
1 bay leaf
salt and black pepper
¾ cup dry white wine
3 egg yolks
½ cup heavy cream

Heat 4 tbsp. of the butter in a large saucepan and put in the chopped vegetables and half the parsley. Cook gently for 5 minutes, stirring now and then. Then pour in enough hot water to come level with the vegetables, adding bay leaf, salt and pepper. Bring to the boil, then remove from heat.

Preheat the oven to 300°F. Heat the remaining butter in a casserole; sprinkle the chicken with salt and pepper, and lay it in the hot butter, turning until golden brown on all sides. Then add the vegetables and their stock. Pour over the wine and bring to the boil. Cover the casserole and cook in the oven for 1½–1¾ hours, until the bird is tender.

When done, remove to a warm place.

Strain the stock into a bowl (retaining the chopped vegetables in the strainer). Let stand for a few minutes to allow the fat to rise to the surface, then extract the fat-free stock from below with a bulb baster, and transfer to a clean saucepan or double boiler. Reheat until almost boiling.

Beat yolks and cream in a bowl, then beat in a few spoonfuls of hot stock. Tip the chopped vegetables back into the stock, then add the egg mixture. Stir constantly over a very low heat until the egg yolks have slightly thickened the sauce. (If nervous of overheating, use a double boiler, or a china bowl standing over simmering water.) Once it has thickened enough to coat the back of a spoon, remove from the heat, or it may overcook.

To serve: carve the bird and lay in a large shallow dish. (If you have overcooked it, don't panic; simply take the meat off the bones and divide into neat pieces.) Pour the hot vegetable cream sauce over the chicken, and sprinkle with the remaining parsley. Serve with plain boiled potatoes. This dish needs no first course, nor other vegetables, nor even a salad. Eat in large soup plates or bowls with knife, fork, and spoon.

Variation: for a simpler version, don't bother to thicken the stock with egg yolk and cream but simply serve the chicken in its vegetable stock, sprinkled with parsley.

AVGOLEMONO SOUP

Serves 5–6

¼ cup long-grain rice
5 cups chicken stock, homemade and free from fat
salt and pepper
2 eggs
juice of 1 large lemon (3–4 tbsp.)

Boil rice in lightly salted water for 10 minutes and drain. Heat the stock, adding salt and pepper to taste. When it boils, add the rice and cook 5 minutes. Beat eggs in a bowl, add lemon juice, and beat again. Pour a large ladleful of boiling soup on to the eggs, beating with a wire whisk. Then pour the egg mixture into the stock, having lowered the heat as much as possible, and whisk constantly 3–4 minutes. (Don't let it boil: this would make the eggs cook in shreds, spoiling the soup.)

GREEK LAMB FRICASSEE

Serves 6

1 boned leg or shoulder of lamb
1 medium onion, thinly sliced
1 carrot, thinly sliced
1 stalk celery, thinly sliced
about 3 cups light chicken stock
2 bunches large scallions, cut across in 1 inch pieces
1 Romaine lettuce heart, cut across in 2 inch chunks
can artichoke bottoms, drained
Sauce:
3 tbsp. butter
3 tbsp. flour
2 egg yolks
salt and black pepper
juice of 1 lemon
3 tbsp. chopped dill

Cut lamb in neat squares, discarding all fat. Place in a casserole with the onion, carrot and celery. Add enough stock to barely cover. Bring to the boil, skimming until the surface is clear, cover, and simmer 1 hour. Add the scallions, bring back to the boil, and cook 5 minutes. Add the lettuce and artichoke bottoms, bring back to the boil, and simmer 2 minutes. (When artichokes are cheap, you can use fresh ones, trimmed and parboiled until tender, see step-by-step instructions above.) When all of them are cooked, lift the meat and vegetables into a serving dish, using a slotted spoon, and keep warm.

Make the sauce: strain stock and measure 2 cups. Let the fat settle and skim it off. Melt butter in a saucepan, add flour and cook 1 minute, stirring. Add fat-free stock, stir until blended and simmer 3 minutes. Beat egg yolks in a bowl, add lemon juice, and beat again. Add 3 tbsp. of simmering sauce, beating constantly, then tip the contents of the bowl into the saucepan. Beat steadily, keeping heat just below boiling, for 3 minutes, until it has very slightly thickened (if you allow it to boil, the egg will curdle and ruin the sauce).

To serve: pour the sauce over the meat, add the dill, and mix gently. Serve as soon as possible, with boiled rice and carrots.

SCRAMBLED EGGS

Serves 2

4–5 eggs
sea salt and black pepper
1 tbsp. butter

Use a heavy pan with a rounded bottom and smooth surface. Beat eggs lightly, adding salt and pepper. Melt butter in pan over a low heat, then pour in the eggs. Leave them a moment, until they start to set, then begin scraping the bottom of the pan with long, slow, regular strokes using a metal spoon with a fairly sharp edge. As the egg sets, the scraping of the spoon lifts the soft curds and liquid egg takes its place at the bottom. Remove from the heat before all the egg has set, and continue scraping and stirring gently; the egg will continue to cook in the heat of the pan.

To serve: spoon gently on to hot plates and eat at once.

Scrambled eggs used to be a popular first course for luncheon parties, served on a huge dish, garnished with broiled mushrooms, tiny broiled tomatoes and croûtons of fried bread. Alternatively, they can be served with some addition (chopped smoked ham, scraps of smoked salmon cut in strips, or a few cooked green peas) stirred in at the very end.

FRENCH OMELETTE

Serves 2

5 eggs
salt and black pepper
½ tbsp. butter

Beat eggs lightly, adding salt and pepper, while the omelette pan heats up. When it is very hot, turn heat down to moderate and put in the butter. Swirl it round once, then pour in the eggs before it has time to brown. Leave them alone for a moment or two, then start to lift the edges gently, using a small spatula and tilting the pan so the liquid egg runs underneath to take its place. When there is only a thin layer of runny egg on top, fold the omelette over in half and slide it on to a hot dish.

Ingredients for Greek Lamb Fricassée

Serve immediately, with a green salad. It should be still runny in the center, what the French call *baveuse*.

Variations: use any of these fillings:

a 2 tbsp. chopped fresh herbs: tarragon, chervil, parsley and chives.

b 3 tbsp. grated Gruyère or Emmental cheese.

c 1 slice dry white bread, cut in cubes and fried in butter with a clove of garlic, well drained.

d 2 tomatoes, peeled, chopped and gently softened in 1 tbsp. butter.

e A red or green pepper, grilled, skinned, and cut in strips.

If using the first filling, add the herbs to the eggs just before pouring them into the pan. All the other fillings are added to the omelette just before folding it over. (They are all already cooked, and so only need reheating.) Don't use more than the recommended amount: an omelette should never be stuffed so resist the temptation to overwhelm the delicate flavour of the eggs. 133

SPANISH OMELETTE
or TORTILLA DI PATATES

A much more solid dish than the French omelette, less delicate but easier to make and good in its own way.

Serves 3–4

½ large Spanish onion, cut in half again and
    thinly sliced
peanut oil, for frying
1 lb. waxy potatoes, peeled and sliced
4 eggs
salt and black pepper

Heat a layer of oil about ½ inch deep in a heavy frying pan or sauté pan. Add onion and cook 2 minutes, then add potatoes. Cook gently, stirring often, about 15 minutes, without allowing them to brown. When they are soft, turn the contents of the pan into a colander standing over a bowl, and leave for a few moments to drain off the oil.

Clean the pan, then put back just enough of the same oil to coat the pan. Beat eggs, adding salt and pepper, and stir the cooked potatoes and onion into the mixture. Heat the pan and pour in the egg mixture. Cook gently without stirring until set, about 8 minutes. Then slide the tortilla on to a plate, clean out the pan, and add another thin layer of oil. Invert the plate over the pan so that the tortilla falls upside down. Cook another 4 minutes, then slide it on to a flat dish. Leave 45–60 minutes.
Serve cut in wedges like a cake. I serve this as a light main dish with two salads: one of lettuce and watercress, and one of tomato.

SOUFFLE OMELETTE

Serves 2

4 eggs, separated
3 tbsp. cold water
1 tsp. sugar
1 tsp. butter
2 tbsp. black cherry jam, warmed

Beat egg yolks with the water, adding sugar. Beat whites until stiff, then pour beaten egg yolks over them, stirring gently until they are incorporated. Heat the omelette pan and add the butter. When it starts to brown, turn the heat down very low and pour in the eggs. Don't stir them, just wait until the omelette becomes puffy and small bubbles burst on the surface. Now spoon the jam over the omelette, fold it over and slide it on to a warm dish.
Serve with extra jam if you like, and cream. This dish has to be eaten immediately, once made.

SMOKED HADDOCK SOUFFLE

Serves 4

½ lb. smoked haddock
1 cup milk
3 tbsp. butter
3 tbsp. flour
3 tbsp. grated Parmesan
4 eggs, separated
black pepper

Cut the fish in four and put in a broad pan. Add milk and enough cold water to almost cover. Bring to the boil, cover, and poach gently for 12 minutes. Remove the fish, strain the stock, measure ¾ cup and set aside.

Preheat oven to 350°F. When the fish is cool enough to handle, flake it, discarding skin and bone. Weigh 6 oz. and chop finely (use the rest for another dish). Melt the butter in a clean pan, add flour, and cook 1 minute, stirring. Then pour in the measured fish stock and bring to the boil, stirring. Simmer for 3 minutes, adding pepper and the Parmesan. Finally, stir in the chopped fish. Remove from the heat and stir in the egg yolks, one by one. Cool a little, then beat the whites until stiff and fold in. Pour into a buttered soufflé dish and bake for 25 minutes, until risen and just set. Serve immediately.

Soufflé Omelette with cherry jam

Variation: Once learned, the process of making a soufflé can be adapted again and again. To make a Cheese Soufflé, omit the fish, use milk instead of fish stock for the sauce, double the quantity of grated cheese and add a little cayenne.

OEUFS SOUBISE

Serves 5–6 as a first course, or 3–4 as a light main course

2 Spanish onions, halbed and thickly sliced
3 tbsp. butter
3 tbsp. flour
2 cups chicken stock
½ cup light cream
½ cup grated Gruyère, or Emmental
sea salt and black pepper
¼ tsp. mace or nutmeg
6 hard-boiled eggs, shelled

Cook the onions slowly in the butter, allowing about 10 minutes to soften without going brown. Add the flour, stir to blend, cook another minute, then heat the stock with the cream and add to the pan. Stir until blended, then simmer 15 minutes. Add cheese, stirring until it blends with the sauce, then add salt, pepper and mace or nutmeg.

Heat the broiler. Cut the eggs in quarters and stir gently into the sauce. Reheat over a low flame, then pour into a shallow, flameproof dish, well buttered, and brown the surface under the broiler.
To serve: if serving as a main course, accompany with a green salad.

PETIT POTS DE CREME AU CAFE

Serves 6

scant ½ cup very strong black coffee
2 cups heavy cream
3 egg yolks
3 tbsp. castor sugar

Start a day in advance. Preheat the oven to 300°F. Heat coffee and cream in a small pan. Beat egg yolks with sugar and pour on the coffee cream when it is almost boiling. Mix well, then strain into 6 little fireproof dishes – small oeuf en cocotte dishes work well. Stand them in a baking pan with hot water coming halfway up the sides and bake 25 minutes, or until just set. Cool, and chill overnight.
Variation: to make Petits Pots de Crème au Chocolat, melt 3 oz. semi-sweet chocolate in 3 tbsp. double-strength coffee. Use instead of plain coffee and use vanilla sugar.

CREME BRULEE

Serves 6

2 cups heavy cream
½ vanilla pod
6 eggs
2 tbsp. vanilla sugar or plain sugar
superfine sugar for topping

Start several hours, or a day, in advance. Preheat the oven to 300°F. Heat cream in a small pan with vanilla pod. Stop just before it reaches boiling point and remove the pod (keep it for another time). Beat eggs in a bowl, add the sugar, and pour in the hot cream, beating steadily. Stand bowl over simmering water, making sure the bowl is above the water, and stir constantly until it has thickened just enough to lightly coat the back of a spoon. Remove from heat and pour into an ovenproof dish, or 6 custard cups. Put in the oven for 10 minutes, or 5 minutes for small dishes, to form a skin which prevents the sugar sinking into the crème. Remove and cool.

To make the topping: spread an even layer of superfine sugar about $\frac{1}{16}$ inch thick over the surface. This can now be *brûlée*, or burnt, by a number of different methods:

a Under the broiler: heat thoroughly in advance to its highest possible setting. Place dish(es) under it, and turn to brown the sugar evenly.

b By salamander: these are round flat irons on a long-angled handle. Heat over a gas flame until almost red-hot, then move over the surface of the dish, holding it as close as possible without actually touching, until the sugar has melted and browned evenly.

c By blowtorch: although this sounds alarming, it is surprisingly easy. Protect the edges of the dish(es) with foil, and simply play the flame over the surface for a few seconds until evenly browned.

d There is an alternative method: draw a circle around the edge of your dish(es) on a piece of lightly oiled foil, and spread an even layer of superfine sugar just inside its margins. Melt and brown the sugar by any of the above methods, then leave to cool. Peel off the foil and drop the disc of brown caramel on to your dish(es).

Leave to cool, then chill your crème brûlée for several hours.

This is a very rich dessert, and should follow the purest and simplest of dishes – possibly a consommé and steamed fish, or roast joint of meat or game.

Variation: put a layer of white seedless grapes, peeled, halved, in your dish before pouring in the crème.

FLOATING ISLANDS

Serves 6

4 egg yolks and 3 egg whites
scant ½ cup homemade vanilla sugar, or
  plain sugar
2½ cups milk
½ vanilla pod

Beat the 3 egg whites until thick, then fold in half the sugar, and beat until stiff. Bring a broad pan of unsalted water to the boil and adjust heat so it barely simmers. Drop tablespoons of the meringue on to the surface of the water, a few at a time, so that they can float freely without touching. Poach gently for 3 minutes, turn with a slotted spoon, and poach another 2 minutes. Lift out and drain on a cloth. (Don't use paper towel: it sticks to the meringue.) Poach the rest of the meringues in batches. When all are done, transfer them from the cloth to a flat tray and put in the refrigerator for a few hours, or overnight.

To make the custard: heat milk with vanilla pod until almost boiling, then turn off heat and let stand, covered, for 20 minutes. Strain the milk and reheat it. (Rinse and dry the vanilla pod: you can use it again.) Beat egg yolks with the remaining sugar in a china bowl until thick and creamy, then pour in the almost boiling milk as you continue to beat. When all is mixed, stand the bowl over simmering water – don't let the water touch the bottom of the bowl – and stir constantly until it has thickened very slightly. It should just coat the back of the spoon. You can use a metal double boiler if you like; it will thicken faster but you risk overheating it. If this happens, and the eggs start to scramble, turn into a food processor and purée; this should save it. Once thickened, stand the bowl in very cold water and stir now and then while it cools, to prevent a skin forming. Then chill for a few hours, or overnight.

To serve: pour the custard sauce into a large shallow dish and lay the poached meringues on it. If you prefer, it can be served in individual bowls, with a meringue floating on custard sauce in each one.

Variation: this sauce is the classic English boiled custard, or *sauce à la vanille*, that used to be served with desserts before the advent of custard powder gave custard a new meaning. It is a delicious accompaniment to hot steamed puddings or compôtes of fruit instead of cream, and can be served hot as well as cold.

—MENUS—

Some suggestions for well balanced meals based on the egg recipes

BOURRIDE

BONED LEG OF LAMB, GRILLED
served cold
green salad

BLACKCURRANT FOOL
with Oatmeal Biscuits

CLAMS IN ASPIC

AÏOLI GARNI
with poached chicken, hard-boiled eggs
and vegetables

FRUIT SALAD WITH CREAM

ZUCCHINI FRITTERS
with Garlic Sauce

GREEK LAMB FRICASSEE
noodles, carrots

WHITE WINE JELLY
with whipped cream

Vegetarian Menu
TOMATO JELLY WITH CELERY
REMOULADE
made with vegetable stock

OEUFS SOUBISE
Potato Bread, lettuce salad

ELDER FLOWER FRITTERS

ASPICS & JELLIES

Aspic may seem somewhat daunting to the learner, with its connotations of haute cuisine and classic dishes. A true aspic takes two days to make, with lengthy simmering and clarification. Yet a simple version can be made by adding gelatine to homemade stock, while chaudfroid sauce can also be simplified. Traditionally made with velouté sauce, aspic, cream and egg yolks, a light version can be made by adding gelatine to reduced chicken stock mixed with cream. Gelatine is a marvellous product, easy to use, and with much to offer anyone who enjoys decorating food, for it protects it – and its garnish – from drying out, while adding its own translucent quality to the finished dish.

Fish and shellfish respond particularly well to aspic, for the jelly recreates the liquid quality of their original habitat. Almost all aspic dishes are best served with a complementary sauce. These can be quite simple, based on mayonnaise mixed with cream or yogurt, and flavored with mustard or herbs, saffron or curry powder. A beaten egg white can be added to give a foamy quality that goes well with the texture of the jelly, while spicy flavors contrast with its blandness.

Like aspics and chaudfroids, sweet jellies have also fallen out of favor in the last few decades, their image spoiled by the introduction of the commercial product with its synthetic flavor, lurid colors, and rubbery consistency. A true jelly should be soft and shivery, only just set and made with the purest of ingredients.

Some of the *nouvelle cuisine* chefs have recently reinstated fruit jellies, serving them like sorbets, in different flavors, garnished with tiny pieces of fruit. Sweet jellies also benefit from serving with a sauce: an almond sauce, a vanilla custard, or lightly-whipped cream flavored with vanilla.

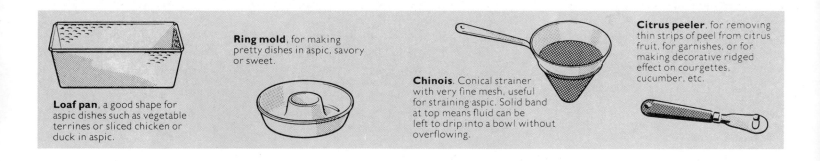

Loaf pan, a good shape for aspic dishes such as vegetable terrines or sliced chicken or duck in aspic.

Ring mold, for making pretty dishes in aspic, savory or sweet.

Chinois. Conical strainer with very fine mesh, useful for straining aspic. Solid band at top means fluid can be left to drip into a bowl without overflowing.

Citrus peeler, for removing thin strips of peel from citrus fruit, for garnishes, or for making decorative ridged effect on courgettes, cucumber, etc.

SEASONINGS
I feel lost without my favorite seasonings. Almost without exception, I use sea salt, both for cooking and serving, and black peppercorns ground in a mill. For cooking, I use a smooth Dijon mustard, usually Grey Poupon. On the table, I have a whole grain mustard, or one made with green peppercorns. This might be one of five or six different brands, for I like to vary them. Some of the best are the French Celine Corcellet, Bornibus and Pommery Moutarde de Meaux, or the excellent Urchfont Black Mustard made by the English firm British Tracklements. Other good English mustards are those made by Gordon's, Elsenham, and Crabtree & Evelyn.

"Le Dejeuner," 1873, by Claude Monet. Picture by Scala/Vision International.
Courtesy Jeu de Paume, Louvre, Paris

TIPS ON MAKING ASPIC AND JELLY

✳️*Any stock, if sufficiently concentrated, will set to a jelly when cold. However, for a jelly firm enough to turn out, or to contain solid ingredients, it is best to increase the setting capacity by including calves' or pigs' feet or veal bones, especially knuckle. When this is too slow, or inappropriate to the flavor of the dish, use powdered gelatine. (Leaf gelatine is rarely seen nowadays.) Don't use commercial aspic powder. One pint aspic or jelly will serve four people.*

✳️*Canned Beef Consommé can be used as a substitute for aspic when only a small amount is needed, but the taste will become over-familiar if used too often.*

✳️*To make herb-flavored aspics, infuse sprigs of the herb in the stock, strain before using, and garnish with leaves of the same herb. Use with soft-boiled eggs or poached fillets of fish.*

✳️*$\frac{1}{2}$ oz. gelatine will set $2\frac{1}{2}$ cups liquid, but half as much again may be needed if the liquid has a high acid content (e.g. if made with citrus fruit, raspberries or unripe tomatoes), or if it contains alcohol.*

✳️*As an alternative to gelatine, which is made from animal protein, vegetarians can use agar-agar or carrageen, made from seaweed and sold in health food shops.*

✳️*You do not need to buy special molds: find suitable dishes already in your cupboards: straight-sided ones are best. Soufflé dishes and small ramekins are good (china works just as well as tin). Rectangular loaf tins make handsome jellies and oval oeuf en gelée molds are perfect for individual jellies of all sorts. Old china and copper jelly molds look charming in antique shops, but are best left there, in my opinion. Their intricate indentations make it very hard to unmold the jelly, while a plain flat surface offers scope for garnishing.*

✳️*Some jellies look pretty roughly chopped and piled in glasses. Try combining an orange jelly, chopped and piled in mounds, with sliced oranges, on a flat dish.*

137

MASTER RECIPE

*LAYERED VEGETABLE TERRINE
IN ASPIC
WITH TOMATO PUREE AND
MUSTARD SAUCE*

Serves 6 as a first course

Aspic:
$\frac{1}{2}$ *chicken, or* $1\frac{1}{2}$–*2 lb. chicken pieces*
*1 calf's foot, or 1 pig's foot, or 1 large piece
  knuckle of veal*
*2 medium onions, halved, plus extra onion
  skins*
2 large carrots, halved
2 leeks, halved
3 stalks celery, halved
$\frac{1}{2}$ *bay leaf*
$\frac{1}{2}$ *tsp. salt*
6 black peppercorns
1 egg white, plus shell
Terrine:
$\frac{1}{4}$ *lb. zucchini, unpeeled*
$\frac{1}{4}$ *lb. carrots*
$\frac{1}{4}$ *lb. broccoli*
$\frac{1}{4}$ *lb. show peas, or string beans*
2 bunches large scallions

Tomato Purée and Mustard Sauce: *see
following recipes*

Start at least 36 hours in advance. Put
chicken and calf's foot (or alternative) into
a stock pot and cover generously with cold
water. Heat slowly, skimming frequently as
it nears boiling point. When it boils, reduce
heat and continue to skim until surface is
clear. Then add the flavoring vegetables,
herbs, and seasonings. Bring back to boil,
skim again, then adjust heat so it boils
gently; half cover and leave for 3 hours,
skimming from time to time. (The constant
skimming and gentle boiling should ensure
a clear stock.) When the time is up, strain
the stock, cool, and chill overnight in the
refrigerator. You will need about a quart; if
there is more, reduce it by fast boiling
before chilling. Throw away the meat and
vegetables.

Next day, prepare your mold. I use a
rectangular bread pan holding exactly 5
cups. Chill it in the freezer while you cook
the vegetables. Cut zucchini and carrots
into long thin wedges. Divide broccoli into
flowerets. Trim showpeas or string beans
but leave whole. Trim scallions, leaving on
most of the green leaves so they look like
little leeks. Keep vegetables in separate

piles. Heat stock (after carefully removing
fat) and poach vegetables separately, removing each variety as soon as it is tender.
Replenish the stock with boiling water as it
reduces, to keep roughly the same amount.
As each vegetable is cooked, drain it, then
transfer to a plate, still keeping them
separate.

When all are done, beat the egg white
until foamy, but not stiff, add its crushed
shell (reserving the yolk for the mustard
sauce), and throw into stock. Bring back to
boil, beating with a wire whisk, then remove from heat and leave to settle a few
moments. Return to the heat and boil up
once more. Have a strainer lined with a
piece of muslin standing over a bowl. After
it boils up for the second time, pour it
slowly through the strainer, leaving to drip
through. The egg white will have formed a
crust, trapping all the small particles of
sediment, and the resulting liquid should be
clear and golden. If not, put the egg white
back into the stock and boil up once more,
then pour through the muslin again.

When the stock has passed through the
cloth (you may squeeze it through gently,
but don't force it or it will be cloudy),
measure it: you need about 2 cups Taste for
seasoning and adjust. When cool, pour a

thin layer into your chilled mold and put in the refrigerator (or freezer, if you watch it carefully) to set. The additon of calf's foot (or equivalent) means it will set to a firm jelly without using gelatine. If you are unable to buy any of these, you may add 1 envelope of gelatine, dissolving it in a little of the clarified stock.

Once the first layer of jelly has set, make a layer o scallions on top of it, interweaving them prettily. Then add the other vegetables in layers, in any order you please. When full, pour in the liquid jelly and chill several hours, until firmly set.

The Tomato Purée and Mustard Sauce may be made any time in the interim, preferably 1–2 hours before serving.

To serve: run a small knife around the edges of the terrine, then stand in a sink with hot water halfway up the sides. Leave 1½–2 minutes, then take out, dry, and invert over a shallow serving dish. Shake hard, giving a few sharp jolts, and see if it will come out. If not, wring out a cloth in very hot water and lay over the pan for a few minutes, then try again. (If you use a china dish as a mold, it will be harder to turn out, and must stand longer in warm water.) Once it is out, remove the pan. Don't despair if some has got left behind; it can usually be eased out and replaced fairly satisfactorily. (If not, you can mask the whole terrine with Tomato Purée). Spoon the Tomato Purée around it, and serve the Mustard Sauce separately, in a small bowl. Cut across in thick slices with a very sharp knife; the combination of just-cooked vegetables with soft jelly makes it hard to cut neatly.

The dish takes a long time to prepare, but it can all be done 2 or 3 days beforehand, and the result is delicious and spectacular. If making a day or two ahead of time, leave it in its pan until the last moment, and only make the sauces on the day itself.

MUSTARD SAUCE

1 egg yolk, at room temperature
a pinch of salt
2 tbsp. Dijon mustard
1 tbsp. white wine vinegar
¼ cup sunflower seed oil
⅓ cup yogurt, beaten till smooth

This is simply a mayonnaise flavored with mustard and yogurt. Break egg yolk into a bowl and stir with wooden spoon, adding salt and mustard. Continue to stir steadily while adding oil, drop by drop at first, then faster. When all oil is absorbed, slowly stir in vinegar. Finally fold in the yogurt.

TOMATO PUREE

1 lb tomatoes

Skin tomatoes, cut in quarters, chop in food processer until reduced to a thick, slightly lumpy purée, and chill.

Jancis Robinson's Wine Choice:
The subtle flavors of the vegetable terrine and its sauces need to be flattered rather than overwhelmed by any vinous accompaniment. White wine from Loire – Muscadet, Côteaux du Layon, Anjou Blanc, Savennières, Saumur, Sauvignon de Touraine, Vouvray, Sancerre, Pouilly-Fumé and most white Vins de Pays – are all light in body and high in refreshing acidity. Of these, Vouvray is probably the most under-priced and a good one has a delicate smell reminiscent of honey and flowers.

FAMILY OF RECIPES

TOMATO JELLY WITH CELERY REMOULADE

Serves 6 as a first course, or 4–5 as a light main dish

1¼ lb. ripe tomatoes
½ onion, sliced
1 stalk celery, sliced
½ carrot, sliced
2 stalks parsley
½ bay leaf
½ tsp. salt
½ tsp. sugar
6 black peppercorns
2 cups chicken stock (homemade
1 tbsp. tomato paste
juice of ¼ lemon
2–3 dashes Tabasco
3 envelopes gelatine
Celery Remoulade:
1 hardboiled egg yolk
1 raw egg yolk
a pinch of salt
2 tsp. Dijon mustard
½ cup sunflower seed oil
1 tbsp. white wine vinegar
1 tbsp. lemon juice
2 tbsp. yogurt
1 head celery, sliced

Make jelly a day, or several hours, in advance. Don't peel the tomatoes; simply chop roughly and put in a pan with the vegetables, herbs, salt, sugar, and peppercorns. Add stock and tomato paste, bring slowly to boil, and simmer 30 minutes. Strain and measure: make up to 3¾ cups by adding more stock. Add lemon juice and Tabasco to taste. Soak gelatine in a cup with ⅓ cup cold water, then stand in a pan of very hot water until melted. Stir into the tomato liquid, mix well, and strain again. Pour into a 4 cup ring mold and chill until set.

Next day, or in the evening, make the remoulade. Mash the hard-boiled egg yolk in a bowl with a fork, add the raw egg yolk, mix to a paste with a wooden spoon, then add salt and mustard. Start adding oil drop by drop. When the oil is used up, add vinegar and lemon juice and adjust seasoning. It should be quite sharp, tasting quite strongly of mustard. Stir in the yogurt. Slice the best parts of the celery, and stir into the sauce. Chop some of the best leaves and reserve.

To serve: turn out the ring mold on to a flat plate (see step-by-step instructions on page 141), and fill the center with the celery remoulade. Scatter chopped celery leaves over the top.

OEUFS EN GELEE

Serves 4 as a first course

1 cup aspic, or homemade beef or chicken stock
1 tbsp. dry sherry, or vermouth
1 envelope gelatine
salt and pepper
4 leaves tarragon, or tiny sprigs chervil or dill
4 poached eggs
2 slices ham, not too thin

Start several hours, or a day, in advance. If using aspic, warm it just enough to make it liquid, add sherry (or vermouth), and adjust seasoning. If using stock, make sure it is absolutely clear and free of fat, heat to boiling, then turn off heat and shake in gelatine, whisking until smooth.

Have eggs poached in advance, and left to cool. Trim edges neatly. Pour a thin layer of cool aspic into 4 small molds or dishes (oval are best, but round will do). Chill until set, then lay a sprig of herb in each one. Choose the best side of each egg, and lay best side down in dishes. Cover with liquid jelly, leaving about ⅓ inch empty. Chill until set, then cut small slices of ham to fit each dish, and lay them over the eggs. Cover with more aspic, and chill in refrigerator a few hours, or overnight. 139

CHAUDFROID OF CHICKEN

Serves 6

4–4¼ lb. roasting chicken
1 onion, halved
2 cloves
1 carrot, halved
1 leek, halved
1 stalk celery
1 small bay leaf
3 stalks parsley
1 sprig thyme
2 tsp. sea salt
8 black peppercorns
2 envelopes gelatine
5 tbsp. butter
⅓ cup flour
1 cup heavy cream
3 sprigs tarragon or dill
a small bunch chives

Start a day in advance. Poach the chicken with the flavoring vegetables, herbs, salt and peppercorns. (Follow Master Recipe on the previous page). When tender, remove bird and leave to cool. Boil up stock until reduced to about 3 cups, then strain and chill until the fat has solidified.

Remove all fat from stock, reheat, and measure 2 cups. Take a quarter of it and shake in the gelatine, whisking with a fork until it has dissolved. Set aside. Melt butter, stir in flour, and cook 1 minute, stirring. Add the rest of the stock and stir until blended. Simmer gently 15 minutes, stirring now and then. When it has finished cooking, stir in the gelatine mixture and cream. When well mixed, taste and adjust seasoning. Pour into a bowl standing in very cold water. Stir often while it cools, to prevent a skin forming.

While sauce is cooling, carve the chicken into neat pieces, removing the skin, and lay them side by side (but not touching) on a flat plate. When the sauce is on the point of setting, pour a layer over the chicken, letting it run smoothly over the pieces of its own accord as much as possible. Chill until set. Keep the rest of the sauce from setting by standing over a pan of hot water. Make a second layer, and as it sets, decorate the chicken with tarragon leaves or feathery sprigs of dill, and some spiky chives. Chill again until completely set; allow 2–3 hours, or overnight.

To serve: cut around each chicken piece carefully, and lift on to a clean dish with a spatula. Accompany with a potato or rice salad, and lettuce salad.

DUCK IN ASPIC

Serves 8

2 ducks, 4½–5 lb. each
1 large onion, cut up
2 carrots, cut up
2 stalks celery, cut up
4 stalks parsley
1 bay leaf
2 tsp. sea salt and 8 black peppercorns
½ bottle dry white wine
2–3 tbsp. orange juice
2 envelopes gelatine
1 small orange
1 lemon

Start a day in advance. Put ducks in a casserole that fits as closely as possible, and strew them with the cut up vegetables, herbs, salt and peppercorns. Add wine and enough hot water to half-cover them, about 4–5 cups. Bring to boil slowly, removing any scum, and when it is clear cover and cook 35 minutes. Turn ducks over and cook another 35 minutes. Test to see if they are done by pulling a leg away from the body: if it resists, cook another 5–10 minutes. Lift out ducks and cool. Strain stock and measure 4 cups; if you have much more, reduce by boiling it up. Let it cool, then chill quickly in the freezer to solidify the fat. Once this is hard, lift it off and warm the stock, just until it turns liquid. Add a little orange juice, and adjust the seasoning. Take about ½ cup of the stock and bring to the boil in a small pan. Turn off the heat and shake in the gelatine, whisking with a fork until it has melted. Then mix with the rest of the stock, and leave to cool.

Carve the birds into neat fillets, discarding skin and bone. Slice orange and lemon thinly. Pour a thin layer of cool aspic into an oval dish, or rectangular loaf pan, and chill quickly in the freezer until just set. Make a pattern of orange and lemon slices on the jelly, and pour another thin layer over them. Chill again. Fill the dish with layers of sliced duck and aspic. If pressed for time, this can be done at one time, but it will not be quite so elegant, nor so evenly distributed. Chill overnight.

To serve: turn out onto a flat plate and divide at the table. Don't try to serve it already cut in slices, for the jelly is so much softer than the duck that it is impossible to do it neatly. Accompany with salads.

Variation: to make <u>Chicken in Aspic</u>, use two large roasting chickens (4½ lb.) and leave out the orange juice.

SHELLFISH IN ASPIC WITH SAFFRON SAUCE

Serves 6

<u>Aspic Jelly:</u>
Fish trimmings: cod's head, bones, etc.
1 onion or leek, halved
1 carrot, halved
1 stalk celery, halved
½ bay leaf
3 parsley stalks
¼ tsp. salt
6 black peppercorns
½ cup white wine
1 envelope gelatine
<u>Fish:</u>
1 monkfish tail
1¼–1½ lb. halibut
6 scallops
¼ lb. shelled shrimp
juice of 1 small lemon
salt and black pepper
2–3 shakes Tabasco
<u>Garnish:</u>
1 bunch watercress
<u>Saffron Sauce:</u> *see right*

Start a day in advance. Put fish bones in a pan with flavoring vegetables, herbs, salt, peppercorns, white wine, and 3 cups cold water. Bring slowly to boil and simmer 25

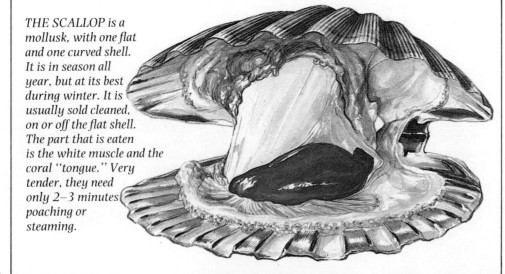

THE SCALLOP is a mollusk, with one flat and one curved shell. It is in season all year, but at its best during winter. It is usually sold cleaned, on or off the flat shell. The part that is eaten is the white muscle and the coral "tongue." Very tender, they need only 2–3 minutes poaching or steaming.

Shellfish in Aspic with Saffron Sauce

SAFFRON SAUCE

1 egg yolk
a pinch of salt
¼ tsp. saffron (powder, not stamens)
¼ tsp. ground cumin
¼ tsp. ground coriander
½ cup sunflower seed oil
1½ tsp. white wine vinegar
1½ tsp. lemon juice
½ cup yogurt

Break egg yolk into a bowl and stir in salt and spices. Add oil drop by drop, stirring constantly. When half the oil has been amalgamated, the rest can be added a little more quickly. When all of it has been absorbed, stir in the vinegar, lemon juice, and finally the yogurt.

FOAMY YELLOW SAUCE

This light sauce is good with all aspic dishes, especially those containing fish, shellfish or soft-boiled eggs.

Serve 4–5

1 large egg, separated
a pinch of salt
1 tsp. Dijon mustard
½ cup sunflower seed oil
1 tbsp. white wine vinegar
2 tbsp. yogurt

Put the egg yolk into a bowl standing on a damp cloth to keep it steady. Beat with a wooden spoon, adding the salt and mustard. Start to add the oil drop by drop, as if making a Mayonnaise. Once it has formed an emulsion, you can add it slightly more quickly, adding a teaspoon of vinegar if it gets too thick. When all the oil is absorbed, add the remaining vinegar.

Beat the egg white until stiff, and fold 2 tbsp. of it into the sauce. Beat the yogurt until smooth and fold that in also.

minutes; then strain into a clean saucepan.

Put monkfish tail into the hot stock, bring back to boil, lower heat, and poach gently until cooked, about 15–20 minutes. Remove monkfish and put in halibut, bring back to boil, lower the heat, and poach about 15 minutes, until cooked. Remove it, drop scallops into stock; poach for 3 minutes, then remove.

Strain stock, measure it, and leave to cool. Calculate how much is needed to make it up to 2½ cups and put that much cold water into a bowl. Shake gelatine into it, and leave to soak 5 minutes. Then stand bowl in a pan of very hot water until it has melted. Stir into fish stock, mix well, and strain into a bowl. Leave to cool.

Take monkfish and halibut off the bone, discarding skin, and flake it. Cut scallops into round horizontal slices; keep back 6 and mix rest with monkfish and halibut, adding the orange tongues; reserve a few shrimp, and mix the rest with the other fish. Squeeze lemon juice over all, and add salt and pepper, mixing it in lightly.

Chill a 4 cup ring mold in the freezer for 15 minutes, then pour in a thin layer of liquid jelly. If you don't have a ring mold, use any round dish or bread pan holding 4 cups. Chill a few moments in the freezer until set, then arrange reserved scallops and shrimp on it. Pour on a little more jelly, and chill again until set. Then fill mold with the rest of the fish and jelly, and chill in refrigerator 3–4 hours.

To serve: turn out following step-by-step instructions below. Fill center with sprigs of watercress, and serve with Saffron Sauce handed separately, as a first course, or as a light main dish with a green salad.

Unmolding a jelly from a ring mold

1 Run a thin knife around the inner and outer edges of the mold.

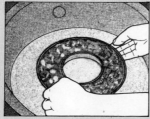
2 Stand mold in a few inches of warm water for 1–2 minutes.

3 Invert on to a flat plate standing on a cloth. Bang down once or twice, then remove the mold.

4 If jelly refuses to come out, leave upside down and cover with a cloth wrung out in very hot water.

FILLETS OF SOLE IN ASPIC

Serves 6

3 fillets Dover sole, or lemon sole, skinned,
*   with bones*
1 onion, halved
1 carrot, halved
1 stalk celery
3 stalks parsley
1 bay leaf
2 tsp. salt
6 black peppercorns
½ cup dry white wine, or ¼ cup vermouth, or
*   2 tbsp. white wine vinegar*
1 envelope gelatine
¼ lb. white seedless grapes, peeled, and
*   halved*

Skin fillets (or get the fish store to do it), and put skins into a pan with bones, flavoring vegetables and herbs. Add salt and peppercorns, wine (or substitute), and enough cold water to cover. Bring slowly to the boil and simmer, half covered, for 25 minutes. Strain into a smaller pan and bring back to boil.

Divide fillets in half and roll them up. Lower into the simmering stock and poach gently for 5 minutes. Remove them carefully and leave to cool.

Taste the stock; you only need 1¼ cups, so reduce it by fast boiling if the flavor is weak. When flavor is good, strain again and measure 1¼ cups exactly. Shake gelatine into hot stock and whisk with a fork until dissolved. Then leave to cool.

Pour a thin layer of stock into 6 oval *oeuf en gelée* molds, or dishes, and chill until set. Cut 6 perfect slices from the grapes, and chop the rest. Lay one slice on top of each dish of jelly, cover with another thin layer of aspic, and chill again. Once set, lay a rolled fillet of fish in each mold, and surround it with chopped grapes. Fill the molds with jelly and chill for a few hours, or overnight.

To serve: turn out on to a flat dish, or individual plates, and serve with a Saffron Sauce (see previous page), or Mustard Sauce (see page 139) as a first course.

CLAMS IN ASPIC

Serves 5–6 as a first course

12 large clams
1¼ cups dry white wine
1¼ cups chicken stock
1 stalk celery, chopped
1 shallot, chopped
2 envelopes gelatine
salt and black pepper
a dash Tabasco
1 tbsp. parsley, very finely chopped

Put clams in a broad saucepan with just enough water to cover the bottom, not more than ½ cup. Bring to boil, cover, and cook about 6–8 minutes, until shells have opened. (Some clams are very stubborn, and have to be forced open.) Take them out of their shells, and save the liquid. Chop the clams finely by hand and set aside.

Take 1 cup strained clam broth and heat in a pan with wine and stock, adding celery (leaves included) and shallot. Simmer until reduced to 2 cups, remove from the heat, and shake in the gelatine. Whisk until it dissolves, then strain and leave to cool. Stir in minced clams and chill until set.

To serve: scrub 18 of the empty half shells. Break up the clam aspic with a fork and pile into as many of the shells as it will fill. Sprinkle with a little parsley, and serve on a large flat dish. (Or put back in the refrigerator until required.) This is an unusual dish which I love, and have only ever had in New York, or in my own house. It can be made with canned clams, but is far better with fresh, if you can find them. It can be served alone, as a first course, allowing about 3 clam shells per person, or combined with one or two other cold fish hors d'oeuvres. These might include a dish of large shrimp, shelled after cooking and dressed with olive oil, lemon juice, and chopped herbs, or small fillets of smoked eel, trout, or haddock.

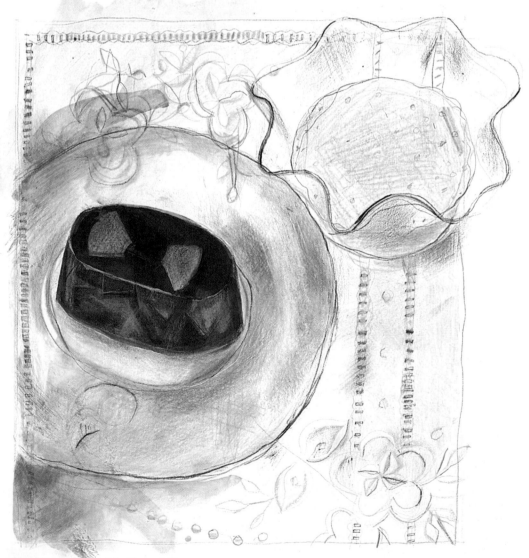

Blackberry Jelly with Almond Sauce

ORANGE JELLY

Serves 6

8 large oranges
6 tbsp. castor sugar
3 envelopes gelatine
¾ lb. white seedless grapes, peeled
⅔ cup whipping cream
⅔ cup yogurt
1 egg white
1 tbsp. sugar or vanilla sugar

Pare the rind of 3 of the oranges, using a potato peeler, and put in a bowl. Squeeze juice of all the oranges, measure, and pour over rind. Take enough water to make the juice up to 3¾ cups, and put it in a saucepan with the sugar. Bring to boil and simmer a minute or two, until the sugar melts, then add the juice and rind. Bring back to boil and skim until the surface is clear. Add 1 tbsp. cold water, bring back to boil, and skim once more. Strain into a bowl and shake in gelatine. Whisk with a fork until it melts, then leave to cool. Pour into a ring mold holding 4 cups and chill overnight, or for several hours.

To serve: turn out on to a flat plate and fill center with grapes. Whip cream, beat yogurt until smooth, and fold into cream. Beat egg white until stiff and fold in also, adding the sugar. Serve in a bowl, or pile on top of the grapes if you like. If you don't have a ring mold, make a layer of grapes in the bottom of a soufflé dish, pour jelly over them and serve in the dish.

BLACKBERRY JELLY WITH ALMOND SAUCE

Serves 6

1 lb. blackberries, fresh or frozen
scant 1 cup sugar
2 envelopes gelatine
4 crisp apples
Almond Sauce: *see below*

Put blackberries in a pan with the sugar; don't add water. Heat slowly until the juice runs, then increase heat slightly and boil for 10 minutes. Strain, crushing berries with the back of a spoon, measure juice, and make up to 18 fl. oz. with water. Soak gelatine in ⅓ cup cold water for 5 minutes, then stand in a pan of very hot water to dissolve gelatine. Mix with blackberry juice, strain again, and cool.

Chill 6 small molds in freezer while you prepare apples (oval *oeuf en gelée* molds are perfect, or china *oeuf en cocotte* dishes). Pour a thin layer of liquid jelly into each one and put back in freezer for a few minutes to set. Cut apples in quarters, peel and core, then cut each quarter across into thin slices. Make a pattern of apple slices on the set jelly, and cover with more jelly. Chill again until set, then fill up with apple slices and jelly, and chill for about 2 hours, until set.

To serve: turn out on to individual plates, and serve with Almond Sauce.

Variation: Raspberry and Peach Jelly
Make as above, substituting raspberries (fresh or frozen) for blackberries, and 2 ripe peaches (pitted, skinned, cut in quarters, then sliced) for the apples. Increase the gelatine by 1 envelope to compensate for the acidity of the raspberries.

ALMOND SAUCE

2 egg yolks
¼ cup milk
2 tbsp. sugar or vanilla sugar
1 tbsp. ground almonds

Break egg yolks into a china bowl sitting over a pan of simmering water. Beat with a wire whisk, then add milk, sugar, and almonds. Continue to whisk about 5 minutes, until light, foamy, and very slightly thickened – it should lightly coat the back of the spoon. Stand bowl in cold water to cool, stirring often to prevent a skin forming. Then pour into a pitcher and serve, preferably still warm, with the jellies.

WHITE WINE JELLY

This must be made with a good wine: a slightly fruity or flowery one is best. I usually use Muscadet, or Vouvray.

Serves 6

2 cups white wine
scant 1 cup sugar
4 envelopes gelatine
¼ cup lemon juice
¼ cup orange juice
1 cup whipping cream

Start a day in advance. Put sugar in a pan with 1¼ cups water. Bring to boil, and simmer until sugar melts. Remove from heat, and shake in gelatine, whisking with a fork until it also dissolves. Set aside and leave to cool. Then add wine and fruit juices. Strain into a ring mold and chill overnight in the refrigerator.

To serve: turn out on to a flat plate and fill the center with lightly whipped cream.

—MENUS—

Some suggestions for well balanced meals based on the aspic and jelly recipes

LAYERED VEGETABLE TERRINE
IN ASPIC
with Tomato Purée and Mustard Sauce

WATERZOÏE
boiled potatoes

COMPOTE OF PEACHES

SHELLFISH IN ASPIC
with Saffron Sauce

GRILLED DUCK WITH ORANGE JUICE
green salad

STRAWBERRY ICE CREAM
with Raspberry Sauce

FILLETS OF SOLE IN ASPIC
with Mustard Sauce

CARBONADE OF BEEF
boiled potatoes, green salad

PINK GRAPEFRUIT SORBET

Vegetarian Menu

RAVIOLI WITH SPINACH FILLING

MIXED VEGETABLE SALAD

BLACKBERRY JELLY
with Almond Sauce

ICE CREAMS, FOOLS, SORBETS

Nothing can beat freshly-made ice cream. Just because it *can* be kept for long periods in the freezer, it doesn't mean it *has* to be, and even commercial ice creams are infinitely better eaten soon after making. When I was a child, homemade ice cream was the greatest treat, since commercial brands were so bad and came in only two flavors, pink and white. It is the old favorites that I like best: ice creams made with a single fruit, or with chocolate, coffee or, best of all, pure vanilla.

I feel differently about sorbets. The absence of cream enhances subtle combinations, and many blends can be both elusive and mystifying. Some of my favorites are half-way between a fragrance and a taste; both elder flowers and blackcurrant leaves make almost identical and magical sorbets, tasting faintly of muscat grapes.

There are a number of different ways of making cream ices. When using a liquid flavoring such as coffee, chocolate or vanilla-flavored milk, I use an egg custard mixed with whipped cream. When the base is a fruit purée, however, a much simpler ice can be made by adding whipped, or very thick, cream. This is basically a frozen fool, and is also good served chilled, or semi-frozen.

The best sorbets are made with an Italian meringue mixture added half-way through freezing to improve texture, but this is tricky: I compromise by stirring in one or two beaten egg whites half-way through the freezing. This prevents the formation of crystals, and gives a pretty opaque white look to the finished ice. When a sorbet is based on a scent or flavor alone, it is best infused in a thin syrup made with sugar and water, sharpened with lemon juice.

Ice cream machines or sorbetières are helpful and come in a range of sizes and prices but they are not essential. The alternative is to freeze ices in metal trays, and to purée them frequently while freezing.

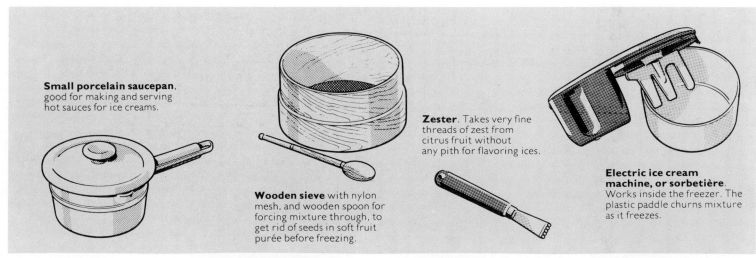

Small porcelain saucepan, good for making and serving hot sauces for ice creams.

Wooden sieve with nylon mesh, and wooden spoon for forcing mixture through, to get rid of seeds in soft fruit purée before freezing.

Zester. Takes very fine threads of zest from citrus fruit without any pith for flavoring ices.

Electric ice cream machine, or sorbetière. Works inside the freezer. The plastic paddle churns mixture as it freezes.

"A Day of Celebration (Namnsdag)," 1902, by Fanny Brate. By courtesy of Nationalmuseum, Stockholm, and Mrs Astrid de Wolfe.

TIPS ON MAKING ICE CREAMS AND SORBETS

✳ If planning to buy an ice cream machine, study the alternatives carefully and then decide which best suits your needs. There are three main types on the market. The most expensive does its own freezing, but takes a lot of space and makes only about $1\frac{1}{2}$ quarts at a time. A cheaper model, which can be operated electrically or by hand, makes more, but has to be packed with crushed ice and rock salt. The least expensive makes about a quart and works inside the freezer.

✳ When making ice cream without a machine, a food processor is almost essential to achieve a good texture.

✳ Have a supply of suitable containers – the thinner the better for quick freezing. Foil food containers are good, or metal ice trays (after removing the dividers). Cover ice trays with foil while freezing.

✳ A scoop is helpful for serving ices decoratively. A new design, called the Superscoop, releases the ice cream as if by magic, thanks to a liquid incorporated within the handle.

✳ Ices look especially good in frosted glass. Have two bowls for serving different flavors.

✳ Some people find that eating sorbets can give them a headache. This can be avoided by serving small cookies such as Tuiles d'Amandes or Chocolate Chip Cookies, with the sorbet. The various cookie doughs (see receipes on pages 123–4) can be made in advance and then frozen until needed.

✳ Try using eaux de vie and other spirits over sorbets. This intensifies the flavor when used with an ice based on the same fruit or a complementary taste. Poire, or Williamine, is good over a pear sorbet; rum goes well with a tea sorbet.

✳ Liqueurs based on chocolate or coffee can be served as a sauce for cream ices. Try Ashanti Gold (chocolate), or Kahlua (coffee), over a vanilla ice.

✳ Good ices and sorbets can be made with fruit syrups. Excellent French ones are available from good food shops. Grenadine, made from pomegranates, and cassis, which is made from black currants, can be bought from good wine merchants.

146 *Strawberry ice cream with Raspberry Sauce, Peppermint ice cream with chocolate chips, Vanilla ice cream with Praline; and Pinwheel Cookies.*

MASTER RECIPE

VANILLA ICE CREAM

Serves 6

1¼ cup milk
1 vanilla pod
2 eggs plus 2 egg yolks
5 tbsp. vanilla sugar (see p. 123)
1¼ cup heavy cream
Praline Garnish (optional):
2 tbsp. unpeeled almonds
2 tbsp. sugar

Put milk and vanilla pod into a small pan, bring slowly to boil, turn off heat, cover. Let stand 30 minutes to infuse, then remove pod (it can be used again).

Choose a large china bowl that fits inside a saucepan. Heat some water in this pan while you beat the eggs and egg yolks in the bowl. When eggs are pale and creamy, add sugar and beat 2–3 minutes. Reheat milk until amost boiling, pour on to eggs, beating steadily a minute or two more, then place the bowl over, but not touching, the simmering water. Stir constantly with a wooden spoon until it has slightly thickened (it may take 10 minutes): it should lightly coat the back of a spoon. If you use a metal double boiler, the custard will thicken quite quickly but may overheat, giving you a sort of scrambled egg.

Once thickened, remove immediately from the heat and stand bowl in very cold water, stirring frequently to prevent a skin forming. When it is quite cool, whip the cream, stopping before it is solid, and fold it into custard.

To freeze: pour into a shallow cake pan or metal ice tray (without dividers). Unless using an ice cream machine, pour mixture out every 45 minutes, preferably into a food processor, and beat before returning to pan. If using an ice cream machine, the paddles will stop turning when the ice cream has almost set. Remove them, smooth out the ice cream with a spatula, and return to freezer, covered with lid. Remove from freezer roughly 1 hour before serving.

Praline garnish: if you want this, make it in advance. Preheat oven to 300°F. Put almonds on a baking tray and toast in oven 20 minutes, until pale golden. Then put them in a heavy-bottomed saucepan, add sugar, place over moderate heat and stir furiously until the sugar has melted and caramelized to a deep brown. Turn on to an oiled piece of foil and cool. Put praline in a plastic bag, crush it with a rolling pin and place in a bowl. When ice cream has half set, fold in the praline (keeping back 1 tbsp.) then return ice cream to freezer. Scatter rest of praline over top just before serving.

Jancis Robinson's wine choice:
There's not much point in serving a delicate wine with ice cream, which tends to chill the taste buds into insensibility. The rich, almost spicy sweet Muscats of southern France are sufficiently high in alcohol and therefore full-bodies that they could probably make their mark on the senses even between mouthfuls of ice cream. Muscat de Beaumes-de-Venice, intense and almost orangey-gold, is a good choice, though. Be sure to drink these Muscats well chilled. An opened bottle will keep well in the refrigerator.

FAMILY OF RECIPES

PEPPERMINT ICE CREAM

Serves 6

3 tbsp. Crème de Menthe (1 miniature bottle)
1½ tsp. peppermint extract
3 drops green food coloring (optional)
2 oz. bitter chocolate, finely chopped

Make as for Vanilla Ice cream (see left), but omit vanilla pod, and substitute plain sugar for vanilla sugar. Just before freezing, stir in Crème de Menthe and peppermint extract. When half-frozen, tip into a bowl, stir in the chopped chocolate, and return to freezer.

CARAMEL ICE CREAM

Serves 6

½ cup granulated sugar
3 tbsp. water
1¼ cups milk
¼ cup superfine sugar
2 eggs plus 2 egg yolks
1¼ cups heavy cream

Find a wide saucepan with a heavy bottom. Put in half the sugar and water, and heat slowly until the sugar melts and turns light golden. While it heats, bring the milk almost to boiling point and keep hot. When sugar has turned color, remove from heat and pour in the boiling milk. Be very careful: it will boil and foam wildly. Stir furiously, until milk and sugar have amalgamated. Beat eggs and egg yolks together, add the superfine sugar, then pour into the hot caramel, stirring until blended. Stand bowl over a pan of simmering water, and stir until it has slightly thickened. Cool quickly, standing the bowl in iced water, and stirring often to prevent a skin forming. When it is room temperature, fold in partially whipped cream, and freeze following instructions in the Master Recipe (left).

Caramel is tricky to make, but unsurpassed as a flavoring and garnish. It has a warm natural flavor, a golden color, and it can be broken into tiny shards, like transparent tortoiseshell, to make the prettiest of garnishes.
Variation: if you like, make extra caramel by using 6 tbsp. granulated sugar and 4 tbsp. water. Pour one-third on to an oiled piece of foil before adding milk and continuing with recipe. When set, it can be peeled off the foil, broken into tiny pieces, and scattered over the finished ice cream as a golden garnish.

PLUM ICE CREAM

Serves 5–6

1½ lb. plums
½ cup sugar
juice of 1 orange
2 large egg yolks
1¼ cups heavy cream

Pit the plums and cut in thick slices. Put them in a pan with 3 tbsp. water, 2 tbsp. sugar, and the orange juice. Bring to boil, and simmer until plums are soft. Lift out plums with a slotted spoon, leaving juice in

pan, and push them through the medium mesh of the food mill (this holds back the skins). Add 6 tbsp. sugar to plum juice, and boil until reduced to about $\frac{3}{4}$ cup. Beat egg yolks and pour plum juice, still boiling, on to them, beating until frothy. Then fold in plum purée and leave to cool. Finally, fold in lightly whipped cream, turn into an ice cream machine – or ice trays – and freeze as usual.

CHOCOLATE ICE CREAM

Serves 6

3 oz. semi-sweet chocolate
1½ cups milk
2 eggs plus 2 egg yolks
5 tbsp. sugar
1½ cups heavy cream

Break the chocolate into small bits and put in a small pan with the milk. Heat slowly, until the chocolate has melted, then set aside. Put the eggs and egg yolks into a china bowl. Find a saucepan that the bowl fits into and bring some water to the boil. Whisk the eggs for 2–3 minutes. Reheat the chocolate milk until almost boiling and pour it on to the eggs, continuing to whisk for another 2 minutes.

Set the bowl over the simmering water and stir constantly with a wooden spoon until the mixture has very slightly thickened. Once this happens, remove from the heat and cool quickly by standing the bowl in a sink half full of very cold water. Stir frequently to prevent a skin forming.

Beat the cream until semi-whipped and fold into the cool chocolate mixture. Pour into an ice cream machine, or ice trays and freeze, as in the Master Recipe.

STRAWBERRY ICE CREAM WITH RASPBERRY SAUCE

Serves 6

1½ lb. strawberries
6 tbsp. sugar
1¼ cups cream

Put hulled strawberries and sugar in food processor and reduce to a purée. Push through a fine food mill to catch the seeds. Whip cream until thick, but not solid, and fold into purée. Pour into a shallow pan or metal ice tray and freeze, following the Master Recipe (see previous page). Serve with Raspberry Sauce.

This simple method of making ice cream works well with soft fruit: it is simply a frozen fruit fool. It is also good served half-frozen. Simply pour the fruit purée into a dish and place it in the freezer for 1–1½ hours, stirring once or twice.

RASPBERRY SAUCE

Serves 6

½ lb. raspberries, fresh or frozen
about 3 tbsp. sugar
1–2 tbsp. heavy cream

Purée the raspberries and sugar in a food processor; if frozen, thaw first in a colander. Push through a fine food mill to catch the seeds, then add sugar and a drop of cream to taste. Chill in refrigerator for a couple of hours before serving.

CITRUS FRUIT SORBET

Serves 4

1 pink grapefruit
2 limes
3–4 large oranges, or 5–6 small ones
¼ cup sugar
1 egg white

Take thin strips of peel from half of 1 grapefruit, 1 lime, and 1 orange. Squeeze juice of grapefruit and limes into a measuring cup, and make up to 2 cups with orange

Blackcurrant Fool with homemade biscuits

juice. Put sugar in ½ cup water in a small pan and boil until the sugar dissolves. Pour boiling syrup over strips of peel, and leave to cool.

Pour the syrup through a strainer on to fruit juice, mixing well. Pour into an ice cream machine, or ice tray, and freeze a couple of hours, until almost solid. Then transfer to a food processor and reduce to a mush. Beat egg white until stiff, add to sorbet, process again, then return mixture to freezer for another hour, or until set. It should be a smooth creamy texture, without crystals. If limes are not available, substitute 1 lemon and extra orange juice.

Variations:

For pink grapefruit sorbet: make as above, substituting 2 cups grapefruit juice (made from 3–4 pink grapefruits) for the mixed citrus fruit juice.

For blood orange sorbet: substitute 2 cups blood orange juice (from about 12 blood oranges) for the mixed citrus fruit. Ordinary oranges can be used instead of blood oranges, but it makes a less unusual sorbet, both in flavor and in color.

TROPICAL FRUIT SORBET

Serves 6

2 ripe mangoes
6 passion fruit
4 limes
¼ cup sugar
¼ cup water
2 egg whites

Cut mangoes in 3 pieces (see step-by-step illustration), and scoop flesh into a food processor, discarding skin. Cut passion fruit in half, and add flesh and seeds to mangoes. Add lime juice, and process to a mush. Boil sugar and water together until sugar melts, cool, and add to fruit purée. Process again, then pour into an ice cream machine or ice trays (following Master Recipe) and freeze about 2 hours, until mushy. Beat egg whites stiff. Put half-frozen sorbet into a food processor and purée, add egg whites, and process again. Pour back into ice cream machine and freeze until done. If using trays, purée twice more during the freezing.

Variations:

For passion fruit sorbet: use 12 passion fruit and the juice of 4 large oranges and 2 limes.

For pineapple sorbet: use the puréed flesh of 1 large ripe pineapple, and the juice of 4 oranges and 1 lime. (First purée the pineapple in a food processor, then push through a sieve or fine food mill.)

Preparing a mango

1 Cut a thick slice, as close to the flat pit as possible.
2 Repeat on the other side, discarding the central section with the pit.
3 Using a pointed knife, make diagonal cuts through flesh, right down to skin.

4 Using both hands, push up mango slices from below.
5 Mango is now domed, convex shape, a little like a hedgehog.
6 Serve on a small plate, sprinkle with fresh lime juice and eat with a spoon.

ELDER FLOWER SORBET

Serves 6–8

1 cup sugar
3¾ cups water
16 elder flower heads
juice of 2 lemons
2 egg whites

Wash elder flower heads and shake them dry. Next, make the syrup. Put sugar and water into a broad pan and bring to boil. Simmer until sugar has dissolved. Put the elder flowers in the hot syrup, cover, and let stand 30 minutes to infuse. Strain syrup into a bowl, discarding the flowers, stir in lemon juice, and leave to cool. When cold, freeze following the Master Recipe on page 147. When mushy, pour into food processor, purée and add egg whites (beaten until thick and foamy without being stiff), process again, then return to freezer.

Citrus Fruit, Pink Grapefruit and Blood Orange Sorbets served in fruit skins

Chocolate ice cream with Chocolate Sauce and Tuiles d'Amandes; Blackcurrant Leaf Sorbet and Chocolate Chip Cookies; Pink Grapefruit Sorbet; Strawberry Fool; and Pinwheel Cookies.

TEA SORBET

Serves 6

2 cups weak tea
1 orange
1 lemon
5 tbsp. sugar
½ cup white wine
2 egg whites

Take thin strips of peel from half the orange and half the lemon. Put in a bowl with the sugar. Pour hot tea over them almost immediately; on no account let it sit. Stir until all the sugar has melted, then leave it to cool.

Later, strain and mix with wine. Pour into an ice cream machine or ice tray and freeze about 2 hours, until mushy. Turn into food processor and process. Beat egg whites until stiff, add to sorbet and process again, then continue freezing until set. If

using ice tray, turn out and process twice more during freezing; this breaks up crystals, giving a better texture. This sorbet has a subtle flavor; it is hard to guess what it is made of.

BLACKCURRANT LEAF SORBET

Serves 3–4

6 tbsp. sugar
1¼ cups water
16 young blackcurrant leaves
juice of 1 lemon
1 egg white

Make as for Elder Flower Sorbet (see previous page), substituting blackcurrant leaves – picked young and before they have been sprayed – for elder flowers.
Variation: use leaves of scented pelargoniums, or a mixture of mints, instead of blackcurrant leaves.

HOT CHERRY SAUCE

Serves 5–6

1 can (12–14 oz.) black cherries
grated rind of 1 orange
grated rind of ½ lemon
2 tbsp. orange juice
1 tbsp. lemon juice
1–2 tbsp. brandy

Drain cherries and put the juice in a small pan with orange and lemon rind. Simmer 10 minutes, strain and reheat, adding fruit juice and brandy. Do not boil again. Add sugar if needed. Just before serving, stir in the black cherries, reheat, and serve with Vanilla ice cream.

HOT CHOCOLATE SAUCE

Serves 5–6

3½ oz. semi-sweet chocolate
½ cup water
2 tsp. vanilla sugar, or plain sugar
½ cup heavy cream

Break chocolate into squares and put in a small pan with the water. Bring to boil and simmer until chocolate has melted. Add sugar and stir until it has melted, then pour in the cream. Stir until blended, then serve with Vanilla ice cream.

RASPBERRY FOOL

Serves 6

1 lb. raspberries, fresh or frozen
⅓ cup sugar
1 cup heavy cream

If using frozen raspberries, thaw them first in a colander. Then purée the raspberries in the food processor, and rub through a fine food mill or sieve to catch the seeds. Stir in the sugar. Whip the cream until slightly thickened without being stiff, and fold into the purée. Pour into a china soufflé dish and chill for about 1½ hours in the freezer, taking it out and stirring once or twice.

This will give you a semi-frozen fool. If you prefer, simply chill in the refrigerator for a few hours, or freeze it completely and serve it as an ice cream.

Hot Cherry Sauce

RASPBERRY MERINGUE ICE CREAM

Serves 6

3 egg whites
¾ cup sugar
1 pint of Vanilla ice cream
¼ lb. fresh raspberries
½ cup heavy cream, lightly whipped

Turn the oven on to its lowest possible setting. Have a lightly oiled piece of foil laid on a baking sheet (use almond oil or sunflower seed oil, not olive oil). Whisk the egg whites until firm but not stiff, then fold in the sugar, continuing to whisk until they stand in peaks. Spread on the foil in a fairly even circle, using a spatula, and cook very gently for about 2 hours. Check several times to make sure it is not browning. By the end of the cooking the meringue should be a pale straw color. Take it out of the oven and leave to cool, then remove the foil (don't worry if the meringue breaks; it won't show).

Take the ice cream out of the freezer 1 hour before serving. At the last moment, lay the meringue on a flat dish and cover with the ice cream. Spread the raspberries over it, and spoon the lightly whipped cream over them in thin whirls.

BLACKCURRANT FOOL

This is a dish for those lucky enough to have wild blackcurrant bushes.

Serves 6

1 lb. blackcurrants
¾ cup sugar
2 cups whipping cream

Take currants off stalks (best done with a small fork). Put sugar in a heavy saucepan with ½ cup water. Bring to boil and cook slowly, until sugar has melted. Add currants, and simmer 5 minutes, then push through a fine food mill. Leave to cool.

Whip cream until thick but not solid. (If very thick already, it will not need whipping.) Pour fool into a glass bowl, and swirl in cream. Do not mix thoroughly; it is prettier to leave a marbled effect.

To serve: this ia rich fool, and is best served with some little cookies.

Variation: to serve semi-frozen: place in freezer 1–1½ hours before serving, stirring once or twice. To make ice cream: pour mixture into an ice cream machine, or shallow dish, and freeze, following Master Recipe on page 147. (You will lose the marbled effect.)

—MENUS—

Some suggestions for well balanced meals based on the ice cream and sorbet recipes

AMERICAN FISH CHOWDER

GRILLED PORK LOIN WITH SESAME SEEDS
noodles, snowpeas

PEPPERMINT ICE CREAM

SPINACH CROQUETTES
with Tomato and Pepper Sauce

CALF'S LIVER WITH ORANGE JUICE
broccoli

CARAMEL ICE CREAM

SMOKED CHICKEN SALAD

GRILLED SALMON STEAKS
WITH PARSLEY BUTTER
new potatoes, peas

BLACKCURRANT LEAF SORBET

Vegetarian Menu

CREAM CHEESE SALAD

PIROG WITH CABBAGE FILLING

CITRUS FRUIT SORBET

SALADS & SNACKS

As we grow more and more pressured, we tend to cook fewer full meals, and snacks and salads play a role of growing importance in our daily lives. Even the most dedicated cook doesn't always want to prepare a proper meal, nor even eat one. Snacks can be delicious, appetizing, and healthy. They can stave off pangs of hunger before a theater show, or give fresh energy during a busy working day. And drinks always taste better when accompanied by something to eat.

Salads, too, have changed their role in recent years. Formerly, they were used solely as the vegetable accompaniment to cold meat or fish dishes. Nowadays, however, they are more often served on their own, either as a first course, or after the main dish. When treated in this way, they become much more interesting. With cooked dishes, far the best salad to serve, in my opinion, is the simplest. But when served alone, more complex mixtures of vegetables and garnishes come into their own.

Raw spinach can be used as a base, and raw mushrooms, cubes of mozzarella or bean curd, crisp bacon dice or garlic-flavored croutons all make delicious additions. Oranges are good with watercress and with olives, while orange and lemon juice can be used to advantage in salad dressings. And *nouvelle cuisine* salads are pretty and appetizing, garnished with a few minuscule slices of goose liver, or chicken livers, smoked chicken, or tiny slices of raw ham.

CREAM CHEESE SALAD

Serves 4 as a first course

1 large bunch watercress
1 lb. tomatoes, peeled and sliced
4 Petit Suisses
4 tbsp. chopped chives
sea salt and black pepper
a pinch of sugar
½ tsp. Dijon mustard
1 tbsp. white wine vinegar
3 tbsp. olive oil

Pick off the tender sprigs of watercress, wash and shake dry. Lay them around the rim of 4 small plates. Arrange the tomatoes within the watercress. Unwrap the Petit Suisses and roll them in the chives. Lay on top of tomatoes and sprinkle with salt and pepper. Mix sugar, mustard, vinegar and oil. Pour over the individual salads; do not toss, just lift the tomatoes slightly.

SPINACH AND MOZZARELLA SALAD

Serves 4–6 as a first course

½ lb. spinach
1–2 mozzarella cheeses
sea salt and black pepper
6 tbsp. olive oil
1 tbsp. white wine vinegar
1 tbsp. lemon juice

Wash spinach and shake dry. Tear into pieces, discarding stalks. Cut cheese into cubes, if using one, or into thick semi-circular slices, if using two. Mix with spinach. Sprinkle with salt and pepper. Mix oil, vinegar and lemon juice and pour over, tossing well.
Variation: add ¼ lb. bacon, fried until crisp and broken into small pieces, and/or 1 large ripe avocado, peeled and cut into cubes.

ORIENTAL SALAD

Serves 3 as a first course

1 large bunch watercress, trimmed
1 cake tofu (bean curd)
sea salt and black pepper
2 tbsp. soy sauce
2 tbsp. white wine vinegar
1 tbsp. sugar
1 tbsp. sesame oil

Pile washed and drained watercress loosely in a bowl. Drain tofu, cut in small cubes, and scatter over watercress. Put salt and pepper in a small bowl, add soy sauce, vinegar, sugar and oil, and beat thoroughly until amalgamated. Pour over salad and toss well.

If you can't get tofu, a mozzarella cheese would make a good substitute.

"Le repas trois Petits Tahitiens," by Gauguin. Photo by Museés Nationaux, Paris. Courtesy of Jeu de Paume, Louvre.

SALAD OF GARDEN THINNINGS

Serves 4

4 handfuls of mixed young green leaves
  (lettuces, summer spinach, sorrel, rocket,
  dandelions, mustard, etc.)
freshly ground black pepper
a pinch of sugar
½ tbsp. lemon juice
2 tbsp. sunflower oil

Wash leaves and shake dry in a cloth, being careful not to bruise them. Pile in a bowl. Put pepper and sugar in a bowl, add lemon juice and oil, and whisk. Pour over salad and toss gently.
Serve immediately. This delicate salad is best served alone, either as a first course, or after the main dish.

CARROT SALAD WITH SESAME SEEDS

Serves 4

1 lb. carrots, grated
¾ oz. 3 tbsp. sesame seeds
2 cups yogurt
2 tbsp. sunflower oil
2 tbsp. lemon juice
sea salt and black pepper

Pile carrots in a bowl. Toast seasame seeds gently in a dry frying pan, turning them so they color evenly. As soon as they are pale golden, remove from heat. Beat yogurt until smooth, then stir in oil and lemon juice. Pour over carrots and toss lightly, adding salt and pepper. Scatter seasame seeds over carrots and fold in.
Serve with cold meats, hard-boiled eggs, or other vegetarian dishes.

COLESLAW

Serves 4

1 lb. white cabbage
1 medium carrot
1 crisp eating apple, cored
3 tbsp. mayonnaise
3 tbsp. yogurt
3 tbsp. lemon juice
sea salt and black pepper

Grate cabbage, carrot and apple finely, using a food processor for preference. Mix mayonnaise and yogurt until smooth, stir in lemon juice, salt and pepper, then stir into the coleslaw, mixing thoroughly.
Serve with frankfurters, cold ham, or hard-boiled eggs.

153

SPINACH, BACON AND MUSHROOM SALAD

Serves 4 as a first course

½ lb. spinach
½ lb. small mushrooms
juice of ½ lemon
¼ lb. bacon
sea salt and black pepper
½ cup olive oil
3 tbsp. white wine vinegar

Wash spinach and drain well. Cut leaves into strips, discarding stalks, and pile in a bowl. Slice mushrooms, caps only, and squeeze lemon juice over them. Fry bacon slowly until crisp, then drain on paper towels. When cool, break into small bits. Put salt and pepper in a small bowl, add olive oil and vinegar, and whisk until blended. Scatter mushrooms and bacon pieces over the spinach, pour dressing over all, and toss thoroughly.
Variation: use a mixture of escarole curly endive or raddichio instead of the spinach.

DANDELION SALAD

Serves 4

6 oz. dandelion leaves
¼ lb. bacon
2 slices dry white bread
2 tbsp. butter
1 clove garlic, peeled
sea salt and black pepper
¼ cup olive oil
1 tbsp. white wine vinegar

If using wild dandelions, blanch them before you pick them by standing an inverted flower pot over them to 7–10 days, otherwise they will be bitter.

Wash dandelion leaves and pat dry. Cut them across in thick strips and pile in a bowl. Fry bacon slowly until crisp; drain on paper towels. When cool, break or chop into small pieces. Cut crusts off bread, and cut each slice into small cubes. Add butter to the bacon fat in the frying pan, and when it is hot put in the bread, together with the garlic clove. Toss until bread cubes have turned an even golden brown. Discard garlic, and drain bread on paper towels. Put salt and pepper in a small bowl, add the oil and vinegar, mix well, and pour over dandelions. Toss, then scatter the bread cubes and bacon pieces over all; toss again, lightly.
Serve alone, either as a first course or after the main dish.
Variation: this salad is also good made with spinach, or spinach mixed with sorrel.

CAPONATA

Serves 4–5

1 lb. small eggplants
salt
1 small onion, chopped
about ½ cup olive oil
3 stalks celery, diced
½ lb. tomatoes, peeled and chopped
12 green olives, pitted
1 tbsp. capers, drained
freshly ground black pepper
1 tbsp. sugar
2 tbsp. white wine vinegar

Cut eggplant into cubes, about ½ inch square. Make layers of the cubes in a colander, sprinkling each layer with salt. Weigh down with a plate and leave for 1 hour. Fry onion in 2 tbsp. oil; when it starts to color, add celery. After 2–3 minutes add tomatoes. Cook gently until thickened, about 10–15 minutes, adding olives, capers, black pepper, sugar and vinegar halfway through.

Dry eggplant and heat remaining oil in a clean pan. When hot, put in eggplant and cook until golden, turning as the cubes brown. When soft and golden brown, lift them out with a slotted spoon, leaving the oil in the pan, and mix them with the other vegetables. Pour into a shallow dish and leave to cool.
Serve at room temperature. Although not strictly speaking a salad, this cold vegetable dish makes a delicious first course, or part of a spread of vegetarian dishes.

MIXED VEGETABLE SALAD

Serves 4

½ Iceberg lettuce
1 ear of corn
¼ lb. shelled peas
¼ cucumber, peeled
2 tomatoes, peeled
1 tbsp. yogurt
1 tbsp. light cream
2 tbsp. sunflower oil
1 tbsp. lemon juice
½ tsp. soy sauce

Tear lettuce into bite-sized pieces and pile in a bowl. Cook corn for 5 minutes, then drain and cool. Slice off the kernels (see page 87), dividing them up and scattering over the lettuce. Cook peas briefly, then cool and scatter them over corn. Dice cucumber and add. Dice peeled tomatoes, discarding juice and seeds (see pages 46–47), and add. Mix yogurt, cream, oil, lemon juice, and soy sauce, whisking until blended. Pour over salad and toss just before serving.

CHICKEN SALAD

Serves 3–4

½ large chicken, or 1 small chicken, poached
1 round lettuce
2 tsp. lemon juice
2 tbsp. sunflower oil
3 stalks celery, chopped
12–16 white grapes, peeled and seeded
Dressing:
3 tsp. mayonnaise
2 tbsp. yogurt
2 tsp. mild curry powder
3 tbsp. sunflower seed oil
3 tbsp. lemon juice

Cut the cold chicken into cubes, discarding skin, bone, and gristle. Discard outer leaves of lettuce, using only the tender inner ones. Lay them in a bowl, and sprinkle with lemon juice and sunflower seed oil. Put the chicken in another bowl with the celery and most of the grapes, keeping back a few for the garnish. Mix mayonnaise and yogurt until smooth, then stir in the curry powder, oil and lemon juice. Pour over the chicken and mix well. Pile in the center of the lettuce leaves, scattering the extra grapes over the top. If you want to prepare the salad in advance, dress only the lettuce leaves and assemble at the last moment.
Serve at room temperature, as a light main dish with toasted pita bread.

DUCK SALAD

Serves 3–4

½ large roast duck
1 head escarole, curly endive, or ½ lb. spinach
1 small bunch watercress
3 kiwi fruit, peeled and sliced
sea salt and black pepper
¼ tsp. Dijon mustard
1 tsp. soy sauce
1 tbsp. orange juice
1 tbsp. lemon juice
¼ cup olive oil

Cut duck into small cubes, discarding all skin, bone and fat. (Keep skin and bones for stock; melt down fat for frying.) Take the inner leaves only of escarole, endive or spinach, wash, pat dry and pile in a shallow bowl. Pick tender ends of watercress off and scatter over leaves. Pile the duck in the center, with sliced kiwi fruit over and around it. Put salt, pepper and mustard in a small bowl, add soy sauce, fruit juices, and oil, and whisk together until blended. Pour over salad just before serving. Don't toss it, just lift to allow dressing to penetrate.
Serve alone, as a light main dish. For 4–5 people, use a whole duck.

FOR THE PERFECT SIDE SALAD

MACHE
a small leaf, slightly bitter
also called corn salad,
or lamb's lettuce.
Expensive: mix
with other leaves

ICEBERG
very crisp lettuce; good texture,
unremarkable flavor

WEBB'S
firm lettuce, quite substantial

BATAVIA
similar to curly endive
in color and flavor, but with larger leaves

RADDICCHIO
Expensive, but a small
head goes a long way
mixed with other leaves

CURLY ENDIVE
slightly bitter.
Use tender pale leaves only

CABBAGE
the ordinary round lettuce, good in
summer; winter variety not worth its price

ROMAINE or COS
firm lettuce with a lot
of character. Good flavor

WINTER SALAD SELECTION

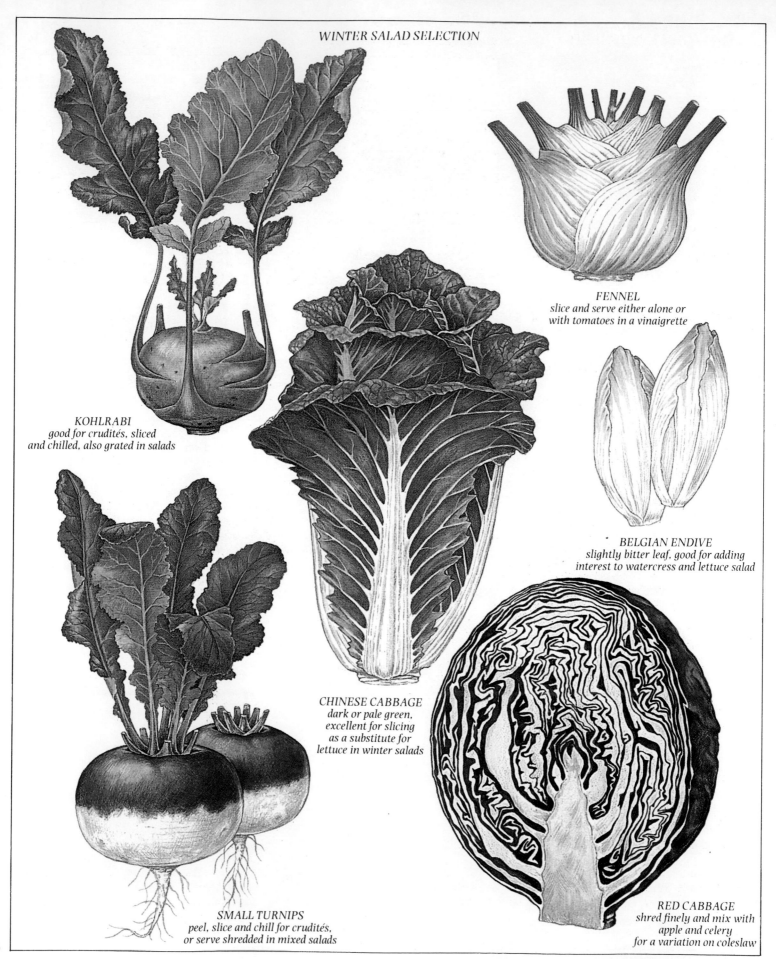

KOHLRABI
*good for crudités, sliced
and chilled, also grated in salads*

FENNEL
*slice and serve either alone or
with tomatoes in a vinaigrette*

BELGIAN ENDIVE
*slightly bitter leaf, good for adding
interest to watercress and lettuce salad*

CHINESE CABBAGE
*dark or pale green,
excellent for slicing
as a substitute for
lettuce in winter salads*

SMALL TURNIPS
*peel, slice and chill for crudités,
or serve shredded in mixed salads*

RED CABBAGE
*shred finely and mix with
apple and celery
for a variation on coleslaw*

LETTUCE, ORANGE AND ALMOND SALAD

Serves 4–5

1 head Romaine
2 medium oranges
1 oz. flaked almonds
sea salt and black pepper
a pinch of sugar
1 tbsp. chopped shallot
1 tbsp. orange juice
1 tbsp. lemon juice
3 tbsp. olive oil

Cut lettuce across in 1 inch pieces, and pile in a bowl. Peel oranges carefully, removing all white pith. Divide them in half, then cut each half in semi-circular slices. Lay over lettuce, and scatter almonds over all. Put salt, pepper, sugar and shallot in a small bowl, add fruit juices and oil, and mix well. Pour over the salad just before serving, and toss well.
Serve with cold roast duck, goose, or game.

WATERCRESS AND ORANGE SALAD

Serves 4

2 bunches watercress
3 small oranges
2 tbsp. chopped shallots
1 tbsp. orange juice
1 tbsp. lemon juice
¼ cup olive oil
sea salt and black pepper

Use the tender sprigs of watercress, discarding the tough stalk ends. Wash and pat dry. Pile in a salad bowl, preferably a wooden one. Peel oranges very carefully and divide into sections free from all pith. Mix with the watercress. Mix fruit juices and oil, adding salt and pepper. Pour over the salad and toss just before serving. This is particularly good with roast duck.

CUCUMBER AND YOGURT SALAD

Serves 3–4

2 cups yogurt
salt and black pepper
1 clove garlic, crushed, or a dash Tabasco
½ large cucumber, peeled and chopped

Beat yogurt until smooth, and add salt and pepper to taste. Stir in garlic or Tabasco, then mix in cucumber, leaving some on the surface.
Serve as a fresh-tasting accompaniment to grilled or roast lamb, or with curries.

Cutting an orange into sections

1 Using a sharp stainless steel knife, cut off one end to make a flat base.

2 Standing orange on cut end, remove peel and pith together, cutting downwards.

3 Continue until orange is completely free from skin and pith.

4 Holding orange in left hand, slide knife between sections.

5 Cut them out, leaving white inner membrane behind.

6 Finally, squeeze out any juice remaining in membranes.

POTATO SALAD I

Serves 4

1½ lb. new potatoes
4 tbsp. olive oil
1 tbsp. white wine vinegar
sea salt and black pepper
5 tbsp. chopped herbs (chives, chervil, tarragon and parsley mixed, or chives and parsley alone)

Boil poatoes in their skins and peel as soon as they are cool enough to handle. If tiny, leave them whole; otherwise cut them in halves, quarters or thick slices. Pile in a bowl and pour 1 tbsp. olive oil over them while they are still hot, mixing it in gently.

Before serving, stir in remaining oil and vinegar, salt and pepper and most of the herbs. Mix very gently, trying not to break up the potatoes.
To serve: transfer to a clean bowl and scatter a few more chopped herbs over the top. Do not prepare too long in advance: this is at its best about an hour after making.

POTATO SALAD II

Serves 4

1½ lb. new poatoes
2 tbsp. olive oil
1 large bunch scallions, sliced
2 tbsp. each mayonnaise and yogurt
sea salt and black pepper

Boil the potatoes in their skins, drain, and peel as soon as they are cool enough to handle. If they are tiny, leave them whole. Otherwise cut them into halves, quarters or thick slices. Pile them in a bowl and pour the olive oil over them, mixing it in gently. Set aside and leave to cool.

After about 30 minutes, add scallions (leaves as well as bulbs), reserving some of as a garnish. Mix mayonnaise and yogurt together and fold very gently into potatoes, adding salt and pepper. Turn into a clean dish and scatter reserved scallions over the top.

HOT POTATO SALAD

Serves 4

1½ lb. new potatoes
2 tbsp. onion, finely chopped
4 tbsp. olive oil
1 tbsp. white wine vinegar
sea salt and black pepper
5 tbsp. chopped chives

Cook potatoes in their skins, drain, peel, cut into quarters or thick slices, and stir in the onion. Pour over oil and vinegar and mix very gently. Add plenty of salt and pepper and stir in three-quarters of the chives. Turn salad into a clean dish and scatter remaining chives over the top.
Serve soon after making. This is delicious served with Poaching Sausage en Croûte.

SMOKED CHICKEN SALAD

This, and the following three recipes, are *salades composées*, useful as first courses and quick to make since they require only the minimum of cooking. These are one of the inventions of the *nouvelle cuisine* that I think worth adopting, for they make light, healthy and pretty dishes.

For each person:

2 leaves escarole, or curly endive
2–3 leaves raddichio, when available
½ oz. leek, white part only, or scallions
½ oz. carrot or turnip
½ oz. fennel, or celeriac, or kohlrabi
3 sprigs watercress
½ oz. small mushrooms, caps only, sliced
1 oz. smoked chicken, off the bone
Dressing:
1 tsp. lemon juice
1 tsp. white wine vinegar
2 tsp. olive oil
2 tsp. sunflower seed oil
sea salt and black pepper

Wash leaves and shake dry. Cut leek, carrot and fennel (or alternatives) into slices 1½ inches thick, then cut each slice lengthwise into slivers, like split matchsticks. Put in a small strainer and suspend in boiling water for exactly 1 minutes, then hold under cold tap to cool. Cut chicken into strips 1½ inches long, leaving on the skin.

To assemble: lay out plates and arrange salad on each. Using scissors, snip batavia and raddichio into small squares and pile in the center of each plate. Pinch leaves of mâche off the root, or the tender sprigs of watercress off the stalk, and lay over salad. Arrange mushrooms over and among the leaves, and lay blanched vegetables over all. Arrange chicken around the edge of the salad. Mix dressing in a small bowl, and spoon it over individual salads (do not toss) just before serving.

Variations: instead of smoked chicken you can use thin fillets of smoked trout or eel, small pieces of Parma or Serrano ham, of *bresaola* (dried beef). I was once given a whole goose liver, preserved in its own fat, and served it this way, in thin slices laid around a salad.

If the extra salad leaves are washed and shaken dry, then stored in separate plastic bags in the refrigerator, they will last for a week, so a whole series of such salads can be made for little extra cost.

Smoked Chicken Salad

MUSHROOMS STUFFED WITH EGGPLANT SALAD

Serves 6

6 large flat mushrooms, caps only
2 small eggplants
½ large Spanish onion, chopped
½ lb. tomatoes, skinned and chopped
sea salt and black pepper
3 tbsp. olive oil
1 tbsp. lemon juice
2 tbsp. parsley, finely chopped

Mushrooms with Aubergine Salad

Preheat oven to 350°F. Lay mushrooms on a baking tray, gills up, brush with oil, and bake about 20 minutes, until soft. Remove and leave to cool. Drop eggplants into lightly salted boiling water and cook 20 minutes; drain. When cool enough to handle, peel and chop. Mix with the chopped onion and tomatoes – these should be drained for a little after chopping – and add salt and pepper to taste. Stir in olive oil and lemon juice, pile on to the mushroom caps, and sprinkle with parsley. **Serve** on a flat dish, as a first course or as part of a vegetarian meal. Or make eggplant salad in double quantities, and serve as a dish on its own, with hot pita bread.

SCALLOP, ARTICHOKE AND AVOCADO SALAD

Serves 6

10 large scallops
½ cup dry white wine
4 artichoke hearts, fresh, frozen, or canned
1 large avocado
1 endive
Dressing:
⅓ cup lemon juice
¼ cup olive oil
¼ cup sunflower oil
sea salt and black pepper
2 tbsp. finely chopped dill

If still on the shell, cut off the scallops, wash well, and cut away black strips and any slimy parts. Bring wine to boil with ½ cup water. Drop in the scallops, adjust heat, and poach gently, covered, for 4 minutes. Drain and cool.

If using fresh artichokes: trim by following the step-by-step guide on page 132, but leaving in choke (this is much easier to remove after cooking, if recipe permits); cook 20–25 minutes in lightly salted water, then drain and cool; pull out inner core of leaves from artichoke and scrape out the choke with a teaspoon. If using canned artichoke hearts, drain. Cut each in half, then cut each half across in $\frac{1}{4}$ inch slices.

When scallops are cool, detach red tongue and cut white part horizontally into 3 round slices. Prepare the avocado last, or it will discolor. Cut it in half, remove the stone, and peel off the skin. Cut each half in quarters, then cut them across in $\frac{1}{4}$ inch slices.

Serve as a first course: lay a few leaves of curly endive on each plate, and arrange sliced scallops and red tongues, artichokes and avocados over them. Mix the dressing and spoon over, scattering dill over the finished dish.

WALNUT AND ENDIVE SALAD

Serves 6

2 heads Belgian endive
1 head escarole, or curly endive
$\frac{1}{4}$ lb. fresh walnuts or $\frac{1}{2}$ cup packaged walnuts
sea salt and black pepper
a pinch of sugar
$\frac{1}{4}$ tsp. Dijon mustard
2 tbsp. white wine vinegar
3 tbsp. walnut oil
2 tbsp. sunflower seed oil

Cut chicory across in $\frac{1}{2}$ inch slices. Cut escarole into squarish pieces, or curly endive leaves into 2 or 3 bits. Chop nuts coarsely. Pile leaves in a bowl and scatter nuts over them. Put seasonings in a small bowl and add vinegar, stirring until they are blended to a smooth paste. Stir in the walnut and sunflower seed oils, mix well, and pour over the salad.

Serve alone, either as a first course or after the main dish. This is delicious to make when the new crop of fresh walnuts, sometimes called "wet" or "green," appears in the shops for a few short weeks. You can use walnut oil alone, but I prefer to lighten it with sunflower seed oil.

A SIMPLE GREEN SALAD

To make the salad: use lettuce alone, or with watercress, escarole, curly endive or cress. Wash the leaves, spin dry and leave in the spinner until required.

Make the dressing in advance: put a pinch each of sea salt and sugar in a small bowl. Add freshly-ground black pepper, $\frac{1}{4}$ tsp. Dijon mustard and 2 tsp. each, lemon juice and white wine vinegar. Stir to dissolve mustard, then add 3 tbsp. best olive oil and a whole peeled clove of garlic (optional).

To serve: tear the leaves in pieces and pile them in a salad bowl. Remove garlic from dressing, mix well, pour over leaves and toss.

TOASTED PITA BREAD

It may seem extravagant to heat the oven just for toasting pita bread, but this makes an elegant and delicious accompaniment to a *salade composée*, and is worth doing for a party. Heat oven to 400°F. Put in pita bread as it heats, just long enough to warm and soften it. (This makes it easy to split the pita without breaking it.) Using a small knife, split open each pocket. Butter the soft sides well, lay on baking trays, and replace in oven. Remove as soon as they are crisp and brown; this will take about 6 minutes.

Serve immediately, piled on a flat dish.

EGGS TONNATO

Serves 4 as a first course, or 3 as a main dish

6 large eggs, hard-boiled
2 tbsp. chopped chervil, tarragon, dill, chives, or parsley
Tonnato Sauce:
2 egg yolks
a pinch of salt
1 cup olive oil
1 tbsp. white wine vinegar
2 tbsp. lemon juice
3½–4 oz. can tuna fish, drained
1 tbsp. capers, drained and roughly chopped
1 tbsp. green peppercorns, roughly crushed
2 tbsp. yogurt

Make Mayonnaise (page 164), with the egg yolks, salt, olive oil, vinegar, and half the lemon juice. Pound the tuna fish in a mortar to a smooth paste, then add the mayonnaise gradually, pounding until amalgamated. Stir in remaining lemon juice, capers, and peppercorns. Finally, stir in the yogurt. Spoon the sauce on to a flat dish in a thick layer. Shell eggs, cut in half lengthwise, and lay, cut side down, in the sauce. Sprinkle with chopped herbs.
Serve as a first course, or with a green salad as a vegetarian main dish.

SPICE MIXTURE FOR HARD-BOILED EGGS

½ cup sesame seeds
¼ cup hazelnuts
2 tbsp. ground coriander
2 tbsp. ground cumin
½ tsp. sea salt
¼ tsp. black pepper

Toast sesame seeds in a dry frying pan over a low heat, shaking and turning until they are lightly and evenly colored. Set aside and do the same with hazelnuts, then pour in a cloth and rub off skins. Set aside. When both are cool, put them in a food processor with spices, salt and pepper and process until finely ground. Store in a tightly covered jar.

Eaten with warm hard-boiled eggs and wholemeal bread and butter, this makes a handy snack. It also makes good sandwiches.

HAMBURGERS

Serves 4

1 lb. chuck steak
sea salt and black pepper

If you have a food processor, buy the steak in one piece and chop it at home. Mix lightly in a bowl, adding only salt and pepper. Divide in four, and shape lightly between hands: whatever you do, don't press it hard. Heat a broiling pan or heavy frying pan, and grease lightly with a little fat. When hot, add hamburgers and cook quite fast, until slightly charred outside and still pink in the center.
Serve with hamburger relishes, chili sauce, or tomato ketchup, either alone or in soft buns (don't toast them) or with a salad.

DOLMADES

Serves 8–10

onion, chopped
½ cup olive oil
½ cup Italian risotto rice
¼ cup pine nuts
sea salt and black pepper
about 30 vine leaves, preserved or fresh
about ¼ cup lemon juice

Start the day before, or several hours in advance. Heat ¼ cup oil in a deep frying pan and cook onions until softened and pale golden. Add rice (washed and drained) and stir round for 2–3 minutes. Add 1 cup boiling water and stir, add pine nuts, salt and pepper, and bring to the boil. Simmer gently about 6 minutes until water is absorbed. Transfer to a plate and cool. (Don't worry that the rice is still raw; it finishes cooking in the vine leaves.)

If using vine leaves from packets or cans, drain them, rinse well, and soak a little while in cold water. Separate them carefully, drop into a pan of boiling water, cook 5 minutes, then drain. If using fresh vine leaves – only young ones are suitable – blanch them for 10 minutes in boiling water, then drain.

Lay 1 heaped tsp. stuffing on each leaf and roll up, squeezing gently in the palm of the hand so it does not unroll. Put any unused leaves in the bottom of a sauté pan, or deep frying pan with lid, and lay the stuffed leaves over them. Pour ¼ cup oil over, then add 2 tbsp. lemon juice and 1 cup hot water. Lay a small plate over them to weigh them down, cover pan, and simmer gently for 45 minutes. Check once or twice if they need more water. Leave to cool in the pan.
To serve: lay the stuffed vine leaves on a flat dish and sprinkle with a little more lemon juice. Serve at room temperature, not chilled. These may be served with drinks, or as part of an hors d'œuvre. They are hardly worth making in small quantities, as they keep well for several days in the refrigerator, but bring them back to room temperature before serving.

FALAFEL

Serves 15

½ lb. dried chick peas
1 Spanish onion, cut in chunks
1–2 cloves garlic, chopped
1 slice fresh white bread, with crusts removed
¼ cup chopped parsley
½ tsp. ground cumin
½ tsp. ground coriander
¼ tsp. baking powder
salt and black pepper
frying oil

Start 2–3 days beforehand. Soak chick peas 48 hours, drain, and rinse. Put in a food processor and process to a fine purée. Add onion and garlic and process again until blended, scraping down sides 2 or 3 times. Tear bread in pieces and soak 10 minutes in cold water. Squeeze dry, add to chick peas, and process again. Then add herbs and spices, baking powder, salt and pepper. Process once more, then place in a bowl and stand for 1 hour.

Heat a pan of frying oil; I use a wok. While it heats, shape the *falafel* into balls about 1 inch across, either round or slightly flattened. When oil is about 360°F drop in a few at a time, and cook 3–4 minutes, turning once. When golden, lift out and drain on paper towels, while you fry next batch.
Serve hot if possible, or at room temperature. Delicious with drinks or as part of a vegetarian or a Middle Eastern hors d'œuvre.

CROQUES MONSIEUR

Serves 4–5

½ cup Gruyère, grated
½ cup heavy cream
sea salt and black pepper
8–10 thin slices dry white bread
¼ lb. thin slices ham
about 6 tbsp. butter

Mix grated cheese with cream to a thick paste, adding salt and pepper to taste. Cut crusts off bread, and spread each slice with cheese paste. Lay slices of ham on half the slices, removing fat and trimming to fit. Make sandwiches, pressing together, and cut in half diagonally. Heat half the butter in a large frying pan and fry half the sandwiches until crisp and golden. Drain on paper towels while you add more butter and fry the rest.

160

CHICKEN LIVER TOASTS

Serves 6

½ lb. chicken livers
1 tbsp. butter
2 tsp. olive oil
½ clove garlic, finely chopped
2–3 leaves sage, finely chopped
sea salt and black pepper
juice of ½ lemon
12 slices French bread
2 tsp. finely chopped parsley

Chop livers, cutting away discolored bits. Heat butter and oil and cook garlic until it starts to color, then add livers. Cook 2–3 minutes, adding sage, just until livers lose their pinkiness. Remove from heat and add salt, pepper, and a squeeze of lemon juice.
To serve: spread on lightly toasted slices of French bread, sprinkled with parsley.

MOZZARELLA TOASTS

Serves 6

6 flat anchovy fillets
¼ cup milk
12 slices French Bread
1 mozzarella

Soak anchovies in milk for 10 minutes, rinse, and pat dry. Toast bread on one side only, under broiler. Cut cheese in half, and then in slices. Lay one on untoasted side of each piece of bread, and toast gently until cheese starts to melt. Then remove, lay an anchovy on top of each one, and serve immediately.

MUSHROOMS ON TOAST

Serves 4

½ lb. small mushrooms, flat or button
5 tbsp. butter
1 tbsp. flour
1 cup milk
⅓ cup heavy cream
salt and black pepper
4 slices toast

Wipe mushrooms, remove stems, and slice them. Leave the caps whole. Heat 3 tbsp. butter in a frying pan and cook mushrooms until softened. Drain, reserving juices, and chop coarsely. Melt remaining butter in a small pan and stir in flour. Cook for 1 minutes, stirring, then add heated milk. Stir until blended, then add mushrooms juices, cream, salt and pepper to taste. Cook gently for 3 minutes then add mushrooms and reheat.
To serve: pour over thick slices of toast and serve on hot plates.

ANCHOÏADE

4 oz. anchovy fillets
¼ cup milk
2 cloves garlic, crushed
¼ cup olive oil
2 tsp. white wine vinegar

Soak anchovy fillets in milk for 10 minutes, drain, rinse under cold tap, and squeeze dry. Chop finely, then pound to a pulp in a mortar. Add garlic and continue to pound until smooth. Add oil very gradually, beating it into the paste, then add vinegar. When all is smooth and well blended, pile into a small jar, cover with plastic wrap, and store in the refrigerator.
To serve: spread on lightly toasted slices of French bread and eat with drinks, or while waiting for meat to barbecue.

TAPENADE

3 oz. anchovy fillets
2 tbsp. milk
6 oz. black olives, pitted
6 oz. capers, drained
3½ oz. can tuna fish, drained
1 tbsp. mustard powder
1 cup olive oil
2 tbsp. brandy
½ tbsp. ground mixed spice (black pepper, cloves and nutmeg or mace)

Soak anchovy fillets in milk for 10 minutes then drain. Put in food processor with olives, capers, tuna fish and mustard. Process to a smooth paste, then turn into a bowl and stir in oil very gradually, as if making mayonnaise. Finally, stir in brandy and ground spices. Pile into a jar, cover with lid or plastic wrap, and keep in refrigerator until needed.
To serve: spread on lightly toasted slices of French bread and eat with drinks. *Tapenade* is also good served with hard-boiled eggs as a first course; either mash the yolks with a little *tapenade* and pile back into the whites, or simply cut the eggs in half and lay, cut side down, in a layer of *tapenade*.

SANDWICHES

Boiled Beef
May be made with salted or fresh beef (brisket or rump). Slice while still hot, and put between lightly buttered light rye bread (not pumpernickel). Dab with mustard and serve with gherkins. If using fresh beef, accompany with cups of the beef bouillon.

Bacon, Lettuce, and Tomato
Make sandwiches of toasted white bread, lightly buttered, and layer of crisp bacon, sliced tomatoes, and crisp lettuce dabbed with bottled mayonnaise (better than home-made for this purpose). Cut off crusts before serving for a really neat sandwich.

Turkey or Chicken
Make as above, substituting sliced turkey or chicken breast for the bacon.

Mushroom
Make with buttered wholewheat bread, sliced raw mushrooms sprinkled with lemon juice and black pepper, and crisply fried bacon.

Potted Shrimp
Make with thinly sliced brown bread and butter filled with potted shrimps sprinkled with lemon juice and black pepper. Remove crusts before serving.

SIMPLE SNACKS
NEEDING NO COOKING

A Hot Weather Snack
Feta cheese, cut in cubes and piled on one half of a flat dish. On the other half, a pile of cubes of pink watermelon. Eat with a fork.

Broad Beans with Salty Cheese
Raw broad beans, preferably fresh from the garden, served still in their pods so you can eat them as you pod them, with little cubes of salty cheese – *feta*, *pecorino* or *sardo*.

Prosciutto and Grissini
Thin slices of raw ham (Spanish *serrano* ham is cheaper than *prosciutto*, if you are lucky enough to live near a Spanish shop) wrapped round *grissini* (crisp Italian breadsticks).

STOCKS & SAUCES

Stocks and sauces are not dishes in themselves, but an integral part of many great recipes. For that reason we have usually included them as part of a complete recipe in the earlier pages. Some sauces, however, are classics which can be used with many different dishes: mayonnaise is an obvious example.

Good homemade stock, too, can be used to give flavor to different dishes – to a soup, a braised dish or a poached one. So here is a brief collection of classic stocks and sauces which you can used in different ways. For a comprehensive list of all the sauce recipes in the book, look under Sauces in the index.

CHICKEN STOCK

1 chicken carcass, raw or cooked, plus skin, neck, feet and giblets (but not the liver)
1 onion, halved
1 carrot, halved
ends of leek and celery
1 bay leaf
2–3 stalks parsley
1 tsp. salt
6 black peppercorns

Put all the ingredients into a deep pot or pressure cooker. (If making stock for aspic, don't use a pressure cooker as this makes a cloudy stock.) Cover with cold water and bring slowly to boil. Skim off any scum that rises to the surface. When it boils, cover, and cook for 3 hours (or, if using a pressure cooker, bring to pressure and cook for 1 hour). When the time is up, strain the stock and leave to cool. Chill overnight in refrigerator and next day remove fat from the surface.

The stock will keep 3 days in the refrigerator; any longer and it is best to freeze it. Boil to reduce the quantity and concentrate the flavor, cool, and pour into ice trays. Freeze, then transfer the cubes to plastic bags, and store in the freezer. Frozen this way, you can use as little as you need without thawing the whole lot.

The best chicken stock is the by-product of Poached Chicken. An excellent stock can also be made with a raw chicken carcass after the primary pieces have been removed for another dish. Chicken wings, with no breast attached, are cheap, and also good for stock.

Variations:
For Duck Stock substitute a duck carcass for the chicken: excellent for making borscht.
For Game Stock use carcass(es) of game birds instead of, or mixed with, the chicken, for Lentil Soup, and braising vegetables.

BEEF STOCK

some beef and veal bones, cut up by the butcher
1½ lb. shin of beef, roughly chopped
1 large onion, halved
1 leek, halved
1 stalk celery, halved
1 bay leaf
3 stalks parsley
2 tsp. salt
10 black peppercorns

Put bones and beef in a stock pot or pressure cooker, cover generously with cold water, and bring slowly to boil, skimming until surface is clear. Add flavoring vegetables, herbs and seasonings, bring back to boil, half cover pot (or bring to pressure if using a pressure cooker), and boil gently but steadily for 3 hours (or 1 hour under pressure). When time is up, strain stock, cool and chill overnight. Then remove the fat (it can be used for frying).

The resulting stock may be reduced by boiling, to concentrate the flavor. It will keep 3 days in the refrigerator, or may be reduced and frozen in ice trays or plastic containers. The reduced stock makes an excellent consommé, while the unreduced form is excellent for soups such as Borscht, onion soup, Minestrone, and Lentil Soup.

The best beef stock is a by-product of Boiled Fresh Beef or Pot-au-feu. A cheaper version can be made by using a mixture of beef and veal bones with a cheap cut of beef. This is a lighter version of the brown stock, made with fewer ingredients and without browning them first.
Variation: for Veal Stock, make as for beef stock, substituting veal bones for beef, and veal for shin of beef. This gives a pale stock, nearer to chicken stock than beef, good for using in vegetable or egg dishes.

STOCK SUBSTITUTE: crumble 3 bouillon cubes into 3 cups cold water in saucepan; add half a sliced onion and carrot, ends of leek and celery, sprig of parsley and 3 black peppercorns. Bring to boil, cook half covered, 30–40 minutes; strain.

FISH STOCK

fish bones, heads, tails, skins, etc.
1 onion, halved
1 carrot, halved
ends of leek and celery
½ bay leaf
2–3 stalks parsley
½ tsp. salt
6 black peppercorns
½ cup dry white wine, or 5 tbsp. vermouth,
*   or white wine vinegar (optional)*

Put washed fish bones into a pan with flavoring vegetables, herbs, and seasonings. Add wine, vermouth or vinegar, if used, and cold water to cover. The amount of water should be calculated in relation to the dish you require it for, but there must always be enough to cover the fish. Bring slowly to boil and cook gently, half covered, for 20–25 minutes. Strain and cool. If you have more than you need, boil it up to reduce before cooling.

It is now ready to use, but may be kept up to 3 days in the refrigerator or frozen, if necessary. A fish stock is usually only required in small amounts, often for making a sauce to accompany the fish. (A court-bouillon is not a fish stock; it is a flavored liquid for poaching fish.) When making dishes with fillets of sole or cod, the stock can be made with the fish bones, head, skin, etc., otherwise you will have to ask for extra fish bones. Bones of sole, flounder, or other flat fish make the best stock; a cod's head is good for making a large amount, but avoid mackerel, or other oily fish.

BROWN STOCK

3 lb. mixed beef and veal bones
2 tbsp. lard, or beef dripping
1 lb. shin of beef, roughly chopped
¼ lb. bacon rind, roughly chopped
1 large onion, roughly chopped, plus a few
*   extra skins*
1 large carrot, roughly chopped
1 large leek, roughly chopped
1 stalk celery, roughly chopped
½–1 cup dry white wine, or ⅓ cup medium
*   dry vermouth*
1 tomato, halved
1 bay leaf
1 tsp. sugar

First brown the bones. If already using the oven, brown them in the fat in a roasting pan, turning them 2 or 3 times, allowing 10–15 minutes at 400°F. Transfer them to a stock pot, and put beef, bacon rinds, and all the vegetables except the tomato into the roasting pan. Brown these also, turning now and then, for 5–10 minutes, then add to the bones in the stockpot. If the oven is not in use, brown bones in a heavy casserole, melting fat first, adding the other meat and vegetables 10 minutes after the bones, and browning all together for a further 10 minutes, stirring now and then.

Then proceed: pour in the wine or vermouth and boil a few minutes, until reduced, then add enough cold water to cover the bones, probably 3 or 4 quarts. Sprinkle cut tomato with sugar and grill until slightly blackened, then add to the pot with the bay leaf. Bring very slowly to the boil, allowing 45–60 minutes, skimming the surface as it approaches boiling point. Boil steadily, half covered, for 3–4 hours, continuing to skim frequently to get a clear stock.

Strain and leave to cool, then chill overnight in the refrigerator. Next day, remove the fat which will have solidified on the surface. The stock is now ready for use. The amount will vary according to the degree of reduction; if you have more than you need, it can be reduced by fast boiling which will also concentrate the flavor. Only add seasoning when adding to the dish you are making.

VEGETABLE STOCK

1 large onion, unpeeled and roughly
*   chopped*
1 leek, roughly chopped
2 large carrots, roughly chopped
2 stalks celery, including leaves, roughly
*   chopped*
2 large tomatoes, unpeeled and roughly
*   chopped*
2 stalks parsley
a few sprigs watercress (optional)
a few outer lettuce leaves (optional)
1 tsp. sea salt

Put all ingredients in a pressure cooker with 6 cups water. Cover, bring to pressure, and cook for 40 minutes. (If using an ordinary pan, use about 2 quarts water to allow for evaporation – liquid hardly reduces at all in a pressure cooker – and cook for 2 hours.) Strain. This gives a clear golden stock, which does not need degreasing or clarifying. It may be used as it is, as a basis for soups and sauces, or for egg and vegetable dishes, or reduced by 5 minutes' fast boiling to about 1 quart, when it will make a delicious consommé, ideal for convalescents or those on diets.

INSTANT STOCK

1 onion, halved
1 carrot, halved
ends of leek and celery
½ bay leaf
2 stalks parsley
6 cups water
6 bouillon cubes

Put vegetables in a pan, cover with cold water, bring slowly to the boil, then add the crumbled stock cube and simmer for 30 minutes. Do not add salt or pepper. When time is up, strain stock and throw away vegetables. This makes a quick stock, useful for steaming meatballs, couscous, etc.

ROUILLE

2 slices dry bread, crusts removed
a little milk
2 dried chili peppers
2 pinches sea salt
1 pinch saffron, stamens or powder
1 head of garlic, peeled and chopped
½ cup best olive oil

Soak the bread in milk for 10 minutes then squeeze dry. Chop the chilies and pound them in a mortar with salt and saffron until reduced to a paste. Add garlic and bread and continue to pound until blended to a smooth paste. Add the oil drop by drop, pounding until all is blended.

This cannot be made without a mortar and pestle, but it is a delicious adjunct to any fish soup and the traditional accompaniment to a bouillabaisse.

TOMATO AND PEPPER SAUCE

3 tbsp. butter
1 small onion, finely chopped
1 tsp. flour
14 oz. can tomatoes, chopped
¾ cup canned red peppers, drained and
*   chopped*
½ tsp. sugar
salt and black pepper
A few shakes Tabasco

Melt butter and cook onion until golden. Add flour, stirring until blended, then stir in tomatoes and their juice. Cook gently for 4 minutes, then add peppers and simmer for 8 minutes, adding salt and pepper to taste. When cooked, stir in Tabasco, to taste. This is a useful spicy sauce for serving with bland foods such as croquettes.

MAYONNAISE

2 fresh egg yolks
a pinch of salt
$\frac{1}{4}$ tsp. Dijon mustard
$1\frac{1}{4}$ cups olive oil
1 tbsp. white wine vinegar
1 tbsp. lemon juice

By hand: have all the ingredients at room temperature. Place the egg yolks in a large china bowl set firmly on a damp cloth so it cannot slide around (you need both hands to make the sauce). Stir them vigorously for $\frac{1}{2}$ minute, add the salt and mustard, and stir again. Have the oil in a cup with a good pouring lip (one that drips will drive you mad). Holding the cup in your left hand, start adding the oil literally drop by drop, stirring constantly. When about a third of the oil has been absorbed, you can start to add it a little faster, and when two-thirds has been amalgamated, start adding it in a thin stream. When it is all blended in, stir in the lemon juice and vinegar. Taste, and add a drop more if required. Cover with plastic wrap and store in a cool larder, or in the refrigerator.

If at any time the mayonnaise curdles, start again by breaking a fresh egg yolk into a clean bowl, and add the separated mayonnaise to it, drop by drop. When that is amalgamated, start adding the rest of the oil, as before. Add an extra $\frac{1}{2}$ cup oil to compensate for the extra egg yolk, and more lemon juice and vinegar to taste. *In the food processor:* break the egg yolks into the processor and add the salt and mustard. Process for $\frac{1}{2}$ minute, then start adding the oil through the lid, drop by drop, while continuing to process. You can add it more quickly as the sauce progresses. Then add the vinegar and lemon juice, and thin it by adding 2 tbsp. boiling water, while processing. Turn into a bowl, cover with plastic wrap and keep low down in the refrigerator, or in a cool larder.

SAUCE HOLLANDAISE

Serves 2

3 egg yolks
a pinch of salt
8 tbsp. unsalted butter
1 tbsp. lemon juice

This is easiest to make in a food processor. heat container by filling with very hot water and standing 5 minutes. Drain and dry. While it is heating, put butter in a small pan and heat until almost boiling, then add lemon juice. Put egg yolks in processor, add salt, and process for 30 seconds, then pour the hot butter through the lid, while continuing to process. Stop as soon as all is added.

The heat of the butter should be enough to cook the egg yolks, thus thickening the sauce very slightly. If this has not happened pour into a small china bowl sitting in a saucepan over very hot water, and stir until slightly thickened.

Serve as soon as possible, in a warm bowl (the sauce does not need to be hot) with poached fish, asparagus, or artichokes. Or pour it over poached eggs sitting on a slice of ham on half a toasted muffin to make Eggs Benedict.

SAUCE BEARNAISE

Serves 2

$\frac{1}{2}$ cup white wine vinegar
1 tbsp. shallots, chopped
3 black peppercorns
4 egg yolks
12 tbsp. unsalted butter
a pinch of salt

While the container of the food processor is heating (see previous recipe) boil vinegar in a small pan with the shallots and peppercorns until it is reduced to $\frac{1}{3}$ cup. Strain, return to pan, and add butter, cut in small bits. Stir until very hot without actually boiling.

Break egg yolks into food processor, add salt, and process for 30 seconds. Then pour hot vinegar and butter mixture through the lid, continuing to process, stopping as soon as all is added. If successful, the sauce will have thickened very slightly; otherwise rescue as in previous recipe.

To serve: pour into a warm bowl and serve with roast beef or grilled steaks.

VELOUTE SAUCE

$1\frac{1}{4}$ cups chicken stock (or veal, fish, or vegetable)
2 tbsp. butter
2 tbsp. flour
salt and black pepper
$\frac{1}{2}$ cup heavy cream

Heat stock, using whichever is appropriate to the dish. Melt butter, add flour, and cook 1 minute, stirring, over a low heat. Remove from heat and start adding hot stock by degrees, stirring until each addition is blended. Halfway through, replace pan over low heat, and continue until all stock is added. Increase the heat slightly, stirring until boiling point is reached,then lower heat and simmer for 3 minutes, stirring now and then. Towards the end of the time, stir in the cream, and salt and pepper to taste.

This is made in the same way as béchamel sauce, using stock (or stock and cream) instead of milk. I use it in preference to a béchamel, except with egg dishes, since they produce no stock of their own. With dishes of poached chicken, fish, or vegetables, the use of the relevant stock instead of milk makes a much more cohesive and flavorsome dish.

Variations:

Curry velouté: add 1 tsp. light curry powder with the flour, and proceed as above.

Saffron velouté: $\frac{1}{4}$ tsp. saffron in the stock while heating. If the saffron is in stamens, strain the stock before adding to the roux (butter and flour paste).

Watercress velouté: chop $\frac{1}{4}$ cup watercress leaves with the cream in a food processor, before adding to the sauce.

Herb velouté: chop 3–4 tbsp. fresh herbs – tarragon, chervil, dill, etc. – with the cream in a food processor, and add to sauce at the end of its cooking. Do not allow to boil after adding herbs.

BECHAMEL SAUCE

2 cups milk
½ small onion
2 cloves
¼ bay leaf
¼ tsp. salt
5 black peppercorns
2 tbsp. butter
4 tsp. flour

Put milk in a small pan with the onion stuck with cloves, bay leaf, salt and peppercorns. bring slowly to boil, cover, remove from the heat, and stand for 20 minutes. (This is only necessary when making a béchamel without added flavorings, so it is not too bland.) Then reheat milk and strain into a cup.

Melt butter in a clean pan, add flour, and stir until blended. Cook over a low heat for 1 minute, stirring constantly, then remove from heat and add hot milk, little by little, stirring till each addition is amalgamated. When half the milk is used, replace over a low heat and stir in remaining milk. When all is added, bring to the boil, stirring, and cook over a very low heat for 3 minutes, stirring now and then. Taste and adjust seasoning.

Variation: if using to accompany a boiled vegetable, use some of the vegetable stock, reduced, in place of some of the milk.

Sauce Mornay: make as above, but without flavoring the milk. Simply heat it and add to the roux (butter and flour paste). When sauce is almost finished, stir in 1 cup grated cheese – Gruyère, Emmental, or Cheddar are best – and stir over a low heat until melted and smooth. If serving with cauliflower, etc., use the vegetable stock, reduced to a good flavor, in place of half the milk.

BREAD SAUCE

1½ cups milk
½ medium onion
2 cloves
¼ bay leaf
sea salt and black pepper
pinch of mace or nutmeg
about 8 tbsp. soft white breadcrumbs
1 tbsp. butter
2 tbsp. cream (optional)

Put milk in a small pan with onion, stuck with cloves, bay leaf, salt, pepper and mace. Bring to boil, turn off heat, cover and stand 20–30 minutes to flavor milk. Strain and reheat. As it approaches boiling point, shake in crumbs gradually, stirring, and stop as soon as it reaches the right consistency (remember it will thicken slightly on cooking). Simmer 3 minutes, stirring often, adding more salt and pepper if required. Just before serving, stir in butter, and cream if you have it.

Serve as a traditional accompaniment to roast chicken, turkey and game.

APPLE SAUCE

2 large cooking apples, peeled, cored and quartered
½ tsp. sugar
2 tsp. lemon juice
1 tbsp. butter (optional)

Slice apples thickly and put in a pan with just enough water to cover the bottom. Bring to boil, cover, and cook gently until soft, stirring now and then so they do not stick. Push through a coarse food mill, or mash with a fork. Stir in lemon juice, and butter if serving hot. If serving warm or cold, omit the butter. This is good with roast pork, duck or goose.

HORSERADISH AND APPLE SAUCE

2 large cooking apples, peeled, cored and quartered
¼ cup sour cream
about 4 tbsp. grated horseradish
a little lemon juice

Slice apples and cook in very little water (do not add sugar) until soft. Push through a coarse food mill and leave to cool. Stir in sour cream and add horseradish gradually, tasting as you do so. Stop as soon as the two flavors are evenly blended. Add lemon juice to taste.

Serve cold with rich meats like cold roast duck, goose or pork.

HORSERADISH SAUCE

½ cup yogurt
½ cup mayonnaise (a good bottle one will do)
2–3 tbsp. grated horseradish, fresh or preserved
1–1½ tbsp. lemon juice or to taste

Beat yogurt until smooth, then mix with mayonnaise. Add horseradish to taste, then a little lemon juice. Serve cold with braised or roast beef.

MUSTARD AND HORSERADISH SAUCE

½ cup yogurt
½ cup mayonnaise
2 tsp. Dijon mustard
2 tsp. grated horseradish
1 tsp. lemon juice
2 tsp. tomato paste and 5–6 dashes Tabasco

Beat yogurt, mix with mayonnaise, and stir in mustard, horseradish, lemon juice and tomato paste mixture. Serve with grilled breast of lamb, or Sausage en Croûte.

YOGURT AND MINT SAUCE

1 cup yogurt
1 tbsp. chopped fresh mint or ½ tsp. dried mint
½ tsp. sea salt

Beat yogurt until smooth then stir in mint and salt. This is good served with grilled lamb or curry.

FRESH HORSERADISH, easy to grow if you can't find it in stores; just peel and grate it to use

ENTERTAINING

MELANIE DE BLANK'S
WEDDING FEAST FOR 50

Melanie de Blank: You have to start off with the best possible ingredients you can afford. For instance, I always use the most expensive butter in my pastry: I don't think anything else gives the same results. I talk to my butcher twice a week and to the fish seller every day, to see what is coming in. I would decide the ingredients of the seafood salad the day I made it, according to what was best.

I think food ought to look honest, to be what it is, not all dressed up. It has to look appetizing, of course, but it should still look like food. I try to think of color schemes, so that when the food is laid out, it looks pretty. And if you're making a feast, it's got to be fun to do or you'd get bored. I immediately thought of things I enjoy making.

For 50 people I think it's best to sit them at round tables for 10, with the starter already on the table, then lay out the rest. So guests would start with the chicken terrine and sauce, and help themselves to the seafood salad, lamb cutlets and potato pie, and green salad.

I didn't ice the cake myself, as that's a very special skill and I'm not much good at it, so I got someone else to do it. Inside, the cake is madeira. I don't like fruit cake and I had a chocolate cake at my own wedding. With it I would serve rosé champagne and a still, medium dry cider, with apple juice or homemade lemonade for the children.

Melanie de Blank stands behind the Layered Chicken Terrine, whole and cut into slices, with the Sauce Verte.
Left are the desserts: Pineapples Filled with Fruit, and Fruit Tartlets. In front of them are the Seafood Salad, Puff Pastry Potato Pies, and Lamb Cutlets in Herb Breadcrumbs.
166 *Right, a mixed green salad.*

LAYERED CHICKEN TERRINE
WITH SAUCE VERTE

10 chicken breasts
1 onion, chopped
1 carrot, chopped
1 stalk celery, chopped
½ cup mushrooms, chopped
2 tbsp. butter
1 tbsp. olive oil
3 stalks parsley
1 bay leaf
6 black peppercorns
½ cup dry white wine
1½ lb. spinach
salt and black pepper
4 bunches fresh tarragon
1 bunch fresh chervil

Start 48 hours in advance. Bone each breast and set the flesh aside. Brown the bones in a heavy roasting pan in the oven, allowing 10–12 minutes at 400°F. Soften the onion, carrot, celery, and mushrooms in the butter and oil in a heavy pan, adding parsley, bay leaf, and peppercorns. Add the browned bones to the vegetables after a few minutes, leaving their fat in the pan. Add the wine and boil up for a moment or two, then cover with water and bring to the boil. Simmer for 3 hours, covered, checking from time to time and replenishing the water as required. Skim the surface frequently, removing any scum. When the time is up, strain, and refrigerate over night.

Next day heat oven to 300°F. Remove the fat from the surface of the stock and boil up until reduced to ¾ cup. Cook the spinach 4–5 minutes in lightly salted boiling water, then drain in a colander and leave to cool. When cool enough to handle, squeeze dry in the hands. Cut each chicken breast horizontally into 2–3 slices. Oil a 2 lb. loaf pan lightly and make a layer of sliced chicken breasts in the bottom. Sprinkle with salt and pepper and cover with a layer of half the tarragon, then half the spinach. Add more salt and pepper, then a second layer of chicken, and the remaining tarragon and spinach, seasoning each layer. Finish with chicken, making 3 layers of chicken, and 2 each of the spinach and tarragon.

Pour the reduced stock over the terrine, shaking it so that it penetrates right through. Cover loosely with foil and put in a roasting pan half full of water. Bake for 1½ hours, until the chicken has turned an opaque white in the center, and the edges have shrunk away from the sides of the pan. Remove from the oven and leave to cool in the bain marie. Later, place in the refrigerator overnight. This terrine does not really need weighting down, but if the center has domed slightly, you can lay two 1½ lb. weights on a piece of foil on the terrine as it cools. Otherwise don't bother; on no account weight it down heavily.
To serve: run a knife around the edges of the pan and turn out on to a flat dish. Don't worry if half remains in the pan; simply ease it out gently on top of the rest. Garnish with chervil. Serve with a Sauce Verte.

SAUCE VERTE

6 egg yolks
a pinch of salt
3¾ cups olive oil
about ⅓ cup lemon juice, or half lemon
    juice/half white wine vinegar
1 clove garlic, crushed (optional)
black pepper
2 bunches watercress
2 oz. parsley
3 bunches fresh chives
3 bunches fresh tarragon
3 bunches fresh chervil

Make the mayonnaise as usual (see page 164). Stir in garlic (optional), and pepper to taste. Pinch the leaves off the watercress and put in the food processor with the parsley heads, chives, tarragon, and chervil. Process until quite finely chopped, then stir into the mayonnaise by hand. Turn into a bowl and serve with the Chicken Terrine.

LAMB CUTLETS
IN HERB BREADCRUMBS

20 lamb cutlets, trimmed
¼ French loaf, cut in slices and toasted
6 tbsp. chopped herbs: one each of
    rosemary, thyme, tarragon, chives,
    chervil, mint; or a mixture if all are not
    available
1 tbsp. chopped parsley
¼ cup flour
salt and black pepper
2 eggs, beaten
butter
olive oil

Break the toast in pieces and reduce to crumbs in the food processor. Mix with the chopped herbs. Lay out three shallow dishes, filling one with seasoned flour, one with beaten egg, and one with the herb mixture. Cut every scrap of fat off the cutlets, then dip them first in flour, then in egg, and lastly in the herb breadcrumbs. Heat a mixture of butter and olive oil in a frying pan and cook the cutlets on both sides until golden brown. Try to time it so they are still slightly pink in the center. Lay them on paper towels to drain. They can be served hot or cold.

PUFF PASTRY POTATOES

1 lb. puff pastry
1 lb. new, or waxy potatoes
sea salt and black pepper
grated nutmeg
2 cloves garlic, finely chopped
4 tbsp. butter
1 egg, beaten
2 tbsp. single cream, or milk

First prepare the potatoes, cutting them in thin, even slices. Drop them into boiling salted water and cook 4 minutes, or until just tender, then drain in a colander, rinse under cold water, and drain again.

Heat the oven to 425°F. Grease a shallow, round cake pan measuring 10 inches in diameter. Divide the pastry into 2, one piece slightly larger than the other. Roll out the smaller part and line the pan. (If you don't have a suitable pan, cut the pastry into a 10-inch circle using a saucepan lid as a guide, and lay on a greased baking sheet.) Arrange the potato slices on the pastry in layers, overlapping, leaving a ½ inch border

Pasta and Seafood Salad.

around the edge. Dot each layer with butter and sprinkle with garlic, salt, pepper and nutmeg. Beat the egg with the cream, or milk, and brush the border.

Roll out the second piece of pastry into a slightly larger circle and lay it over the potatoes. Press the edges together to seal. Brush all over the top with the beaten egg and bake for 25–30 minutes, until puffy and golden brown. If it starts to get too brown, lay a piece of foil loosely over it. Take out of the oven and leave to cool. Do not chill. **Variation:** this pie is also delicious served hot. In this case, cut a small circle in the center of the pastry lid before baking. After baking, remove it, and pour in ½ cup heavy cream, with 2 tbsp. chopped chervil or dill mixed into it, and serve.

PASTA AND SEAFOOD SALAD

Pasta:
4 cups all-purpose flour
5 large eggs
⅓ cup olive oil
1 tsp. salt
Seafood:
1 lb. filleted white fish, (halibut, turbot, cod or haddock), roughly chopped
1 lb. unshelled shrimp
6 oz. smoked salmon
1 clove garlic, crushed
sea salt and black pepper
3 tbsp. lemon juice
½ cup olive oil
⅓ cup chopped chives
⅓ cup chopped parsley

First make the linguine (narrow-cut noodles). Mix all the pasta ingredients

together, and allow to rest for 1 hour before rolling out the dough. Roll it through the pasta machine on the thinnest-but-one roller, then cut it on the narrow cutter. Cook the noodles as usual: 1–2 minutes will be enough. Drain, refresh in cold water and put in a large bowl, with 2 tbsp. olive oil to stop it sticking together.

Drop the chunks of white fish into simmering, lightly salted water or fish stock and poach 1–2 minutes. Shell the shrimp, and cut the smoked salmon into thin strips, about 1 inch long.

Mix fish into the pasta with the shrimp and smoked salmon (keeping a little of each back to garnish), using fingers so as not to break up the fish. Combine garlic, salt, pepper, lemon juice and olive oil in a small bowl. Mix into the noodles shortly before serving, stir in the herbs, and scatter the reserved seafood over the top.

169

FRUIT TARTLETS

Rich sweet pastry:
2 cups flour
2 tbsp. ground almonds
a pinch of salt
2 tsp. sugar
8 tbsp. unsalted Normandy butter
1 egg yolk
a few drops iced water
Filling:
2 cups whipping cream
2 tbsp. vanilla sugar, or sugar plus a few
  drops vanilla extract
24 green grapes, peeled
12 black grapes
6 strawberries
2 kiwi fruit

Put the flour into a large bowl, make a well in the center and add the almonds, salt, sugar, butter, egg yolk and water. Work them together with fingertips, then draw in the flour and work it all together, bringing in the flour to make a nice ball of pastry. Chill, roll out, line 10–12 small round tart pans, prick once with a fork then chill again before baking. Heat the oven to 400°F.

Tiny Fruit Tartlets

Bake the tarts 12–14 minutes, remove and cool.

Later, whip the cream until thick and fold in the vanilla sugar. Put a generous dollop of cream into each tartlet, and then into each one put 2 peeled green grapes. 1 unpeeled black grape, cut in half, a strawberry slice, with a few leaves left on for decoration, and half a slice of kiwi fruit.

PINEAPPLE FILLED WITH RED AND GREEN FRUIT

1 large pineapple, cut in half
2½–3 lb. mixed red and green fruit:
  strawberries, raspberries, kiwi fruit,
  melon, green grapes, etc.
6 passion fruit
juice of 3 oranges
sugar, to taste
8–10 sprigs mint

Scoop the flesh out of the pineapple, discarding the core, and cutting the flesh into small cubes. Mix with the other fruit in a large bowl. Cut the strawberries in halves or quarters, slice the peeled kiwi fruit, cut the melon in cubes. Leave the raspberries and peeled grapes whole. Add sugar to taste and then chill in the refrigerator for 1–2 hours.

When you are ready to serve, pile the mixed fruit into the halved pineapple. Cut the passion fruit in half and squeeze the juice into a small bowl. Add the orange juice and mix, with sugar to taste. Pour over the fruit and decorate with a few tiny sprigs of mint.

Arabella Boxer's variations: Melanie de Blank shows us the ideal wedding lunch, but few of us would contemplate making a seafood salad for 50 with home-made pasta, as well as coping with bridesmaids' tantrums, a tearful bride, and wedding guests who have lost their way. I suggest making the seafood salad with bought fresh pasta, using linguine, the narrow-cut noodles, if possible, or dried pasta twists (fusilli) or spaghettini. Melanie says it looks pretty made with green pasta, which is often better bought than made since adding the spinach can make the dough heavy. Alternatively, you could make the pasta in advance and freeze it. Easier still, you could forget it altogether and use saffron rice instead.

A terrine makes an ideal first course for a luncheon party. They are easier to handle and less filling when served in slices, with a complementary sauce or jelly, and eaten with a fork, rather than with bread and butter. Melanie's lamb cutlets in breadcrumbs could not be easier. You might prefer a simpler potato dish however. A homemade version of Russian salad is delicious, especially when the vegetables are still slightly warm, and the mayonnaise flavored lightly with garlic.

If pressed for time, a simple wedding feast can be made memorable simply by concentrating on a really good mayonnaise, quickly made in a food processor, and all the different foods that go with it. The main ingredient could be poached salmon or sea trout if you can afford it, or rare roast beef. The other foods could be hard-boiled eggs, new potatoes in their skins, hearts of romaine lettuce, and small skinned tomatoes, with plenty of crusty French bread and unsalted butter. This could be followed by a thick strawberry fool, semi-frozen, with a raspberry sauce, and the cake. If you want to make the cake yourself, use the fruit cake recipe (page 124). Instead of the cake, you could serve homemade cookies with the fool for any occasion other than a wedding – say a christening party or wedding anniversary.

FISH TERRINE

Serves 10

1 lb. salmon
black pepper
juice of 1 lemon
1 lb. spinach
2 slices dry white bread, crusts removed
*3 lb. whiting, filleted (approx. 1½ lb. after
    filleting)*
½ cup heavy cream
3 eggs, lightly beaten
1½ tsp. sea salt
coarsely-ground black pepper
¼ tsp. mace, or nutmeg

Start 24 hours in advance. Cut the salmon into strips, free from skin and bone. You should have about 13 oz. Lay them in a dish, sprinkle with pepper, squeeze lemon juice over them and leave 1 hour.

Cook the spinach 4–5 minutes in lightly salted boiling water, drain, and cool. When cool enough to handle, squeeze out and chop coarsely, by hand. Tear the bread into pieces and reduce to crumbs in the food processor. Add the white fish, cut in small pieces, and the cream, eggs, salt, pepper and mace or nutmeg. Process until thoroughly blended, then turn into a bowl and fold in the chopped spinach by hand.

Heat oven to 300°F. Line a 2 lb. loaf pan with wax paper (nonstick baking parchment is best) so that only the short ends are unlined, and leave the ends of the paper sticking up on either side (for lifting out the terrine after cooking). Fill the pan with alternate layers of fish forcemeat and drained salmon strips, finishing with forcemeat. Fold over the waxed paper to cover the top and stand in a roasting pan half full of water. Bake for 1½ hours, then remove from the oven. Cool, then chill overnight.
To serve: run a knife along the short ends of the pan, and lift the terrine out, using the ends of the paper. Invert on to a flat dish, cut in slices and serve with a Sauce Verte.

DUCK PATE

Serves 8–10

1 duck
¾ lb. unsmoked bacon, in 1 piece
*¾ lb. fatty pork (belly, throat, or boned
    spareribs)*
¾ lb. veal
2 tbsp. green peppercorns
2 cloves garlic, crushed
1 tbsp. sea salt
½ tsp. ground mace
¾ cup dry white wine
4 tbsp. brandy

Garnish:
*a few strips bacon fat, or a few small bay
    leaves and cranberries, or juniper berries*

Preheat oven to 400°F. Put the duck upside down in a rack in a roasting pan and roast for 25 minutes; remove and leave to cool.

If you plan to garnish the pâté with bacon fat, cut about 5 thin strips off the piece of bacon. Then cut the pork, veal, and the rest of the bacon in pieces and chop finely in a food processor, or put through a grinder. Mix all together in a large bowl. Cut the flesh off the duck, discarding skin and bone (keep for making soup). Cut into small neat dice, by hand, and stir into the mixed meats. Add the peppercorns, garlic, salt and mace, then stir in the wine and brandy. Mix very well and leave for 1–2 hours, if convenient.

Preheat oven to 300°F. Line a bread pan or terrine with the strips of bacon fat laid diagonally across it (or decorate with tiny bay leaves and a few cranberries, or juniper berries). Then pile in the pâté mixture, smoothing it with a spatula. Stand in a roasting pan half full of hot water and cook for 1¾ hours. Remove and leave to cool, then lay a piece of oil over it with a 2 lb. weight on top. Leave overnight in a cool place. Next day, remove the weight and chill in the refrigerator. Make 1–2 days before eating. Turn out on a flat dish to serve.

PLUM SAUCE

Serves 10

2 lb. canned plums, drained and pitted
1¼ cups red wine
½ tsp. ground cinnamon
½ tsp. ground cloves
½ tsp. ground nutmeg
½ tsp. ground ginger
½ cup red currant jelly
5 tsp. Dijon mustard
5 tsp. orange juice

Put the plums in a pan with the red wine. Add the spices and bring to the boil. Simmer, uncovered, for about 10 minutes, until thick and somewhat jammy. Meanwhile, melt the jelly in a bowl over simmering water. Sieve it, then mix with the mustard and orange juice. Stir into the plums, mix and leave to cool.
Serve cold with pâtés or cold meats, hot, with roast duck, turkey or goose, or with hot baked ham. This keeps for 1 week in the refrigerator.

GAME PATE

Serve 8–10

1 cock pheasant
¼ lb. unsmoked bacon, in 1 piece
1½ lb. fatty pork (belly, throat, or boned spareribs)
2 cloves garlic, crushed
1 tbsp. sea salt
10 black peppercorns
10 juniper berries, roughly crushed
3 tbsp. brandy
¾ cup red wine
½ lb. chestnuts (optional)
Garnish:
5 thin strips bacon fat or a few small bay leaves, and a few cranberries

Preheat oven to 400°F. Put the pheasant in a rack in a roasting pan and cook for 15 minutes, then remove and leave to cool.

If using bacon fat to decorate the pâté, cut 5 long strips off the bacon. Then cut the rest in pieces, together with the pork, and chop finely in the food processor, or put through a grinder. Turn into a large bowl. Carve the pheasant, stripping the meat from the bones, and cutting by hand into neat dice. Mix with the pork and bacon, adding the garlic, salt, peppercorns and juniper berries. Stir in the brandy and wine, and mix well. Leave 1–2 hours, if possible.

Preheat oven to 300°F. Decorate the terrine or mold with the strips of bacon fat diagonally across it, or the little bay leaves and berries. Pile the pâté mixture on top, smoothing it evenly, and stand in a roasting pan half full of hot water. Cook for 1¾ hours, then remove and leave to cool. 1–2 hours later, lay a piece of foil over the pâté, and stand a 2 lb. weight on it. Leave in a cool place overnight. Next day, remove the weight and chill in the refrigerator for 1–2 days.
To serve: turn out onto a flat dish and serve alone, or with Cumberland Sauce or Cranberry Sauce (page 214).

CUMBERLAND SAUCE

Serves 10

2 shallots, finely chopped
4 oranges
2 lemons
1 lb. redcurrant jelly
2 tsp. Dijon mustard
1¼ cups port
2 tsp. arrowroot

Put the chopped shallots in a small pan. Pare the rind of 2 oranges and 2 lemons; cut it in thin strips and add to the pan. Cover the shallots and rind with cold water, bring to the boil and simmer 5 minutes. Drain, discarding the water.

Squeeze the juice of all the fruit and reserve. Melt the jelly over simmering water, then push through a small sieve, or baby food mill. Return to clean bowl, still set over boiling water. Stir in the mustard, port, fruit juice, rind and shallots. Cook gently for 5 minutes, then mix the arrowroot to a paste in a cup with 2 tbsp. water. Stir into the sauce and cook for another 3 minutes.

Pour into jars and leave to cool. Seal tightly and keep for 1 week before eating. It will keep for 2 months, but keep it in the refrigerator once opened. Serve with cold turkey or ham, pâtés etc.

SEAFOOD AND SAFFRON RICE SALAD

Serves 10

2 cups long grain rice
¼ tsp. saffron
⅓ cup olive oil
sea salt and black pepper
¼ cup white wine, or 2 tbsp. white wine vinegar
1½ lb. monkfish
10 scallops, or ½ lb. white crabmeat (frozen)
1½ lb. shrimp, unpeeled, or ½ lb. peeled
2 tbsp. lemon juice
⅓ cup chopped chives (optional)

Cook the rice in lightly salted boiling water until tender – about 12 minutes. While it cooks, put the saffron in a cup and pour ¼ cup boiling water over it and leave 5 minutes to infuse. When the rice is cooked, drain it in a colander, rinse under cold running water, and drain again. Then turn into a large bowl and stir in the saffron-flavored water, pouring it through a strainer if using stamens. Mix well, until it is evenly colored, then stir in half the olive oil and plenty of salt and pepper.

Bring some lightly salted water to the boil, add a drop of wine if you have it, or 2 tbsp. wine vinegar, and put in the fish. Cook for about 12–14 minutes, until cooked, then remove and drain. If using scallops, drop them into the simmering water and poach 2–3 minutes, depending on size. Drain. If using frozen crabmeat, thaw it, drain, and break into small chunks. Shell the shrimp. Flake the fish, discarding skin and bones. Cut the scallops in quarters, and the tongues in half.

Stir the remaining olive oil into the rice, then the lemon juice. Mix the fish very gently into the rice, trying not to break it. Finally, stir in the chopped chives. (The chives are not essential if you have used saffron but are very important if the rice is plain white.) Serve as soon as possible after cooking; do not chill, If you have to make it much in advance, put in the refrigerator but take it out 2 hours before serving.

RUSSIAN SALAD

Serves 10

3 lb. new potatoes
1 lb. small carrots
1 lb. green beans
4 lb. peas
4 lb. broad beans
2 cups mayonnaise
2 cloves garlic, crushed
sea salt and black pepper

Boil the potatoes in their skins. Drain and peel while still hot. Cut in halves or quarters according to size, or in thick slices. Leave the carrots whole if tiny, or cut in halves, quarters, or thick slices, so they resemble the potatoes in size. Cook until just tender in lightly salted boiling water, drain, and mix with the potatoes. Cut the green beans in 1 inch chunks, and cook in a little lightly salted boiling water until tender. Drain, and add to the other vegetables. Shell the peas and beans and cook separately; drain and add to the others.

Make the mayonnaise in advance. Stir in the garlic, and fold gently into the vegetables, trying not to break them. Turn into a dish and serve, when possible, within 1–2 hours of making, while still slightly warm.

RASPBERRY MERINGUE

Serves 10

6 egg whites
1½ cups sugar
2½ cups heavy cream or whipping cream
2 lb. raspberries

Make as for Raspberry Meringue Ice cream (page 151) but in double quantities and substituting whipped cream for the ice cream. Make two separate rounds, using more fruit and less cream than in the other version. This can be made a few hours in advance and kept chilled until needed.

CLAUDIA RODEN'S
HOT PICNIC FOOD

Claudia Roden: In the Middle East people don't think of picnics as being different food; they bring their saucepans along and cook on the spot. There is a tradition of cooking food out of doors.

Pita is the best food for a bonfire party, because you put the whole meal into one parcel. It is like a sandwich really, only it is shaped like a pouch so it holds the filling better and keeps it warm. You can buy different shapes of pita, large and small, round and oval, and sometimes you can find wholemeal pita, but for this purpose the large oval shape is best.

You can prepare the stuffed pita breads ahead of time, wrapped in foil, and warm them up in the bonfire or over the barbecue, or pack them into an insulated bag for a picnic. They are very versatile: I would make some and leave them in the refrigerator, wrapped up, for the children to warm up themselves in the oven if they were coming home late.

You should mark each little parcel according to the fillings, perhaps with colored stars on the foil wrapping, so people can choose a different one for their second helping.

Afterwards I would probably offer a cake packed with fresh fruit, rich, but firm enough to cut up outside. Sometimes we bake fruit, like bananas, over the fire, and grown-ups can cut a slit in the top and add some dark rum, but it might not be safe for children. To drink, I would like something warm and spicy: hot orange juice with a dash of cinnamon for the children, and a mulled wine for the adults. And if the barbecue or bonfire was in my own garden, I would finish with Turkish coffee.

Claudia Roden with her stuffed pitas wrapped in foil:
the different colored stars on the foil indicate different fillings. 173

The pitas (left) and the fillings: top left. Eggplant and Pepper; right, the Chicken; and in front, the spicy meat filling.

CHICKEN FILLING OF MOROCCAN INSPIRATION

To fill 14–16 pita halves

*1 chicken
1 lb. onions, grated
1½ tsp. cinnamon
¼ tsp. allspice
½ tsp. ginger
2 cardamom pods, cracked
the juice of 1 lemon
salt and pepper to taste
a large bunch of parsley or fresh coriander,
   finely chopped
7 eggs
¼ lb. blanched almonds
7–8 pita breads, warmed*

Put chicken in a large saucepan, cover with water and bring to the boil. Remove any scum as soon as it appears, then add onions, spices, lemon, salt and pepper and simmer 1½ hours, or until the chicken is so tender the flesh falls off the bone.

Remove chicken, strain stock, add parsley or fresh coriander and reduce to 1 cup. Beat eggs lightly, add to the stock over a very low flame and stir constantly until the mixture is a thick cream (it does not matter if it curdles). Toast the almonds and chop or break them into largish pieces with a pestle and mortar. Skin, bone and coarsely chop the chicken, as late as possible so it does not dry up, then stir it into the egg and stock mixture with the almonds; taste and adjust the seasonings.

Cut each pita across in two, then open each half out gently to form a pouch. Put 2 tbsp. of the chicken mixture in each half and wrap it in foil. Warm up in the fire.

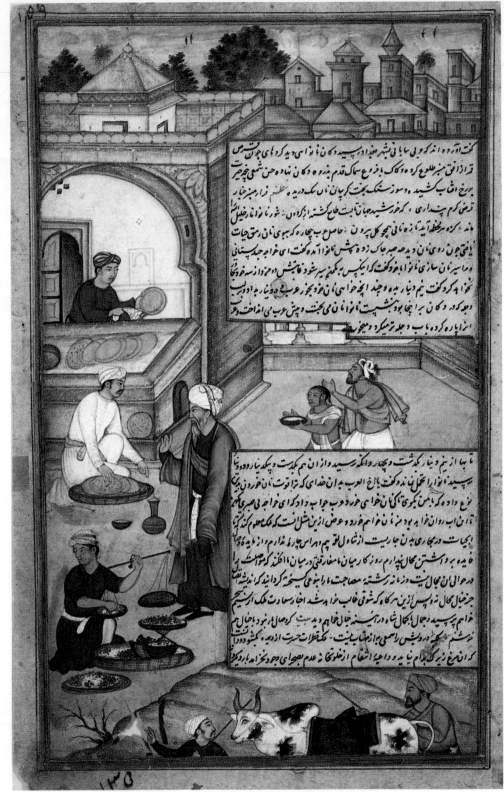

*The Arab and the baker, c. 1590, attributed to Dharm Das
The Chester Beatty Library and Gallery of Oriental Art, Dublin*

175

MEAT FILLING OF ARAB INSPIRATION

To fill 8 pita halves

2 tbsp. oil
2 tbsp. pine nuts
1 onion, chopped
1 lb. ground lamb, beef or veal
2 tbsp. raising or golden raisins, or 5 dried
   apricots, chopped
1 tsp. cinnamon
½ tsp. allspice
salt and pepper to taste
a small bunch of parsley, finely chopped
4 pita breads, cut in half across

Fry the pine nuts in oil, shaking the pan until lightly browned. Remove them and fry the onion, stirring occasionally until softened, then add the meat and crush it with a fork. Add the dried fruits and flavorings and stir until the meat changes color. Take off the heat and add the parsley and the fried pine nuts.

Put 2 tbsp. in each pouch of bread and wrap in foil. Warm up in the fire.

AN EGGPLANT AND PEPPER FILLING

To fill 14 pita halves

2 eggplants, weighing about 1 lb.
1 onion, coarsely chopped
⅓ cup light oil
2–3 cloves of garlic, crushed
1 large green pepper, chopped
1 × 1 lb. 13 oz. can of peeled tomatoes
2 tbsp. wine vinegar
1 tbsp. sugar
salt and pepper
1 tbsp. dried mint
¼ lb. mature cheddar, coarsely chopped
1 small bunch of parsley, chopped
7 pita breads, cut in half across

Trim and dice the eggplants, sprinkle with salt and leave for an hour in a colander until the bitter juices are released. Rinse and squeeze a few pieces at a time in your hands, shaking off as much water as possible. Fry the onion in oil until lightly colored, add the eggplant, and stir a few minutes until lightly browned. Add garlic and, when the aroma rises, add the green pepper, tomatoes with their juice, vinegar, sugar, mint, pepper and salt (only a little salt to allow for the saltiness of the cheese). Cook until the eggplants are done and the liquid is much reduced (too much would make the bread soggy). Stir in the cheese and parsley.

Put 2 tbsp. in each pouch of bread and wrap in foil. Warm up in the fire.

Spooning the Eggplant and Pepper Filling into the pita pouch before wrapping it in foil.

APRICOT CAKE

½ lb. dried apricots (preferably a sharp
   variety)
¼ lb. hazelnuts (preferably with their skins)
¾ cup sugar
6 eggs

Preheat the oven to 325°F. Put the apricots in a saucepan with ½ cup water and simmer a few minutes until they soften; drain. Grind or chop the hazelnuts finely, but not too finely, so that they are not a mush and one can feel them. Blend the slightly-cooled apricots to a paste and mix them in a bowl with the nuts and sugar. Separate the eggs and add the yolks to the mixture. Beat the whites and fold into the mixture; stir in three or four tablespoons first as this makes it easier to fold in the rest. Pour the mixture into a buttered and floured 9-inch cake pan and bake for 1 hour. Cool in the pan before turning out.

MULLED WINE

½ gallon, or 2 liters robust red wine
¾ cup sugar
1 stick cinnamon
2 tsp. ground cinnamon (optional)
4 cloves

Put the wine, sugar and spices in a saucepan and heat to nearly boiling. Cover and leave to infuse 5 minutes, then strain, and serve if the party is in your own garden, or pour into a vacuum bottle.

FRESH FRUIT CAKE

This cake is so full of fresh fruit that it makes a good dessert. All sorts of fruit may be used – apples, bananas, pineapples in the winter; apricots, plums, greengages, cherries, gooseberries, peaches and dates in the summer.

2¼ lb. fruit (I used 3 apples, 2 small pears,
   2 bananas and 12 dates)
1 cup unsalted butter
scant 1½ cup sugar
5 eggs
2½ cups sifted flour
½ tsp. salt

Preheat oven to 325°F. Keep 2 apples and 7 dates for the top, and wash or peel, top and tail, core or pit the rest as necessary and cut into largish pieces. Cream the butter, add the sugar then the eggs, one at a time, beating well to a pale, light cream. Stir in the flour and salt and mix well. Fold in the fruit and pour the mixture into a buttered and floured 9-inch cake pan. Peel, core and slice the remaining apples and cut the dates into four, removing the pit. Arrange on top of the cake mixture and press down lightly. Bake for 1½–2 hours or until the cake seems firm when you press it. Cool for 5 minutes before turning out on to a rack.

   You can carry the cake to the bonfire in its pan and cut it up there. It is moist but firm enough to hold in your hand, without needing a plate.

Fresh Fruit Cake decorated with apples and dates.

Arabella Boxer's variations: Claudia's first suggestion for a bonfire night picnic was to stuff three different fillings into filo pastries each made in a different shape – to enable guests to identify the different fillings in the dark. But as filo is not always easy to find, she chose a simpler version, using pita bread. For those who can buy filo, however, here are some suggestions.

   Filo pastry, or strudel leaves – the same pastry can be used for either purpose – can be bought in Greek Cypriot shops and Middle Eastern stores. It comes in 1 lb. packages, but freezes well, so that half may be used and the remainder frozen. The important thing is to remember that while you are filling and folding one sheet, the unused sheets must be kept covered with a damp cloth or they will dry out and become brittle, making them impossible to fold without breaking.

   I might start with a thick soup – pheasant and lentil, pasta and bean, or corn chowder, carried in a vacuum bottle. In this case, I would make only one or two

pastry fillings, or I might substitute a spinach pie, or small cheese pastries. As a dessert, I would probably fall back on a cake, popular with adults and children and easy to carry out. The Carrot Cake (page 125) could be carried to the picnic site in its pan and the frosting taken separately in a plastic carton and spread on to the cake with a spatula before it is cut up. Or you might just offer fruit: take a watermelon and 2 or 3 limes; cut the melon into narrow wedges at the site, sprinkle it with lime juice and eat in the fingers. A honeydew type of melon is best cut up before leaving into 1 inch cubes and sprinkled with lemon or lime juice; pack it into large plastic cartons and, on arrival, stick 3 or 4 cubes each on to wooden skewers. For a dessert that is hot, delicious and also great fun, you could offer toasted cheese: pack 2 lb. of feta, cut into 1 inch cubes in plastic cartons. Unpack on to a flat dish with a bundle of long metal skewers and let each guest toast his own around the bonfire.

Arabella Boxer's suggestions
for a hot Winter Picnic

First course

PASTA E FAGIOLI
(see page 107;
make double quantities and carry
in a wide-necked vacuum bottle)
or
CORN CHOWDER
or
PHEASANT AND LENTIL SOUP
or
CABBAGE SOUP WITH SAUSAGES

Main course

SPANAKOPITTA
or
TIROPITAKIA
or
FILO PASTRIES

Third course

TOASTED CHEESE

MELON ON STICKS

WATERMELON WEDGES

CARROT CAKE
(see page 125)

CORN CHOWDER

Serves 10

8 ears corn
3 oz. salt pork, chopped
1 Spanish onion, chopped
2 leeks, sliced
4 cups chicken stock
black pepper
4 cups milk
1 cup light cream

Cut the kernels off the corn cobs on to a chopping board, transfer to a bowl, and scrape the juices off the cobs with the back of the knife, mixing with the kernels. Fry the soft pork in a heavy saucepan or casserole; when the fat has melted, put in the onion and leek, and cook gently 3–4 minutes. Add the corn and stir around the mix well. Heat the stock and add to the pan. Bring to the boil, taste and add black pepper, and salt if needed. Cover, lower the heat, and simmer for 20 minutes. When the time is up, add the heated milk and cream, and pour into a vacuum bottle. Serve with Matzos or water biscuits.

CABBAGE SOUP WITH SAUSAGES

Serves 10

12 oz. kidney beans
1½ lb. shin of beef, cut in large pieces
1 large carrot, halved
1 stalk celery
1 bay leaf
6 oz. salt pork, or fatty bacon
2 large onions, chopped
1 large green cabbage, quartered and cut in strips
salt and black pepper
3 medium potatoes, peeled and cut in chunks
3–4 Polish sausages, cut in thick slices.

Soak beans overnight. Put the beef in a pan and cover with 2½ quarts cold water. Bring slowly to the boil, skimming until the surface is clear, then add the carrot, celery, and bay leaf. Simmer gently, half covered, for 1½ hours. Chop the pork or bacon, heat slowly in a casserole and cook gently 12–15 minutes, until all the fat has melted. Lift out the solid parts with a slotted spoon and discard.

Cook the chopped onions in the fat until soft and translucent, then add the sliced cabbage. Cook gently about 5 minutes, stirring now and then, until the cabbage has wilted. Then add the contents of the other pan (beef, flavoring vegetables, and stock), and heat. Drain the kidney beans and add to the casserole with the potatoes, bring to the boil, half cover the pan, and simmer 45 minutes. Take out the beef, carrot, celery and bay leaf; stir in the sliced sausages, and stand for a little before serving. If making in advance to carry out, only add the sausages shortly before pouring into a vacuum bottle or their strong taste will overpower the cabbage.

PHEASANT AND LENTIL SOUP

Serves 10

1 large cock pheasant
2 large onions, halved
2 large carrots, halved
3 leeks, trimmed
3 stalks celery, trimmed
1 bay leaf
4 tbsp. olive oil
1 lb. brown or green lentils, washed and drained
salt and black pepper

Start a day in advance. Put the bird in a deep pot or pressure cooker with ½ an onion, ½ a carrot, the ends of leeks and celery, and the bay leaf. Cover with 3 quarts cold water and bring slowly to the boil. Skim until the surface is clear, then

cover and cook for 45 minutes (or 15 minutes under pressure). When it is cooked take out the pheasant, and leave to cool a little. Then cut off all the white meat, the breasts and wings, and return the carcass to the pot or pressure cooker. Cover again, and cook for a further 2¼ hours (or 45 minutes under pressure). When the time is up, strain the stock, and leave to cool. Later, chill overnight in the refrigerator.

Next day, remove all fat from the surface of the stock and measure it. You should have about 2½ quarts; if much less, make up with water. Chop the remaining vegetables and cook gently in the oil in a heavy pan for 10 minutes. Add the lentils, and stir around 1 or 2 minutes, then heat the stock and add to the pan. Bring to the boil, half cover the pan, and cook 45–50 minutes, or until the lentils are tender. In the meantime, cut the pheasant meat off the bone, discarding the skin, and dice. Add it to the soup when the lentils are soft, and heat through for 5 minutes, without allowing it to boil. Adjust seasoning, and pour into a vacuum bottle.

SPANAKOPITTA (SPINACH PIE)

Serves 8–10, with other dishes

2 lb. fresh spinach
2 bunches scallions
1 tbsp. sea salt
10 tbsp. butter
2 onions, finely chopped
2 large eggs, beaten
¼ lb. feta cheese, crumbled
freshly ground black pepper
8–10 leaves filo pastry

Wash spinach, drain, then chop it quite finely in the food processor, with the scallions. Tip them into a colander in layers, sprinkling each layer with salt. Leave 15–20 minutes.

Heat 6 tbsp. butter and cook the chopped onions gently until they start to change color and soften. Squeeze the spinach and spring onions between the hands to get rid of all the moisture, then put the mixture in a large bowl. Place the fried onions over it and mix well. Beat the eggs and stir in the crumbled feta, adding lots of pepper, and stir into the spinach.

Heat oven to 350°F. Find a suitable pan; a round flan ring about 11 inches broad would do nicely, or a square one 10 inches wide × 1½ inches deep. Melt the remaining butter and brush the pan with some of it. Lay 1 sheet of filo in the pan, trimming the edges with scissors so they overlap the pan by 1–2 inches. (If using a round pan, don't round off the filo sheets; they should have square corners overlapping each other.

which are later folded back over the top.)
Brush the filo all over with melted butter,
and cover with another sheet, trimming
and brushing with melted butter as before.
Continue until you have used 4 or 5 sheets;
keep the rest covered with a damp cloth.

After the last one has been brushed with
butter, fill the lined pan with spinach,
spreading it out evenly. Cover with another
4–5 sheets filo, trimming these to fit exactly
inside the pan, and brushing each with
melted butter as before. Finally, fold the
corners of the bottom sheets back over the
top layer, brushing with butter to stick
them down. Brush all over once more with
butter, and make a diamond pattern of
diagonal lines, with a pastry wheel or the
point of a sharp knife, through the first 2 or
3 layers of filo. Bake for 40 minutes. Wrap
in foil. Cut and serve just before eating.

TIROPITAKIA
(SMALL CHEESE PASTRIES)

Makes about 24

½ lb. feta cheese
4 oz. cream cheese
2 medium eggs
2 tbsp. chopped mint
black pepper
3 sheets filo pastry (about 4 oz.)
about 6 tbsp. butter, melted

Heat oven to 350°F. Grate the feta into a
bowl and mash the cream cheese into it
with a fork: it does not need to be absolutely smooth. Beat the eggs and stir in the
mint and pepper. It will not need salt, as the
feta is very salty. Take 1 sheet filo at a time
and cut into 8 strips about 2½ × 10 inches.
Brush them with melted butter and lay a
small teaspoonful of the filling in one
corner. Fold into a triangular shape (see
the step-by-step drawings, right). Brush all
over with melted butter, sticking down the
ends, and lay on a baking sheet. When all
are done, bake for 15 minutes or until
golden brown. Wrap all together in a foil
parcel and pack in an insulated box.

FILO PASTRIES

Makes 12 pastries

6 sheets filo (about 8 oz.)
8 tbsp. butter, melted
Claudia's chicken filling, meat filling, or
* eggplant and pepper filling*
* (see pages 175–6)*

Heat the oven to 350°F. Unwrap the filo,
and count out 6 sheets. Separate one, and
roll up the others, covering them with a
damp cloth. Cut the first sheet into 2 strips,

15 × 5 inches. Brush with melted butter and
lay 2 tbsp. filling at one end of each strip.
Fold into triangles, squares or rolled, according to the step-by-step instructions
below (use a different shape for each
filling).

Once folded, brush all over with melted
butter to seal the ends. Lay on a baking
sheet and proceed with the next piece of
filo. When all are done, bake for 20–25
minutes, or until golden brown. Wrap in
foil for transporting to the picnic. Reheat
in the edges of the fire.

To make filo pastries

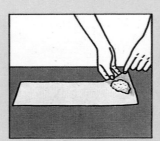

To make a triangle:
1 Take a 5-inch wide strip of
filo, brush with melted butter
and lay 2 tbsp. of filling in one
corner.

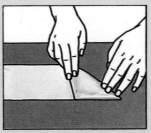

2 Fold the bottom corner over
the filling to make a triangle.

3 Continue folding: at right
angle, then down, at right
angle, then up, along the strip.

4 Brush the top with melted
butter.

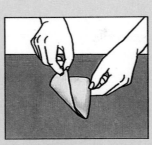

5 Fold the final corner over
and stick down.

To make a square:
1 Brush filo strip with melted
butter, lay 2 tbsp. of filling at
one end and fold over the
edges of the strip to hold in the
filling.

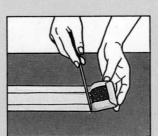

2 Fold over the end to make a
neat square, and continue
along the length of the strip.

3 Brush all over with melted
butter, sticking down the
edges.

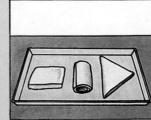

Use different shapes for
different fillings: for the roll,
fold in the edges as for squares,
then roll up.

ANTONIO CARLUCCIO'S
BUFFET PARTY FOR 25

Antonio Carluccio: To organize a buffet party for 25 or so people takes careful planning if it is going to be a pleasure for you and your guests. This menu would take a day for one person to prepare single-handed.

I feel it is important to have food that is exciting and easy to eat. Here there's a good balance between fish, meat, vegetables, salad (in the vine leaves), fruit and cheese; between fresh and cooked food; and between hot and cold dishes. You can eat all of it with your fingers, you don't need forks, only plates. I think that's the most practical thing when you're standing up.

You can gently reheat the shrimp, rice balls, spinach fritters, chicken livers and spiced turkey breasts – you can leave the skewers in place as the wood won't get too hot. The point to remember is to cook in advance the food that won't lose in appearance, and leave the fruit to the last minute because that must be fresh or it will look unattractive. It's important to use only good olive oil in the cooking, rather than butter or solid fat, because oil looks and tastes nice if you serve the items cold.

Antonio Carluccio holding the Enveloped Prawns.
In front, from the left, are: Exotic Fruits on Skewers; Spinach Fritters;
a bowl of Chicken Livers with Sherry; a pyramid of
Crudités in Vine Leaves; fried Arancini;
Spiced Turkey and Chicken Breasts on skewers, and Parma Ham Fingers.

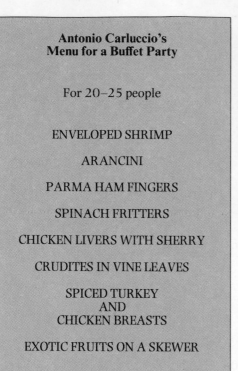

**Antonio Carluccio's
Menu for a Buffet Party**

For 20–25 people

ENVELOPED SHRIMP

ARANCINI

PARMA HAM FINGERS

SPINACH FRITTERS

CHICKEN LIVERS WITH SHERRY

CRUDITES IN VINE LEAVES

SPICED TURKEY
AND
CHICKEN BREASTS

EXOTIC FRUITS ON A SKEWER

HAPPY MARY

SPARKLING WINE

Making Crudités in Vine Leaves: one spoonful of the mixture of raw and cooked vegetables in lemon mayonnaise is placed in the center of each vine leaf and folded into a small parcel.

ENVELOPED SHRIMP

*2 lb. good frozen puff pastry
30 unpeeled, uncooked giant shrimp
1 bunch fresh dill
3 eggs
salt and pepper, and a little flour
1 tbsp. breadcrumbs*

Defrost pastry, roll out to $\frac{1}{8}$ inch thick, and cut into 4 inch squares. Peel the shrimp and drain. Beat 2 of the eggs with salt and pepper and the finely chopped dill, then stir in the breadcrumbs to make a soft paste.

Place one shrimp in the middle of each pastry square, and add a teaspoon of egg and herb mixture. Beat the remaining egg and brush along the edge of the pastry. Fold the pastry into the shape of an envelope; make sure it is sealed. Brush the top with more egg and bake at 400°F. for 15 minutes.

The envelopes can be prepared the day before, and gently reheated before serving.

ARANCINI
(RICE BALLS)

*$\frac{1}{2}$ cup olive oil
1 small onion, finely chopped
$\frac{1}{4}$ lb. chopped mushrooms
1$\frac{1}{2}$ lb. Italian arborio rice (for risotto)
5 cups stock
3 eggs beaten
$\frac{1}{4}$ cup grated Parmesan cheese
salt and pepper to taste
1 cup dried breadcrumbs
olive oil for deep frying*

Place olive oil in a large pan over moderate heat and brown the onion and mushrooms. Add the rice, stirring almost continuously, and add the stock, ladle by ladle, until the rice is cooked 'al dente' (chewy), remaining almost dry. Place rice to cool on a large surface, spreading it out to help the cooling process.

When cool, place it in a mixing bowl, add the 3 beaten eggs, cheese, salt and pepper and mix well. Form rice into balls about the size of an apricot in the palm of your hand. Roll them in breadcrumbs and deep fry until golden. They can be served hot or cold, and can be gently reheated in the oven the next day.

PARMA HAM FINGERS

This is a very sinple but effective dish to prepare for any sort of party.

*40 small slices of Parma ham, preferably from the end of the ham. This way they will be smaller and cheaper! (or 20 large slices, halved)
1 tbsp. fresh (or dried) mixed herbs
salt and pepper to taste
3 Mozzarella cheeses*

Spread the Parma ham out. Cut the Mozzarella first into thick slices lengthways and then into fingers and mix carefully in a bowl with the herbs, salt and pepper, to coat the cheese. Roll each Mozzarella finger up in a slice of Parma ham.

Arrange then on a plate with some green garnish, such as a bunch of fresh herbs, or with radicchio leaves, if in season.

SPINACH FRITTERS

2½ lb. fresh spinach
2 large eggs
a dash of nutmeg
2 tsp. grated Parmesan cheese
¼ cup dried breadcrumbs
olive oil for frying

Wash spinach thoroughly and place in a pan of boiling water. Boil for 5 minutes. Drain and cool, and squeeze the excess water out.

Chop the spinach coarsely and place in a mixing bowl with eggs, nutmeg, salt and pepper, cheese and breadcrumbs. Mix well, and with the help of a tablespoon form 20–25 mounds of spinach, then flatten slightly. Gently fry until brown, and serve hot or cold.

CHICKEN LIVERS WITH SHERRY

2 lb. chicken livers, thoroughly cleaned and
    cut into two.
¼ cup olive oil
a pinch of ground sage
1 tbsp. sesame seeds
1 tbsp. dried garlic
salt and chilli sauce to taste
1 small glass of dry sherry

Mix the livers with all the other ingredients except the sherry, and leave for one hour. Preheat oven to its maximum heat, place the livers on a baking tray and roast until cooked (about 15–20 minutes). Shortly before taking them out of the oven, stir in the sherry. (If you are making these in advance and going to reheat them the next day, omit the sherry until you are almost ready to serve them.)

Pile in a dish, and serve hot or cold with wooden toothpicks.

SPICED TURKEY AND CHICKEN BREASTS

This recipe is inspired by the Eastern dish *Satay*.

1½ lb. breast of chicken
1½ lb. breast of turkey
1 tsp. fresh minced garlic
1 tsp. mixed herbs (dry or fresh)
1 dash Worcestershire sauce
salt and chili powder to taste
¾ cup olive oil
juice of 1 lemon
30–40 long wooden skewers

Cut the breasts into 1 inch cubes, mix all the herbs and spices with a little olive oil

Fruit dessert: thread banana, grape, strawberry, melon, paw paw or grapefruit, and pineapple on to skewers at the last possible minute and sprinkle with lemon juice.

and marinate the meat for a couple of hours.

Heat the remaining oil in a non-stick frying pan; when hot, add the meat mixture and stir fry for 10 minutes, adding the lemon juice at the last minute.

When the mixture is cool, thread the chicken and turkey cubes on the skewers alternately, and serve hot or cold.

CRUDITES IN VINE LEAVES

This is the refreshing dish of the party, and is similar in appearance to the Greek Dolmades.

2 carrots
1 parsnip
4–5 spring onions
1 red pepper
3 celery stalks
2 small ripe avocados
1 small bunch of parsley and 1 of dill, both
    finely chopped
⅓ cup lemon mayonnaise
juice of ½ lemon, and the grated rind
1 package vine leaves (which usually
    contain 40–50 leaves)

Boil the carrots and parsnips, and drain. Cut all the vegetables, cooked and raw, into very small cubes, and mix with the mayonnaise, lemon juice and lemon rind,

salt and pepper.

Cook the vine leaves in boiling water for 5 minutes (if fresh, add salt to the water and boil until tender). Spread the leaves on a board, and place a teaspoon of the mixture in the center of each. Fold as shown in the photograph opposite, and serve.

EXOTIC FRUITS ON A SKEWER

This is very refreshing. Many fruits can be used, but they must be ripe. I chose:

1 mango
1 melon (choose what is in season)
4 peaches
1 paw paw
2 pink grapefruit
6 kiwi fruits
1 bunch black grapes
25–30 strawberries
5 bananas
juice of 1 lemon

Peel fruit and cut into large chunks. Place on the skewer in a colorful order: you can use the same type of skewers as in the chicken and turkey recipe.

This is the only recipe that it is necessary to prepare at the last minute, just before the party, to avoid oxidization of the fruits. To improve the appearance of the fruit, sprinkle with a little lemon juice.

HAPPY MARY

For each drink:

5 oz. good tomato juice
a dash of celery salt
a dash of Tabasco
a dash of Worcestershire sauce
juice of ¼ lemon
1 measure of gin

Mix together all the ingredients and serve poured over ice.

The Happy Mary is supposed to favor the initial conversation at a party, and at the same time prepare the stomach for the feast. The sharpness of the drink and the alcohol content depend on how fast you wish to reach the chosen atmosphere. It would taste just as good on its own, with no alcohol at all, for non-drinkers or drivers.

For the rest of the evening I suggest serving Champagne, or a good sparkling wine. An extremely good 'sparks' for relatively little money, which is not dissimilar from a conventional Champagne, is Longlais Château Saumur.

A Happy Mary garnished with celery and lemon, with sparkling Saumur behind.

Arabella Boxer's variations: Antonio is a most expert cook. For others less accomplished, however, I suggest moderating his menu, for it is challenging for one person. The enveloped shrimp are tricky to make, and even threading things on skewers takes longer than you might think unless you have help. Some of his dishes, like the Parma ham and Mozzarella, or the fruit on skewers, could not be simpler, for they don't even need cooking; even so they do take time to peel, chop and assemble neatly.

The arancini can be simplified by using plain boiled rice mixed with beaten eggs and chopped herbs, in place of the risotto. Or you could serve falafel, made with ground chick peas. Instead of the shrimp in pastry I might take small fishballs using a salmon. mixture.

Barbecued spareribs can be eaten in the fingers so long as they are cooked until dry and crisp. One very simple dish is tiny new potatoes baked in their skins and served with a dipping sauce. Quails' eggs make charming Scotch eggs in miniature. Grilled chicken wings make another tasty snack, served as they are, or with garlic sauce. To save time at the last moment, you could substitute bowls of cherries or grapes for the fruit on skewers, or serve a chocolate cake made the day before.

If I had enough large pitchers, I would make a white wine punch to serve throughout, so that only one lot of glasses were needed. This is especially good in summertime, when a little fresh fruit – but not too much – can be added.

SCOTCH QUAILS' EGGS

4 dozen quails' eggs
2 lb. fatty pork (belly or boned spareribs),
   finely minced
2 lb. veal, finely minced
1 medium onion, cut in chunks
2 inch square piece of ginger
3 large cloves garlic
2 tsp. soy sauce
2 tsp. lemon juice
8 shakes Tabasco
2 tsp. sea salt
black pepper
4 eggs, beaten
dry breadcrumbs
frying oil

Put the eggs in a pan, cover with lightly salted cold water, bring to the boil, and cook 2½ minutes. Drain, and plunge the eggs into cold water. Later, shell them.

In a large bowl, mix the pork and veal, beating with a wooden spoon. (Ask the butcher to put it through the grinder twice, if he is agreeable.) Put the onion chunks in a garlic press and squeeze the juice into the meat. Do the same thing with the ginger and the garlic, mixng the juice in well. Finally, stir in the soy sauce, lemon juice, Tabasco, salt and pepper.

Divide the mixture in quarters, and roll out each quarter as thin as possible on a lightly floured board. Divide each piece into 12. Put one in the palm of your hand,

dip an egg in flour, and lay it on the meat. Gradually work the meat around it, until the egg is completely enclosed. Repeat with all the other eggs.

Heat the pan of oil to about 360°F. Dip the eggs in beaten egg, then in breadcrumbs, drop them into the oil, a few at a time, and cook until they are golden brown all over, turning once with a perforated spoon. They will take about 4 minutes. Drain on paper towels while you cook the next batch. If possible, serve before they have cooled, either alone, or accompanied with a bowl of Tomato and Pepper Sauce. Or cut them in half and put a dab of sauce on each.

FISHBALLS

Makes about 4 dozen

2 lb. freshly mashed potatoes
1 cup butter
sea salt and black pepper
4 egg yolks, lightly beaten
2 lb. cooked salmon
8 tbsp. finely chopped parsley
3 eggs, beaten
1 cup breadcrumbs
butter and oil, for sautéing,
   or oil for deep frying

Have the hot mashed potato in a large bowl. Stir in the butter, in small bits, then plenty of salt and pepper and the egg yolks. Flake the fish, discarding skin and bone, and chop it by hand. Stir it into the potato, beating with a wooden spoon until blended. Finally stir in the parsley. Divide the mixture into quarters, them make each quarter into about 12 round balls, rolling them between lightly floured hands. Dip in beaten egg and breadcrumbs. They may be sautéed or deep fried, whichever is most convenient; I usually cook them in a mixture of butter and olive oil, in a large frying pan. Cook until golden brown all over, turning frequently, then drain on paper towels. Serve warm, either alone, or with a bowl of Sauce Verte.

BAKED NEW POTATOES
WITH DIPPING SAUCE

5 lb. small new potatoes
Dipping Sauce:
2½ cups mayonnaise
2½ cups sour cream
¼ cup tomato paste
Tabasco, to taste

Preheat oven to 400°F. Brush the potatoes; do not peel them. Rub dry in a cloth and lay them on baking sheets. Bake 45–60 minutes, depending on size. (Even tiny

potatoes take a surprisingly long time to bake.) Test by piercing one with a skewer.

Make the sauce while they are baking. Beat the mayonnaise and sour cream until smoothly blended, then stir in the tomato paste, and Tabasco to taste. Serve the potatoes in a large dish, stuck with toothpicks if you like, although this won't be necessary if they are warm, rather than hot, and serve the sauce separately in a bowl.

BARBECUED SPARERIBS

See the recipe on page 95. Buy double quantities, leaving them whole. Use the tomato-based marinade, and cook in the oven until very crisp and slightly charred. Leave to cool before cutting up into ribs.

GRILLED CHICKEN WINGS

Chicken wings sold without any of the breast attached, are quite cheap. 1–2 hours before cooking, rub with olive oil and lemon juice, crushed garlic and black pepper. Grill or broil slowly, until charred and blackened outside, and just cooked within. Serve as a snack with drinks, or as part of an hors d'œuvre. If you prefer, omit the garlic, and serve with Garlic Sauce.

WHITE WINE PUNCH

Makes enough for 20–25

1½ cups water
1¼ cups sugar
1½ cups lemon juice
1 quart orange juice
¾ cup orange curaçao
¾ cup brandy
4 bottles white wine, from the Loire or
   Rhine (Vouvray, Muscadet, Moselle or
   Reisling)
peel of 1 cucumber, in long strips
2 peaches, sliced (optional), and/or ½ lb.
   strawberries (optional)
2 large bottles Perrier, or other fizzy
   mineral water or club soda

Make the sugar syrup in advance; put the water and sugar in a pan, bring to the boil and cook 2–3 minutes. Then pour into a jug and leave to cool.

Some hours before the party, mix the sugar syrup, fruit juices, spirits and wine in large jugs. Add cucumber peel and chill, either in the refrigerator or in a sink packed with ice, for 3–4 hours. Just before serving, add the mineral water, plenty of ice, and the fruit. (Omit the fruit if you prefer and just use the cucumber peel.)

DINAH MORRISON'S
TEA PARTY

Dinah Morrison: We often have tea parties when we're in the country, where people do go visiting a lot. It's a very good way of entertaining where there is a wide range of people you want to see. Friends can bring along their parents, or children, or visitors if they have them staying; it's easy to include an extra guest at tea.

I think it should be fairly traditional: scones or tea bread or perhaps muffins, with homemade jam, some cookies and a good cake. You don't have to cook it all on the day, though scones always taste better the day you make them. Here you can make the brandy snaps, meringues and shortbread in advance and keep them in an airtight tin. The éclairs can be made a day ahead too, but only add the cream and icing at the last minute. And the sponge cake is actually better if left for a day or two first, otherwise it can be very crumbly and falls to bits when you cut it.

If you're a bit unsure about how best to decorate the cake, try spreading the crystallized petals on a white plate about the same size as your cake, and move them around with tweezers to decide the arrangement you want. Then transfer them to the cake.

Dinah Morrison with her Iced Sponge Cake.
Scones with Strawberry Jam and cream, Shortbread, Meringues.
Brandy Snaps, Éclairs and Tea bread.

TEA BREAD

3 cups white bread flour
¾ cup milk
½ oz. fresh yeast
2 tbsp. honey
4 tbsp. butter
½ tsp. mixed spice
pinch of salt
½ cup raisins, soaked in warm water
about ½ cup chopped nuts: hazelnuts,
*   walnuts or almonds*

Sift flour into a large warm bowl and make a well in the center. Gently warm the milk to about 110° and mix 3 tbsp. with yeast. Put this into the well in the flour and cover with a sprinkling of flour. Melt the honey and butter together, adding the mixed spice and salt. Stir the honey mixture into the flour and yeast, and half the milk, adding the rest of the milk slowly, and mixing hard until it makes a soft, manageable dough. You may not need all the milk, you may need a little more, depending on what flour you are using. All this can be done very quickly in a food processor, and in my experience this uses less liquid. Knead the dough on a floured surface until smooth and put to rise in an oiled bowl covered with oiled plastic wrap.

When the dough has doubled in size, knead again incorporating the drained raisins and the chopped nuts. Cover with plastic wrap again and let the dough relax 10–15 minutes. Then flatten out and fold the two sides towards the middle. Turn a quarter circle and fold the other two sides to the middle to make a neat sausage shape, with the folds underneath.

Put this in a greased, floured bread pan, 4 × 8 inches, cover with the greased plastic wrap once more and let the dough rise. When it reaches just above the rim of the pan put the loaf in a preheated oven at 400°F and bake for 10 minutes. Turn the oven down to 375°F and continue cooking for 15 minutes. Take the loaf out of the oven and remove gently from the pan, then put back into the oven for 5 minutes to dry off the crust.

This loaf is delicious when it is new, and it also makes excellent toast when it is a day or two old.

SCONES

Makes 8–10

2 cups all-purpose flour
½ tsp. salt
1 tsp. cream of tartar
½ tsp. baking soda
4 tbsp. butter
about ½ cup fresh or sour milk

Sift the dry ingredients together and rub in the butter. (This can be done in a food processor.) Gradually mix in the milk until a soft dough is formed. If you use sour milk the scones will be lighter and even more delicious. Roll the dough out to a depth of about ¾ inch, cut with a 2 inch biscuit cutter and put the rounds of dough on a greased baking sheet.

The top of the scones can be brushed with egg or milk to make them shiny, or you can rub some sugar lumps over the skin of an orange until they take up some of the oil in the skin and press one lump into the top of each scone before you cook them. Bake in a preheated oven at 425°F. for 12–15 minutes.

Serve hot with clotted cream and home-made jam.

STRAWBERRY JAM

Makes 3 lb.

2 lb. small strawberries (not too ripe)
3¼ cups sugar
juice of 2 lemons
small knob unsalted butter

Wash and hull the strawberries and cut any large ones in half. Warm the sugar in a low oven. Put the strawberries and lemon juice in a large pan over a gentle heat until the juice runs. When the sugar is hot, stir it gently into the fruit and let it dissolve. Then raise the heat and let the jam boil, stirring gently from time to time to prevent it burning. Test the set of the jam by putting a small blob on a saucer and allowing it to cool rapidly in the freezer. (If it wrinkles when pushed gently with a finger tip, setting point has been reached.) Or you can test the temperature: it will set at just a fraction over 220°F. on a candy thermometer. (Don't rest the thermometer on the bottom of the pan, but take the temperature in the middle.)

When the jam is cooked, skim off any froth (preserving sugar or superfine sugar forms the least scum and so is not as extravagant as it might seem). If it is hard to remove every last bit, a small knob of butter about the size of a hazelnut, stirred into the jam, will remove the last few bubbles. Let the jam cool a little before putting it into warm, clean jars. (Full details for covering jam jars are given in the recipe for Raspberry Jam on page 191.) Wipe the jars, cover and label them, and store in a cool, dark cupboard.

ECLAIRS

Makes 16–18

6 tbsp. butter
1 cup water
pinch salt
1 cup all-purpose flour, sifted
3 large eggs
1 egg yolk for glazing

Heat butter in the water, with a pinch of salt. When the butter melts add the flour. Stir the mixture until smooth, and continue to stir gently over a low heat until a film of mixture sticks to the bottom of the pan. Turn into a bowl and leave to cool for 5 minutes. Beat in the eggs one at a time until the mixture is smooth and glossy.

Transfer to a large pastry bag with a plain round nozzle. (It's easier to do this if you support the bag, nozzle down, in a jar, the sides folded over the rim, while you spoon in the mixture.) Pipe 2½–3 inch lengths of the mixture on to a greased, floured baking pan, allowing room for expansion. Beat the extra egg yolk with a teaspoonful of water and paint the top of the uncooked éclairs. Dry for a quarter of an hour while you preheat the oven to 375°F. Cook 35–40 minutes until golden brown.

Quickly slit the éclairs on one side and open out a little. Scoop out any uncooked mixture and put them back in the oven to dry while the oven cools down. This makes sure they are not soggy.

Fill the éclairs with whipped cream, and dip them in glacé icing, flavored with coffee or chocolate.

Variation: the same mixture will make cream puffs if piped in mounds on the baking sheet and cooked in the same way. Filled with whipped cream, these are very good piled into a pyramid to make a spectacular dessert. Dribble the chocolate or coffee icing over the completed pyramid.

Sponge cake filled with butter icing and topped with glacé icing and crystallized flowers.

SHORTBREAD

Makes 8 pieces

½ cup butter
¼ cup sugar or vanilla sugar
1 cup all-purpose flour
½ cup rice flour

Cream the butter and sugar together. When pale and fluffy, add the two flours, sifted together. Press the mixture into a greased pan 7½–8 inches in diameter. Prick the shortbread with a fork and mark into 8 pieces, then press around the edge of the shortbread with a finger or wooden spoon to make a wavy pattern. Cook in a pre-heated oven at 325°F for 45–50 minutes. Let the shortbread cool in the pan and recut the wedges before storing in an airtight container until needed. It will keep 7–10 days.

ICED SPONGE CAKE

3 eggs, well beaten
¾ cup sugar
2 tsp. lemon juice
¾ cup all-purpose white flour
¼ cup cornflour

Preheat oven to 325°F. Add sugar to eggs and put the bowl inside a larger bowl full of hot water. Beat the mixture hard (with an electric beater if you have one) until thick. Add lemon juice and fold in the two flours sifted together. Put the mixture in a greased, floured cake pan 9 inches in diameter and 2–3 inches deep. Bake in the middle of the oven for 1 hour. Cool the cake slowly in the pan. When it is cool, split the cake in two, spread the bottom layer with butter icing; replace the top layer and decorate.

Butter Icing:
6 tbsp. unsalted butter
scant 1 cup confectioner's sugar
flavoring: 1 tsp. vanilla extract, or 1 tbsp. lemon or orange juice, or 1 tsp. instant coffee dissolved in 1 tbsp. boiling water, or 1 tbsp. cocoa powder

Beat the butter and sifted sugar together and stir in the flavoring of your choice.

Glacé icing:
1½ cups confectioner's sugar
about 5 tsp. liquid: fruit juice, coffee liquer or, for a harder icing, egg white.

Gradually add warm liquid to the sifted icing sugar. Stop when the mixture is wet enough to spread on the cake (if it becomes too wet, add more sifted sugar to stiffen it again). Spread over the top of the cake with a wet spatula.

Crystallized Flower Decoration:

Choose small flowers, or just use petals (rose petals are ideal) and make sure that they are not damp. Beat an egg white with a pinch of salt until just a little more fluid; if the egg is a bit stale you may have to add a splash of cold water. Paint the petals with this, using a tiny paint brush, then dip them into superfine sugar. Use a teaspoon to pour sugar into any folds or cracks. Shake the petals and put to dry on a cake rack. A pair of tweezers can be a great help with this rather fiddly work. Let the flowers dry overnight in a warm dry room and use to decorate a cake. They can be stored in an airtight box for a little while: a little silica gel in the box will keep them really dry.

BRANDY SNAPS

Makes about 36

6 tbsp. butter
6 tbsp. light brown sugar
6 tbsp. light corn syrup or Golden Syrup
1 tsp. ginger
¾ cup all-purpose flour, sifted
1 tsp. brandy, or lemon juice

Put the butter, sugar, syrup and ginger into a saucepan and heat gently until butter is melted. Add flour and brandy or lemon juice, and stir together. Put teaspoons of the mixture on to a heavy greased baking sheet, leaving enough room for them to spread. You will have enough mixture for 3 or 4 batches. Bake for about 10 minutes at 350°F.

When done, lift the brandy snaps off the baking sheet with a spatula and roll them up quickly while they are still pliable. (If they cool and stiffen, put the pan over a very low heat for a moment or two.) Allow the brandy snaps to cool on a cake rack, and store until needed in an airtight container. They will keep well for a week.

MERINGUES

Makes 10–12

4 egg whites
pinch salt
1¼ cups superfine sugar

Preheat oven to 225F. Whisk egg whites with a pinch of salt until they start to form soft peaks. Add half the sugar and continue to whisk until it forms stiff peaks. Fold in the rest of the sugar and put the mixture into a large pastry bag with a serrated nozzle. Pipe mounds of the mixture on to a heavy greased and floured baking sheet and bake for 2½ hours. At the end of the cooking time, lift the meringues from the tray, turn them over, and leave them in the oven as it cools down. Store in an airtight container and serve as they are, or sandwiched together with whipped cream.

You can use the instructions for Crystallized Flowers (above) to frost small fruit like redcurrants, wild strawberries and grapes, and tiny leaves like currant leaves, as well as rose petals and, in the springtime, primroses and violets.

Arabella Boxer's variations: Tea must be the one meal at which the English excel. There are so many irresistible teatime foods that it becomes almost impossible to choose between them, Cucumber sandwiches or toasted muffins, drop scones or fruit bread, sponge cakes or brandy snaps – each seems more tempting than the last. Good as they are, however, few can beat freshly baked bread with unsalted butter and homemade jam.

We also have a wider range of teas to drink than any other country I know. There are varieties to suit every taste, from smoky Lapsang Souchong to somber Darjeeling, flowery Earl Grey to subtle Oolong Tips. China tea, in particular, gains from drinking out of thin china, with a choice of milk or lemon.

By tradition, tea has always been an informal meal. It probably reached its zenith in the first half of this century in the English country houses. While the other meals were eaten in the dining room, tea was usually served on a round table spread with a cloth in a corner of the drawing room, in the library, or in the nursery. In the winter, it was often near the fire, as in our photograph, while in summertime, it might be laid on the lawn under a shady tree. Guests came and went as they pleased, helping themselves to whatever took their fancy. Each house had its own teatime speciality that regular guests grew to expect and look out for. Here are some of my own favorites.

Arabella Boxer's suggestions for a Tea Party

DROP SCONES

POTATO SCONES

BRACK, or FRUIT BREAD

RASPBERRY JAM

GINGERBREAD

ICED TEA

DROP SCONES

Makes 16–18

2 cups all-purpose flour
½ tsp. baking soda
1 tsp. cream of tartar
¼ tsp. salt
1 egg, beaten
1¼ cups sour milk

Sift the flour, baking soda, cream of tartar and salt into a large bowl. Stir the milk into the eggs, then stir into the flour, using as much as is needed to make a thick batter. (Different flours absorb different amounts so it is impossible to be exact.) Rub a griddle or large frying pan with a small piece of butter, and heat. When it is hot, pour on large spoonfuls of the batter, three at a time, being careful they don't run into each other. Cook until bubbles form on the top surface, then turn and cook the other side until nicely browned. Serve warm, or after cooling, with unsalted butter.

BRACK, or FRUIT BREAD

1¼ cups strong tea, cold
¾ lb. mixed dried fruit
¾ cup brown sugar, packed
2–4 tbsp. whisky (optional)
2 cups all-purpose flour
a pinch of salt
1½ tsp. baking powder
4 tbsp. butter, cut in small bits
1 egg, beaten

Start a day in advance. Soak the dried fruit and the sugar overnight in the cold tea, adding the whisky, is used. Next day, heat oven to 300°F. Sift the flour, salt, and baking powder into a large bowl. Rub in the butter then stir in the egg. Stir in the dried fruit, and add the tea gradually, stopping when you have a soft dough. You may not need it all. Have a loaf pan lined with non-stick baking parchment, or oiled foil. Fill it with the dough and bake 1½ hours. Turn out to cool; do not eat until it has cooled completely. It is delicious spread thickly with unsalted butter.

RASPBERRY JAM

2 lb raspberries
2½ lb. sugar
1 tsp. unsalted butter (optional)

Cook the raspberries in a heavy pan over very low heat, without adding any liquid. Crush them with the back of a wooden spoon to release all the juice. While they are cooking, warm the sugar in a low oven. When the berries have yielded all their juice, stir in the warmed sugar and continue to cook until it has dissolved, stirring often. Once it has completely melted, boil rapidly for about 10 minutes. Test for setting, either with a sugar thermometer, or by cooling a tiny bit rapidly in the freezer. (If it wrinkles when pushed gently with a finger tip, setting point has been reached.) Take off the scum on the surface of the jam, adding – if you like – a tiny bit of butter to help remove the very last of the foam.

Let it cool slightly before spooning into warm sterilized jars. Allow to cool before covering, first with a small circle of wax paper dipped in brandy, or liquid paraffin – this helps prevent mold forming – and the lid. If your jars don't have lids, simply cover with parchment or wax paper, tied with string. Wipe off any drips, label carefully, and store in a cool dark cupboard.

POTATO SCONES

Makes 12–16

4 tbsp. butter
¾ cup water
1 cup all-purpose flour, sifted
2 eggs
scant 1 cup freshly mashed potato
sea salt and black pepper

Heat the butter and water together in a small pan. When the butter has melted, remove from the heat and stir in the sifted flour. When smooth, break in the eggs one at a time, beating until amalgamated. (Use an electric hand beater if you have one.) Then beat in the hot mashed potato, continuing to beat until smooth. Add salt and pepper to taste, turn out on a lightly floured board, and leave to cool. Sprinkle with flour, wrap in plastic wrap and chill in the refrigerator for a few hours, or overnight.

Shortly before serving, take the dough out of the refrigerator and roll out until about ½ inch thick. Either cut in rounds or ovals with a metal cutter, or roll into a neat circle and cut in triangular wedges, like slicing a cake. Oil a large griddle or frying pan and heat. When it is hot, cook the scones until golden brown on both sides. Serve as soon as possible after cooking, with unsalted butter.

GINGERBREAD

2½ cups all-purpose flour
1 tsp. baking soda
1 tsp. baking powder
1½ tsp. ground ginger
½ tsp. ground allspice
½ tsp. ground cinnamon
½ tsp. sea salt
2 eggs, beaten
½ cup dark molasses
½ cup corn syrup Golden Syrup
6 tbsp. dark brown sugar
¾ cup butter
⅔ cup milk
¾ cup whipped cream (optional)

Heat oven to 350°F. Sift the flour, baking soda, baking powder, spices and salt into a large bowl. Stir in the beaten eggs. Warm the molasses, syrup, sugar and butter in a small pan until the sugar has melted; do not let it get hot. Stir into the flour, beating until well mixed, then stir in the milk. You should have a thin mixture, just capable of pouring. If not, add more milk. Pour into a shallow square pan lined with baking parchment or buttered wax paper, about 9½ inches square, and 1½ inches deep. Bake for 45 minutes. Cool on a wire rack, and serve in squares, topped with whipped cream. This is also good served warm, as a pudding.

ICED TEA

Serves 6

6 tsp. Indian breakfast tea
⅓ cup sugar
2 lemons, sliced
12 sprigs mint

Put tea in a heatproof pitcher, add sugar, 6 lemon slices and 6 sprigs mint. Pour in 6 cups boiling water, stir and leave 5 minutes. Stir again and strain into 6 glasses filled with ice cubes. Garnish with fresh lemon slices and mint. In 4–5 minutes the tea will be ready to serve. It should be made just before serving, but if you must make it in advance, strain it into a pitcher with lots of ice (no mint or lemon), cool and chill. Then serve by pouring into glasses over ice cubes, and garnish as above.

GLYNN CHRISTIAN'S
DELICATESSEN DINNER

The storecupboard where dinner began: left, a package of filo pastry, frozen spinach, frozen shrimp, canned clams and canned mussels; center, cans of cannellini beans, chick peas and plum tomatoes; right,

canned lychees, bottles of rosewater and rum, and frozen blackberries.

Glynn Christian: All the main ingredients of this meal can be bought in advance, so you don't have to fit in shopping on the day you're cooking. The only things you have to buy at the last minute are the main vegetable and salad ingredients and, of course, you should buy whatever is freshest. On this occasion I bought zucchini and served them with a sauce based on canned tomatoes.

I chose a dip for the first course as I like the idea of people having something to do, while I just have one thing to worry about: assembling the pastry. I might serve the first course in the living room so the guests can carry on talking there while I finish cooking, and move into the dining room for the main course. You can use different fish for the pastry filling, but it must have a good contrast of taste, texture and color to surprise people. You could use all shrimp if your budget allows, but mussels are good and cheaper. Size is important, and if you're using shrimp they must be large, not cocktail size, so it looks nice, not just a white sauce with little bits in it.

I would offer dry Madeira with the first course, and follow it with a New Zealand white wine, Cooks 1980 Chardonnay. Afterwards I would serve blue cheese with iced sweet white wine: it's just an extension of the idea of eating Stilton with port. You can serve the cheese before the sorbet if you are confident enough to make that the final *pièce de résistance*, or serve it last if you just want to relax.

Glynn Christian: at the front of his table is the main course, Seafood Pastry, with Zucchini in Tomato Sauce; the Mixed Salad that will accompany them is at the back. In the center is his first course: White Bean and Chick Pea Salad with hot pita bread.

WHITE BEAN AND CHICK PEA SALAD

Bean Purée:
2 14 oz. cans cannellini beans
1 clove garlic, crushed
2 tbsp. olive oil
5 tbsp. lemon juice
salt and black pepper
Chick Pea Salad:
1 14 oz. can chick peas
1 tbsp. olive oil
1 tbsp. lemon juice
1 Polish sausage, sliced
2 oz. feta cheese, crumbled, or white Stilton
    or white Cheshire
black pepper
1 small handful flat parsley

Drain the beans (reserving the juice in case
you need a little of it to thin the purée) and
put them in the food processor with the
garlic, olive oil and lemon juice. Process to
a purée, adding salt and pepper to taste.
Drain the chick peas and place in a bowl.
Stir in the olive oil and lemon juice, and the
kabanos sausage cut in slices about the
same size as the peas. Then stir in the
crumbled cheese and some black pepper
(salt won't be needed if you use the feta, as
it is already salty). Tear parsley leaves into
pieces and scatter among chick peas.
To serve: pour the purée on to a flat dish
and pile the chick pea salad in the center.
Serve with hot pita bread cut into pieces, as
a first course or dip.

SEAFOOD PASTRY

¾ lb. filo pastry (¾ package)
2 tbsp. butter
2 tbsp. olive oil
Filling:
1½ lb mixed seafood, canned and/or frozen.
    I used 1 can baby clams, 2 cans mussels,
    and 1 lb. frozen shrimp
2 packages frozen leaf spinach
4 tbsp. butter
2 heaped tbsp. flour
1¼ cups milk
1 small onion, halved
1 small carrot, halved
1 small bay leaf
4–5 black peppercorns
2 tsp. ground cumin
1 tsp. ground coriander
1 tsp. paprika

Preheat oven to 350°F. Take the filo pastry
and cut the sheets (5 or 6) in half across.
Take half and trim them to fit your serving
dish. Lay them one by one on a buttered
baking sheet, brushing each one with
melted butter and olive oil before laying the
next one on top of it. Bake 10–15 minutes,
until light golden. Then remove from the
oven and repeat the process with the remaining sheets of filo, but this time score a
diagonal criss-cross pattern through the
top 2 or 3 with the point of a knife. When
both are baked, set aside. (This can be done
the day before.)
To make the filling: defrost frozen shellfish
and spinach. Drain the canned shellfish,
pouring the liquid into a saucepan, and boil
until reduced to about ½ cup; set aside.
Heat the milk with the onion, carrot, bay
leaf and peppercorns. When it reaches
boiling point, turn off the heat, cover the
pan, and let stand 15–20 minutes to infuse,
then strain and reheat. Melt the butter, stir
in the flour, and cook for 1 minute. Pour in
the reheated milk and stir until blended,
then add the reduced shellfish liquid and
the spices and simmer for 3 minutes, stirring now and then. Add all the shellfish and
fold gently into the sauce, being careful not
to crush the mussels, and heat through
gently, stirring as little as possible. Squeeze
out the spinach to get rid of the moisture
and spread in a big frying pan (with no
added oil or butter) to dry and warm it.
Reheat the pastry for 10 minutes at 350°F.
  Remove filo from the oven and lay the
bottom half on your dish. Spread the
spinach carefully all over (it not only tastes
good, it prevents the sauce making the
pastry soggy) and spoon the shellfish over
all. Cover with the pastry lid and serve.

ZUCCHINI IN TOMATO SAUCE

1½ lb. zucchini
2 tbsp. butter
1 14 oz. can tomatoes
1 tbsp. olive oil
salt and pepper
1 tbsp. chopped mint

Slice the zucchini diagonally about ¾ inch
thick. Stew them gently in the butter 2–3
minutes, then add the crushed tomatoes
and their juice, olive oil, salt and pepper,
and cook about 15 minutes, until the
zucchini are tender and the sauce slightly
reduced. Stir in the mint and serve.
Variation: when serving on its own, or
with a simple main dish, add 1 tsp. each
ground coriander and cumin with the
tomatoes and omit the mint.

Lychee Sorbet with Blackberry Sauce.

MIXED SALAD

$\frac{1}{3}$ lb. mâche, or other leaf lettuce
3–4 oz. radicchio
$\frac{1}{3}$ lb. large mushrooms, sliced
salt and pepper
4 tbsp. olive oil
1–1$\frac{1}{2}$ tbsp. wine vinegar or lemon juice

Mix the mâche, radicchio leaves, and thickly sliced mushrooms (caps only) in a bowl. Mix the dressing and pour it over the salad: toss well and serve.

LYCHEE SORBET WITH BLACKBERRY SAUCE

2 1 lb. 4 oz. cans lychees
2–3 tsp. rose water
2 egg whites
Blackberry Sauce:
$\frac{1}{2}$ lb. frozen blackberries
3 tbsp. sugar
3 tbsp. dark rum

Drain the lychee juice into a saucepan and boil it up until reduced by half. Cool. Put the lychees into a food processor or blender and purée, then push through a sieve, return the residue in the sieve to the pulp, and sieve again. Mix with the reduced juice and add the rose water. Freeze as usual. When totally frozen, transfer to a food processor and reduce to a mush. Beat egg whites until stiff, but not dry, and fold into the mush. Freeze again.

To make the sauce, put blackberries in a food processor (reserving some for the garnish) and blend. Push through a sieve, then stir in the sugar and rum. Chill.

To serve: pour some sauce on to small plates, lay a scoop of sorbet on top and garnish with a few berries.

Variation: as an alternative to the sauce, serve the sorbet garnished with chilled orange slices sprinkled with vodka.

Arabella Boxer's variations: There are times when it's just not possible to cook, even for those who enjoy it. Yet it seems insane to spend hard-earned money in restaurants when our own homes are often prettier and more peaceful. One answer is to buy food that is already prepared, or partly so.

An important part of serving delicatessen food is in the presentation, for it can look both cheap and messy. The solution is, first to buy plenty of it, and second to add some first-rate fresh ingredients. For freshness is what is missing and what are needed are generous additions of good olive oil and wine vinegar, fresh lemon and lime juice, scallions, ginger, garlic, fresh herbs, sea salt and black pepper, spices, fresh bread and unsalted butter.

Glynn chose to make a conventional three course meal from his delicatessen food, which is interesting for it shows what can be done. I find it easier to treat delicatessen food in a more casual way, however, making buffet-type meals in the Scandinavian style, even for small numbers. I might start with a selection of fish dishes eaten with tiny chilled glasses of Schnapps; follow with some smoked chicken or turkey, salami-type sausages or good ham, with two or three salads: and serve one dish only to finish, either a broiled goat's cheese if you can find one, or broiled grapefruit to cleanse the palate. Or you could serve some good cookies or chocolates with the coffee instead. Amaretti di Saronno (tiny macaroons wrapped in pretty paper) would do well, while strips of ginger dipped in chocolate, creamy peppermints, or chocolate truffles all make good substitutes for dessert.

TONNO E FAGIOLI

Serves 6

2 cans cannellini beans
¼ mild Spanish onion, thinly sliced in rings
sea salt and black pepper
5 tbsp. best olive oil
2 tbsp. white wine vinegar
2 7½ oz. cans tuna fish, drained
1½ tbsp. chopped parsley

Pour the beans into a colander and rinse under cold running water. Drain well, then tip into a bowl. Stir the onion rings into the beans with plenty of salt and pepper. Stir in 3 tbsp. oil and 2 tbsp. vinegar, being careful not to break the beans. (Do not prepare too long in advance, or they will absorb the oil and you will have to use more.) Pile on to a shallow dish. Drain the tuna fish and break up into large flakes. Pile on top of the beans. Pour 2 tbsp. olive oil over it, and sprinkle parsley over all. This makes a substantial first course for 6; if serving with other dishes, make half the quantity.

ANCHOÏADE OR TAPENADE TOASTS

1 loaf French bread
1 jar anchoïade, anchovy paste, or tapenade

Cut the French bread in fairly thin slices and toast them lightly on one side only under the broiler. Spread the untoasted side with anchoïade, anchovy paste, or tapenade and replace under the broiler for a moment or two. Serve with drinks, or as a first course, alone or with other dishes.

QUAILS' EGGS ON SWEET CORN

Serves 6

24 quails' eggs
2 12 oz. cans sweet corn, whole kernel
¼ lb. bean sprouts
½ cucumber, peeled
5 tbsp. single cream
5 tbsp. sunflower seed oil
5 tbsp. lemon juice
sea salt and black pepper
1–2 dashes Tabasco

Put the little eggs in a small pan, cover with lightly salted cold water, and bring to the boil. Simmer for 2½ minutes, then drain and plunge into cold water. Drain the corn well, then place in a bowl. Rinse the bean sprouts in a colander, drain, then mix with the corn. Chop the cucumber into dice and add to the corn. Put the cream in a bowl and add the oil gradually, beating it in with a small whisk. Then beat in the lemon juice, adding salt and pepper and a couple of shakes of Tabasco. Pour over the corn salad and mix carefully, then spoon on to six small plates. Shell the eggs and lay four on top of each plate.

MARINATED KIPPER FILLETS

Serves 6

2 packages kipper fillets
¼ mild Spanish onion, thinly sliced in rings
½ cup good olive oil
2 tbsp. lemon juice
black pepper

Make 24 hours in advance, if possible. Take the fillets out of their bag, and rinse under the cold tap. Pat dry with paper towels. Make a layer of kipper fillets in a rectangular dish, and scatter some of the onion over them. Sprinkle with pepper but don't add any salt. Spoon over the oil and lemon juice and stand in a cool place for 24 hours, or overnight at least. If stored in the refrigerator, place low down and remove 1–2 hours before serving so it is not too chilled. Baste now and then, or move the fillets round. Serve with brown bread and butter.

RYE BREAD CANAPES

Excellent sliced rye bread from Scandinavia or Germany, very good for making canapés, can be bought in good delicatessens. Cut each slice in half and spread with unsalted butter. On a third of the slices pile black lumpfish roe, with a squeeze of lemon juice and a little black pepper. on another third, put thin slices of Gruyère or Emmental cheese, sprinkled with a tiny bit of paprika. On the remaining third, spread skinned red peppers cut in strips. (Ideally, these should be grilled fresh peppers – see page 98 – but canned red peppers can be used instead.) Arrange the canapés on a large dish; the combination of black. yellow and red makes a pretty dish.

SPICED HERRING SALAD

Serves 6

6 hard-boiled eggs
1 lb. new potatoes, boiled
4 gherkins, chopped
1 large bunch scallions, sliced
5 tbsp. mayonnaie
5 tbsp. yogurt
1 tsp. mild curry powder
salt and black pepper
6 marinated herring fillets

Chop the hard-boiled eggs in large pieces, and mix with the freshly boiled potatoes, peeled and thickly sliced. Stir in the gherkins and most of the scallions, keeping back some for garnish. Mix the mayonnaise with the yogurt, stirring in the curry powder and salt and pepper to taste. Fold into the egg and potato mixture, mixing gently. Pile on a dish, scattering the remaining scallions over the top. Skin the herring fillets and cut each one in three pieces. Lay them over the salad, or around the edges. Serve with buttered rye bread.

HERRINGS IN SOUR CREAM

Serves 6

12 salt herring fillets
½ cup milk
juice of 1 lemon
2 tbsp. grated horseradish
1 cup sour cream
1–2 apples, unpeeled and coarsely grated

Start 24 hours in advance. Open the jars of salt herrings, drain them, and soak in a mixture of half milk-half water. Leave overnight. Drain, remove the skins, and lay them in a shallow dish. Pour over the lemon juice and leave for 1–2 hours in the refrigerator. Stir the horseradish into the sour cream, and mix with the coarsely grated apples. Spoon over the herrings and chill another 1–2 hours before serving.

LENTIL SALAD

Serves 6

2 14 oz. cans lentils
½ bunch scallions, sliced
1 tbsp. sunflower seed oil
5 tbsp. yogurt
sea salt and black pepper

Rinse the lentils under cold running water and drain well. Tip into a bowl and stir in the sliced scallions, oil and yogurt; add salt and pepper to taste. Serve at room temperature, with smoked meat, sausages, or hard-boiled eggs.

CARROT SALAD

Serves 4–6, with other dishes

4 tbsp. sesame seeds
1½ lb. carrots, grated
4 tbsp. sunflower seed oil
4 tbsp. yogurt
4 tbsp. lemon juice
sea salt and black pepper

Toast the sesame seeds lightly by putting them over a moderate heat in a dry frying pan. Stir now and then, watching them carefully. When they have colored lightly, remove from the heat and leave to cool. Pile the grated carrots into a bowl and stir in the oil, yogurt, and lemon juice, adding salt and pepper. Mix lightly. Finally, stir in the toasted sesame seeds. This salad goes well with smoked meat of all kinds, and with hard-boiled eggs.

GRILLED CHEVRES WITH WALNUT OIL SALAD

Serves 6

6 small round individual goats' cheeses
a few leaves mixed escarole, curly endive, and mâche
sea salt and black pepper
2 tbsp. walnut oil
2 tbsp. sunflower seed oil
1 tbsp. white wine vinegar

Heat the broiler. Make a small salad of mixed leaves and pile in a bowl. Mix the oils and vinegar with salt and pepper, pour over the salad and toss. Grill the cheeses gently on both sides, just until the tops brown and they are heated through. Serve after the main course on individual plates, with a few leaves of mixed salad on the side, and French bread. It is quite filling, and no sweet course is needed.

ICED PEACH DESSERT

Serves 6

2 cans white peaches
1 can frozen concentrated orange juice
1 large Granny Smith apple, cored
1 tbsp. sugar
⅔ cup heavy cream
⅔ cup yogurt
2 tbsp. vanilla sugar or plain sugar

Drain the peaches and put them in a soufflé dish. Mix the syrup from the peaches with the frozen orange juice, whisking until blended (or blend in a food processor). Grate the unpeeled apple and stir it into the orange syrup. Add 1 tbsp. sugar and spoon over the peaches. Chill for 1–2 hours. Just before serving, whip the cream. Beat the yogurt smooth and fold it into the cream, then fold in the vanilla or plain sugar.
To serve: spoon the cream over the peaches in big blobs, without covering them completely or smoothing it out.

Arabella Boxer's suggestions for a Scandinavian-style Delicatessen Dinner

First courses
(choose 3 or 4)

QUAILS' EGGS ON SWEET CORN

MARINATED KIPPER FILLETS

HERRINGS IN SOUR CREAM

SPICED HERRING SALAD

RYE BREAD CANAPES

TONNO E FAGIOLI

ANCHOÏADE
or
TAPENADE TOASTS

Main courses
(choose 3 or 4)

SMOKED CHICKEN
or
TURKEY

SLICED HAM, SALAMI, COPPA, ETC.

PROSCIUTTO E GRISSINI
(see page 161)

LENTIL SALAD

CARROT SALAD

TOMATO JELLY
WITH
CELERY REMOULADE
(follow recipe on page 139, but make double quantities)

Third courses

GRILLED CHEVRES
WITH
WALNUT OIL SALAD
or
GRILLED GRAPEFRUIT
(see page 99)
or
ICED PEACH DESSERT

CAROLINE CONRAN'S
BRITISH LUNCH

Caroline Conran: It's often pleasant to entertain friends from abroad at home, and I started planning this menu with the most English dish I could give them, the steak and kidney pudding. Everything else is planned around that, as it is rather massive, so the other things have to be light and delicate.

Oysters would probably be the best thing to eat before steak and kidney, but they are hard to open, and some people find it impossible "to risk the living morsel down their throats". Another possibility, but very extravagant, is half a freshly cooked lobster for each person, with a little fresh mayonnaise flavored with chopped tarragon. But if you don't want to invest in lobsters, then sea trout is another good choice.

You can leave the steak and kidney pudding to cook itself, or prepare it the night before and leave it, ready for cooking, in the refrigerator overnight. You can make the mousses the day before, too, but the sea trout is best cooked that morning and not chilled otherwise I find it goes hard. The sea trout and the pears would be done and cooling before you sit down to have a drink with your guests, and only the cabbage needs last minute attention. If you wanted to avoid that, you could cook it, drain, and then heat (don't fry) it in melted butter.

If you prefer, you could decide on baked apples instead of the pears, but you must avoid a stodgy pudding after the steak and kidney. The English serve their cheese after the dessert. Of course this isn't a hard and fast rule, but it is rather pleasant and luxurious to sit late into the afternoon, talking and eating grapes and cutting little pieces of cheese while you drink a sweet Vouvray, or chilled champagne, or port.

Caroline Conran with her Steak and Kidney Pudding and Cabbage.

Sea Trout, and Salmon Mousses garnished with a watercress leaf, and Horseradish Sauce.

SEA TROUT AND SALMON MOUSSES WITH HORSERADISH SAUCE

Sea Trout:
1 whole sea trout, weighing 3–4 lb.
2 tbsp. dry white wine
salt
a little oil

Heat oven to 325°F. Ask the fishseller to clean the fish, paying great attention to the dark channel along the inside of the spine, which is bitter and spoils the look of the fish when cooked.

Rub it with salt inside and out, and sprinkle with a little oil. Place a large piece of foil on a table and bend up the sides and ends. Put in the fish, pour in the wine and fold the foil into a parcel. Bake for 30–40 minutes. Pierce the trout behind the head with a knife to see if it is cooked. A compact fish will take longer than a long thin one.

When it is ready, remove it carefully, slide it on to a long dish and let it cool.

Little Salmon Mousses:
¾ lb. raw salmon, or sea trout, skinned and
*   boned (about 1 lb. with bones)*
2 eggs
5 egg yolks
pinch nutmeg
1 cup heavy cream
1 cup milk, boiled and chilled
salt and pepper
8 leaves of watercress or tarragon

Preheat oven to 300°F. Cut the salmon into cubes, put into a blender or food processor with all the other ingredients and blend. Strain through a wire sieve and pour into 8 little buttered pots (I use coffee cups). Put into a baking pan containing an inch or so of boiling water (which will stand in for a *bain marie*), and put into the oven for 18 minutes. Allow to cool a little before turning out, or keep ready in the refrigerator, and stand the pots briefly in boiling water before turning them out.

Horseradish Sauce:
3 tbsp. grated horseradish
1 tsp. mild Dijon mustard
1 tsp. tarragon vinegar
¾ cup cream
pinch salt

Mix the ingredients together and add more cream (light will do) if it seems too hot.

To serve: carefully turn out each little mousse on to a plate around the sea trout and put a leaf of watercress (or tarragon) on each. Put the horseradish into a separate bowl. Present the fish at the table, and then strip off the skin from head to tail in one piece. The flesh is removed in segments, cutting along the central line. Give each person a quarter of one side of the sea trout (or less), a salmon mousse and some horseradish: the horseradish is a little fierce, so eat it sparingly. A good Sauvignon is excellent with this.

STEAK AND KIDNEY PUDDING

Filling:
1½ lb. chuck steak, or other juicy stewing
    steak
¼–½ lb. ox kidney (or pig's, or lamb's)
¼ cup all-purpose flour
1½ cups button mushrooms, cleaned and
    trimmed (optional)
1 tbsp. Worcestershire sauce
2 tbsp. red wine or port
salt and plenty of coarsely ground black
    pepper
beef stock or water to three-quarters fill the
    bowl
Suet-crust:
¼ lb. suet
2 cups self-rising flour
salt

Trim the meat of fat and sinews and cut
into cubes. Cut the kidney into pieces the
size of a small walnut.

Make the pastry by mixing the suet, flour
and salt in a bowl and then adding just
enough cold water to bind it – don't add
too much as first, this mixture should be
light and spongy, not wet. Roll it out,
keeping back about a quarter for the lid,
and line a buttered 1 quart pudding basin
or bowl.

Roll the meat in seasoned flour, mix it
with the mushrooms and put it into the
bowl. Mix the Worcestershire sauce and
wine and pour it in, then add enough well-
seasoned beef stock or water to come two-
thirds to three-quarters of the way up the
sides. Moisten the top edge of the crust.
Roll out the remaining pastry to make a lid,
cover, press firmly to seal, trim and roll the
edges over inwards, pressing lightly.

Pleat a piece of foil and cover the top of
the pudding loosely with it, tying it around
under the rim of the bowl with string. Make
a handle by passing the string across the
top two or three times – not too tightly as
the pudding must have room to expand.
Lower into a large pan of boiling water
with a close-fitting lid; the water should
come two-thirds of the way up the basin,
and must be topped up as it boils away. If
the pudding leaks a bit, don't worry. Boil,
covered, 4–5 hours.

Then lift out of the pan, remove the foil
and wrap the basin in a clean white napkin,
with the top crust showing fluffy and
slightly browned from its collar of white
linen. If the crust has come in contact with
water, it may be pale and glistening, but it
will still be delicious to eat.
Serve the fragrant pudding with a green
vegetable such as cabbage, and a good
claret to drink with it.

Compôte of Pears.

CABBAGE

1 large green cabbage
salt and black pepper

I cook this cut in quarters, with the stalks
cut away. Drop the pieces, carefully
trimmed of the dark green outside leaves,
and washed, into a large pan of well-salted
boiling water and cook, uncovered, until
they start to look transparent and to sink.
Drain at once, cut in pieces very coarsely in
the colander, to get rid of as much water as
possible, and heat through very, very gently in melted butter for 10 minutes, turning
from time to time. Season with very coarse
freshly ground black pepper.

COMPOTE OF PEARS

6 large, firm winter pears
Syrup:
1½ cups sugar
2 quarts water
1 vanilla pod, or 1 tbsp. vanilla sugar
½ lemon rind
juice of a whole lemon

Simmer all the syrup ingredients together
for half an hour.

Peel pears thinly with a stainless knife:
they look prettier if you leave their stalks
on. As each is peeled, slip it into the
simmering syrup. Poach them gently 30–40
minutes, turning them over once or twice.
Leave to cool in their liquid. Drain and
serve with a pitcher of cream.
Variation: ripe peaches can be poached in
the same syrup. Skin them first like
tomatoes by pouring boiling water over
them. Cook for 20–30 minutes. Serve cool,
drained, with a pitcher of cream.

Alternatively, after removing the fruit,
you can reduce the syrup by boiling it until
it measures about a cup. Serve it poured
over the pears or peaches: it will make them
glisten.

Arabella Boxer's variations: Caroline's English meal would certainly delight any foreign guest, served in the elegant dining room of the Conrans' London house. Yet I can't help thinking wistfully of a dinner she cooked for Michel Guerard, the brilliant young French chef who invented *cuisine minceur* and helped introduce the *nouvelle cuisine*, which finished with a most delicious hot apple pudding. These hot puddings are so intrinsically English; they don't even exist in the cuisine of other countries, and foreigners love them.

Planning a meal around a hot pudding obviously excludes the suet pudding for the main course, so I would substitute a classic English roast, probably a saddle of lamb. This is a splendid joint, typically English in its simplicity. Composed of two loins of lamb, still joined together, it is to my mind infinitely preferable to the showy crown roasts and guards of honour contrived by clever butchers. The meat benefits from being left on the bone, which keeps it moist and full of flavor.

As a first course, I would serve a soufflé or a selection of smoked fish garnished with lemons, and accompanied by a creamy horseradish sauce, and brown bread and butter. If anyone wanted cheese after this meal, I would serve an unusual English cheese: a Single Gloucester made on a Hereford farm.

Arabella Boxer's suggestions for an English Lunch

SMOKED FISH PLATTER
or
EGGS IN SPINACH SOUFFLE

ROAST SADDLE OF LAMB
with
MINT SAUCE and REDCURRANT JELLY
(or rowan or crab apple jelly)
new potatoes
peas, carrots, and broad beans

EVE'S PUDDING
or
QUEEN OF PUDDINGS
or
BREAD AND BUTTER PUDDING
or
CASTLE PUDDINGS

EGGS IN SPINACH SOUFFLE

Serves 4

8 eggs
1/2 lb. frozen leaf spinach
3 tbsp. butter
3 tbsp. flour
3/4 cup milk
sea salt and black pepper
5 tbsp. grated Parmesan or Gruyère

Poach 4 eggs an hour beforehand; lay them on a plate and chill in the refrigerator (this helps to prevent them overcooking in the soufflé). Cook the spinach as usual, drain well and chop by hand. Heat the oven to 350°F. Melt the butter, add the flour, and cook for 1 minute, stirring. Heat the milk and add it, stirring until blended. Simmer for 3 minutes. Add salt and pepper to taste, stir in the spinach and half the grated cheese. When all is well mixed, remove from the heat and cool 2–3 minutes.

Separate the 4 remaining eggs and beat the whites until stiff. Beat the yolks and stir into the mixture, then fold in the beaten whites. Spoon a little of the soufflé mixture into a buttered soufflé dish. Lay the eggs on the spinach, remembering where they are placed. Then tip the rest of the soufflé mixture over them. Scatter the remaining cheese over the top, making a pattern to indicate the position of the eggs. Bake for 30 minutes and serve immediately.

SMOKED FISH PLATTER

Serves 4

Arbroath Smokie Pâté (see below)
6 oz. smoked salmon
2 smoked trout
1 smoked mackerel, or 2 fillets
4 pieces smoked eel
a few smoked sprats
2 lemons
Horseradish Sauce (see page 165)

Make the smokie Pâté (see below). Divide the smoked salmon into 8 small slices, and roll around dessertspoonfuls of the pâté. Skin the trout and divide into 8 thin fillets. Repeat with the mackerel, or mackerel fillets. Arrange all the smoked fish on a large flat platter and garnish with lemon quarters. Serve Horseradish Sauce and a plate of brown bread and butter separately.

ARBROATH SMOKIE PATE

Americans don't often see smokies, but any smoked haddock such as Finnan Haddie can be substituted.

1 large smokie or other smoked haddock
2 oz. cream cheese
1 tbsp. sour cream
1 tbsp. lemon juice
sea salt and black pepper

Take the flesh off the bones (discarding the skin), and weigh it. You should have $3\frac{1}{2}$–4 oz. Chop finely then purée in a food processor. Add the other ingredients, processing until well blended. Chill for 1–2 hours to firm before serving.

ROAST SADDLE OF LAMB

Serves 6

1 saddle of English lamb
1 cup red wine

Heat oven to 425°F. Stand the lamb on a rack in a roasting pan and roast 20 minutes, then turn oven down to 350°F. Allow 20 minutes per lb. from the time you turn down the oven for slightly pink meat; if you prefer it well done, allow an extra 15–20 minutes.

Halfway through the cooking, heat the wine. Take the roasting pan out of the oven and pour off most of the fat, just leaving the juices that lie beneath it. Pour the wine over the meat and return to the oven, basting two or three times during the remainder of the cooking. When the time is up, take the meat out of the oven and let stand in a warm place, loosely covered, for 20–30 minutes. Remove the rack, and place the roasting pan over a low flame. Scrape all the meat juices and sediment together, letting them bubble for a moment or two, then strain into a sauceboat and keep hot.

Carve the lamb in long strips, running from one end of the joint to the other, and serve it with its gravy, fresh mint sauce, and a fruit jelly, either rowan, crab apple, or redcurrant. Serve the best young vegetables with it, depending on the season: perhaps in summer, new potatoes, peas, carrots and broad beans; in winter, Glazed Onions or Leeks and Carrots, and turnips.

MINT SAUCE

Serves 6

5 tbsp. mint leaves, chopped
4 tbsp. sugar
5 tbsp. lemon juice

Put the mint in a bowl with the sugar and lemon juice. Add $\frac{3}{4}$ cup boiling water, stir once or twice, and stand for 1 hour before serving.

LEEKS AND CARROTS

Serves 4

2 lb. leeks
1 lb. carrots
3 tbsp. butter
sea salt and black pepper
2 tbsp. chopped parsley

Cut the leeks in 1 inch slices and cook for 10 minutes in $\frac{1}{2}$ inch lightly salted water in a covered pan. Drain well. Cut the carrots in $\frac{1}{2}$ inch slices and cook until soft in lightly salted water. Drain well. Melt the butter in a heavy pan and put in the carrots and leeks. Mix gently, adding lots of sea salt and black pepper. Cook gently over a low heat for 2–3 minutes, until reheated and well mixed, then place in a serving dish and sprinkle with chopped parsley.

REDCURRANT JELLY

Redcurrants are found wild in America.

Makes about 3 lb

3 lb. redcurrants
$3\frac{3}{4}$ cups water
about 3 cups granulated sugar

Strip the currants off the stalks, using a small fork. Put them in a heavy saucepan with the water. Bring to the boil and simmer for 15 minutes, until mushy, pressing them against the sides of the pan with the back of a wooden spoon. Pour into a jelly bag, or a strainer lined with muslin, and leave to drip overnight. Do not try to hurry it by squeezing, or the jelly will be cloudy.

Next day measure the juice. For every $2\frac{1}{2}$ cups allow 2 cups granulated sugar. Put the sugar in a clean pan and warm it slightly over gentle heat. Add the juice and bring to the boil. Cook steadily until setting point is reached, which will probably take about 8 minutes. Skim until the surface is clear, then pour into warm jars. Cover after cooling, wiping off any drips, and label. (Full details for covering are given in the recipe for Raspberry Jam on page 191.) Store in a cool, dark cupboard.

BREAD AND BUTTER PUDDING

Serves 4

10–12 slices of a dry French loaf, $\frac{1}{4}$ inch thick
unsalted butter
1 tbsp. raisins or golden raisins
1 cup milk
1 cup light cream
3 eggs
6 tbsp. sugar

Heat oven to 350°F. Butter the bread and arrange in layers in a buttered baking dish, sprinkling each layer with raisins. Heat the milk and cream together in a small pan. Break the eggs into a bowl and beat, adding the sugar gradually. When the milk and cream reach boiling point, pour them on to the eggs, continuing to beat. Pour through a strainer on to the bread. Bake, standing in a baking pan half full of water, for 40 minutes, then remove and leave to cool slightly, for about 30 minutes. Serve warm with cold cream.

The best bread and butter pudding I have ever eaten was one of this sort, made by Anton Mosimann, Chef de Cuisine at the Dorchester Hotel in London and served with his own superlative vanilla ice cream.

CASTLE PUDDINGS

Makes 6

3 eggs
6 tbsp. sugar
1 tsp. grated lemon rind
$\frac{3}{4}$ cup flour, sifted
6 tbsp. butter, half-melted
1 cup light corn syrup or Golden Syrup
1–2 tbsp. lemon juice

Heat oven to 350°F. Beat eggs until very light and almost frothy, adding the sugar and lemon rind by degrees, beating continuously. Then shake in the flour gradually, and finally add the butter. (This is quickly done in a food processor.) When well mixed, pour into buttered molds, shaped like tiny pails (sometimes called dariole molds). Place on a baking tray and bake for 20 minutes.
To serve: turn them out and hand a sauceboat of maple syrup or Golden Syrup, warmed and sharpened with lemon juice. You may like to have a pitcher of cream also.

QUEEN OF PUDDINGS

Serves 4

$1\frac{1}{4}$ cups milk
2 strips lemon peel
2 tbsp. unsalted butter
$\frac{1}{2}$ cup sugar
1 cup soft white breadcrumbs
3 eggs, separated
4 tbsp. raspberry jam

Heat the milk with the lemon peel. When it boils, turn off the heat, cover the pan, and let stand for 10 minutes. Heat the oven to 325°F. Discard the lemon peel and replace the pan over the heat. Add the butter and 2 tbsp. sugar, stirring until they have melted. Remove from the heat and stir in the breadcrumbs. Cool for 10 minutes, then stir in the lightly beaten egg yolks. Pour into a buttered baking dish and bake 30 minutes. Take out of the oven and leave to cool.

Turn down the oven to 250°F. Warm the jam and spread it over the pudding. Beat the egg whites until firm, fold in the remaining sugar to make a meringue mixture. Spread over the jam so that the pudding is completely covered. Bake another 30 minutes or so, or until the meringue is firm and lightly colored. This lovely pudding can be served hot, warm, or after cooling, but do not chill. Serve with cream.

EVE'S PUDDING

Serves 4

1 lb. cooking apples, peeled and sliced
generous $\frac{1}{2}$ cup sugar
6 tbsp. butter, at room temperature
1 cup self-rising flour, sifted
2 eggs, beaten

Heat oven to 350°F. Put just enough water in a heavy pan to cover the bottom. Add the sliced apples and 3 tbsp. sugar and cook gently until soft. Turn them into a buttered soufflé dish holding about 1 quart. Cream the butter with the remaining sugar, in the food processor or by hand. Fold in the beaten eggs and the sifted flour in alternate spoonfuls, or process until blended. Spoon over the apples to completely cover them. Bake 30 minutes until golden brown and puffy. Serve immediately with a pitcher of thick cream.

JOCASTA INNES'S
VEGETARIAN DINNER

Jocasta Innes: I greatly enjoy ceremonious dinner parties when other people give them, but the most I can aspire to as a single parent with two young children and a job is a much less ambitious style of entertaining. The food I provide is invariably simple – robust rather than refined, bistro food rather than three star.

I am not a vegetarian, but if I were to become one I would live on Indian food because its spiciness and earthiness make up for the slightly pinched, "thin" feeling standard vegetarian dishes give me, without on the other hand going over into the bloating stodginess of all those beans.

Mattar panir is delicious, looks appetizing, is absurdly cheap, and can be prepared up to the last stages ahead of time.

Dips of various sorts are my favorite start to my sort of meal, not just because they are easy to make with a blender, but because they can be spread out to look like a feast and because people so enjoy all that licensed unmannerliness, stretching across each other and using their fingers; it always breaks the ice and keeps the company busy while I chase around putting the main course together.

Steamed lemon mousse is unusual enough to seem partyish for a dessert, with an extraordinary "short" texture, both rich and light, and the lemony sharpness clears one's palate after a rich muddle of spices. One last point: I do like to produce an unexpectedly home-made item, which makes guests feel a bit spoiled, here it is the water biscuits. When making things like biscuits it is important not to make them too perfectly regular, so that everyone realizes they are your own work. You can always tell my biscuits are homemade.

Jocasta Innes sits behind the dips, Guacamole and Patlican Kebabi, with a bowl of black olives and homemade Water Biscuits. Left, Saffron Rice, and in front Mattir Panir, pickles, yogurt sprinkled with paprika, and Indian Salad with Ginger.

GUACAMOLE

2 large or 3 medium ripe avocados
2 medium tomatoes
2 cloves garlic, peeled
1 small onion, peeled
small pinch cayenne, or chili powder
salt and pepper
juice of 1 lemon
few sprigs parsley

Remove flesh from avocados, peel and seed tomatoes, and put both in blender with the onion and garlic. Blend until fairly smooth. Add a tiny pinch cayenne or chili (or chopped fresh chili if you prefer), salt, pepper and lemon juice to taste. Pile into bowls and dust with chopped parsley.

PATLICAN KEBABI (EGGPLANT PUREE)

2 or 3 small eggplants
2–3 cloves garlic, peeled
2 tbsp. olive oil
¼ cup yogurt
juice of 1 lemon
salt and pepper
few sprigs of parsley, coriander or mint,
  chopped

Preheat oven to 350°F and bake eggplants until soft. Then slit open and scoop out pulp. Blend this with the remaining ingredients and season to taste. Pile into bowls and sprinkle with parsley, coriander or mint.

WATER BISCUITS

2 cups all-purpose flour
1 tsp. baking powder
pinch salt
4 tbsp. butter or margarine
about 5 tbsp. water
rock salt and/or sesame seeds

Sift together flour, baking powder and salt. Rub in fat finely and add just enough water to make a firm dough. Roll out as thinly as possible on a floured surface with a floured rolling pin. Stamp out rounds with a cup, prick them all over with a fork, sprinkle with a little coarse salt and/or sesame seeds and arrange an oiled baking sheet. Cook in a preheated oven at 300°F for 20 minutes or until crisp and lightly colored. Store in a tin and crisp them up in a low oven if necessary before eating.
Note: If you are in a hurry, use pita bread, torn into strips and dried off in the oven.

MATTAR PANIR

A dish of cubes of homemade curd cheese, fried and added to an Indian-style ragoût of tomatoes, onions and peas. The curd cheese, or *panir*, needs to be started the day before or at least 8 hours before you start preparing the rest of the dish. Some of the whey is added to the rest of the dish, giving a slightly acid flavor which is excellent and unexpected.

Panir
2½–3 quarts milk
1 cup plain yogurt
juice of 1 small lemon, or 2 tbsp. vinegar

Bring milk to boiling point, remove from heat and stir in yogurt and lemon juice or vinegar. In a few seconds the milk separates dramatically, into solids and clear whey. Stand a colander lined with muslin or a clean napkin over a bowl and into this pour the contents of the pan. Leave overnight, or for 8 hours. Reserve the whey. Fold muslin around the little packet of rubbery white curd, place between two boards, and weight with 10 lb. weights, or full jam jars, or whatever. Leave 6–8 hours at room temperature. Unwrap, cut into ½ inch cubes and store in refrigerator until needed.

Mattar
2 medium onions
3 cloves garlic
1 small knob fresh ginger root
1 tsp. turmeric
2 tsp. freshly ground coriander berries
2 tsp. garam masala
1–2 fresh green chillies, seeded and
  chopped, or ½ tsp. chili powder

1 lb. 13 oz. can peeled tomatoes
10 oz. package frozen peas (thawed)
pinch sugar
½ cup ghee or vegetable oil

To prepare the ragoût: in a large heavy pan, gently fry chopped onion, garlic and ginger in ghee or vegetable oil, until soft and golden, but not browned. Add a splash of reserved whey, then turmeric, coriander, garam masala and chili. Stir, cook for a moment or two. Add a further cupful of whey and the drained tomatoes, and bring to the boil. Lower the heat and simmer 10 minutes, stirring occasionally. Add peas and a pinch of sugar, and simmer another 5 minutes or so. You can stop at this point (or before adding peas) if you are cooking the dish ahead.
To fry cheese: heat ⅓ cup ghee or oil in a heavy pan until a drop of water flicked in sizzles immediately. Add curd cubes and fry until golden brown, turning them over with a slotted spoon to fry evenly, and transfer to a warm dish as they cook.
To complete the dish: add the fried cubes of cheese to the ragoût, cover and cook over a low heat for 20 minutes to allow the bland curd to absorb the other flavors.

Although Mattar Panir is not hot enough to need a cooling counterpoint, I usually serve yogurt (plain, or with chopped cucumber added) with it, and Saffron Rice.

SIMPLE SAFFRON RICE

2–3 tbsp. Indian rice per person
1 tsp. turmeric
¼ tsp. saffron threads
1 large lime or lemon
1 tbsp. butter or ghee
salt and pepper
chopped coriander or parsley

Bring a large pan of salted water to a fast boil, add rice and turmeric and boil fast for 11 minutes, until tender but just firm in the center of each grain. Pour into sieve and run hot water over rice for ½ minute to wash off starch. Shake rice into a shallow ovenproof dish. Steep the saffron threads in 2 tbsp. hot water while the rice cooks. Pour the saffron threads and steeping water over the rice, squeeze in lime or lemon juice, add a few nuts of butter or ghee, cover with foil and heat through 20 minutes or so in the bottom of a 350°F oven. Just before dishing up, sprinkle with chopped coriander or parsley.

Steamed Lemon Mousse.

STEAMED LEMON MOUSSE

6 eggs
1 large lemon
10 tbsp. butter
⅔ cup sugar

Separate eggs, put yolks into the top of a double boiler, and whites into a large mixing bowl. Grate lemon rind finely, then cut lemon and squeeze out the juice. Add lemon rind, juice, butter (cut in bits) and sugar to egg yolks in top of double boiler and cook over simmering water, stirring all the while until it thickens dramatically. Transfer the top half with egg mixture to a bowl of cold water and continue stirring until it cools – this prevents a skin forming on top. Now whisk egg whites until firm, and fold gently but thoroughly into the cooled custard mixture.

Oil a 1 quart custard dish lightly but thoroughly, pour in the mousse mixture, cover with plastic wrap, then a cap of foil. Bring 1 inch of water to boiling point in a pan large enough to take the bowl. Find a saucer to stand it on; wearing gloves, slip saucer into the pan, upside down, stand bowl on the inverted saucer, replace lid, and simmer gently for an hour. Check now and then to see the pan has not boiled dry. Leave pudding to cool in its bowl.

To turn it out, remove foil and plastic wrap, then slip a knife blade gently around the sides to loosen any clinging bits, and invert on to a plate. It should come out whole and firm, but if it doesn't spoon it into individual bowls – it will taste just as good.

INDIAN SALAD WITH GINGER

1 cucumber
4–5 firm tomatoes
1 green pepper
1 onion
<u>Dressing</u>:
juice of 1 lemon or lime
2 tbsp. oil
small knob fresh ginger
salt
1 clove garlic (optional)

This salad should be chunky, in contrast to the soft texture of the Mattar Panir. Peel cucumber, slice lengthwise into 4, then into 1 inch long chunks. Salt lightly, and drain in colander for 30 minutes. Cut tomatoes into segments, seed and dice the green pepper, peel and roughly chop the onion. Combine all the ingredients in a glass bowl. Dress with lemon or lime juice and oil, to which you add a little ginger juice (made by squeezing ginger in a garlic press), salt, and garlic if you like.

Arabella Boxer's variations: Preparing a vegetarian meal is no hardship for me. Several of my friends and one of my children are vegetarian, and I love this sort of food. I am very fond of grains – buckwheat, cracked wheat, and couscous especially – and usually plan the main course around one of these. They are fairly cheap, substantial, and adaptable; one or two extra vegetable dishes can always be added for unexpected guests. For a more elaborate meal I might make a Spinach Roulade, with one or two fillings and sauces.

First courses are easy: hot or cold vegetable soups, pastry dishes, vegetable vinaigrettes, eggs, or assorted crudités and dips are all eminently suitable. And, for the sweet course, my first choice would always be fresh fruit, prepared as simply as possible. I find people are lazy about preparing their own fruit, and will rarely take the trouble to peel an orange or cut up a pear. Yet if they are presented with it already done, they fall upon it with delight. What could be more appealing than two or three different fruits – peaches, melon, and strawberries, for example – simply cut and laid out on a flat dish, sprinkled with fresh lime or orange juice?

A VEGETABLE COUSCOUS

Serves 6

$\frac{3}{4}$ lb. couscous
6 cups vegetable stock
6 small onions, peeled
4 leeks, thickly sliced
4 carrots, thickly sliced
2 stalks celery, thickly sliced
4 small zucchini, thickly sliced
6 tomatoes, skinned
$\frac{1}{4}$ teaspoon ground saffron
salt and black pepper
$\frac{1}{2}$ lb. chick peas, cooked or canned
Hot Sauce:
1 tsp. ground cumin
1 tsp. ground coriander
$\frac{1}{2}$ tsp. chili powder
$\frac{1}{2}$ tsp. celery salt
2 tbsp. tomato paste
2 tbsp. hot vegetable stock (see above)

Put the couscous in a bowl and add 2 cups cold water. Leave for 10 minutes by which time it will have been absorbed. Put the stock in a couscousière, or deep pot. Add the whole onions and bring to the boil. When it boils, add the leeks, carrots, and celery. Put the soaked couscous in the top half of a couscousière, or in a strainer that fits inside the pot, lined with muslin. Set it over the simmering stock, cover with the lid and boil gently for 30 minutes. Then lift the strainer and add the zucchini to the stock, replace the couscous and cook 10 minutes. Then add the whole tomatoes to the stock, replacing the couscous, and cook 5 minutes more. Remove the couscous and tip onto a large dish, breaking up any lumps. Keep it hot while you add the chick peas to the stock, with saffron and salt and pepper to taste. Reheat, then let stand beside the heat for 5 minutes before serving.
To serve: lift out the vegetables with a slotted spoon and lay on top of the couscous. Serve the stock in a large tureen, and make the hot sauce at the last moment, by stirring 3 tbsp. of the hot stock into the spices, in a small bowl. Serve with soup plates, knife, fork, and spoon. If you prefer, serve the couscous alone, and the vegetables in the stock.
Variation: for non-vegetarians, replace the vegetable stock with water, and add a cut up chicken at the same time as the onions. Serve the chicken pieces laid over the couscous, and the vegetables in the tureen with the stock.

COLD SPINACH AND LENTIL SOUP

Serves 6–8

$\frac{1}{4}$ lb. brown or green lentils
$\frac{1}{4}$ lb. spinach
1 medium onion, chopped
2 tbsp. sunflower seed oil
1 clove garlic, finely chopped
2 cups buttermilk
sea salt and black pepper
juice of $\frac{1}{2}$ lemon

Pick over the lentils, wash and drain. Put them in a pan and cover with cold water. Bring to the boil and cook until almost tender, about 45 minutes. In the meantime, wash the spinach, removing the stalks if tough, and cut in slices. When the lentils are almost ready, add the spinach and cook for another 15 minutes. Cook the onion in the oil until pale golden, adding the garlic halfway through. When spinach and lentils are both soft, turn off the heat and stir the onions and their oil into the soup. Cool for 10–15 minutes, then process in a food processor or blender. Pour into a large bowl and leave to cool completely.

Later, stir in the buttermilk; there should be roughly twice as much soup as buttermilk, but the proportions are not vital. Add sea salt and black pepper to taste, and a little lemon juice. Chill before serving.

This makes an unusual cold soup, and is quite filling.

CRACKED WHEAT RISOTTO

Serves 6

$\frac{3}{4}$ cup butter
1 large onion, chopped
1 lb. cracked wheat (sometimes called bulgur)
about 1 quart chicken stock, homemade
sea salt

Melt the butter in a flameproof casserole and cook the chopped onion until pale golden. Add the cracked wheat and cook gently over low heat for 10 minutes, stirring often. Heat the stock and pour on enough to cover generously. Bring to the boil, lower the heat, add the salt and cover the pan. Simmer gently for about 10 minutes, until all the stock is absorbed. If this happens before the cracked wheat has softened, add a little more stock.
Serve with other vegetable dishes. When this is served with simple dishes, a bowl of yogurt can be handed separately; if you are serving Mushrooms in Sour Cream with it, this is not necessary.

PEPERONATA

Serves 6

1 large onion, chopped
½ cup olive oil
3 cloves garlic, finely chopped
2½ lb. mixed red, green, and yellow peppers
  (when available), cut in strips
1½ lb. tomatoes, skinned and chopped
salt and black pepper

Cook the onion gently in the oil in a heavy pan. After 5 minutes, add the garlic and the peppers. Cover and cook slowly for 15 minutes, stirring now and then. Add the tomatoes and continue to cook gently another 10–15 minutes, stirring occasionally. Add salt and pepper to taste.

This Mediterranean dish is best served warm, or after it has cooled; whatever happens, however, don't chill it in the refrigerator.

MUSHROOMS IN SOUR CREAM

Serves 6

1½ lb. mushrooms, trimmed and sliced
6 tbsp. butter
2 cups sour cream, or crème fraîche
sea salt and black pepper
dash lemon juice (optional)

Cook the mushrooms gently in the butter in a deep frying pan, stirring occasionally, about 8 minutes, until softened. Boil up for a moment or two to reduce the juices, then lower the heat and stir in the sour cream or crème fraîche. Reheat, adding salt and pepper, and a drop of lemon juice if you want to sharpen the taste.

BAKED AUBERGINES

Serves 6

3 large eggplants
1 large Spanish onion
1½ lb. tomatoes
olive oil, for frying
salt and black pepper
½ tsp. sugar
1 Mozzarella, thinly sliced

Cut the unpeeled eggplants in ½ inch slices, sprinkle with salt, and leave to drain in a colander. Cut the onion in half, then in ¼ inch slices, and divide into rings. Skin and slice the tomatoes, drain off the seeds and juice, and cut into strips similar to the onions.

Heat oven to 350°F. Heat a thin layer of olive oil in a broad frying pan. Dry the eggplant slices and fry until golden brown on both sides. Drain on paper towels, lay them in a shallow baking dish and keep warm. Add more oil to the pan and fry the onion rings until soft, then add the tomatoes and cook 2–3 minutes more, adding salt, pepper and the sugar. Spoon the tomatoes and onions over the eggplant slices and lay the sliced cheese over all. Bake 30 minutes, just until the cheese has melted nicely.

ZUCCHINI, CARROTS AND TOMATOES

Serves 6

⅓ lb. young carrots, sliced
olive oil
1¼ lb. zucchini cut in ½ inch slices
¾ lb. tomatoes, skinned and thickly sliced
sea salt and black pepper

Cover the carrots with lightly salted water, bring to the boil, cook 5 minutes and drain. Make a layer of olive oil in a deep frying pan or sauté pan, with a lid. Cook the zucchini for 10 minutes, covered, stirring often. Add the drained carrots and cook another 10 minutes, then add the sliced tomatoes and cook for 15 minutes, until all is soft and slightly mushy. Season with salt and pepper and serve with a simple grain dish, such as Cracked Wheat Risotto or as a filling for pancakes.

SPINACH ROULADE

Serves 4

1½ lb. spinach
¼ cup heavy cream
1 tsp. sea salt
black pepper
5 large eggs, separated
¼ cup grated Parmesan
Mushroom Filling:
½ lb. mushrooms
2 tbsp. butter
2 tbsp. flour
½ cup sour cream
⅔ cup milk, heated
sea salt
Ricotta Filling:
½ lb. ricotta
2 tbsp. yogurt
sea salt and black pepper
2 tbsp. chopped scallions, or chives
2 tbsp. chopped parsley
Tomato Coulis: (see page 109)

First choose and make your filling.
Mushroom filling: slice the mushrooms and soften in the butter. As they yield their juices, boil up for a moment or two to reduce, then lower the heat and stir in the flour. Cook 1 minute, stirring, then add the heated milk and sour cream. Season to taste and simmer for 3 minutes.

Ricotta filling: moisten the ricotta with the yogurt, add salt and pepper to taste, and stir in the scallions (or chives), and parsley.

Make the Tomato Coulis and set aside.

Prepare a 12 × 8 × ¾ inch jelly roll pan by lining it with non-stick baking parchment, or oiled wax paper. Heat the oven to 400°F. Cook the spinach 4–5 minutes in lightly boiling salted water. Drain in a colander and leave to cool. Then squeeze dry and chop by hand. Put it in a bowl and stir in the cream, salt and pepper, and the egg yolks, lightly beaten. Beat the whites until stiff and fold in. Spread the mixture in the lined pan and sprinkle the grated Parmesan over the top. Bake for 10–12 minutes, or until firm.

Take out of the oven and invert over another piece of baking parchment, or lightly oiled paper. Remove the pan and peel off the first piece of paper. Spread the prepared filling over the spinach. Roll up, using the paper, and slide on to a flat dish. Serve as soon as possible, with a Tomato Coulis.

FRESH FRUIT SALADS

Some of my favorite desserts are very simple dishes of sliced fruit, sprinkled with superfine sugar and citrus fruit juice:

Sliced **oranges** (see step-by-step instructions on page 157) sprinkled with orange juice; sliced oranges with cubed orange jelly (see page 143); mixed sliced oranges and pink grapefruit, with orange juice mixed with pulped passion fruit.

Sliced **peaches** with lime juice; sliced peaches in a raspberry sauce (see page 148); sliced peaches, strawberries and cubed melon with lime juice.

Three sorts of **melon**, cubed with lime juice; watermelon, cubed, with lime juice; cubed honeydew melon, pink grapefruit sections and sliced kiwi fruit, with lime juice.

Sliced **pineapple**, alone or mixed with oranges, with blood orange juice.

Mangoes (see step-by-step instructions on page 149); with lime juice.

A **mixed fruit salad** in shades of pink and green, cut up very small: honeydew melon, strawberries, white peaches, kiwi fruit, redcurrants etc., all in orange and lime juice.

FESTIVE DINNER

Patricia Lousada: I'm terribly influenced by what I see. I go out with a list but if I see something else beautiful, I'll buy that instead. In general, I think about the main course first, and work from there. Entertaining is always something of a dilemma for me. Often I'd like to cook something very new and can't because then I'd be in the kitchen the whole time. Sometimes I feel I have to do a casserole because then I know I'll enjoy the whole evening more.

This is the traditional dinner for an American Thanksgiving. The usual dish is turkey, and I've tried to find a new way of cooking it, by boning it first. It isn't really as difficult as it sounds and can be done a couple of days ahead. Even if it takes the best part of an hour, it is worth doing because it looks impressive, it takes less time to cook than an unboned bird and it's simple to carve at the table. And you can then use the bones to make a delicious gravy in advance.

I do think that everybody doesn't want too much food nowadays, and being American I worry about cholesterol, so I tend not to put butter and cream in more than one course. The pumpkin soup is fairly light, and an easy first course for a big gathering, and though I've used butter for the vegetables in the main course, you could easily cook them more simply. With the meal I would drink a simple French red wine, as white would not stand up to the strong flavors of the turkey and its sauces.

Patricia Lousada sits by her Pumpkin Soup and Clover Leaf Corn Rolls. In the center of the table is the boned, stuffed turkey, with Glazed Carrots, and Cucumber and Snow Peas and, in front are Madeira Sauce, Spiced Kumquats and Cranberry Sauce.

**Patricia Lousada's
Menu for a Festive Dinner**

For 10–12 people

PUMPKIN SOUP
with
CLOVER LEAF CORN ROLLS

BONED STUFFED TURKEY
with
MADEIRA SAUCE,
and
CRANBERRY SAUCE
and
SPICED KUMQUATS

GLAZED CARROTS
CUCUMBER AND SNOW PEAS

BLUEBERRY AND RASPBERRY PIES

PUMPKIN SOUP

*6 lb. piece of pumpkin or good-sized whole
    pumpkin
4 tbsp. butter
2 onions, finely chopped
5 cups chicken stock
2½ cups milk
⅓ cup fresh basil, roughly chopped
salt and freshly milled black pepper*

A whole pumpkin can be used for the soup and can also provide a charming serving bowl. Cut a circle in the top of the pumpkin around the stalk. Scrape out the seeds and stringy bits and discard. Then scrape out the flesh to use for the soup. If you are using a piece of pumpkin, scrape out the seeds and stringy center and discard; cut the rest into chunks and peel.

Sauté the onion in the butter until translucent but not browned. Add the pumpkin flesh and stock and simmer, covered, until the pumpkin is tender. Purée in a processor or blender and return to the pan. Add the milk and taste for seasoning. Before serving, reheat to just below boiling point, add the basil, pour into the shell, if you have it, and serve with Clover Leaf Corn Rolls.

CLOVER LEAF CORN ROLLS

Makes about 18 rolls

*3 tbsp. lemon juice
⅔ cup lukewarm milk
¼ cup lukewarm water
¾ oz. fresh yeast or ⅛ oz. dried yeast
3 cups white unbleached flour
¾ cup cornmeal
1 tbsp. sugar
2 tsp. salt*

Add the lemon juice to the milk and set aside. Add the water to the yeast and leave to dissolve. Place the flour, cornmeal, sugar and salt in a large bowl and put in a very low oven for about 5 minutes to warm the flour slightly.

Pour the yeast mixture and the soured milk into the flour and stir first with a spoon and then with your hand until the dough comes away from the sides of the bowl. If it is too sticky, add more corn meal, if too dry add a little warm water. Knead on a lightly floured surface until the dough is smooth and elastic. Put back in the bowl, cover with a plastic bag and leave in a warm place until doubled in volume.

Punch down the dough. Pinch off small pieces and shape them into 1½ inch balls by rolling them between your palms. Place 3 balls in each well of a greased muffin tin and put in a warm place until they have at least doubled in size. (They will by then have merged into each other to give you the clover leaf shape.)

Preheat oven to 400°F and bake rolls for 25 minutes. Turn the rolls out on to a wire rack to cool. They can be reheated briefly just before serving.

"The King of Pumpkins receiving the homage of his subjects," 1865. Honoré Daumier: lithograph, le Charivari.

STUFFING AND ROASTING THE TURKEY

The stuffings can be prepared a day ahead, but the turkey should only be stuffed on the day of cooking.

For a boned turkey weighing about 12 lb. dressed

Mushroom Stuffing:
4 tbsp. butter
2 cloves garlic, very finely chopped
1½ lb. mushrooms, very finely chopped
good squeeze of lemon
salt and freshly ground black pepper
⅓ cup parsley, chopped

The mushrooms can be chopped in a processor in several batches using an on/off technique. Heat the butter in a large frying pan, add the garlic and cook until translucent. Add the mushrooms, lemon juice and some salt and pepper. Cook over a high heat, stirring occasionally until all the moisture has evaporated; this can take about 20 minutes. Stir in the chopped parsley, scrape into a bowl and reserve.

Spinach Stuffing:
1½ lb. fresh spinach
a handful of sorrel leaves (optional)
pinch salt

Wash the spinach and sorrel in cold water and remove the stalks and any large center ribs. Place in a saucepan with a pinch of salt and only the water that is still clinging to the leaves. Cook, covered, for 5 minutes or until the spinach is just wilted. Drain and squeeze out some of the excess moisture.

Rice Stuffing:
⅔ cup each of brown rice and wild rice, or 1⅓
*   cups brown rice*
2 large eggs, lightly beaten
2 tbsp. lightly toasted pine nuts, or slivered
*   almonds*
salt
freshly ground black pepper

Place the brown rice in a saucepan filled with plenty of boiling salted water, return to the boil, cover and simmer for 25 minutes, or until barely tender. Drain, turn into a bowl and mix with half the beaten eggs and the pine nuts.

    Wash the wild rice, if you are using it, under cold running water. Place in a saucepan and barely cover with water. Simmer very gently, covered, until the rice has absorbed the water, about 15 minutes. It should still be quite crunchy. Drain, turn into another bowl and mix with the remain-

Boning the turkey

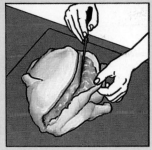

1 Cut off the wings at the elbow, leaving the largest wing bone on. Cut off the ankle joint on the legs if necessary.

2 Place the bird on its breast, slit the skin down the backbone from neck to tail. With a fairly short, sharp knife, using short strokes, scrape the flesh and skin away from the carcass, easing the skin and flesh back as you go. Work on one side at a time.

3 Cut the flesh from the saber-shaped bone near the wing. Wiggle the wing to find the ball and socket joint and sever it where it meets the carcass. Do the same with the thigh bone, so that the wing and thigh are separated from the carcass but still attached to the skin. Repeat on the other side.

4 Cut against the ridge of the breastbone to free the skin, being very careful not to pierce it.

5 Hold the end of the wing bone in one hand, cut through the tendons and scrape the meat from the bone, drawing the skin inside out and using the knife to cut the bone free. Repeat the process with the thigh and drumstick bones, then do the other side. It is much easier to find the joints if you wiggle the bones well.

6 Push the skin from the legs and wings right side out. Remove the flaps of breast meat and place them in front of the breast where there is no meat. Tidy up the turkey by cutting away any excess fat and sinews. The bird is now ready to be stuffed.

ing egg. Season both bowls of rice with salt and pepper to taste.

Stuffing and roasting the bird

Preheat oven to 350°F. Spread the boned turkey skin side down and rub a bit of salt and pepper into the flesh. Cover with a layer of wild rice or half the brown rice if you are only using one sort. Spread the spinach over the rice, then cover this with the brown rice. Finally heap the mushrooms in a dome down the center of the turkey. Bring the side edges of the turkey over until they meet, and sew them together with a needle and thick black thread (black is easy to see for removal). Fold the neck skin over and stitch across. Turn the bird over and mold into a good plump shape. Place a few rounds of loosely tied string around the bird in order to help it keep its shape.

    Cover the breast with a piece of muslin soaked in 4 tbsp. of melted butter and place in a roasting pan. Cook for 1 hour 15 minutes. Uncover the bird and remove the strings and roast for a further 30 minutes. Transfer to a serving dish, and allow the bird to rest in a warm place for 10 minutes before carving.

Serve with Madeira Sauce, whole Cranberry Sauce and Spiced Kumquats and fresh vegetables in season.

MADEIRA SAUCE

The sauce is made in two stages but can be made ahead of time except for the last minute addition of the roasting juices and alcohol.

Turkey Stock:
turkey bones, neck, gizzard, heart (not the liver)
1 onion, quartered
1 carrot, sliced
1 stick of celery, sliced
bouquet garni (bayleaf, sprig each of parsley, thyme and tarragon)
10 peppercorns, lightly crushed

Place all the ingredients in a large saucepan with 2½ quarts water. Cover and simmer for 3 hours. Strain and return to the pan. Boil hard, uncovered, to reduce the stock to about 5 cups. Cool, then remove all traces of fat from the surface of the stock.

Madeira Sauce:
6 tbsp. butter
6 shallots, very finely chopped
¼ carrot, very finely chopped
¼ stick of celery, very finely chopped
1 tbsp. each fresh tarragon, parsley and thyme, finely chopped
a few peppercorns, lightly crushed
7 tbsp. sercial Madeira
turkey stock (above)
3 tbsp. brandy
roasting juices

Sauté the shallots, carrot and celery, herbs and peppercorns in 4 tbsp. butter for 15 minutes. Deglaze with 4 tbsp. Madeira. Then add the stock and simmer, uncovered, for about 1 hour. Strain, pressing the vegetables through a fine sieve with a wooden spoon. Return to the pan and taste for seasoning. The sauce can be done ahead of time up to this point.

During the last half hour of the turkey roasting time, reheat the sauce, add the remaining Madeira and the brandy and simmer gently. You should have about 2½ cups of sauce. Add the roasting juices, which you can deglaze with a few spoons of sauce. Adjust the seasoning – it should have quite a strong flavor. Swirl in the remaining butter, cut into small pieces, and serve in a pitcher.

CRANBERRY SAUCE

12 oz. fresh or frozen cranberries
1 cup sugar
1 cup water

Stir the sugar and water in a saucepan over a low heat until the sugar is dissolved. Bring to the boil, add the cranberries and return to the boil. Reduce the heat and boil gently, uncovered, for 10 minutes, stirring occasionally. Turn into a serving bowl and serve at room temperature.

SPICED KUMQUATS

Keep for 8 weeks before using.

2 lb. kumquats
2 lb. sugar
1 stick cinnamon
2 tbsp. whole cloves
6 blades mace
4 cardamom pods
2½ cups cider vinegar

Place the kumquats in a saucepan, barely cover with water and simmer, covered, for about 1 hour, or until the skin is tender. Meanwhile, dissolve the sugar with the spices in the vinegar over gentle heat. Bring to the boil and boil for 5 minutes.

When the kumquats are tender, drain them and reserve the cooking liquid. Place the kumquats in the syrup and, if necessary, add some of the reserved liquid to just cover the fruit. Simmer together for 30 minutes. Remove pan from heat and leave uncovered for 24 hours, turning the fruit in the syrup once or twice.

Next day bring the kumquats and syrup to the boil, drain the fruit and pack in sterilized jars. Bring the syrup back to the boil and boil hard to thicken slightly. Pour over the kumquats, distributing the spices between the jars, and seal.

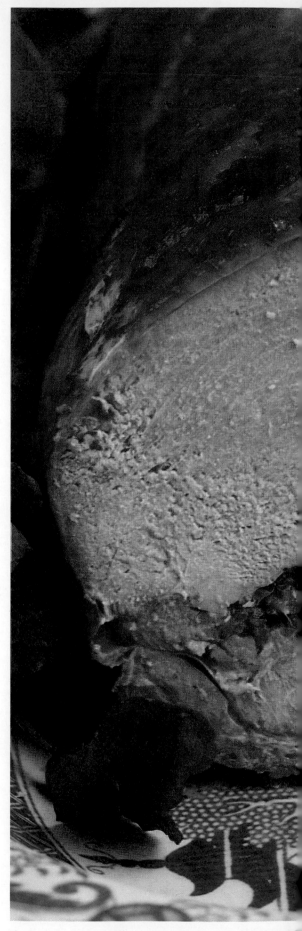

The boned turkey, easily cut into slices, stuffed with wild

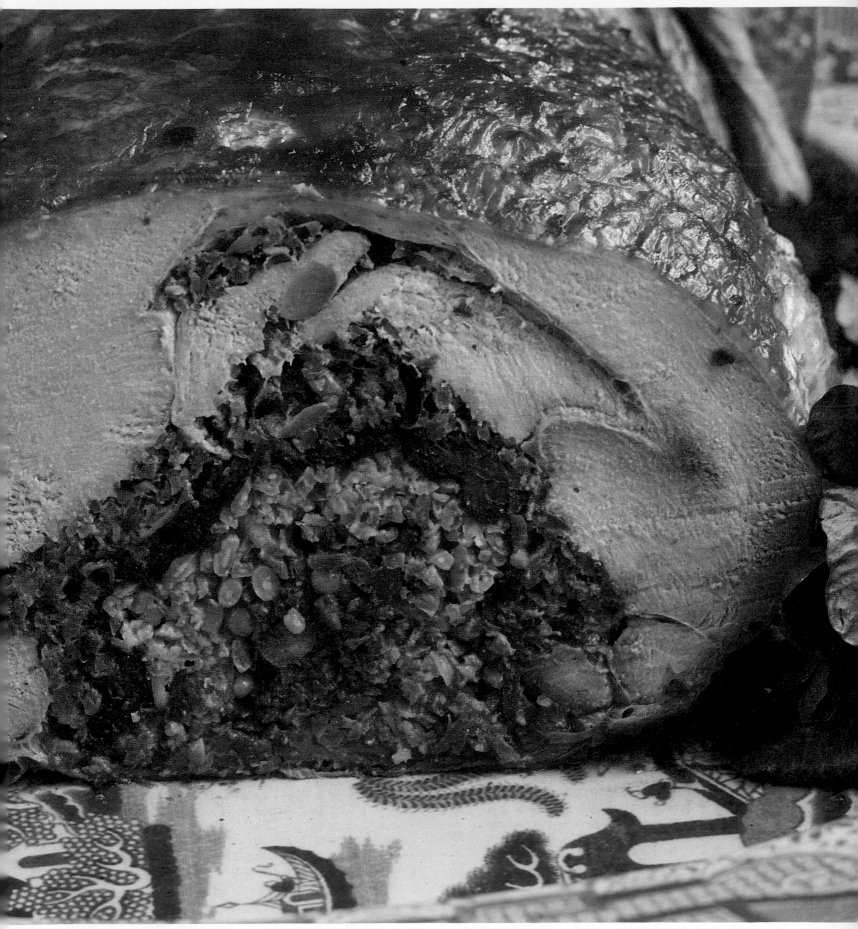

rice in the outer ring, then spinach, then brown rice, with dark mushroom stuffing down the center.

GLAZED CARROTS

2 lb. carrots
knob of butter
pinch of sugar
salt and pepper
chopped parsley

Peel the carrots and cut them into round slices. Place them in a saucepan, add water to come halfway up the carrots. Add butter, sugar, and salt. Cover and cook for 10 minutes, then uncover and continue cooking until all the water is absorbed. Shake the pan from time to time towards the end to avoid scorching. They can be cooked ahead and reheated with an additional knob of butter and served with pepper and parsley sprinkled over the top.

CUCUMBER AND SNOW PEAS

3 cucumbers
2 lb. snow peas
2 tbsp. butter
salt and pepper
fresh dill if available

Pinch off the ends of the snow peas and blanch 1 minute in lots of boiling salted water. Drain and refresh under cold running water and set aside. Peel the cucumbers, slice in half lengthwise and scoop out the seeds. Cut into 3-inch sections and slice lengthwise into thin slivers. Toss them in a frying pan in butter. Stir for a few minutes, until they become opaque, then add the snow peas and heat together before placing in a hot serving dish. Sprinkle with dill or another fresh herb that is in season.

BLUEBERRY AND RASPBERRY PIES

Pastry to line two 10-inch pie pans:
$3\frac{1}{4}$ cups flour
$\frac{1}{2}$ tsp. salt
1 tsp. baking powder
5 tbsp. sugar
grated rind of one orange
7 oz. unsalted butter, left at room
    temperature for 1 hour
2 large egg yolks
$\frac{2}{3}-\frac{3}{4}$ cup heavy cream

Fillings:
1 lb. fresh blueberries
scant $\frac{1}{2}$ cup sugar
1 tbsp. butter
1 lb. fresh raspberries
$\frac{3}{4}$ cup redcurrant jelly
$\frac{1}{4}$ cup orange juice

Sift flour, salt and baking powder together. Stir in sugar and orange rind. Cut butter into small pieces and rub in with your fingertips until mixture looks crumbly. Blend in egg yolks and half the cream with a fork. Add just enough remaining cream for the dough to cling together in a ball. Divide into 2 equal pieces, wrap separately in plastic wrap and refrigerate for at least 30 minutes.

Roll out dough when ready to use and line two pie pans. Prick the base with a fork and fill the center with a piece of crumpled aluminum foil weighed down with dried beans. Refrigerate for 15 minutes before baking in a preheated oven at 400°F for 10 minutes. Remove the paper and beans and bake one shell a further 5 minutes (or until the bottom and sides are firm and only very slightly colored) and bake the other shell fully, until it is a golden brown all over. Remove to a rack to cool.

Mix the blueberries with the sugar and add to the partially baked shell. Dot with butter and bake at 375°F for 40 minutes: cover the pastry with a piece of foil if it browns too much.

As near serving time as possible, assemble the raspberry tart. Melt the red currant jelly with the orange juice and paint the bottom of the fully-cooked shell with some of it. Arrange the raspberries over the glazed shell and paint them with the remaining jelly.

To serve: cut each tart into 8 equal pieces (have the knife very hot; rinse it in boiling water). Rearrange the slices so that they alternate and you have 2 red and blue pinwheel colored pies.

216 *Alternate slices of Blueberry and Raspberry Pie.*

Raspberry Pie.

Arabella Boxer's variations: One of the hardest things for a cook is to take a traditional occasion, and produce a meal that is appropriate without being predictable. With her Thanksgiving meal, Patricia Lousada has achieved this *par excellence.* The familiar foods are there, but presented in original ways. The pumpkin is served as a soup rather than the familiar pie. She boned the turkey herself, and filled it with layers of wild rice – an indigenous American food – brown rice, spinach, and mushrooms. And in addition to the usual cranberry sauce, she made a preserve of kumquats that was almost the best thing of all.

Many of the same foods are relevant at Christmas; the pumpkin soup could be replaced by a classic consommé. For those who don't feel up to boning a turkey, it can be roasted in the usual way, but using Patricia Lousada's stuffing for added interest. For a smaller party, a capon or goose can be used. A goose is an uneconomic bird, for it is shaped like a duck, with only a shallow layer of flesh covering its bones. An average goose will only feed 6 (or 8 at a pinch) while a turkey the same size will feed 10 to 12. It does yield considerable benefits, however, in its liver, a true delicacy in its own right, and in its fat. It is the best fat of all for frying and roasting potatoes, braising vegetables, or making soups of fresh or dried vegetables. Carefully strain off the fat from the roasting pan and chill until solid, when it can be scraped free of meat jelly. It will keep in the refrigerator for weeks.

A hot baked ham is another handsome dish for a festivity and is especially useful for a holiday since it is as delicious cold as hot. It goes well with all the usual accompaniments, the fruit sauces and preserves. Whatever you do, try to include the preserved kumquats, for they are beautiful, and so delicious.

If you feel you must end with the traditional plum pudding, here is the recipe. And here, also, is home-made lemonade, a welcome addition to family festivities, both for children and for drivers who want to limit their intake of alcohol.

**Arabella Boxer's suggestions
for food for
the Christmas Season**

ROAST TURKEY
or
ROAST GOOSE

GLAZED HAM

CHRISTMAS PUDDING

BRANDY BUTTER

LEMONADE

ROAST TURKEY

Serves 10–12

14 lb. turkey (drawn weight)
1 cup butter, melted
sea salt and black pepper
*5 cups turkey stock, made in advance and
    degreased*

Make the turkey stock according to Patricia Lousada's recipe, using the giblets, neck, etc., but not the liver, and adding a chicken stock cube to strengthen the flavor. If, instead of the Madeira Sauce, you want to serve a simple gravy, you will only need about 2 cups.

Heat the oven to 350°F. Remember to weigh the bird before stuffing to calculate roasting times. Stuff both ends of the bird, using one or two stuffings as you prefer. I usually put a Bread Stuffing in the body of the bird, and a Sausage and Chestnut one (see page 67) in the crop; next time, I shall use Patricia Lousada's Rice, Spinach and Mushroom Stuffing, and make my own Sausage and Chestnut mixture into small forcemeat balls, frying them separately to serve around the bird.

Brush the turkey all over with melted butter and sprinkle with salt and pepper. Lay it in a roasting pan; it will probably be too big to sit on a rack. Take a square of clean cloth (a piece of muslin, or an old linen napkin or dish towel, will do nicely) and dip it in melted butter. Lay it over the breast of the bird so that it is completely covered. Roast for 20–25 minutes per lb., testing it at the end of the shorter time as you would a chicken, by wiggling a leg rather than piercing it with a skewer, to see if it is done.

Remove the cloth to uncover the breast for the last 30 minutes, basting with the melted butter. While it is cooking, make the Madeira Sauce, adding the pan juices at the end. Let the bird stand, loosely covered and in a warm place, for about 15 minutes before carving.
Serve with Madeira Sauce or gravy, and Cranberry Sauce, as well as all the usual and traditional accompaniments.

ROAST GOOSE

I like goose best with a simple Potato Stuffing, or – perhaps better still – without a stuffing, for this allows the fat to escape. Instead of stuffing the bird itself, a Sausage and Chestnut mixture can be made into small balls and fried separately.

Serves 6

*1 goose, approximately 13 lb. (about 11 lb.
    after drawing)*

Heat oven to 400°F. Weigh the bird and calculate the roasting time, allowing 25 minutes per lb. weighed before stuffing. Prick the skin all over with a sharp skewer, lay upside down on a rack in a roasting pan and roast 20 minutes. Turn the oven down to 350°F. Take the bird out of the oven and remove, pour off the fat in the roasting pan. Then return to the oven and continue roasting. If using a stuffing, remove the bird from the rack at this point, cool slightly and stuff it as soon as the bird is cool enough to handle. Then return to the oven and proceed. (The preliminary roasting without stuffing allows more of the fat to run out.) Turn right side up for the last 30 minutes, but do not baste.

While it cooks, make a stock with the giblets and a few flavoring vegetables: onion, carrot, and celery. Strain stock and degrease. When the bird is roasted, stand it in a warm place for 15 minutes, loosely covered. Pour off the fat in the roasting pan, leaving the juices. Put the pan over a moderate flame and scrape all the juices together, adding the stock. Let the gravy bubble away for a moment or two, then strain into a sauceboat.

Serve with Cranberry Sauce, or a tart Apple Sauce, or Horseradish and Apple Sauce. Since goose is such a fatty bird, I think it best to serve plainly boiled potatoes rather than roast, or a potato purée made with less butter than usual and more milk. A green vegetable like broccoli or green beans, or tiny brussels sprouts goes well with the richness of the goose.

GLAZED HAM

8–10 lb. country ham (a small ham, or ½ large one)
3 large onions
4 stalks celery
3 large carrots
2 turnips
2 parsnips
4 stalks parsley
2 bay leaves
15 peppercorns
1¼ cups cider vinegar
1 cup brown sugar, packed
Glaze:
⅔ cup brown sugar, packed
½ cup soft brown breadcrumbs
2 tsp. Dijon mustard
1 tbsp. cider vinegar

Start a day in advance. Scrub the ham all over and soak for 24 hours. Scrub the vegetables, cut them in chunks and lay them in a thick layer in the bottom of a large pan or casserole. Add parsley and bay leaves, peppercorns, vinegar and sugar. Lay the ham on top, and cover with cold water. Bring to the boil and make a note of the time the first bubbles reach the surface. Skim until the surface is clear, then cook steadily, keeping the water just below boiling point, for 20 minutes per lb.

When the time is up, turn off the heat and leave the ham to cool partially in its stock. An hour or so later, lift it out and remove the skin. Mix the sugar and breadcrumbs to a paste with the mustard and vinegar. Spread this all over the fatty surface of the ham, using a spatula and pressing well on to the fat. Heat the oven to 350°F. Bake for 45 minutes, uncovered, basting once halfway through with a little extra vinegar. When the time is up, turn off the oven, open the oven door, and leave the ham for 15 minutes before carving.

Serve hot with Plum Sauce, Cumberland Sauce or Cranberry Sauce, a purée of potatoes and assorted vegetables, or cold with salad and baked potatoes.

CHRISTMAS PUDDING

Best made a few weeks in advance.

Makes 1 large and 1 small pudding, or 3 small ones

1½ lb. seedless raisins
½ lb. mixed and candied peel, chopped
½ lb. glacé cherries
¼ lb. almonds, peeled and chopped
¾ lb. shredded suet
¾ lb. soft white breadcrumbs
8 eggs, beaten
½ cup stout or dark beer
½ cup brandy
Accompaniments:
¼–⅓ cup brandy
Brandy Butter (see following recipe)

If the raisins are large, cut them in half. Mix with the peel, cherries, almonds, suet and breadcrumbs in the largest bowl you have. Stir in the beaten eggs, stout or beer, and ½ cup brandy. Leave for a few hours, or even overnight.

Choose your pudding basins and butter them well. This mixture will fill one holding 2 quarts, and one holding 1 quart; or you can make three 1 quart puddings. Divide the mixture between them, leaving at least an inch empty at the top for the pudding to swell. Cover with buttered foil, then wrap the whole basin in a square of cloth, knotting the corners over the top to serve as a handle.

Have a very large pan – or 2 smaller ones – with small cake pans or old saucers laid upside down in the bottom. Stand the pudding basins in them, and add cold water to reach halfway up the sides of the basins. Remove the basins and bring the water to the boil. When it is boiling fast, replace the basins and bring back to the boil. Adjust the heat so that it boils steadily, cover the pan(s), and cook for 6 hours. Check the water level every now and then, and replenish it with more boiling water, pouring it down the sides of the pan from a kettle. When the time is up, lift out the puddings and leave to cool.

Next day, remove the cloths and replace with clean ones. Keep in a cool cupboard until needed. Formerly, Christmas puddings were made one year for the following year, but this is only possible in old houses with cool larders. In stuffy centrally heated houses, the puddings cannot be kept for very long without growing mold; six to eight weeks is long enough.

On Christmas day, the pudding should be boiled again for as long as is convenient. If to be eaten in the evening, give it another 6 hours, but if to be served at lunch, 4 hours will do. This second boiling is not essential; we often used to eat the smaller pudding the day it was cooked, but it does make the puddings darker and richer.

To serve: turn the pudding out on to a hot plate and stick a tiny sprig of holly in the center. Warm ¼–⅓ cup brandy in a ladle, holding it above a gas flame, then set light to it and pour it, flaming, over the pudding. Serve with Brandy Butter.

BRANDY BUTTER

Makes 1 cup

½ cup unsalted butter
½ cup superfine sugar
¼–⅓ cup brandy

Take the butter out of the refrigerator 45–60 minutes beforehand. Cut it in pieces and put in the food processor. Process, add the sugar, and process again until thoroughly blended. Then add the brandy very slowly through the lid, while processing. Stop after adding ¼ cup and taste; add a little more if you want, but don't be tempted to add more than ⅓ cup or it will separate. Pile into a small dish and chill in the refrigerator. Cover with plastic wrap and keep refrigerated until needed. (It can be made days, or even weeks in advance.) If you prefer you can substitute rum for the brandy, in which case you may prefer to use soft brown sugar instead of superfine sugar.

LEMONADE

3 large lemons
4 tbsp. superfine sugar
5 cups water

Wash the lemons and cut them in quarters, without peeling. Then cut each quarter in half, and put the pieces in the food processor. Add sugar and water, and process briefly, until the lemons are roughly chopped. Pour through a strainer into a large pitcher and chill in the refrigerator. Add ice cubes just before serving.

GUIDE TO WINE, APERITIFS AND AFTER-DINNER DRINKS

APERITIFS

Aperitifs should open the mind to the prospect of social pleasure and the body to the gastronomic joys ahead.

Most hosts know that alcohol is a mild stimulant and that a little tends to get things off to a good start. Some make the dangerous assumption that a lot will therefore get things off to a *very* good start, with disastrous results. This stage of any social occasion is meant to open the doors of perception rather than close them, and moderation in what is served as an aperitif is thoughtful, rather than niggardly.

Spirits, with an alcohol content of about 40 per cent, have their devotees, but strongly-flavored ones like gin with sweetish mixers such as tonic, may dull rather than sharpen the appetite. A finely blended whisky with soda would be the connoisseur's choice of spirit, though he might substitute Campari for whisky which is only 23.6 per cent alcohol. Whatever the ads say, Campari still tastes best with soda, ice and a slice of lemon or, even better, orange. Pimm's is one of those proprietary drinks that can sit alone with self-confidence on the drinks tray, though it somehow seems rather silly in the middle of winter. This gin or vodka-based concoction has the disadvantage of being dizzily heady, and rather filling if served with the usual lemonade and fruit salad trimmings.

There is a huge range of lower-strength branded aperitifs to choose from, with vermouths Martini, Cinzano and Riccadonna the most successful. These are flavored, fortified wines with an alocohol content of about 17.5 per cent, made chiefly in northern Italy. Vermouth comes in red, white, pink and orange, and in all degrees of sweetness. Most appetizing is the dry white sort that used to be called "French" and, indeed, the most subtly-flavored commercial brand, Noilly Prat, is made in France, though now owned by Martini. Chambéry, made in the French alpine foothills, has even more delicacy than Noilly Prat – though all these dry white vermouths start to get a bit stale once the bottle has been open a month or so.

The French specialize in aperitifs made, not only by fortifying wine, but by adding alcohol to a grape juice base. The assault on the taste buds is much the same as for vermouth, although drinks such as the dry white herb-flavored Lillet have a slightly syrupy undertone, as do Dubonnet and St Raphael. When the grape juice comes from Champagne, the drink is called ratafia, while the Cognac region produces Pineau des Charentes – both sweet, grapey and deceptively strong.

The gentian-based Suze, artichoke-based Cynar and quinine-flavored Byrrh are acquired tastes; Italian Punt e Mes is much more approachable. It is halfway between an extra-herby vermouth and Campari in flavor and, unlike most vermouths, stands up well to the weakening effect of soda.

The archetypal aperitif is a good sherry. Sherry is the same alcoholic strength as vermouth, but the best sherries have a tanginess that seems to act as a starting pistol for the gastric juices: the appetite is whetted and the palate toned up.

Bottles labelled Fino or Manzanilla should contain the lightest, driest form of sherry, which, in its purest form, is as much like the commercial Amontillados as a cup of cocoa. La Ina and Tio Pepe are creditable examples. These very pale, slightly pungent wines are only about 16 per cent alcohol and their appetizing edge of flavor dissipates once the bottle is opened. They are best served well chilled.

More suitable, perhaps, for damp, cool climates, and particularly for winter, are darker, nuttier sherries. Dry Olorosos such as Domecq's Rio Viejo or Harvey's Fine Old Amontillado still have the characteristic sherry tang to sharpen up the appetite, but are more suitable and comforting.

Port and Madeira each have a dry pale version that can be drunk as an aperitif and, like really dry sherry, can take you through many a first course. Madeira is the traditional accompaniment to many soups, for instance, and in its driest form, Sercial, can be enjoyed on its own. White port may

be sweet or dry, and most people would probably find the sweet ones too raisiny to tone up the appetite; however, the dry style responds well to the ice-and-lemon-peel treatment.

More and more people serve wine as an aperitif. The function of the aperitif is to refresh, so the wine should be cool, and there is nothing more refreshing than a cool wine with bubbles in it. Champagne is the most luxurious aperitif and widely served in wine circles.

It is possible to find perfectly respectable dry, white sparkling wines for little more than half the price of champagne however. Sparkling Saumur makes a good aperitif because its flavor is fairly neutral and its bouquet very "clean". France is still the prime source of reliable fizzy wines, such as the frothy Blanquette de Limoux from the deep south, the pungent Crémant d'Alsace, and the slightly honeyed sparkling Vouvray.

The drinking world is divided into those who find bubbles stimulating, and those who find them indigestible. There is an enormous range of still wines that seem designed as aperitifs for those in the second category. The wines made along the Loire are perfect: the hallmark of the Chenin Blanc grape is just a whiff of honey and flowers, and a well-made Vouvray, Savennières or Montlouis makes delicious preprandial drinking. A simple Mâcon Blanc would also be fine. To the east are the dry, Germanic wines of Alsace and the wines of Germany itself – many of them ideal aperitifs. The wines of the Mosel are particularly low in blurring alcohol and high in refreshing acidity, counterbalanced in most cases by the fruitiness of the Reisling grape. Germany's better medium dry wines, labelled Kabinett or Spätlese are difficult to match with food and usually ideal aperitifs.

One of the least financially painful aperitifs is the Kir, or vin blanc cassis. Any old dry white wine will do, though the ultratart Bourgogne Aligoté is traditional in Burgundy where the drink was dreamt up, and French wines do seem to work best. Pour just a dribble of crème de cassis blackcurrant liqueur into each glass before topping up with very cool wine. Substitute red wine and the drink becomes a Cardinale.

Non-alcoholic drinks

The considerate host always offers a non-alcoholic alternative. All of us have the obvious on tap, but mineral waters that fizz may seem more festive and are usually more delicious. Served with ice and lemon, they can even give the illusion of stimulating drinking.

Other favorite non-alcoholic aperitifs include the vodka-less Bloody Mary, though there is a considerable art in spicing it perfectly. A gin-and-tonic without the gin is a simpler variation on this theme, and lime juice can be substituted for gin for those who are determined to have a mixed drink. A single lime, cut artfully, incidentally, can add a note of sophistication to a surprisingly large number of glasses of water or other suitable fizzy drinks.

WINE

It matters either not at all, or enormously, what wine is served with various foods, depending on the occasion and the frame of mind of the drinkers. At a sunny alpine picnic after a long climb, it is difficult to imagine that even the most churlish member of the party would complain that the red rioja was unsuitable for the smoked salmon sandwiches, although at a dinner party organized weeks in advance, such a wine with a smoked salmon starter would seem a curious choice.

Some tricky foods

Most foods can be enjoyed with a wide range of different wines and the host need only be concerned that his choice makes a sensible sequence (see below). However, there are a few foods that make particularly awkward partners for wine, because they are particularly high in one of wine's components, such as acidity, or because they alter the palate's ability to distinguish nuances of flavor. In these circumstances usually all that is necessary is to rinse the mouth fully with water, or to chew on something neutral such as bread, and the tasting faculties will return to their normal, finely-honed state. The foods that call for particular ingenuity in matching with wine are:

Hot, spicy foods These make it physically impossible to taste something relatively delicate, and with spices stronger than cardamom and ginger, beer is probably a more sensible choice than wine. But if it's got to be wine choose an assertive, cooling white such as spicy Gewürztraminer.

Chinese food is usually sweet and salty, with a bit of sourness thrown in for good measure. White feels better than red, and a bit of residual sweetness, as in a good Vouvray, might not come amiss.

Very acid foods "Vinegar" comes from *vin aigre* (sour wine) and the combination of vinegar and any wine makes the taste sour. At the Robert Mondavi Winery in California they use his finest Cabernet Reserve to dress the salads, and any dry wine can be substituted for vinegar if the salad is to be served with a fine wine. Lemon juice is also a gentler substitute. Perfectionists avoid the problem by serving the salad after the main course, and drinking water with it.

Artichokes and asparagus There's something strange about these two vegetables that makes wine taste metallic (just as toothpaste does). A Fino sherry might just stand up to the mystery ingredient, but actually both vegetables are watery enough to allow the eater a few minutes without lubrication.

Very sweet foods Sweetness in food tends to accentuate the acidity in any accompanying wine, and it will only survive if it has even more counterbalancing sweetness. Only a very rich wine can stand up to something as sweet as a crème brulée, say, and a Sauternes, with its alcohol content of at least 13%, seems most suitable. Sweet German wines are often less than half as alcoholic, and best served alone or with some simple fruit. Chocolate is the most difficult sweet food to match with wine and a sweet fortified wine such as Malaga from southern Spain may be called for.

"White wine with fish and red with meat"

It is easy to see how the rule evolved, but sad to see how it has outlawed many interesting and pleasurable combinations. True, tannin, the preservative found most commonly in youthful red wine, makes fish taste metallic. Furthermore we are conditioned to expect a touch of acidity to liven up most fish (vinegar with rock salmon, a sorrel sauce with the real thing), and since white wines tend to be slightly higher in acidity than reds, they are, indeed, the natural partners for most fish dishes.

However, many red wines are low in tannin and high in acidity, and these can be delicious drunk with fish. Beaujolais and any other wine based on the Gamay grape, such as the less expensive examples from Touraine, would be fine with any firm-textured fish, as would most of the southern French red Vins de Pays that are such good value. Rather finer red wines to serve with fish include light red burgundy, Loire reds such as Saumur, red Sancerre, Chinon and Bourgueil, as well as some light reds from northern Italy, especially Alto Adige wines, youthful Chianti and good quality Valpolicella. Fish with the flavor and texture to stand up well to red wine include brill, halibut, red mullet, salmon, sea trout, and turbot.

Many white wines can be enjoyed with meaty dishes, although most German wines are too delicate for a rich stew. A Spätlese and ham might work, on the other hand, on the sweet and salty principle of prosciutto and melon.

The question of weight

Try to match the weight of the wine, in all instances, to the weight of flavor in the dish. A full-blooded steak would call for a very full-bodied wine, white or red. An oak-matured white rioja, California Chardonnay or Australian Semillon would be great – as would a mature white burgundy.

Delicate wine can be overwhelmed by strong-flavored food, like a Muscadet served with a goulash, just as very powerful wines, such as Barolo or Hermitage, would spoil the subtle flavor of an avocado mousse.

Examples of "heavyweight" foods are most forms of charcuterie, especially sausages and boudins; anything very garlicky or smoked; anything very oily, such as sardines, herrings, mackerel or pepperonata; most meaty pâtés and terrines; lobster and other rich shellfish; most casseroles and baked meat dishes; venison, hare and game birds; strong-flavored cheeses; creamy puddings; cakes and rich tarts.

With all these it makes sense to serve a wine that is assertive in flavor and relatively full-bodied, whether white, pink or red, sweet or dry.

Wines that would not stand up to these rich foods are almost any German wine other than some of the firmer products of the Baden Württemberg or Franken regions; most Loire wines, both red and white, such as Muscadet, Anjou, Saumur, Vouvray, Savennières, Coteaux du Layon, Sauvignon de Touraine, Sancerre, Pouilly-Fumé, Bourgueil and Chinon; Vinho Verde; Beaujolais and other Gamays; south almost any Vin de Pays; Coteaux du Tricastin, Côtes de Ventoux and Côtes du Luberon; the wines of Haut-Poitou; Lu-xembourg and Swiss wines; wines of Savoy such as Apremont; most wines labelled Riesling; Galestro from Tuscany; many whites from north-east Italy and most New Zealand wines.

Such wines should not be served with foods stronger in flavor than a vegetable terrine, a gentle salmon mousse, plain roast chicken, low-key fish dishes, sweetbreads, escalopes of veal, fresh goat cheese and cream cheeses, and simple fruit dishes.

Wine with the first course

Soup is usually strong flavored and full-textured and tends to make most table wines taste insipid. There is usually no need to slake a thirst, so wine need not be offered. Dry fortified wines, such as a Fino, Manzanilla or Dry Amontillado sherry, or a Sercial Madeira are better partners.

It is often sensible to continue drinking the aperitif wine during the first course, which usually means it is white and dry. The strong, dry, perfumed wines of Alsace are useful first-course wines. Gewürztraminer and Pinot Gris (Tokay d'Alsace) are even fuller than the classic Reisling, and Pinot Blanc and Sylvaner can stand up to smoked foods well. It often works if the chosen wine is a geographical relative of the food. Light Italian reds, such as youthful Chianti and Barbera, or even Valpolicella, would be perfect with a pasta starter, for instance, while something like grilled sardines suggest Vinho Verde, and a salade niçoise seems sad without a dry rosé from Provence.

Wine and cheese

It's surprising that this combination is considered a classic when the two components vary so enormously; perhaps it has evolved as a by-product of our reverence for all things French, and these two French commodities in particular.

Many people believe that English cheese is a better foil for wine than most French cheeses, which tend to be very fatty and high in ammoniac stink if left a minute past their maturity. Almost any firm English cheese complements almost any wine, and there is an old wine trade adage that you should should "buy on an apple and sell on cheese," highlighting the softening, flattering aspect cheese tends to cast on a wine drunk immediately after it, while something as acid as an apple makes any wine taste sour. Small cubes of cheddar are left enticingly between the bottles at most British trade tastings.

Whatever your preference, only fairly mild cheeses should be served with a fine wine, where delicate complexities of flavor would be overwhelmed by a very pungent cheese. Mild French cheeses, most Swiss and many Italian cheeses are gentle enough to complement either a light-bodied wine or a venerable one.

Very strong cheeses call for a surprising choice of wine. Roquefort and Sauternes is a classic combination: the Sauternes has enough weight to take on the sharpness of the blue cheese, and there is no inherent clash between sweet and salty as combinations such as ham and chutney demonstrate. Port and Stilton is another example of this matching of a very sweet wine with a very salty cheese. A fairly mild Stilton is delicious with a rich Madeira, such as a Bual or Malmsey. All but the most delicate cheeses are enhanced by a full-bodied, sweetish wine, such as port, sweet Madeira, Malaga, Australian liqueur Muscats, good quality California Zinfandel or even red Rhône. The sweeter forms of Hungarian Tokay or even some French Muscats could also take a party through the cheese course and straight into coffee.

Wine with desserts

Sweet foods tend to make any wine taste sour, unless it is considerably sweeter. This puts full-bodied very sweet wines such as Sauternes, Barsac, Monbazillac, Muscat de Beaumes de Venise, Moscatel de Setubal and Château La Salle from California at a premium. Only very simple fruit dishes can really enhance a fine dessert wine from Germany or the Loire. Ice creams and sorbets pose problems. They anaesthetize the taste buds so only very, very sweet wines make any impact. One of the richer Muscats might, but providing any wine at all is really unnecessary.

The sequence and number of wines

For casual entertaining it is enough to keep a running supply of one white and one red wine, but a more formal occasion is especially memorable if some thought has gone into providing different wines to match each course. One wine at a time is quite enough for most people. Yet it is surprising how much more instructive and entertaining it is to serve two related wines together. A claret could be compared with a wine made from the same grape (Cabernet Sauvignon) from Italy, Spain, California or Australia. Two different vintages of the same wine could be examined together; or a couple of similar wines from the same vintage.

The classic order in which wines are served to show their best is dry before sweet, light before full-bodied and young before old.

In practice this tends to be translated into a lightish dry white with the first course, a slightly fuller red with the main, perhaps an even richer red with the cheese, and a sweet white wine with a dessert (though this would be quite a feast). Color is not as important as weight and flavor, and a meal, for instance, of poached salmon preceded by antipasti could quite happily be washed down with a good Beaujolais followed by a fine, white burgundy.

Temperature

A high proportion of wine is served at the wrong temperature. If a wine gets too hot, about 70°F, it starts to turn to vinegar and the process is irreversible. Up to this point, however, the warmer a wine is, the more smell there will be to savor, because more of the volatile elements that convey flavor to the nose are released at higher temperature. Balanced against this, which suggests we should drink wine fairly warm, is our desire to be refreshed, which points to serving it fairly cool. The trick is to find the most suitable temperature between the two extremes.

Low temperature emphasizes tannin, which is a natural preservative that tastes like stewed tea and is found in many youthful red wines, particularly claret and the better Italian reds. This is probably what gave rise to the rule of serving red wine fairly warm. Low temperatures also make wine seem more refreshing, and since we seem to expect white wines to be particularly refreshing, we have evolved the rule of serving white wines fairly cool.

The "reds warm, whites and rosés cool" rule is a very crude system, however. Generally speaking, the more full-bodied a wine, the more difficult it is to vaporize its volatile elements. So a light, aromatic wine (most of which are white) can stand up to chilling better than a rich, full-bodied one (most of which are red). But there are many light reds, such as Beaujolais, which taste

very refreshing when served cool. And there are many white wines, such as a good white burgundy, so full-bodied and complete they need to be served warm to give off their best. These are the ideal serving temperatures for various categories of wines.

Very cool (40°F, or all day in the refrigerator): whites or rosés with an unappetizing smell that needs to be frozen away; ordinary whites and rosés on a hot day.

Cool (45°F, or two hours in the refrigerator): all sparkling wines. Aromatic and light-bodied whites and rosés, eg German and Loire wines. Fino and Manzanilla sherry.

Cellar cool (52°F, or half an hour in the refrigerator): full-bodied, good quality whites and rosés, such as white burgundy and Rhône wines, and Chardonnays from around the world. Light reds such as Beaujolais, Chinon, Bourgueil, red Saumur, Valpolicella and Bardolino.

Cool room (58°F, and perhaps straight from your wine storage area): medium-bodied reds without too much tannin, such as burgundy and rioja. Amontillado and Cream sherry, Tawny port and most Madeira.

Warm room (65°F, or all day in a lived-in room): full-bodied reds, and those with a high tannin content, such as young claret and most Cabernet-based wines. Vintage port.

Careful planning is not always possible. The fastest way to chill a bottle is to put it in the freezer for 15 minutes or to plunge it into an ice-bucket filled with a mixture of water and ice cubes. (Ice cubes alone are slower because they touch only part of the bottle.) The fastest way to warm wine is to put it somewhere very hot, but this could easily push it towards vinegar. It is safer to pour wine and try to warm individual glasses in the hand. The "cellar cool" wines are the most versatile because they are least sensitive to temperature.

Glasses for wine

A wander around any glassware department is enough to suggest that a wide range of expensively-cut crystal is a prerequisite of the sophisticated host. Nothing could be further from the truth. Only one, or at most two sizes of glasses are really necessary and, in order to get the most from a wine, the plainer the glass the better.

Our noses are much more sensitive than our mouths, and at least half of the pleasure a wine can give is in its smell or "bouquet." The most important thing about a wine glass, therefore, is that its shape should make it as easy as possible to savor this bouquet.

The well-designed wine glass has a wide bowl that narrows towards the rim so the bouquet collects above the surface of the wine and stays in the glass, ready to be appreciated by the drinker. Standard connoisseur practice is to serve wine in large glasses, only half to two-thirds full, so there is plenty of room for the bouquet to collect above the wine.

The best way to encourage a wine to give off its bouquet is to swirl it around a bit to put as great a surface of wine as possible in contact with air. This is one reason why wine glasses should have a stem – the stem also stops the drinker from warming up a white wine, and from leaving sticky marks on the bowl.

Style is much less important than shape. To some people the dining table is not complete without the glitter of cut crystal or the shimmer of engraved glass. But the dedicated wine lover believes the wine itself is much more beautiful than any glass. He or she will choose very thin plain crystal, to appreciate his wine's limpidity and exciting variations in color. He would not dream of drinking wine from a substance other than clear glass (never tinted): silver or pottery might change the wine's temperature and affect its flavor.

Fortified wines such as port, sherry and Madeira are up to twice as alcoholic as table wines and suggest a rather smaller glass. Just like cognac, their bouquet is important too, and the traditional shapes for getting the most out of them all narrow towards the top to retain the bouquet.

Champagne and other sparkling wines can be drunk quite happily from a wine glass, but the bubbles are best if they have a long way to travel. This is the logic behind the flûte favored in the Champagne region. But it has twin disadvantages: the bouquet is dispersed easily, and it is also easy to warm up the wine. The ideal sparkling wine glass is probably more like this: it is tall,

From the left are: three glasses for red or white wine, a Paris goblet, a "claret jug" of red wine, three tall glasses for champagne, a decanter of sherry, a smaller glass for fortified wine (sherry or port), a brandy glass, and two smaller glasses for fortified wine or brandy.

but narrows towards the top. The wide, flat coupe is frowned on because it loses both bouquet and bubbles and spills easily.

Detergent can make a sparkling wine less sparkling, and affect the taste of any wine, so thorough rinsing of wine glasses is essential. Storage is even more important, as wine glasses can trap stale air or the smell of the shelf if kept upside down for long.

Decanting
There is only one sort of wine that all wine lovers agree should be decanted: a wine such as a twenty-year-old claret that has developed a sediment yet has enough life in it to stand up to the process of separating it from the inconvenient and unsightly sludge. Whether to decant any other type of wine is a topic of red-hot controversy.

Everyone agrees that if a robust wine has been in bottle so long that it has thrown a deposit, it will not suffer from being poured into another vessel, avoiding any uncom-

fortably chewy aspects of the wine. But the process of moving the wine from one container to another does tend to encourage its precious bouquet to dissipate. So it is standard practice with very ancient wines to open the wine just before serving and pour straight from the bottle. The bouquet of a very old wine is faded and delicate and can rapidly fade into vinegar when exposed to air, so they are kept well away from the decanter.

Some authorities including the revered French wine expert Professor Emile Peynaud, argue that even youthful wines will suffer by being transferred from bottle to decanter by losing some of their all-important bouquet. They argue this loss is only worth while if the wine is so robust that it gives off lots of bouquet, and it has a sediment worth avoiding by decanting. Others argue that decanting wine exposes it to oxygen and so speeds up the ageing process making the wine taste more excitingly mature than if it had been poured

straight from the bottle. This does seem to be somewhat optimistic.

Then there is the question of allowing the wine to "breathe," the popular practice of opening the bottle an hour or so before serving and allowing it to stand, "breathing in" the atmosphere to soften the wine. What is probably happening here is that the "bottle stink" (the unappetizing vapor that may collect between the surface of the wine and the cork) is evaporating, so that what is left is the pure bouquet. It certainly seems unlikely that there is any significant interaction between air and the tiny surface area of wine exposed to it. Decanting a very ordinary wine will probably also have the effect of dispersing any bottle stink, which may be why it has so many devotees.

There are wines that have too much smell. Very traditionally-made full-bodied reds such as the herbier Châteauneuf-du-Papes, or the concentrated Vega Sicilia of Spain and Chateau Musar of Lebanon, can benefit by losing a bit of their bouquet through decanting, and Italians say Barolo is made much more approachable this way. At the other end of the spectrum, it would be a shame to lose any of the delicate aroma by decanting a German wine, for instance.

The best way to store decanters is full of water so they don't get dusty or smelly. Stains may come off with an overnight soak of vinegar or false teeth cleaning preparations, although the decanter must be rinsed very thoroughly after. Some restaurants serve wine bottles in a decanting cradle, a basket that keeps the bottle tipped at a slight angle, as if for take-off. This is a useful angle if the bottle contains sediment, but pointless otherwise.

Cooking with wine

A splash of wine can transform a dish from something edible to something exciting, particularly sauces and savory juices. Wine can also be used as a marinade, as part of a poaching liquid, as macerating liquid for fruit, and as a flavoring ingredient in its own right.

The quality and flavor matters most when the wine is not transformed by reduction or simmering. In such instances, the wine should be perfectly drinkable on its own, but need not be expensive. A pleasant generic Sauternes, for example, would be a more sensible marinade for fresh nectarines than Château d'Yquem.

Fortified wines are particularly useful in cooking. They have a very positive flavor and their extra alcohol level makes them stand up well to different processes. A dash of sherry can bring a terrine or savory mousse to life, and port or Madeira can be a vital ingredient in potted cheese.

When the wine is going to be heated sufficiently to boil off its alcohol and leave only the bare bones behind the considerations are slightly different. Dry white vermouth can be very useful when a dry wine essence is required, provided the slight herb flavor is appropriate. Noilly Prat, in particular, blends well with a dash of lemon juice for fish sauces. Beware of German wines and others with residual sugar: their sweetness and slightly perfumed character may be out of step with a savory dish. The ideal white wine for reductions is very dry and quite full and the wine box can be useful here.

My ideal red cooking wine is not something I would often choose to drink – although it has no off-flavors. The process of reduction seems to burn away much of the character of a red wine, so a very hearty, robust, almost coarse wine is called for. A rich, traditionally-made rioja might fill the bill, or an inexpensive red from Greece or Cyprus. Best of all, perhaps,

would be the cheapest Australian or heartiest Californian wine currently available.

Buying wine

The overheads of excise duty if the wine is imported, bottling, labelling and transport are the same on every bottle of wine. So the wine in a bottle costing $5 will be worth much less than half the wine in a $10 bottle. The more you spend, the better the bargain you get. In addition, a mouthful of good wine has a much longer impact on the senses. It leaves a long, lingering aftertaste that almost demands to be savored, rather than the often non-existent or even unpleasant aftertaste of a cheap wine that encourages gulping if only to wash it away. A bottle of reasonable wine and a bottle of mineral water cost about the same as two bottles of plonk, and should give much more pleasure.

AFTER-DINNER DRINKS

Liqueurs tend to be quite expensive. Many people who travel abroad buy their quota in duty-free shops. A wide range of liqueurs takes a lot of money and effort, but a respectable trio might include one based on oranges such as Cointreau, Grand Marnier or Mandarine Napoléon; one based on whiskey such as Drambuie, Glayva or one of those cream cordials; and one based on a monastic recipe such as Bénédictine or Chartreuse.

Much simpler, and just as stimulating are the great digestif brandies cognac and armagnac. Cognac comes in all states of maturity and all price tags. Delamain and Hine are favorites with aficionados, as are the rare estate bottled cognacs such as Ragnud's and the very special, powerful

British-bottled cognac offered by traditional merchants such as Harveys and Berry Bros & Rudd.

Armagnac is usually rather more fiery than cognac but has lots of character, and a longer history. Like the more northerly brandy, armagnac's two most common quality designations are three-star and the superior VSOP, but it is also easy to find vintage-dated armagnac.

Single malt whiskey comes into its own as an after-dinner drink and should be drunk and enjoyed just like a brandy. Both spirits are aged in oak casks for many years, and are produced by the same distillation process.

All these liquors are high in alcohol, usually about 40 per cent, and seem to demand a withdrawal from the dining table for their consumption. But there are many drinks that are less of a breathalizer liability, and can be enjoyed at table to bring a meal to a close, rather than mark its end. Port is one such drink and the unnecessary "rule" about passing it clockwise should put no one off enjoying its rich lusciousness.

Vintage port throws a sediment and needs to be decanted. Fine old tawny ports and the best-known brands, such as Cockburn's Special Reserve and similarly priced vintage character ports, are designed to be drunk straight from the bottle, however. These are fruity, strapping fortified wines that will keep for weeks even after the bottle has been opened.

Cheese is the traditional solid matter to soak up port, while the often-overlooked Madeira supposedly calls for nuts, especially walnuts. Both drinks stand up perfectly well on their own (and can even tackle the odd mint chocolate) but the richer Madeiras labelled Bual or, even richer, Malmsey, are the ones designed for post-prandial drinking.

Any dark, sweet fortified wine is appropriate here, and that includes the raisiny Malaga from Spain, the rare and sumptuous liqueur Muscats of Australia, and even the Commandaria from Cyprus. There are also many full-bodied sweet wines that can do nicely as both dessert wine and digestif. A really good Sauternes may be rich enough to serve on its own, and there is a host of other liquid riches based on the grapey Muscat, such as the popular syrup from Beaumes de Venise, Moscatel de Setubal from Portugal and the rather lighter grape essences such as Château La Salle which comes from California.

226   *An ideal larder, a cool, north-facing room off the kitchen, in a country house.*

STOCKING UP THE LARDER

The contents of your larder must depend largely on the space you have available, and how close you live to good stores. But they are dictated, too, by one's own personality and finances. An extravagant and generous character might keep a can of *pâté de foie gras*, or a black truffle, so they can throw together a luxurious treat for their friends at short notice. More frugal beings, like myself, prefer to buy such things (if ever) for a special occasion, and keep their larder for basics. This is my selection of provisions that play a vital role in many favorite dishes:

Oils. Olive oil: *either* one relatively inexpensive oil for general use and one green "virgin" oil for special salads; *or* a good comporise for both cooking and salads. Sunflower-seed oil, for frying and light salads. Peanut oil, for deep frying. *Optional extras*: sesame oil, for flavoring Chinese dishes.

Vinegars. White wine vinegar, for constant use – salads etc. Cider vinegar. *Optional extra*: Red wine vinegar, for marinades and pickles.

Pasta. Italian spaghetti, noodles (tagliatelle), and quills (penne). Soup pasta: vermicelli, noodle squares, and risone (rice-shaped pasta). Buckwheat noodles, from health food stores. *Optional extras*: Chinese or Japanese noodles.

Flour. White bread flour. Wholewheat bread flour. All-purpose flour, self-rising flour (small bag only), buckwheat flour (for making blinis and buckwheat waffles). Cornflour, rice flour, potato flour and arrowroot (all for thickening sauces).

Grains. Rice: Long grain, short grain, brown rice, from health food stores. Couscous, Polenta, roasted buckwheat, bulgur (cracked wheat), from health food stores. Semolina and cornmeal.

Pulses. French or Italian ("soissons" or "cannellini") haricot beans, brown or green lentils, chick peas. *Optional extras*: flageolets, red kidney beans, dried broad beans (for Greek and Middle Eastern dishes), orange lentils.

Nuts and seeds. Almonds, pine nuts; Sesame seeds, poppy seeds, mustard seeds. *Optional extras*: hazel nuts, pecans or walnuts.

Whole spices. Black peppercorns, juniper berries, cloves, cinnamon sticks, vanilla pods, nutmeg, ginger, coriander, cardamom, allspice, chili peppers.

Ground spices. Coriander, cumin, turmeric, and chili powder. Mild curry powder, paprika, cayenne, allspice, cinnamon, mace, cloves. Quatre épices (French blend of pepper, cloves, nutmeg, and cinnamon or ginger; may be replaced by ground allspice). Saffron in powder form, from Italian or Spanish shops. Easier to use than stamens.

Dried herbs. Bay leaves, rosemary, thyme, oregano and mint. (Other herbs in freezer, or in garden.)

Dried fruit and vegetables. Prunes, apricots, currants and raisins. Dried apricot paste, from Middle Eastern stores. Porcini (Italian dried funghi). Orange and lemon peel (home-made). *Optional extras*: peaches and apples, from health food stores.

Fresh fruit and vegetables. Strings of onions, shallots and garlic (pink, when available). Potatoes. Pumpkins, in season. Cooking and eating apples, lemons and limes.

Cans. Italian plum tomatoes, tomato juice, red peppers, tomato paste. Black olives, capers, anchovy fillets, green peppercorns in brine. French or Italian white beans, red kidney beans, green flageolets. Tuna fish, clams and clam juice – American or Italian. V8, or mixed vegetable juice. *Optional extras*: Campbell's beef consommé, celery hearts, whole kernel corn.

Jams etc. Preferably homemade, otherwise good bought jams. Ditto marmalade, homemade or Tiptree. Fruit jellies, for eating with cold meat. eg crab apple, rowan, quince, redcurrant.

Honeys and syrups etc. Thick English honey, clear English honey. Golden syrup, or (American) corn syrup or molasses.

Sugar. Granulated sugar, superfine sugar, confectioner's sugar. Moist light brown sugar, dark brown sugar. Brown lump (cane) sugar. Brown coffee sugar. Homemade vanilla sugar (granulated sugar flavored with vanilla beans).

Mustard. Smooth Dijon mustard, eg Grey Poupon. Wholegrain mustard, eg Pommery Moutarde de Meaux.

Salt. Sea salt.

Pickles and chutneys. Homemade: dill pickles, piccalilll, pickled beets, spiced plums (Elizabeth David's recipe). Bought: Sharwood's mango chutney. *Optional extras*: relishes (for hamburgers). Pickled watermelon rind (for eating with ham). Fruit pickles and chutneys.

Sauces. Light soy sauce. Tabasco. Lea and Perrins Worcestershire sauce. Heinz tomato ketchup. Chili Sauce and Vegetable Seasoning. *Optional extras*: mayonnaise. Oyster sauce, for Chinese dishes. Mushroom ketchup, anchovy essence.

Jars. Marmite, Bovril, tahini (sesame seed paste, for making hummus, from Middle Eastern and Cypriot shops).

Cheese. Large piece of Parmesan, wrapped in muslin. Ditto Cheddar.

Biscuits etc. Matzos, oatcakes, Scandinavian crispbread, packets of sliced rye bread, Scandinavian or German.

Eggs. Better kept in a cool larder than in the refrigerator.

Teas, coffees etc. Ground coffee beans, decaffeinated, instant espresso coffee (ordinary and decaffeinated). English Breakfast Tea. Lapsang Souchong. Hibiscus and peppermint herb teas.

Chocolate. Cooking and eating. Drinking chocolate, or cocoa.

Miscellaneous. Chicken and beef stock cubes. Knox gelatine, dried yeast, breadcrumbs (homemade).

A SELECTION OF SAUSAGES

TEEWURST
Highly-spiced pork and beef
Germany

METTWURST
Pork, beef
paprika and
nutmeg
Germany

LANDJAGER
Beef, pork and
caraway seeds
Germany

MERGUEZ
Hard and highly-spiced
Algeria

LOUKANIKA
Pork belly, red
wine and coriander
Greece

LIEBERWURST
Liver sausage
with extras
Germany

COTECHINO
Pork and white wine
Italy

ANDOUILLES DEVIRE
Pig's tripe, pork, and
chitterling
France

SCHINKENWURST
Flaked smoked ham
Germany

MORTADELLA
Pork, white wine and
coriander
Italy

ITALIAN SALAMI
Pork and spices

**SAUCISSON DE
LYON (SEC)**
Pork, fat and garlic
France

ROSETTE
Pork in fatty casing
France

FRANKFURTER
Lean pork and bacon fat
Germany/USA

WIENERWURST
Veal, pork and shallots
Austria/USA

ZAMPONE
Pork wrapped in a pig's trotter
Italy

KNACKWURST
Pork, beef, cumin
and garlic
Germany

KALBSBRATWURST
Veal, bacon and milk
Switzerland

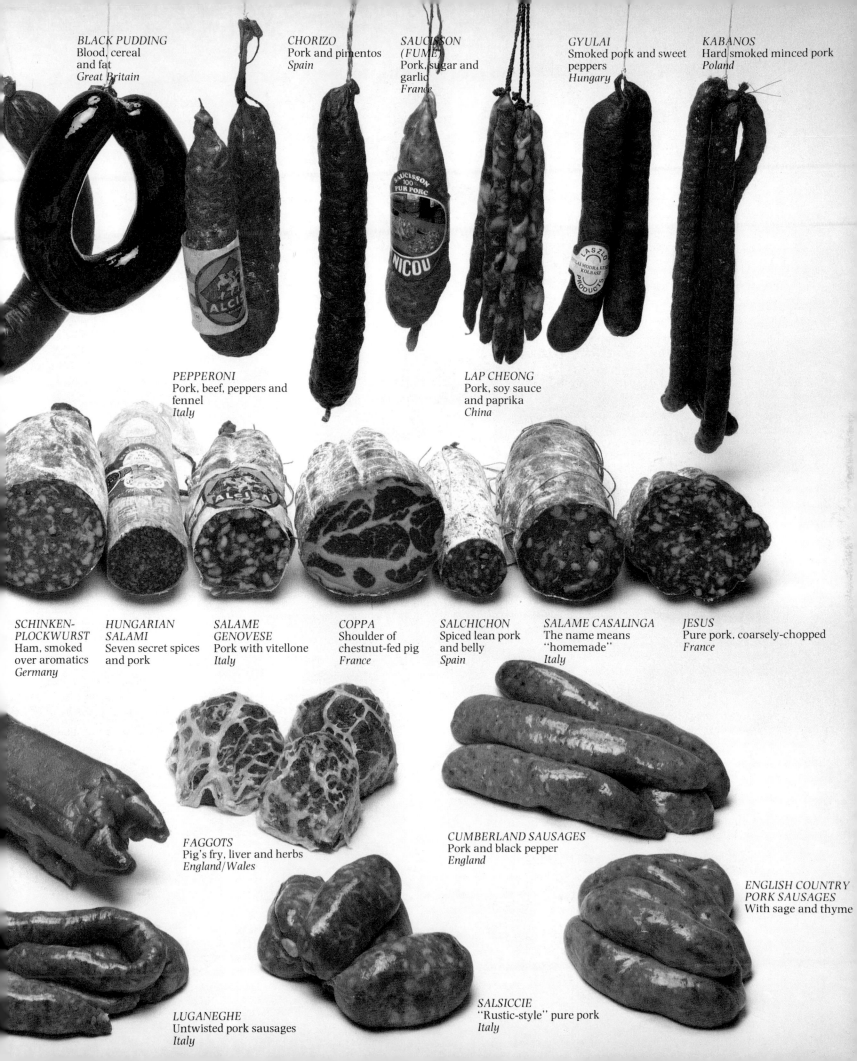

BLACK PUDDING
Blood, cereal
and fat
Great Britain

CHORIZO
Pork and pimentos
Spain

**SAUCISSON
(FUME)**
Pork, sugar and
garlic
France

GYULAI
Smoked pork and sweet
peppers
Hungary

KABANOS
Hard smoked minced pork
Poland

PEPPERONI
Pork, beef, peppers and
fennel
Italy

LAP CHEONG
Pork, soy sauce
and paprika
China

**SCHINKEN-
PLOCKWURST**
Ham, smoked
over aromatics
Germany

**HUNGARIAN
SALAMI**
Seven secret spices
and pork

**SALAME
GENOVESE**
Pork with vitellone
Italy

COPPA
Shoulder of
chestnut-fed pig
France

SALCHICHON
Spiced lean pork
and belly
Spain

SALAME CASALINGA
The name means
"homemade"
Italy

JESUS
Pure pork, coarsely-chopped
France

FAGGOTS
Pig's fry, liver and herbs
England/Wales

CUMBERLAND SAUSAGES
Pork and black pepper
England

**ENGLISH COUNTRY
PORK SAUSAGES**
With sage and thyme

LUGANEGHE
Untwisted pork sausages
Italy

SALSICCIE
"Rustic-style" pure pork
Italy

IDEAL KITCHEN TOOLS

No kitchen should be furnished all at once. It is better to buy the minimum, and then learn by experience and preference what additional items you need. The first things you buy should either be the best – good steel knives, for instance – or the cheapest, which you can replace when you discover what you really want. Here is an ideal set of kitchen tools. Start with the starred items, and build up from there.

★1. Set of three saucepans, heavy aluminum. *Most young cooks start off with a set of saucepans carefully graded in size. In fact, I think it is more useful to have two the same size, and one smaller one.*

2. Milk pan, aluminum lined with non-stick surface. *On the whole, I don't bother with non-stick pans, since with age and maintenance a good quality pan will develop its own semi-non-stick surface; a Teflon-lined milk pan is worth its keep, however, for boiling milk and for making scrambled eggs – both tedious to clean.*

★3. Oval casserole, enamelled cast iron, 4 quarts. *I think a kitchen needs two casseroles, one medium-sized oval one and a much larger round one. The oval one is useful for cooking a whole chicken, or a rolled piece of meat. It is indispensable for braising. The large round casserole (not shown) is essential for making osso buco and oxtail stew.*

4. Very small saucepan, heavy gauge aluminum, 5 inch. *Useful for boiling an egg etc.*

5. Steamer, stainless steel.

★6. Stock pot, black enamel. *This is a relatively inexpensive piece of equipment, considering its size, since it does not have to be of heavy metal. It is never used for frying, only boiling. It is also useful for cooking pasta and rice, which need lots of water.*

7. Flour dredger.

8. Set of metric weights.

★9. Scales. *Old-fashioned scales are the best; they are far more accurate than balance scales, can't go wrong, and can be used with metric weights.*

10. Tefal pressure cooker. *My favorite sort of pressure cooker, the French Tefal cooker cannot be undone by children, or even absent-minded adults, since the lid has to be screwed down very firmly indeed, and needs strength to open it. It is a good size for cooking vegetables, but the larger size is more useful for making stocks and cooking pieces of beef or ham, or chickens.*

11. Fish poacher, stainless steel, 18 inch. *Without a fish poacher, whole fish cannot be poached, except for the very smallest ones. This is a useful size for poaching small salmon, sea trout, large rainbow trout, or pieces of larger fish.*

12. Basting spoon, stainless steel, 14 inch. *A large stainless steel spoon is extremely useful, both in the kitchen and as a serving spoon with large dishes.*

★13. Two ladles, stainless steel, 4 inch and 3 inch. *Two or even three sizes are useful: one very big one for transferring liquids, a large-ish one which holds a bowlful of soup, and a small one for serving sauces, and for rubbing them through a sieve.*

★14. **Perforated spoon, stainless steel, 14 inch.**

15. **Funnel, stainless steel.**

★16. **Fish slice.**

★17. **Colander, aluminum, 9 inch.** *Aluminum colanders are a better buy than cheap enamel ones which chip. Essential for draining pasta and vegetables.*

★18. **Measuring cup, plastic, 1 quart.** *Two or even three measuring cups are useful in different sizes and materials. This one, in plastic, is also useful for measuring dry goods, while the Pyrex ones are better for hot liquids.*

★19. **Food mill, tinned, 9 inch.** *Even if you have a food processor, a food mill or vegetable mill is still a vital piece of equipment. Not only can it be used to give a slightly rough and lumpy texture to certain soups, it is essential when part of the food to be puréed has to be held back, such as raspberry seeds. (The food processor will simply purée everything.)*

★20. **Balloon whisk, wire with wooden handle.** *Should be of the thinnest possible wire, for beating in as much air as possible.*

21. **Sugar and oil thermometer.** *Especially useful for the inexperienced cook, for testing the temperature of liquids from frying oils to sugar syrups.*

22. **Conical sieve, or** *chinois,* **fine.** *As well as two or three strainers, each kitchen should have a conical sieve with a fine mesh. This is called a* chinois, *because of its resemblance in shape to a coolie hat. It usually has a solid band of metal around the top, which prevents the liquid gushing out over the bowl it is being strained into, and strengthens it.*

23. **Small flat whisk.** *Extremely useful for whisking up a sauce in a frying pan, when a balloon whisk would be no use at all.*

★24. **Two sizes of strainers, tinned wire, 8 inch and 5 inch.** *Vital for straining stocks and sauces, draining rice, pasta and vegetables, etc.*

25. **Kitchen scissors.** *Always useful for cutting fins off fish, chopping chives etc. These ones also open screw-top jars and bottles.*

26. **Omelette pan, steel, 10 inch.** *Traditional omelette pans, like this one, are made from heavy forged steel about $\frac{3}{16}$ in. thick. Thin ones are useless. If you look after it well, cleaning it with salt and heating oil in it before using the first few times, it will gradually develop a smooth non-stick surface so that the omelette slides about easily within it. Never use corn oil in it, since this develops into a bumpy surface like blistered varnish. This size will make a 5 egg omelette, for two.*

★27. **Box-shaped grater.** *This shaped grater is most practical – easier to use than a flat one, easier to clean than a round one.*

★28. **Large china bowl.** *One really big mixing bowl, for making bread, pâtés, and puddings.*

29. **Electric beater.** *Get the cheapest available one with three speeds. Avoid those with stands and bowls, they aren't necessary. Nor are dough hooks, which are generally included, since the motor isn't strong enough to beat dough.*

★30. **Mixing bowls.** *A set of three graded mixing bowls is almost essential.*

31. **Food processor.**

32. **Sauté pan and lid, black enamelled cast iron, 10 inch.** *I think that two or even three frying pans are needed in the ideal kitchen: one deep frying pan, or sauté pan, like this one, and one or two shallow ones. This sauté pan is in black enamelled cast iron, and will last for ever. It is excellent for frying onions, frying chickens, making sautés and reducing sauces. The lid, although not essential, doubles its use as it transforms it into a small casserole. It is also good for toasting sesame seeds, which tend to jump around.*

33. **Oval baking dish, glazed earthenware, 12 inch.** *A traditional French baking or gratin dish, very inexpensive.*

34. **Oval grating dish, earthenware, half-glazed, 12½ inch.**

35. **Mortar and pestle, porcelain, 6¾ inch.** *Mortars and pestles must be used with a circular grinding motion, never banged up and down. Enormously useful for many things, such as grinding spices, in small amounts (hard to do in a food processor), making sauces like rouille, etc. Buy the biggest one you can afford; if they are too small the food slops over the edge.*

★36. **Two open flan rings.** *I find open flan rings easier to use than pans, so long as I have a pizza pan or other suitable flat base. They are easy to grease, and to remove after baking.*

37. **Deep cake tin, 8 inch.**

38. **Pizza pan, 11 inch.** *Can also be used in conjunction with open flan rings – and even for serving the flan or quiche on, after removing the ring, if you are nervous about transferring it to a plate.*

★39. **Large baking sheet, aluminum.**

40. **Bulb baster, plastic.** *A good invention, though not aesthetically very pleasing. Useful for basting meat while roasting, also for extracting liquid from narrow apertures where a spoon will not fit, down the side of a meat loaf as it shrinks away from the pan, for instance. It is also invaluable for extracting fat-free stock from below the surface, after the fat has settled.*

★41. **Roasting pan, stainless steel, seamless, 16 inch.** *As soon as you can afford to, invest in a good quality one. This one can be used on top of the stove for making gravy – the cheap ones are too thin and uneven – and for browning bones when making stock. Le Creuset make good looking (but heavy) versions in enamelled cast iron that can double as baking dishes for lasagne and cannelloni.*

42. **Roasting rack, chrome-plated.** *Useful for holding meat or poultry out of the fat while cooking, also for holding rolled meat firmly, and for small birds.*

43. **Large shallow frying pan, black cast iron, 11½ inch.** *This is very heavy, but rarely needs lifting. Extremely useful for frying things that need a lot of space, such as sliced eggplants.*

44. **Tongs, slotted.** *Handy for lifting food in and out of pans, especially when deep frying.*

★45. **Smaller shallow frying pans, black cast iron, 9¼ inch.** *A smaller version of no. 43, for frying bacon and eggs, etc.*

★46. **Lemon squeezer, glass.**

47. **"Racle-tout," plastic scraper.** *An excellent utensil for cleaning pastry boards after making pastry or bread, for lifting chopped herbs etc., and for scraping out bowls.*

48. **Rubber spatula, large.** *Useful for scraping out mixing bowls.*

★49. **Wooden spoons.**

★50. **Pastry brush, flat and round.** *Two shapes of pastry brush, useful not only for glazing pastry but also for basting with marinades etc. Keep one shape for oil, marinades, butter, the other for beaten egg. The round one holds more liquid; the flat one is better for glazing pastry.*

51. **Cake rack.** *A good quality cake rack in heavy wire is useful for a multitude of things as well as cooling breads, cakes and cookies. Can be used as an impromptu barbecue supported over bricks, out of doors or in the fireplace.*

52. **Jam funnel.** *Any wide-necked funnel is useful for transferring dry foods like rice out of packages into storage jars.*

★53. **Peppermill.** *It is not necessary to have a giant peppermill. This is small, cheap and practical.*

★54. **Carving fork, stainless steel.** *All beginners should have a carving fork with a guard to protect their hand in case the knife slips.*

55. **Carving platter, wooden.** *Greatly facilitates carving for the beginner, since it holds the meat securely, and collects the gravy.*

56. **Skewers, flat, stainless steel.** *Tiny skewers are good for making hors d'oeuvres like grilled shrimp, while huge ones protect your hands from getting scorched when barbecueing. They must have flattened shafts; if the metal is round, the skewer will slide inside the food as it cooks, instead of turning it.*

57. **Nutmeg grinder, wooden.**

58. **Garlic press.**

59. **Apple corer, stainless steel.**

60. **Chinese cleaver.** *Once you have learned to use a Chinese cleaver, it seems the best tool for chopping everything, even the smallest things like half a garlic clove, or a tablespoon of parsley. Also useful for lifting chopped foods into the pan.*

★61. **Steel, fine cut.** *For sharpening knives. Ask your butcher to show you how to use it.*

62. **Chopping board, small, wooden.** *Always useful in conjunction with the larger pastry/chopping board (no. 65). Plastic chopping boards are more hygienic than wood, but I will never like them much; the sensation of steel meeting plastic is just not the same.*

63. **Spatula, stainless steel, rosewood handle, 8 inch.** *Useful for shaping croquettes, lifting them from worktops to the pan, smoothing surfaces, etc.*

★64. **Potato peeler.**

65. **Pastry/chopping board, sycamore.** *This is actually a pastry board, but of good enough quality to double as a chopping board. (Large chopping boards are very expensive, and too heavy to move about.) This one is jointed, which prevents it warping. I have one like this, in sycamore, which is 25 years old, but as good as new.*

★66. **Paring knife, stainless steel.** *Having chosen the sort of knife you prefer, four different sizes will cover every eventuality. Paring (no. 66), filleting (no. 68), chopping (not shown here), and carving (no. 67). We have replaced the chopping knife with a Chinese cleaver (no. 60).*

★67. **Carving knife, stainless steel.**

★68. **Filleting knife, stainless steel.**

★69. **Serrated knife, stainless steel.** *A saw-edged knife is very useful for beginners since it facilitates carving as well as cutting bread, tomatoes and citrus fruit. This comes from a good range in stainless steel with plastic handles which can go in the dishwasher.*

★70. **Rolling pin, beech.** *The most useful shape of rolling pin, in my opinion. A long straight one, without handles, in wood.*

71. **Timer.** *Modern stoves have timers, but it is sometimes helpful to be able to take one with you to another room.*

★72. **Can opener, chrome plated.** *If you use as few cans as I do, there is no need for expensive electric or wall-mounted can openers. This is a compromise, comfortable to use and inexpensive.*

★73. **Measuring spoons, plastic.**

74. **Heat diffuser.** *Useful for beginner cooks, and for those with old stoves which cannot be turned low enough to keep food barely simmering.*

★75. **Screwpull, plastic.** *A brilliant new corkscrew, very good-looking, winner of design awards. A good present, it has an exceptionally well-made screw, so fine that it never splits the cork.*

76. **Mouli, rotary grater with 3 drums, stainless steel.** *For grating small amounts of cheese, nuts or chocolate, when it is not worth using the food processor.*

ACKNOWLEDGMENTS

Author's Acknowledgments

I would like to thank the whole team of people who have worked on this project at different stages; some of them work at *The Sunday Times*, some at Weidenfeld and Nicolson, and some are freelance. My special thanks to Michael Bateman, whose idea it was, and who asked me to work on it in the first place, and to my editor, Brenda Jones, who proceeded to control the whole intricate operation with her amazing calm, efficiency, and constant good humor. I believe that the strength of the series, and of the book, lie in the brilliant visual presentation; for this, congratulations and thanks to designer Gilvrie Misstear. Also to picture editor James Danziger, and to the whole team of photographers and illustrators who worked on it, especially David Montgomery, Tessa Traeger, and David Reed, who, between them, took most of the pictures. My sincere thanks also to Sarah Spankie at *The Sunday Times*, who worked on the series throughout, and encouraged me constantly in the nicest possible way. Various others came and went at different times, all contributing something of their own, in particular, Christine Walker and Rosie Atkins. Warm thanks to the subs at *The Sunday Times*, especially Liz Clasen, who helped me throughout the traumatic business of last-minute correcting and cutting of proofs.

I must thank Philippa Davenport, who took over the Marketing section, both for her customary thoroughness and professionalism, and for forbearing to complain when some of her work was cut, due to lack of space. The eight cooks who made up the Entertaining section earned my sincere gratitude for the originality and charm of their contributions. In the final stages, many thanks to Tristram Holland at Weidenfeld's, for all her patience and help with the book proofs. Finally, I'd like to thank the two friends I asked for at the beginning, to help me throughout the course: firstly, Alex Dufort, photographer and chef, who assisted me one day a week and helped immeasurably, both with his technical knowledge and experience, and with his infectious enthusiasm. Secondly, Dinah Morrison, who I feel has contributed more than anyone else to the whole project. Not only did she cook all the food for the photographs in the Techniques section – in itself a mammoth task – and let us use her kitchen one day a week as photographic studio; she also cooked an exquisite English tea for the Entertaining section, wrote the piece on herbs for the marketing section, and, with the help of her friend Judy Lister, set the examinations for *The Sunday Times Magazine*. Apart from all this, I'd like to thank her for her good advice, hospitality, and unfailing support.

Despite the large number of people who have worked on this project, I have been allowed to stick to my own individual attitude throughout, for which I am truly grateful. Everyone who has been involved has worked to reinforce my own views, however idiosyncratic they might seem, and I am happy to find that they have colored the book, just as they have colored my life. *Arabella Boxer*

The authors, the publishers and *The Sunday Times Magazine* would like to thank the photographers and artists whose work appears on the preceding pages:

Paul Bevitt 228–9
Chloe Cheese 142; 150; 159; 190
Alex Dufort 56
Hannah Firmin 95; 123; 136 (bottom)
Colin Frewin 30; 40; 50; 60; 68; 81; 90; 100; 111; 128 (right); 136 (top); 144
Lynda Gray 1; 29; 39; 49 (top); 59 (top); 67; 79; 89 (top); 99 (top); 109 (top); 119; 127; 135; 143; 151 (top); 220; 221; 223; 225
Vana Haggerty 48 (top); 85
Rosalind Hewitt 54
Edwina Keene 33; 35; 46 (bottom); 47; 76 (bottom); 87 (bottom); 88; 94 (top); 98 (center); 104; 106–7; 115; 132; 141 (bottom); 149 (top); 157; 179; 213
Stuart Lafford/Linden Artists 37; 155; 156
Dee McLean/Linden Artists 96; 162; 235; 237; 239
James Merrell 224
David Montgomery 73; 78; 122; 124; 125; 166–7; 169; 170; 173; 174; 176; 177; 180–1; 182; 183; 184; 186–7; 189; 192–3; 195; 198–9; 200; 201; 204–5; 207; 210–1; 214–5; 216; 217
Vivian Monument/The Garden Studio 20
James Mortimer 230–1
David Reed 34; 36; 38; 45; 46 (top); 48 (bottom); 49 (bottom); 55; 58; 59 (bottom); 64; 65; 72; 74; 75; 76 (top); 84; 86; 87 (top); 89 (bottom); 97; 98 (left); 98–9; 105; 108; 109 (bottom); 114; 116; 117; 133; 134; 141 (top); 148; 149 (bottom); 151 (bottom); 158
Richard Solomon 44; 66; 94 (bottom); 128 (left); 165
Tessa Traeger 8; 17; 22; 32; 42; 52–3; 62; 71; 83; 92; 103; 112–3; 130; 138; 146; 226–7; endpapers
Denis Waugh 6
Phil Weare/Linden Artists 140
Harry Willock 25
Janet Woolley 13

They would also like to thank Bruce Bernard, Gunn Brinson and Jenny de Gex, who did the picture research for the paintings; Vincent Page, who cleared the rights on all the pictures; and David Baker, who helped with the art work.

INDEX

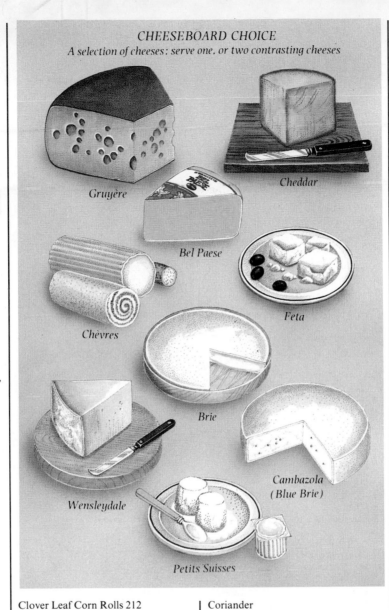

CHEESEBOARD CHOICE
A selection of cheeses: serve one, or two contrasting cheeses

Gruyère

Cheddar

Bel Paese

Chèvres

Feta

Brie

Cambazola
(Blue Brie)

Wensleydale

Petits Suisses

SIMPLE FIRST COURSES

Avocado
and tomato salad

Taramasalata
with pitta bread

Raw spinach
and mushroom
salad

Parma ham
with fresh figs

Smoked mackerel
with horseradish

Artichokes
with
melted butter

Melon with limes

Grapefruit
with cherry

SIMPLE FRUIT DESSERTS

Baked apples

Raspberry tartlets

Pineapple slices
with
blood orange juice

Sliced peaches
with
raspberry sauce

Apple tart

Citrus
fruit sorbets

Fresh fruit

Melon, pink grapefruit
and sliced kiwi fruit with lime juice